Statistics in Social Research: An Introduction

Statistics in Social Research

AN INTRODUCTION

Robert S. Weiss

Brandeis University and
Harvard Medical School

John Wiley & Sons, Inc., New York · London · Sydney

10 9 8 7 6 5 4 3 2

Copyright © 1968 by John Wiley & Sons, Inc.

Library of Congress Catalog Card Number: 67-29571
Printed in the United States of America

Preface

This book is intended to serve in two roles: as a general textbook, coordinating statistical ideas and techniques to the problems of social research, and as a guide to the management of quantitative social research. I have tried to keep in mind its two possible audiences: the student audience—graduates or advanced undergraduates—who may be taking a first course in statistics, and the professional audience, especially those who are embarking on quantitative research for the first time. My assumption has been that the interests of these two audiences will very nearly coincide: that the student will learn most if he is addressed as a professional-in-training, while the uninitiated in research requires, as does the student, that relevant topics be developed from his most elementary ideas. As I point out in the last chapter, it is difficult to direct a report toward two different audiences. This volume, at times, may exemplify the difficulty. My hope is that the needs of the two groups are close enough to justify my not having followed my own advice.

My selection of material differs from the selection in most statistics texts, in that I have included a discussion of the processes of data collection which give rise to quantitative data, a detailed discussion of tabulation, and (in the last part of the book) an extensive discussion of measures and tests which are appropriate for work with nominal and ordinal data. Less than usual space is given to the product-moment correlation coefficient. The measure itself is discussed as a means of representing association in metric data, but there is no discussion of regression equations, errors of estimate, or curvilinear association. The reason for these omissions is that problems that require use of these ideas occur rarely in social research—possibly because an association between two measures, each of which is at least interval in level, is rarely of sufficient interest to justify intensive analysis. On the other hand, I have included material that serves as an introduction to the ideas of the analysis of variance. When a metric (interval or ratio scale) dependent variable is available, this is an extremely useful approach, and one that is increasingly to be encountered in reports of social research. I hope that my discussion clarifies the terms "effects," "treatments," and "interaction," and will prepare a reader to understand an analysis of variance table.

The sequence of chapters is intended to follow the progressive concerns of an investigator engaged in quantitative research. First, there is a discussion of how quantitative data are collected; then a discussion of data processing; then a discussion of tabulation; then material dealing with data description, the logic of inference, and significance tests; and finally, a brief discussion of reporting. Chapter 12, on sampling, from one point of view may be out of place. As it is the first step in data collection, it could have served as the first chapter of the book; instead, I have used it to introduce the topic of inference, to which it is logically related.

An instructor might consider combining the materials of Chapter 6 and Chapter 7, in order to teach together the ways of representing a distribution by a single measure and the ways of communicating variation. Chapters 4 and 5, on tabulation and graphing, also might be combined and dealt with as a single unit.

In Appendix 2 I have included data on 100 respondents in a national sample survey that considered (among other topics) the attitudes of women toward child-raising. All of the respondents were women between the ages of 25 and 65, living in what the Census Bureau considered as an urbanized area of the United States. There were no further restrictions; some women were from the North, some were from the South; some were well educated, some were not; and so on. The original study from which this sample was taken was completed in 1955 by the Survey Research Center of the University of Michigan. I acknowledge their kindness in letting me include them. When teaching a course in statistics I have found it useful to assign, as the examination for the course, the analysis of these data. This has always turned out to be extremely time consuming, but work on real data such as these seems almost necessary for assimilation of the book's materials.

I am grateful to many people who have helped me with this book: Dr. Lillian Cohen (Mrs. Leo Kovar), who first introduced me to the problems of writing a text; Professor Charles Smith; Dr. Elizabeth Hartwell; Professor Howard Freeman; and Professor Richard Hill, among others. Dr. Freeman made a good many editorial comments on the manuscript, which were most useful as guides for revision. Dr. Hartwell read the manuscript several times, and flagged what, I hope, were most of the errors. Brandeis University contributed funds for having the manuscript typed. Dean Charles Schottland of the Florence Heller School of Social Welfare, at Brandeis University, gave me both encouragement and concrete assistance, each at the appropriate point. Mrs. Gina Prenowitz has been a brilliant editor. Much of the final work on the book was done during a leave of absence from teaching, while engaged in research as a member of the Harvard Medical School Laboratory of Community Psychiatry. The Laboratory is directed by Dr. Gerald Caplan to whom I also owe a debt of gratitude.

ROBERT S. WEISS

Contents

Statistics in Social Research: An Introduction

Chapter 1

Introduction

The scientific enterprise is motivated by the desire to learn about our-selves and the world in which we live. Its aim is understanding; its method is the constant comparison of conceptual formulation with relevant experience. Research is the process by which this experience is gained.

Research in the social sciences differs from research in the physical sciences or the natural sciences only in what is studied and not in the methods or motivations of study. There are, of course, techniques of study that are characteristic of the social sciences that are not found in the physical sciences, just as there are techniques for the study of chemical problems that are not used in the study of physical problems; but techniques do not define a field. Social research is investigation of the social world and is not limited to any particular methodology.

Social research can take a wide variety of forms that differ from each other in (1) the nature of the conceptualization at which the research aims; (2) the nature of the study design; and (3) whether the data are used in a qualitative or quantitative fashion. These dimensions are highly interrelated; for example, a study that aims at (1) the production of precise statements regarding the incidence of certain characteristics in a population would (2) select a representative sample of the population of interest, and would (3) deal with the data in a quantitative mode. How-ever, we may find it useful to consider each of these dimensions separately.

1. Kind of Conceptualization

Before we begin the study of a phenomenon it may appear extremely complex to us. It may seem to take many forms, and to be related, or possibly related, to many other phenomena that, in themselves, may be highly variable in form. In our conceptualization, we seek to make this tangle manageable by identifying important elements, stating the levels or values they may assume, and identifying regular interconnections

1

among them. There are two general directions in which we can proceed in this process. After having identified elements and values, we can identify both the frequencies and the interrelations of values of the elements. This is the direction of *analysis*. We can alternatively attempt to identify a system of interrelationships among elements such that the level or state of any element can only be explained in terms of the conditions of all other elements. This would be the direction of *holistic*, or *systemic* research. The difference between the analytic and holistic approach is not in the data collected, although the analytic approach tends to be associated with quantitative data and the holistic with qualitative data, but rather in the kind of conceptualization that is aimed at. In the one case, we are concerned with frequencies and with propositions that can be supported by demonstrating discrete interrelations; in the other, with descriptions of systems of interrelationships. Neither of these approaches is superior to the other; they each have roles in scientific work.

2. Kind of Study Design

The term, "study design," refers especially to the kind of sample selected by the investigator and the degree of control over phenomena that the investigator possesses. Other research questions that are raised in discussion of design include whether data will be gathered over a lengthy period of time, or only in a single encounter; whether research objectives will be formulated and fixed before data gathering begins in earnest, or will be permitted to develop as the research progresses; whether data gathering instruments (for instance questionnaires) will be developed and if so, of what sort, or whether, alternatively, the investigator will rely on informal observation and interview. There can be, obviously, endless combinations of decisions to each of these questions. Yet it does seem possible to identify four general kinds of study designs, recognizing the existence of many subvarieties in each. These are the case study, comparative research, surveys, and experiments.

(*a*) *The case study.* The case study is simply an intensive study of a single instance of a class we want to understand. Almost all community studies, and many studies of organizations, have been case studies. The case study is a good method for developing dense, vivid data from which the organization of elements, in the one instance, may be inferred.

(*b*) *Comparative research.* The intensive study of a small number of comparison cases allows an investigator to consider not only the sort of organization that may be generic to members of a certain class, but also to develop a typology of organizational variations. The intensive study of a number of family structures permits the investigator to discuss not only family structure in general, but also the structure of democratic families, mother-dominated families, disorganized families, and the like.

(c) *Survey research.* A survey gathers information about the same quality from a large number of respondents. Often, when an investigator wants information about a very large population—such as the population of the country—he may choose a sample from this population that he has reason to believe is very nearly representative of it, and study the sample. It is this idea that underlies opinion polls, and that also underlies more ambitious studies of beliefs, attitudes, and behaviors. Survey studies are also of great value in the discovery of interconnections among elements: for example, the personality and social characteristics associated with treatment for mental illness.

(d) *Experiments.* Experiments are research forms in which the investigator controls the occurrence of a few factors—often only one—and so can demonstrate clearly the causal connection between them and their consequents. Experiments, when it is possible to perform them, are ideal ways of testing hypotheses.

3. Quantitative and Qualitative Research

Quantitative research, the research approach with which this book is concerned, may have as its hallmark the production of precise statements. These statements almost always involve measurement. If the fundamental measurement is of a "one-zero" sort, requiring only the decision that something does or does not belong in a certain category (nominal measurement), then the statements will involve counts of the number of instances that fall within the category and the number that do not.[1] We might say at the cost of only a bit of oversimplification that quantitative research aims at the discovery of fact.

Qualitative research, on the other hand, attempts to go directly toward an integrated conceptualization without an intermediate stage of precise statements involving measurements or counts. This research may involve the formulation and test of hypotheses, but both formulation and test are likely to be carried out informally, as an investigator interacts with the phenómena he is studying. Glaser and Strauss say, in reference to *field work*, which is one form of qualitative research, "What the field worker does is to make this normal strategy of reflective persons into a successful research strategy."[2]

---

[1] Another view might be that quantitative research requires standardized data, while qualitative research requires data that are closely interrelated.

[2] Barney G. Glaser and Anselm L. Strauss, "Discovery of Substantive Theory: A Basic Strategy Underlying Qualitative Research," *American Behavioral Scientist*, **8(6)** (February, 1965), p. 9.

Analytic aims tend to lead to quantitative research using survey or experimental designs, and holistic aims tend to lead to qualitative research using case or comparative designs, although occasionally qualitative *data*—appraisals, impressions, attempts at vivid descriptions and quotations—may be used to add depth or color to a study that is basically quantitative, while quantitative data, in turn, may be used to give factual support to one or more points in a qualitative study.

This book, although it is concerned with the management of quantitative research in general, gives more attention to the problems of survey research than to those of experimental research. The reason for this is purely pragmatic; it is difficult to conduct experiments on questions of sociological interest, and many of these questions, indeed, call for description rather than the tests of hypothesis for which the experiment is so clearly the best design.

Steps in Nonexperimental Quantitative Research

A survey, or similar study, begins when an investigator decides to collect measures or frequencies that can be expressed in tables and analysed statistically. Often, although not always, the study design requires information about the same qualities in each member of a population. Questions that might lead to a design of this sort can be as varied as those having to do with the attitudes toward psychiatry of members of an older population; the relationship between size and effectiveness in a group of organizations; or the relationship between crime rate and level of immigration in a population of cities. When studies of populations are done, not with every member of the population, but rather with smaller samples from the populations, the design of the sample is an important aspect of the design of the research.

The second step in this kind of research, after the main outline of the study has been decided, is to develop the techniques by which the attributes in which we are interested will be measured. How shall we determine how effective an organization is, or whether an individual has one attitude or another? The devices that we use to secure our information may be no more complicated than the question, "How old are you?", or may be as intricate as a complex personality test.

Almost always a study will collect information about more than one quality of each case. It is costly to arrange to gather information about an individual case—to get an interviewer to someone's home, or to arrange to collect statistics on an organization—but once the research contact has been made, additional information is inexpensive. Since the additional information may be illuminating, and at worst will do no more than fail to help, the practice is to try to learn about whatever qualities of each case seem likely to be relevant to the aims of the study. The amount of information collected may be limited only by the amount of time subjects can be expected to give, and by cost, which eventually does become appreciably greater when a great deal of additional information is required.

In most studies, information gathering produces a great deal of data, the sheer amount and variety of which would be overwhelming, and paralyzing of any analysis effort, if there were not available some system for handling it. A data-processing stage in the study becomes necessary to bring the data into a manageable form.

The next step in dealing with the data often is to develop detailed tabulations, so that the investigator can see what he has. However, even at this beginning point in analysis investigators have different styles. Some investigators prefer first to study more complex features of the data (for instance, cross-tabulations or correlation charts) to get some sense of overall organization, while other investigators prefer first to give attention to simpler tabulations, from which may be gained a sense of the elements of the structure. Still other investigators may be interested only in a few predetermined features of the data which bear on already formulated hypotheses, but this is perhaps the least frequently encountered style for dealing with quantitative data of any richness. In any event, the aim of all investigators will be the same: to understand the implications of the data and to communicate them to a relevant audience together with the tabulations or other statistical statements which are their evidence.

Once the main lines of the analysis are developed, the investigator has available to him a range of statistical techniques for identifying and communicating to a reader specific features of the data. Charts are useful for communicating in a dramatic way a few features of the data, especially to a nontechnical audience. Measures that identify representative values and other measures that capture variation in the data, when reported together, are compact ways of describing the main features of an entire distribution of information. Methods for measuring the degree of association between characteristics can illuminate underlying connections and direct attention to relationships that may possibly be causal in nature. Methods for establishing the worth of inferences from the data may be used to support assertions about populations much larger than the sample studied.

An Example

To make concrete what quantitative research may be like, let us examine a single quantitative study, one that has been unusually detailed in reporting its methodology.

Mental Health in the Metropolis: The Midtown Manhattan Study[3] is a report of an ambitious project by a multidisciplinary team that had, as its objective, the determination of the incidence, nature, and to a limited extent, etiology, of psychiatric difficulties in a city. The study design required interviews with a large sample of residents of a district in the heart of Manhattan; this made it possible for the investigators to deal with many individuals, as they might have in a national sample survey, and also to consider the effects of a single living environment, an advantage associated with a community study.

By concentrating their interviews within a single geographic region, the investigators also reduced the cost of interviewing below what would have been the cost for a national sample survey, and they were able to reinterview individuals without great difficulty in locating them again. There were disadvantages too in their choice of study design; in particular, they were not able to say with any assurance whether their findings were applicable to other urban areas within the United States.[4]

Once the general design was set, the authors turned to the problem of specifying the composition and size of their sample. They decided to use as a criterion for an eligible repondent: "That the individual be a resident for whom a Midtown dwelling is both his primary 'home base' and the place he now actually occupies." In early discussions among the staff, they report, it had been proposed that only one hundred households within Midtown be sampled, because this would permit intense study of each. However, it was finally decided that group-by-group comparisons were extremely important, and in order to insure large enough samples of useful size within each of the many subgroups, it was agreed that the sample as a whole ought to be large. A minimum size of fifteen hundred was aimed at. A rather complicated sampling procedure was developed,[5] 87% of those approached agreed to cooperate with the study, and the result was a study population of 1666.

Before the interviewers were directed to their respondents, the long process of development of data-gathering devices had taken place. There is no need here to review the steps that must have been involved; this topic is discussed in books more focused on data-gathering methods. Similarly, there is no need here to discuss the problems of interviewing, important as they are, but only to recognize that much work went on in the field in gathering the required data.

[3] By Leo Srole, Thomas S. Langner, Stanley P. Michael, Marvin K. Opler, and Thomas A. C. Rennie (New York: McGraw-Hill, 1962).
[4] See the authors' discussion of this point in their Chapter Five. The questions of which population ought to be represented in a survey and with what assurance extrapolations can be made are recurrent problems of survey research.
[5] *Mental Health in the Metropolis, op. cit.*, pp. 34–35.

When the completed forms were received back in the office, coding was begun. This is the process of assigning values or categories to each of the responses. Of particular importance in the coding was a set of items designed to help two psychiatrists form an opinion about the respondents' mental health. The two psychiatrists classified each respondent within one of six categories: "well," "mild symptom formation," "moderate symptom formation," "marked symptom formation," "severe symptom formation," and "incapacitation." The difficulties in making these judgments were many, and even though the psychiatrists attempted to use criteria in as standardized a way as possible, they state in the report their concern that their measures may not have been entirely valid: that is, that they may have measured something other than mental health.

It is standard practice in writing reports to omit discussion of the methods by which data were analysed; these often are a combination of routine and inspiration that would be difficult to report adequately. It may be assumed that the coded responses to each of the questions were numbered, and the numbers punched into I.B.M. cards; that tables were made up from the cards, and studied and speculated about by the research staff; that new questions led to new tables; and that, finally, as the data were understood, the main lines of the report developed.

The report presents, for the most part, cross-break tables showing the incidence of different degrees of health and illness among various groups. It shows, for example, that among the youngest age group some 24% seem "well," 38% seem to have "mild symptom formation," 24% have "moderate symptom formation," and 15% are "impaired," and that the percentage who are well decreases as one moves into older age groups, while the percentage who are impaired increases dramatically. These results are interpreted, at some length, in the text.[6] Other sections of the report deal with the incidence of health and illness by socioeconomic level, national origin, religion, and number of generations in this country.

Mental Health in the Metropolis is a study that has both exploratory and descriptive aims. It is concerned with learning as much as possible about a previously obscure problem and then describing its results as fully and accurately as possible. An alternative aim might have been that of explaining what was found, making clear why a certain group seemed to be a high risk population, for example. Still another alternative aim might have been that of testing some previously formulated hypothesis, which perhaps itself was an implication of a theory that was of importance, but was not well established.

---

[6] *Ibid.*, p. 160.

The aims of the study will determine the study design. Exploration requires a great deal of information throughout the area of concern. Testing requires precision and rigor. Studies that hope to support causal explanations may have to develop something near an experimental design. The type of analysis required will also be determined, in part, by the aims of the study. Testing and explanation involve inference; description does not. Finally, the aims of the study will determine the type of report that is written.

The main divisions in this text attempt to parallel what are distinct steps in quantitative research: data collection, data processing, description, and inference. Chapter 2 deals with the measurement aspect of data collection; Chapter 3 with data processing, Chapters 4 to 9 with techniques for the description of data, and Chapters 10 to 14 with the establishment of inference. Chapter 15 presents some material on reporting.

PROBLEMS

1.1. Examine some recently published quantitative research studies. You ought to look at a few book-length studies (see the Book Review sections of *The American Sociological Review* and *The American Journal of Sociology* for brief descriptions from which you may choose some which seem of special interest) and also a few article-length studies (for which see *The American Sociological Review*, *Sociometry*, and *The American Journal of Sociology*).

Describe the technical problems encountered by the authors; for example, problems of measurement, sample selection, data processing, analysis of data, and communication of results.

1.2. Select some general problem area, such as the implications of poverty, or the determinants of mental illness. State a specific problem that would lead to quantitative research and a specific problem that would lead to qualitative research. (For example, in a study of the implications of poverty, a quantitative study might be one that would seek the incidence of various diseases among groups of different income. A qualitative study might be one that would seek to describe the different life styles of the poor and not-so-poor, as in Lewis' *Five Families*.)

Discuss briefly the ways each study might contribute to an understanding of the problem area.

1.3. Name two problems for which the data of Appendix 2 might be relevant. Would the analyses be descriptive or explanatory, exploring or testing?

Chapter 2

Measurement

There are at least three quite different processes by which we decide the amount or quantity of something. Later in the chapter these processes are discussed in detail, but in this introductory section we may consider them in a looser way.

First is the process we may use when we have a unit of measure: inches or pounds or calories, for example. We are then able to talk about how many units are contained in whatever we are examining; how many inches of length or pounds of weight or calories of heat. When there is a unit of measure we may say that we are working with a *metric system*, although more frequently we would distinguish between an *interval system*, when we have a scale whose zero point is arbitrary, and a *ratio system*, when we have a scale whose zero point means an absence of the quality that is being measured.

Often, particularly in older books, *measurement* is considered possible only if we have a metric system. This may be justified from a common sense point of view, since it is only when we have a metric system that we may be able to give a numerical answer to the question "How much is there?" In fact, it may be argued that only if we have a ratio system can we truly state a quantity, since in an interval system the numbers assigned to amounts of the quality are to some extent arbitrary. (The Fahrenheit scale for temperature is an interval system in which zero degrees does not mean absence of heat, nor does it represent the same temperature as zero degrees in the Centigrade system.)

A more modern view is to include under the heading of measurement not only the sort of absolute assessment of amount that is possible with a metric system, but also a more *comparative* assessment of amount which may be furnished by a ranking. An example would be a ranking of students in terms of their athletic ability, which would enable us to say that one of the students is first and another second, but not that any

9

student has a certain amount of athletic ability. Measurement of this kind involves use of an *ordinal system*.

Some authors distinguish between quantitative and qualitative data by saying, essentially, that quantitative data is the result of measurement by means of either a metric or an ordinal system, whereas qualitative data is the result of identifying, discerning, or designating. This is one approach and may be developed into a consistent point of view. It seems preferable, however, to recognize still another process (besides statement of quantity and comparison) as yielding measurement, since this third process is also one through which the data of quantitative research may be developed. In fact, in some studies, this process is more important than the preceding two. It is that of categorizing: of deciding whether a particular instance belongs under a heading or does not, whether a quality exists or does not. It is sometimes referred to as "one-zero measurement," to communicate that just two values can be attributed to the quality; either it exists or it does not. (There can be more than just two categories, but each is treated in a "one-zero" fashion: for example, "Is she a red-head; yes or no? A blonde; yes or no? A brunette; yes or no?") This kind of measurement may be said to rely on a *nominal system*.

All three kinds of data—metric, ordinal, and nominal—present us with the same statistical problems. We require techniques, irrespective of the kind of data, for identifying representative values in an array, for describing the degree of homogeneity in the array, for picturing the array, and for deciding the extent to which the data support or invalidate a statistical hypothesis. The particular techniques that we develop to meet these ends differ, however, depending on the level of the data with which we are working. It therefore seems a reasonable procedure to consider metric, ordinal, and nominal data alike to be measurements, but measurements of different kinds.

A definition of measurement which will include all these processes is:

Measurement is any process by which a value is assigned to the level or state of some quality of an object of study.[1]

Notice that this definition is met by processes that may be subjective as well as objective, and whose values may be descriptive terms as well as numbers designating quantities. Notice, too, that the definition requires nothing of the measurement in terms of precision, trustworthiness, or usefulness. Some measurements may be worth making, while others may not. We shall need criteria of the worth of measurements to decide this.

[1] Compare this definition with that offered by Peter Caws, in "Definition and Measurement in Physics," in *Measurement, Definitions, and Themes*, ed. C. West Churchman and Philburn Ratoosh (New York: Wiley, 1959), p. 5. The definition here is similar to Caws' except broadened to include categorization as a kind of measurement.

"Usefulness" depends on the relation of the measurement to the research goal. "Precision" and "trustworthiness" may be evaluated, in part, by assessing the reliability and validity of the measurements. Because these assessments—particularly reliability—sometimes focus attention on the instruments used to produce the data, we might pause to examine what we mean by the term "instrument of measurement."

Measuring Instruments

Suppose that we want to measure the length of a desk top. To accomplish this, we set one end of a tape measure at one edge of the desk top, then unroll it until we reach the other edge. We read the marking on the tape, and say "Fifty-eight inches," or whatever it is. What we are essentially saying is that because a tape measure length of fifty-eight inches matches the table top length, then the table top must be fifty-eight inches too.

The tape measure is an instance of *a measuring instrument;* that is, *a device that permits us to assign values to the level of a quality possessed by objects of study*. It can be unrolled to give us values for the length of anything within a certain range of lengths—desk tops, pictures, shoes—with a certain degree of accuracy. In social research, a questionnaire is sometimes called a measuring instrument, since it can be used to assess the extent to which individuals have some quality, such as information about current events. When a measurement is made subjectively, as when a judge decides which of several candidates seems the most able, we might say that it is the judge himself who is the measuring instrument. Some research groups that have been forced to rely on subjective judgments, but that have also wanted to achieve as much precision as possible, have used terms like "calibrating the observer" to refer to training designed to increase the reliability of judgments. Later in the chapter there is presented a discussion of the most commonly used instruments for developing nominal, ordinal, and metric data.

Reliability and Validity

Two important criteria for judging the goodness of any measurement are the reliability and the validity of the measurement. Conceptually, reliability refers to the extent to which repeated measurement produces the same result, while validity refers to the extent to which the measurements deal with the level of the quality they are supposed to be dealing with, and not something else. Although these are the central meanings of these terms, there are a number of ways of investigating each.

Assessments of reliability may consider either the physical instrument by which the data are collected, or the judge or observer who is inevitably required to read or interpret the results produced by that instrument.

The first type of reliability may be referred to as interinstrument reliability, and is a statement of the extent to which the same instrument, or instruments believed to be identical, will produce the same values when assessing a quality that is constant in amount. A test of interinstrument reliability would be a comparison of responses to an item on degree of religious belief which is placed at the beginning and again at the end of an interview schedule. An example of an instrument that might be expected to have low interinstrument reliability would be a yardstick made out of an easily stretched rubber.

The second type of reliability is interobserver reliability, which is the extent to which different observers or judges agree in their statement of the measurement. A test of interobserver reliability would be the comparison of the decisions made by two coders asked to decide the category within which a statement should be placed. Another would be the comparison of the statements of two chemists regarding the level of liquid in a tube.

A frequently used measure of reliability is the percentage of agreement between different assessments. This measure has some unsatisfactory characteristics, but it may well be as good as any other. Its chief drawback is that its value may increase if the demand for precision is reduced. For example, the percentage of agreement between coders who only have to decide between dark and light will be higher than the percentage of agreement between coders who have to decide among several shades of gray. When the degree of precision aimed at is taken into account, the percentage of agreement seems to be a reasonably satisfactory measure.

There seem to be at least four different ways in which investigators attempt to support the validity of measures. Elinson gives these definitions:

Validity A. Construct validity is what the investigator says the measure is measuring: "Intelligence is what intelligence tests measure" . . . .

Validity B. Consensual validity involves construct validity, but is assessed by the degree of consensus among investigators that a measure is measuring a certain quality. . . .

Validity C. Criterion validity is the association between one measure and a measure of some other variable taken to be the criterion variable. . . . .

Validity D. Predictive validity is the association between one measure and a measure of some other variable taken to be the criterion variable . . . over time—i.e., predictive of some criterion.[2]

[2] Jack Elinson, "Methods of Sociomedical Research," in *Handbook of Medical Sociology*, ed. Howard Freeman, Sol Levine, and Leo G. Reeder (Englewood Cliffs, N.J.: Prentice-

It is easy to see how a measure of, say, self-esteem might first be validated by showing that it is associated with judgments of self-esteem made by close acquaintances (Validity C). The judgments of close acquaintances would be trustworthy in terms of a different idea of validity, Validity B. The investigator might not trust his measure even then, however, if it did not predict which individuals would be likely to experience depression in the face of frustration, and which would be relatively invulnerable to depression (Validity D).

Validity A is a way of escaping the problem of establishing validity by defining the concept in terms of the measure. It is usually an evasion, however; the concept generally means more than just the measure. There is another idea of validity, in addition to the four listed, which also has some aspects of evasion of the problem, called "face validity"; this is simply the appeal to the inherent plausibility of the measure.

Frequently validity, like reliability, is measured by the percentage of agreement between the decisions made by the tested instrument and the decisions made by the criterion. (Of course if validity is argued either by the construct validity or face validity routes, no statistical evaluation is necessary.) Occasionally, we encounter a research report in which the validity of a measure is argued by showing that it corresponds with a criterion measure more often than chance would explain. This is a poor argument; we should hope that a measure of something would correspond to a criterion at better than a chance level, even if the measure were only of slight value. (Imagine a weather forecast that was only a little better than guesswork.) A good measure must not just correspond better than chance—it must correspond regularly.

Nominal Measurement

Suppose that we are able to tell when a quality has achieved different states, but we cannot say anything more about relationships among the states. We know when hair color is blond, brunette, or redhead, but we cannot say that one color is more anything than another, or that the brunette is closer to the blonde in some way than is the redhead, nor can we make any other relational statement.

The basic idea of the kind of measurement that we are now discussing is this: we assign values to qualities of objects only in terms of whether or not the objects are equivalent in the qualities. Where objects are not equivalent in whatever quality we are interested in, we make no

Hall, 1963), pp. 460–461. See also the discussion of reliability and validity in Claire Selltiz, Marie Jahoda, Morton Deutsch, and Stuart Cook, *Research Methods in Social Relations* (New York: Holt, 1959), pp. 146–186.

further statement. A slightly different way of saying this is that we assign values in such a way that we identify which things are alike and which things are different, but do not say that one has more of the quality. Measurement that has these properties is called *nominal measurement*. When not all of our objects of study are unique, we refer to nominal measurement as *categorization*. A system for nominal measurement may then also be referred to as a category system.

How do we construct a category system? Some category systems come to us already constructed. These are the classifications of people or institutions that are already part of our habits of thought: for example, male and female; married, single, divorce, widowed, and separated; or metropolitan, suburban, small town, and rural. When we use such "given" categories, we do not concern ourselves too much about the rules by which we assign values. It would truly be ridiculous to train a survey interviewer in rules for deciding sex. There might be more question about determining race without explicit criteria, but few, if any, research people worry about this.

Often we do not work with "self-evident" category systems, such as those for sex, marital status, race, religion, or type of residence. Instead, we may want to classify individuals according to reason for voting for a certain candidate, or attitude toward education. In these cases, there is no obvious category system ready at hand. The category system must be developed from the data themselves or, alternatively, from theory or from our general grasp of the situation.

A category system that is not based on the data, but instead comes from common usage or theory or intuition, can be characterized as an *a priori system*. Generally, when we do not have some specific hypothesis in mind, and when the quality in which we are interested is not already categorized by convention, we build our category system directly from our data. If we develop categories that are "close" to the data—that is, that require little inference on the part of the categorizers—and which are also clear-cut in their definitions, we should have few problems of reliability, and we may at least claim face validity with better basis than this claim generally has.

A category system that is close to the data will almost always have many separate categories. A reader will not be able to grasp results presented in so many discrete categories, and so the investigator must anticipate having to group these precise low level categories into a small number of more gross categories, probably at a higher level of abstraction. If he can be fairly sure in advance what these more gross categories will be, it may well be advantageous for him to introduce them immediately, and either list the more precise subdivisions of the gross cate-

gories as subcategories, or else dispense with them entirely. No
will work be saved by this procedure, but there will be fewer c
errors, because the coders will be working in terms of the categ
that will eventually be used. However, the investigator must remem͵ʋr
that any precise category (in fact, any category that cannot be formed
by grouping together other categories) which is *not* used at the time of
coding will almost undoubtedly never be available for examination
through the life of the study; it would be too expensive to go back and
recode everything.

If the investigator hopes to test specific hypotheses, it is most useful
for him to introduce their terms into the coding process, rather than
hope to represent them by a combination of lower level categories. The
danger is that otherwise the data may not be coded from the proper per-
spective and the investigator will not be able to coordinate the actual
categories with the concepts he hopes to use. Suppose, for example,
that he hopes to learn in what ways middle-class women differ from
working-class women in their management of their children, and suppose
that he is interested not in differences in specific practices, but rather
in the level of concern they display. Unless the data have been coded
specifically for "expressions of concern," there may be no way of ever
learning about this; if the data were coded only for the child-raising
practices reported by the mothers, or for their apparent goals in child-
raising, or even for the nature of their concerns in child-raising, there
might be no way of ever deducing the mothers' level of concern. Yet
even though we should always code in terms of concepts important to
the aims of the study, it is usually also desirable to build at least some
codes directly from the data. These may serve, if in no other way, as
inventories of what is there.

There are three requirements that a system of categories developed
from data ought to meet, in addition to the requirements of reliability
and validity. These may be referred to as: logical correctness; articulation; and overall organization.[3]

Logical correctness refers to the requirement that here, as in any category system, the set of categories should be exhaustive, and the categories themselves mutually exclusive. That is, any object of study should
be classifiable within the system, and no object of study should be
classifiable more than once. Most category systems attain exhaustive-
ness by including a "wastebasket" category such as "not classifiable

[3] The discussion here is based in good part on the paper, "Some General Principles of
Questionnaire Classification," by Paul F. Lazarsfeld and Allan H. Barton, in *The
Language of Social Research*, ed. Paul F. Lazarsfeld and Morris Rosenberg, (Glencoe,
Free Press, 1955), pp. 83–99.

elsewhere," to insure that the system is logically correct. If a category system is a good one, it will not be necessary to use the wastebasket category often.

Articulation refers to the organization of categories according to level of specificity. The biological classificatory system offers a model; any organism may be classified according to its species, but its species and related species are then grouped by genus, and its genus and related genera are then grouped by phylum.

Lazarsfeld and Barton are very clear on this point:

The basic purpose of classification is to simplify the handling of a great number of individual items by putting them into a smaller number of groups, each group consisting of items which act more or less alike in relation to the problem being studied. This raises the following problem: If the classification is kept very simple, with only a few broad groupings, it will combine many elements which are not very similar. Important distinctions of a more detailed sort will be lost completely. On the other hand, if the classification preserves all distinctions which may be of any significance, it will contain too many groups to be surveyed and handled conveniently.

The solution of this dilemma is to use an "articulate" classification: a classification with several steps starting with a few broad categories and breaking them down into many more detailed categories. In this way one can eat one's cake and have it too: when a few broad categories are sufficient, only the simple first step need be used; when a more detailed study is required, the finer distinctions can be found preserved in the later, final steps of the classification system.[4]

Overall Organization. Finally, the category system should have a structure or organization that makes sense. For example, in a categorization of responses of college students to the question, "What are the advantages of a college education," the broad headings might move from changes in the self, to changes as viewed by others, to possible social benefits of these changes. The point is to make it possible for a user of the code to grasp easily its principle of organization. If the general and specific headings each follow a clear logical sequence, the code is easily dealt with; if the categories are jumbled one after the other with no rhyme or reason, the code will be hard to use.

Building a Code from Data

There is a definite procedure that can be followed in building a code from data. We begin by selecting a sample of the materials to be coded which is large enough so that items that appear in the data with sufficient frequency to require categories will assuredly be represented in the

---

[4] *The Language of Social Research, op. cit.*, pp. 84–85.

sample. A first sorting of the sample materials then suggests what categories are needed, and from this the code itself is constructed. There are three steps in the process: sampling of items; preliminary sorting; and construction of the code.

The process may be illustrated with materials from a study of college students. Students entering a particular school, which we will call X University, were asked "Do you expect that X University will be helpful in your life?" and then, "Why do you expect this?" This question was one of a series intended to produce information about what these students expected of the college. From the total population of protocols, about seventy-five were chosen at random and the responses to the questions were typed out. It should be noted that it did not matter for the adequacy of the eventual code what proportion seventy-five was of the total freshman class; what was important was that seventy-five was a large enough sample of responses to ensure that a response that occurred a significant number of times in the freshman class as a whole would be represented at least two or three times in the sample.

A small number of the responses, a section of the preliminary sorting, and the beginning of the code, are presented as Table 2.1. Notice that in Section C, the code contains not only the headings for code categories, but examples of responses that go into these categories, as well. If only the headings of categories were listed, it would have been easy to forget the types of items the headings were supposed to name. The investigator would then have had to guess just what a particular category meant.

Ordinal Measurement

If we are working with a nominal measurement system, and we have two objects that we are interested in comparing with each other, then there are only two statements that we can possibly make about the objects, and we must choose one or the other. We can say that one object is *like* the other (that is, is equivalent to it in its value of the quality in which we are interested), or we can say the two objects are unlike. Often, however, even though we may not have available a unit of measurement, we may be able to rate some objects as having more of a quality than others. The measurement system in which the magnitudes of qualities can be compared is referred to as *ordinal measurement*.

Ordinal measurement has three characteristics: first, values are assigned to objects in such a way that we can identify which objects are equivalent; second, in any pair that is not equivalent, we can say which object is the greater and which is the lesser in the quality; and third, if one object is greater in a quality than a second, and the second is greater in the quality than a third, then the first object is also greater in

Table 2.1

Material Illustrating Process of Building a Code from Data

A. Responses to the Questions: "Do you expect that X University will be helpful in your life?" and "Why do you expect this?"
   1. Yes. Everything we do and everything we go through leaves an experience in our life.
   2. Yes. Because I'll be able to hold my own in conversations on a lot more subjects, also I'll have a basic knowledge of everything.
   3. Yes, I do. Will advance me in the way of better initiative and industry.
   4. Yes. Due to the newer methods I'll be better suited. (How's that?) How to meet up to conversations. (Anything else?) No.
B. Preliminary Sorting
   Yes, because
   Everything we do and everything we go through leaves an experience in our life; Everything in your life is helpful;*
   Same reason as any college; Any higher education is good; Any kind of education is helpful in your life; I think only as far as getting an education
   The education I receive in liberal arts and humanities couldn't help but be a help in later life; Courses taught will affect me throughout my life and knowledge will affect me
C. Code
   1. *Yes, because of value of education in itself*
       11. *Education is always helpful.* Any higher education is good; any kind of education is helpful in your life; I think only as far as getting an education; the education I receive in liberal arts and humanities couldn't help but be a help in later life; courses taught will affect me throughout my life and knowledge will affect me.
       12. *Broadened because of X University's program.* Broaden me—learn to enjoy arts and music instead of just science; because it's the kind of broad education everyone should have; broadens interests and you need a variety of interests to be adjusted; I will have a general knowledge of most subjects; broaden my environment in natural and social science which I might not acquire in other colleges; get cultured things as well as specifics; cultural aspect; if I wasn't in this college, I wouldn't read Plato.

---

* Semicolons separate responses made by different individuals.

the quality than the third. Stating these three characteristics of ordinal measurement is simply a formal way of stipulating that ordinal measurement is a system that permits us to develop a ranking of individuals in terms of their possession of some quality.

It is worth stressing that ordinal measurement is inherently *compara-*

tive. As an example, to determine which of two substances is the harder, we may see which will scratch the other. This scratch-test comparison will clearly satisfy the first two requirements for ordinal measurement; any two substances will either scratch each other equally, in which case we shall say that they are equivalent in hardness, or else one will scratch the other, in which case we shall say that it is the harder. The third requirement for an ordinal system is that if we take three substances of different hardness, and the first scratches the second, while the second scratches the third, then the first will always also scratch the third. This third requirement for an ordinal scale is called "transitivity."

It may be worth noting that we cannot take transitivity for granted. It must be checked either by reference to the logic of the situation or, more frequently, by reference to empirical data. For example, in trying to rank individuals in terms of dominance, we may find that individual A tends to talk over individual B, and individual B over individual C, but individual C somehow manages to dominate individual A. In this case, "dominance" cannot be measured in an ordinal system, since it is not clear what ranks ought to be assigned to A, B, and C. The three are not equivalent in their degree of dominance, yet neither is one clearly to be ranked above another. There are at least two ways in which this problem might be handled, and an ordinal system, or set of ordinal systems, worked out nevertheless. The simplest is to assert that where such failures of transitivity occur, the objects should be considered to be equivalent in the quality even though, if we take them two by two, they are not. The alternative is to think of the quality as a resultant of the interaction of several factors, which individuals possess in different combinations, and try to work out the rankings of individuals on these hypothesized underlying factors. Although theoretically attractive, this second alternative leads rapidly to very complicated problems: What are the underlying factors? How are they to be measured? How are they to be seen as combining?

A number of techniques have been developed for achieving ordinal measurement of qualities of interest to social research. Bert Green, in a review article, mentions six distinct approaches, of which the first two would seem to be of most importance for sociological work.[5] Arguments are sometimes made that some of these approaches—summated scores, Thurstone scaling, and the unfolding techniques—go beyond ordinal measurement and achieve the level of interval scale measurement. It is not possible here to consider the merits of these arguments; they appear to be persuasive, in various degrees, but not conclusive. The conservative

[5] Bert F. Green, "Attitude Measurement," in *Handbook of Social Psychology*, ed. Gardner Lindzey (Cambridge: Addison-Wesley, 1954).

course is to accept the results of each of these approaches as trustworthy on an ordinal level, and to examine closely the sense in which they may be informative beyond this level.

Green's list of approaches is the following:

1. Summated scores. We develop a set of items, to which we have individuals respond. We rank the individuals according to the sum of their scores on the items. A true-false test would be an example of this approach. Perhaps the best known form in social science work is the "Likert scale," in which are summed responses to a set of items each of which permits the respondent to locate himself on a five-point scale.

2. Scalogram analysis. Here items are developed that are interrelated in such a way that anyone who responds positively to a "difficult" item will almost certainly have responded positively to all easier items. Individuals are ranked according to the most difficult item to which they responded positively, unless there is good reason for interpreting this response as an "error of measurement." This approach was developed by Guttman and is often referred to as Guttman scaling. It is also referred to as cumulative scaling.

3. Ratings. Judges can be asked to rate individuals, or to rank order individuals. The judges may be helped by instructions regarding what to take into account, but the assessments are in any event subjective. When the rankings of several judges are to be combined, we have the problem of the *amalgamation of judgments.*

4. Judgment methods. Items are ranked by judges in terms of the degree to which they exhibit a favorable or positive attitude. Individuals are then asked to identify which of the items they would endorse. They are ranked according to the value of the average item they endorse. This approach was first developed by Thurstone, and is sometimes called Thurstone scaling.

5. The unfolding technique. In this approach, developed by Clyde Coombs, individuals are asked to rank items by the extent to which they agree with them, irrespective of whether an item is too far in a positive or in a negative direction. From this information, it is possible to deduce an ordering of items by the degree to which they represent positive attitudes, and also to deduce an ordering of individuals by the degree to which they possess a positive attitude.

6. Latent structure analysis. Paul Lazarsfeld has proposed a general mathematical model in which individuals who have a certain underlying level of positive attitude are assumed to have a corresponding probability of agreeing with particular items. From the pattern of responses of the entire population, estimates are developed of the way in which individuals of different types are likely to have dealt with the items. It is then possible to state the type to which a particular individual probably belongs by examining the pattern of his responses. The mathematics involved, like the model itself, is extremely sophisticated.[6]

A more detailed discussion of the first three approaches follows.

The Method of Summated Scores

Let us begin with a simple example of a scale based on summated scores. Suppose that an instructor wants to rank his students in terms of the extent to which they understand the material of his course. To make the example more concrete, let us assume that the course is one in statistical methods. How should he do it?

We might think of a single question that might somehow sample a student's knowledge of the course material; "What is a mode?," for example. But this would only allow us to divide our students into those who know, and those who do not, and we should like to be able to make finer distinctions than this. Another problem with this single item approach is that even those who do not know might guess correctly. And there is always the chance that response to the item is not a perfectly valid indication of statistical knowledge; someone with a good general knowledge of the subject may have neglected to learn the particular matter the item tests, or someone with very little general knowledge might happen to know just that one point and no other.

Obviously, what is needed is a large group of items, each of them sampling the students' information about the course. However, just having a great many items is not sufficient. Suppose that every item tested the same level of information about the course. Then students with less than this level would miss most items, and students with more than this level would answer almost all items correctly. Again there would be too little discrimination. We need items that cover the entire range of difficulty. Another point is that it would not do to include in the test questions about early English literature. A student could, with good cause, ask what they had to do with statistics. The items should, of course, deal with the quality being measured. Every item, however, will test some-

---

[6] There is an extensive literature on the construction of indices and scales. In addition to the article by Bert Green, (*ibid.*), see the articles by Stouffer, Guttman, and Lazarsfeld in *Studies in Social Psychology in World War II, Measurement and Prediction*, ed. Samuel Stouffer *et al.* (Princeton, N.J.: Princeton University Press, 1950). Also, Clyde Coombs, *A Theory of Data* (New York: John Wiley, 1964); John and Matilda Riley, *Sociological Studies in Scale Analysis* (New Brunswick, N.J.: Rutgers University, 1954); and Warren Torgerson, *Theory and Methods of Scaling* (New York: John Wiley, 1958). In addition there are manuals describing in detail specific techniques: for example, Paul Lazarsfeld, *Latent Structure Analysis* (New York: Bureau of Applied Social Research, Columbia University, 1960); and almost numberless technical articles in such journals as *Psychometrika*. Further references are given below.

thing in addition to what we want to test; it will have "surplus content." For example, every item will test capacity to understand English. We cannot do away with surplus content, but we must ensure that the surplus content of the items will not produce a biased test. One way of attempting to do this is by trying to vary the nature of the surplus content. For example, an examination on statistics might include data from a wide variety of fields.

Constructing the scale. We begin the construction of the scale by developing a list of a large number of items, as many as fifty, each of which seems likely to have some relationship to the quality that we want to measure. In developing this list, we attempt to include items that vary among themselves in surplus content and which test different levels of the quality in which we are interested, but all of which seem, on the face of it, to have something to do with the quality. Where do items come from? Goode and Hatt suggest: "Possible items should be selected from all available sources—newspapers, magazines, books, motion pictures, and the student's own knowledge of the problem."[7] Clearly, developing this initial sample of items is a fairly arbitrary procedure, although we attempt to achieve as wide a representation of possible items as we can.

The next problem is to select the items that work. To do this, the total test is tried on a sample of about a hundred respondents. A score is given to each respondent by adding up the number of items to which he gave answers which were "correct," which "passed," or which were indicative of a certain attitude. Once this is done, the investigator examines the relation between each item of the test and the total score. He asks of each item whether it separates people in the same way the total scores separate people. If it does, then it is a usable item. If it fails to do so, then it must be rejected.[8] A group of items that are consistent in the way they order respondents makes up the completed scale.[9]

In Likert's handling of the method of summated scores, each item is responded to by checking one of five alternatives; strongly agree, agree, undecided, disagree, and strongly disagree. These are given values from $+2$, for strongly agree, to -2, for strongly disagree, and the values are

[7] William J. Goode and Paul K. Hatt, *Methods in Social Research* (New York: McGraw-Hill, 1953), p. 272. For a more detailed discussion of item selection and scale construction in general, see their presentation, *ibid.*, pp. 261–295. See also McNemar, Quinn, "Opinion-Attitude Methodology," *Psychological Bulletin,* **43** (1946), pp. 289–374, Bert Green; "Attitude Measurement," *op. cit.;* and Allen Edwards, *Techniques of Attitude Scale Construction* (New York: Appleton-Century-Crafts, 1957), pp. 149–171.

[8] Edwards discusses a number of alternative statistical guides for item selection.

[9] A case study of the processes by which some very useful indices were constructed is given in T. W. Adorno, Else Fraenkel-Brunswik, Daniel Levinson, and R. Nevitt Sanford, *The Authoritarian Personality* (New York: Harper, 1950).

summed to give the individual his overall score. Likert showed that this simple scoring system gives results equivalent to scoring systems based on much more complicated assumptions.

Sometimes, in constructing a scale of the sort described here, it may be desirable to weight the contribution of individual items to the total score. For example, in an index intended to measure level of commitment to continuing education, an answer to the question, "Do you intend to continue in school" might be given twice or three times the weight of an answer to the question "All things considered, would you say school is a good institution, or a bad institution?" because the first item is more closely related to the intent of the index. The idea is to reduce the contribution of surplus content to the total score by giving small weights to items whose surplus content seems large. Information on the degree to which an index is reflected in an item may come from the statistical examination of the association of index and item. It may also come through the use of factor analysis, which is a statistical technique that can simultaneously identify items from which indices can be formed, because they all are related to the same quality, and also state the extent to which specific items contain surplus content.

Scalogram Analysis

In the method of summated scores, any item that is responded to positively contributes as much to the total score as any other item. In a test of mathematical ability, a correct answer to the question, "Integrate $(x^2 - 2)$" would contribute no more than a correct answer to the question, "How much is 2 plus 2?" If someone for some reason gave a correct answer to the first and an incorrect answer to the second, he would receive the same score on the pair of items as someone who answered in the opposite pattern.

In the scalogram analysis approach to ordinal measurement, each item in the test is associated with a level of the quality. The ranking of an individual is then based on the pattern of his responses to specific items and not on his total score. In the examples above, an individual who could give a correct answer to "Integrate $(x^2 - 2)$" would get a higher score on mathematical ability than someone who could not, whether or not he had answered correctly "How much is 2 plus 2?" (unless it should be decided that his answer to the difficult question was a fortunate guess).

There are a good many ways in which the idea that the ranking of an individual should be related to the pattern of his performance rather than to a composite score can be worked out in practice. The best known is the Guttman scaling technique, although a technique due to Bogardus antedates it by many years.

Bogardus was concerned with measuring the relative attractiveness or unattractiveness of various entities, including most notably ethnic minorities. To do this, Bogardus worked out what he considered levels of desired social distance. The first level, in which there is no desire for social distance, would be shown by someone who was willing to admit a member of a given minority group to close kinship by marriage. The second level would be shown by someone who would refuse this, but would admit the minority group member to his club as a personal chum. Further levels include: (3) to one's street as a neighbor, (4) to employment in one's occupation, (5) to citizenship in one's country, (6) as visitors only to one's country, (7) would exclude from one's country. The level of dislike of an individual for a minority group is indicated by the point at which he would refuse intimacy.

The chief problem in the Bogardus technique is that the unidimensionality of the test is assumed, rather than demonstrated. *Unidemensionality* means that all items are getting at the same underlying quality. Items can be judged to be unidimensional if—and only if—all those individuals who pass or agree with a difficult item also pass or agree with an easier item. (A "difficult" item is one that few people agree with. An "easy" item is agreed with by many.) For example, the following items represent a unidimensional test of the quality, "willingness to stay in the army after World War II had ended." The items were part of an instrument devised to measure, just after the war had ended, the extent to which enlisted men would want to remain in service.

1. If civilian jobs are hard to get after the war, do you think you might want to stay?
2. If we have a large army after the war (say 2,000,000 men), do you think you might want to stay.
3. Do you think that you might want to stay in the army for *a career* after the war?[10]

An individual with great desire to stay in the army would answer all three questions positively. An individual with some desire would answer the first two positively. An individual with little desire, but without aversion, might answer only the first positively. However, almost no one would answer the second positively but not the first, or the third positively but not the first and second. Because this is the case, the items may be characterized as unidimensional. Of course, this must be decided empirically, and not by arguing that it should be so, as is done here.

[10] Adapted from material presented by Louis Guttman in *Studies in Social Psychology in World War II*, Volume IV, *op. cit.*, pp. 136–137.

Guttman scaling is concerned with selecting items that are unidimensional. Individuals may then be ranked in terms of the most difficult item they passed. When items are unidimensional, the responses of individuals can be shown to follow a simple pattern when (a) the items are listed as columns, and go from the easiest item to pass or agree with to the most difficult, in order; and (b) individuals are listed as rows, and go from the individual who has most of the quality, in order, to the individual who has least.

Suppose we have four items, in order of difficulty A, B, C, and D. Item A might be "What is the square of 15?" or even "How much is two and two?" and Item D might be "Integrate $(x^2 - 2)$." Or we might have a set of items that reflect the seriousness of grief, in which Item A would be "mild insomnia," and Item D would be "hallucinating about grieved-for individual." Now suppose we have five individuals of differing levels of mathematical ability, or differing levels of grief symptomatology. Then we should expect patterns of responses to the items as shown in Table 2.2, if the items are unidimensional.

If the items are unidimensional for our population, we know that the individual who scored "two passes" must have passed just the first two items. So long as the items are unidimensional, we can reproduce the pattern of any individual's answers just by knowing his total score. "Reproducibility" is thus a way of referring to the extent to which the items are unidimensional in a population.

Construction of a Guttman scale can be arduous, if done by hand at one's desk. The general idea is to start with a larger number of items than we shall eventually use, and by examining patterns of responses to reduce the number of items to a small unidimensional set. (Computer programs for accomplishing this are available and of course should be used if

Table 2.2

Responses to Ranked Items by Ranked Individuals

	Items			
Individuals	A	B	C	D
1	Pass	Pass	Pass	Pass
2	Pass	Pass	Pass	Fail
3	Pass	Pass	Fail	Fail
4	Pass	Fail	Fail	Fail
5	Fail	Fail	Fail	Fail

possible.) The following instructions, much simplified from those given by Guttman, will suggest the nature of the procedure.[11]

1. Choose a set of fifteen to thirty[12] items that seem to be unidimensional and also seem to tap different levels of the quality. The items need not be dichotomous, (supplying only two alternatives), but it is helpful if as many are dichotomous as possible.

2. Administer the test to a population of at least thirty respondents. However, too large a population of respondents will make further work time-consuming; it is only necessary to have enough respondents to furnish a reasonable sample of the population that eventually will be studied.

3. Score respondents in terms of the total number of items with which they agree, or the total number of items that they answer correctly. It is necessary to dichotomize those items that were not originally dichotomies. Alternatives should be collapsed in a way that will maximize the usefulness of the item for discriminating among scale types in the population.

4. Score items in terms of the total number of individuals in the population who agree with it, or answer it correctly.

5. Arrange a "scalogram" by listing the individuals, in order of decreasing scores, along the left margin, and the items, in order of increasing difficulty, along the top margin.

6. Identify items that are failed by high-scoring individuals and passed by low-scoring individuals by the number of out-of-order responses that these items receive. An out-of-order response is a failure or disagreement that occurs among the high-scoring individuals in the region of predominant agreement, or a pass or agreement that occurs among the low-scoring individuals in the region of predominant disagreement. Remove the items that have the greatest number of out-of-order responses.

There is sometimes some ambiguity about which response should be called an error when an individual's responses do not follow the population ranking; that is, when he "passes" a difficult item after "failing" an easier one. In such cases, we should identify as errors those responses

---

[11] See the chapters by Stouffer and by Guttman in *Studies in Social Psychology in World War II*, Volume IV, *op. cit.*; Louis Guttman, "The Cornell Technique for Scale and Intensity Analysis," *Educational and Psychological Measurements*, **7(2)**, 1947, pp. 247–280; and the discussion based on the latter article, in Goode and Hatt, *op. cit.*, pp. 285–295.

[12] If a computer program is used there are no limits except computer capacity on the number of items or the size of the population which can be used. It is because of the existence of computer programs that the Guttman technique is likely to be of increasing importance, since without them the amount of work involved in constructing a Guttman scale is nearly prohibitive. Still, it is useful for the student to work out a Guttman scale by hand, even if he will eventually use a machine program, to get an idea of what the procedure is like.

that will make the total number of errors for the individual a minimum. If there still is an ambiguity, then it is probably good practice to take as the error the failure of the easier item, assuming that the true ranking of the individual is more likely to be indicated by his success on the more difficult one. This is not, however, a "conservative" course, and in some research situations an investigator may prefer to risk underestimating an individual's possession of a quality rather than risk exaggerating it.

7. Now rescore individuals on the new test (the original test minus the items removed in Step 6) and adjust their ranking.

8. Calculate the "coefficient of reproducibility." This is simply one minus the ratio of the number of times a response appears out-of-order to the total number of responses. If it is 0.90 or higher, you may stop. If it is not this high, or if you want greater reproducibility, continue by removal of other items that have many out-of-order responses. (The formula for the coefficient of reproducibility is $C = 1 - (e/N)$ where e stands for errors and N for the total number of responses.)[13]

There are a great many problems in Guttman scaling, and although much work has been done, not all the issues have yet been settled. Investigators who want to use the Guttman approach continue to be troubled by the difficulty of finding items that can be scaled, by the possibility that items that scale in one population will not scale in another, and by some uncertainty regarding the meaning of a given level of reproducibility. The question of the relative worth of cumulative and summated scales is still controversial. The clear logic of the Guttman approach is appealing, yet in practical situations summated scales continue to be constructed and used in preference to Guttman scales. They are easier to build, and give finer discriminations. (Whether these finer discriminations can be trusted is another matter.) Perhaps the new possibility of developing cumulative scales by computer is changing the balance.

Rating Scales

Both indices and scales have in common an attempt to produce an *objective* measurement of a quality. The respondent is expected to perform honestly, but once he does, the procedure is entirely "out there," clear-cut, repeatable. The measurement could be performed by anyone, with the same end result. Quite another strategy is, however, available to us. We could propose that some qualities are best measured subjectively, that the subjective judgments of raters in a position to know

---

[13] Under certain circumstances the coefficient of reducibility is not by itself an adequate measure of the worth of the scale. When the modal categories of response, for each item, are very large, then we should also consider the "minimum marginal reproducibility." See the discussion in Edwards, *op. cit.*

would be most likely to give reliable and valid measures. "Happiness," it may be argued, might best be measured by asking individuals to rate themselves. There would be serious problems with such a procedure, to be sure, including differences between individuals in the states they would describe as constituting great happiness or unhappiness, and differences as well in defensiveness, self-knowledge, and ability to perform what may be a difficult task. Yet it is conceivable that at times subjective appraisal, in which the individual himself weighs and combines different elements, and makes his own overall judgment, may be the only way of getting the data. Devices for eliciting such subjective appraisals may be characterized as *rating scales*. For example, in a study of divorced women, the investigator wanted to know how the second marriage of those divorced women in his sample who had remarried compared to their first. The investigator's approach was to ask for a comparative rating: "In general, how does your present married life compare to your former married life? (a) Much better; (b) A little better; (c) About the same; (d) A little worse; (e) Much worse."[14]

Amalgamation of Judgments

In subjective ratings, the response of a judge may be affected by a great many factors not controllable by instructions, no matter how good they are. Investigators may sometimes be able to reduce the possibility of idiosyncratic response by pooling the appraisals of several judges; that is, they may be able to *amalgamate* judgments. There are several methods for achieving this amalgamation. Unfortunately, no two can be relied on to give the same final ranking all the time. The two methods of amalgamation most frequently used are (a) the adding of ranks, and (b) the method of majority rule.

Adding of ranks is perhaps the simplest method of amalgamation. The investigator simply ranks the sums of the ranks assigned each object by each judge, and then considers the object with the smallest total to be the most preferred and so on. An example is given in Table 2.3. The sum of the ranks for organization A is 14, the sum for organization B is 10. Therefore, the composite ranking of organization B places it ahead of the composite ranking of organization A.

The method of majority rule requires that we have each organization compete with every other organization. We compare organization A with organization B, for example, and we find that organization A is ranked higher than B by three judges and lower by two: organization A wins that competition. We then compare organization A with organization C, and so on. Since organization A will win every competition, we

14 William J. Goode, *After Divorce* (New York: Free Press, 1956), p. 365.

rank it highest in the composite ranking. Organization B will win a competition if it runs against any organization other than organization A, and so it is next in the ranking.

The method of majority rule, in the example worked out in Table 2.3, results in a different composite ranking than does the method of added

Table 2.3

Ranking of Six Organizations in Terms of Their Effectiveness

Judges	Organizations					
	A	B	C	D	E	F
Mr. Brown	1	2	4	3	5	6
Mr. Smith	1	2	3	4	5	6
Mr. Green	6	2	1	3	4	5
Mr. Phillips	5	2	1	6	3	4
Mr. Jones	1	2	6	3	4	5

Amalgamation by method of added ranks:

	A	B	C	D	E	F
Total ranks:	14	10	15	19	21	26
Composite ranking:	2	1	3	4	5	6

Amalgamation by method of majority rule:

A compared with B: preferred, 3 out of 5
A compared with C: preferred, 3 out of 5
A compared with D: preferred, 4 out of 5
A compared with E: preferred, 3 out of 5
A compared with F: preferred, 3 out of 5

B compared with C: preferred, 3 out of 5
B compared with D: preferred, 5 out of 5
B compared with E: preferred, 5 out of 5
B compared with F: preferred, 5 out of 5

C compared with D: preferred, 3 out of 5
C compared with E: preferred, 4 out of 5
C compared with F: preferred, 4 out of 5

D compared with E: preferred, 4 out of 5
D compared with F: preferred, 4 out of 5

E compared with F: preferred, 5 out of 5

Composite ranking:	A	B	C	D	E	F
	1	2	3	4	5	6

ranks. We could devise still other methods of amalgamation, which might give still other rankings. For example, we might decide that the first rank in the consensus ranking should be given to A, because it has the most first choices, and the second rank to C, because it follows in first choices, and so on.

Interval and Ratio Scales: Metric Measurement

In order to identify not only which of two objects has the more of a quality, but also just how much more it has, we need a *unit of measure*, such as feet or pounds or degrees, in terms of which we can express the difference in magnitude. Scales in which such units of measure exist possess all the properties of ordinal measurement, plus the additional property that magnitudes have absolute meaning, in terms of the unit of measure, and need not be stated only comparatively.

We say we have an *interval scale* if we have a unit of measurement but the point where the scale begins is arbitrary; there is an arbitrary zero point. The Fahrenheit scale for measuring temperatures is of this sort. We have a unit of measurement, the degree, but the zero point of the scale was arbitrarily fixed as the temperature of freezing brine, which was the coldest temperature obtainable in the laboratory at the time the scale was developed. If the zero point is not arbitrary, but represents an absence of the measured quality (as is true of zero inches, or zero pounds weight, or zero foot-candles of illumination), then we say we have a *ratio scale*.

In an interval scale the unit of measure is based on differences:intervals. We can determine when two observations of temperature are zero degrees different (and here zero does mean an absence—of a difference), or one degree different, or several times one degree different. In a ratio scale we can make these statements, of course, and we can also make meaningful statements about the ratios that obtain between observations; we can say that one building is twice as tall as another, for example.

Some methods that are appropriate when there is a unit of measure may be used equally well with interval- and ratio-scale data. We shall therefore at times employ a single term to refer to both at once, *metric data*, since they each possess a unit of measure, a "metric."

One of the ways in which metric data arise in sociological research is through the process of counting. We can, for example, compare counties in terms of the number of people who live within them, or the number of bushels of wheat grown within them, or the number of crimes committed by their inhabitants; all these counts are metric information. Other data that sociologists may use which may be measured in a metric system include age, income, number of years of schooling, and the like. These are not sociological concepts, but rather are nonsociological measures that are likely to be of sociological importance.

Because metric measurement is powerful, giving us extra information beyond that obtained in other forms of measurement, we prefer it, all things equal. We should prefer to know someone's exact age rather than whether he was older, around middle-age, or young. The utility of metric information leads some investigators to collect metric information that may indicate, or relate to, a quality they want to study, rather than ordinal or nominal information that may capture the quality more directly. They may, for example, collect information on income, when what they want to know about is prestige in the community. The value of this strategy is still sometimes debated. It does seem to have its dubious aspects.

PROBLEMS

2.1. Refer to the data in Appendix 2.
   (a) Choose one item for which an *a priori* category system can be stated, and list the categories.
   (b) Choose one of the open-ended items. Develop a category system for it, working from the data.
2.2. How might you judge the reliability of coding of data into the categories you presented for 2.1a?
2.3. Make up a set of items you think might be unidimensional. About ten items would be a good number to work with. For example, you might develop a test of knowledge of public figures, or a questionnaire on attitudes toward our foreign policy, or a questionnaire on success experiences in athletics. In any event, you will want to include some items which most respondents will "pass," and some items which most will "fail," as well as some intermediate items.

   Ask about twenty individuals to respond to the questionnaire: friends, colleagues, anyone. Using their responses, decide which items together form a useful Guttman scale. (If you were not doing this just for experience, you would be more careful about the sample, of course.)

Chapter **3**

Data Processing

Quantitative research, especially survey research, tends to collect great amounts of information. A survey of modest size might ask forty or fifty questions of two hundred individuals, from which eight thousand different measurements would result. More ambitious studies could easily collect twenty times as much information.

Systems for processing quantitative data range from the primitive handsort card through the edgepunch card to sophisticated electro-mechanical equipment, and on to the modern computer. In the handsort system, information is entered on the face and back of file cards in a way that makes reading and sorting easy. When the cards have been sorted, the numbers in each group are counted by hand. In edgepunch systems, cards are notched along their edges so that sorting can be done by a mechanical device. Once the cards are separated, counting is done by hand. In electromechanical systems, machines read specially prepared cards, automatically sort them into categories, automatically count how many cards fall into each category, and perform a good many more complicated sorts and counts when desired. It is even possible to have the recording of results automated by this equipment and to have the machines type up whatever information is desired. Finally, computers can perform, literally, any operation on data that can be stated with sufficient specificity so that the computer can be told what to do; computers can remember information and instructions as long as desired and they can produce results with a rapidity that is simply stunning. If information or a set of instructions is to be stored, we might not want to burden a computer's memory with it, but it is easy to transfer information from the computer to tape or cards, and back again.

Despite the difference in level of development which separates the Stone Age handsort system from the Space Age computer, some of the same principles hold throughout, and it may be worth beginning our discussion with handsort, just because there the principles are plain to see.

Handsort Cards

Handsort cards are file cards—2 × 4 in., or 3 × 5 in.—around the edges of which has been listed information about a single case. An example is given in Figure 3.1. To make up the cards we need the following:

(1) A code, which will serve to categorize information, and which both names and numbers categories. For example, we might begin a code for a handsort system in this way:

> *1. Sex of respondent*
> 1m. Male.
> 1f. Female.
> *2. Age*
> 2.xx. Actual age. Example; if respondent is aged 23, then list 2.23.
> 2NA. Not ascertained.
> *3. Are you in favor of current American foreign policy?*
> 3a1.   Yes, because we are taking a firm stand.
> 3a2.   Yes, for other reason.
> 3b1.   No, because we are too belligerent.
> 3b2.   No, because we are not belligerent enough.
> 3b3.   No, for other reason.
> 3NA.   Not ascertained.

(2) A scheme for listing codes along the edges of the file cards. In computer language, this might be characterized as a list of *addresses* for information. For example, the respondent's sex is listed in the upper left corner in Figure 3.1.

```
1m                      3a1        4m     2.22
    Economics                             5a4
                     Student #37
11.4             Q.7: "Social security is a    6b1
                 useful anti-inflationary
                 measure."
    economist    Q.10: Hopes to become a   70th.
                 labor economist.
    California                             81
                        9b2
```

Figure 3.1   An example of a handsort card, taken from a study of student attitudes toward government policy. Information was also listed on the back of the card.

There is no problem in regaining information stored in handsort cards, but we might note this, in general, as a third concern, after coding of information and entering it into the proper addresses. Here we develop tabulations by sorting the cards along whatever dimension is of interest, and then counting the numbers of cards in each of the sorted categories. Cross-tabulations (tabulations according to two variables) require sorting again within each of the sorted categories.

Handsort is not a bad system for handling a small amount of data from a sample of not much more than one hundred individuals. And it is, of course, a system that requires no equipment at all. But it cannot handle too many individuals or too much information about each. As the number of cards increases, sorting and counting become increasingly tedious, unreliable, and frustrating.

Edgepunch Cards

The sorting problem, but not the counting problem, of handsort may be managed by moving to an edgepunch system. There are a good many cards manufactured for this system; McBee cards and E-Z sort cards are perhaps the best known, but there are others as well. The cards come with a row of holes (or, in some cards, two or three rows of holes) along their edges. Figure 3.2 pictures a McBee card.

In handsort cards, information was entered by writing in the value of the quality associated with a given position. In edgepunch, the investigator does not write in the value, but instead represents it by punching out the cardboard separating the holes from the edge of the card. Figure 3.3 shows how this way of entering information can be used to sort the

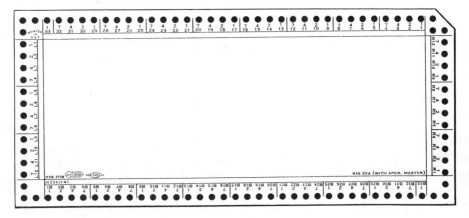

Figure 3.2   A McBee card.

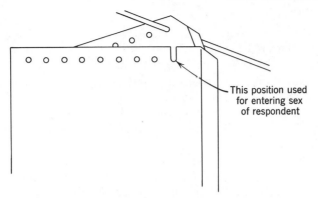

This position used
for entering sex
of respondent

Figure 3.3   Sorting with edgepunch cards. Punches in upper right hand position represent males. When steel rod is inserted through holes in upper right position and then lifted, the slotted cards, all males, drop off the rod, while the cards whose edges have not been punched, all females, are lifted away.

cards. The extreme right-hand punch position has been selected for entering the sex of the respondent. If the respondent is male, the edge is punched out; if female, it is not.

A single punch position on an edgepunch card can represent either of two values: one value if it is punched, the other if it is not. If we had more than two values to represent, we would need more punch positions. If, for example, we had a four-valued code for education, we would need two punch positions which we would associate with each other in a "field." Our code might be:

	Code in First Punch Position	Code in Second Punch Position
Education		
a. Did not complete grade school	0	0
b. Completed grade school	0	1
c. Completed high school	1	0
d. At least some college	1	1

("0" means no punch; "1" means punch.)

Just as four values can be entered in a two-hole field, up to eight can be entered in a three-hole field, up to sixteen in a four-hole field, and so on. Every additional punch position doubles the number of values that can be entered in the field. (Numbering the categories, we can use only two values, one to stand for punch, the other for no-punch. If we use a "1" for the first, a "0" for the second, our categories are being given numbers in the binary system. For a three-hole field, for example, we develop these eight binary numbers; 000, 001, 010, 011, 100, 101, 110, 111.)

The steps required for the edgepunch system are the same as those required for handsort. We code our information, both naming and numbering our categories. We work out "addresses" for specific items. (Sex, for example, might be entered in punch position one.) When we want to produce tabulations we sort mechanically but count manually.

It is difficult to say what the upper limit is to the number of edgepunch cards that can be dealt with. It may be in the neighborhood of four hundred or so. Beyond this, the cards become hard to handle, and the subgroups too large to count by hand. The amount of information that can be entered on an edgepunch card depends on the kind of card with which the investigator works. It is safe to say, however, that edgepunch cards cannot manage the amount of information that is collected in an ordinary survey. With this much information, it is necessary to move on to electromechanical counting and sorting systems.

Electromechanical Sorting and Punching Systems

Machines for sorting and counting punched cards have been developed by a number of firms, including I.B.M., Remington Rand, Underwood and others. I.B.M. equipment was, however, for many years, so dominant in social science research that its firm name became used as a generic term for any electromechanical sorting and punching system.[1]

Up to the mid-1950's, it was only by the use of electromechanical equipment that a great deal of quantitative data could be processed. A counter and sorter would be found in almost every organization that did quantitative research, and those organizations that specialized in quantitative research were likely to have a much more extensive assortment of machines. Today, computers have taken over much of the task of data processing, and in many organizations electromechanical equipment is used strictly as an adjunct to the computer. As such, it is characterized as "off-line" equipment: a clear statement of its secondary role. Where a great deal of social research is done, it is sometimes found that electromechanical equipment is still useful for projects that are limited in

---

[1] The earliest version of the present-day machine for sorting punched cards was developed about 1880, by Dr. Herman Hollerith, for use in connection with the United States Census. For some years, these machines were called Hollerith machines after their developer. I.B.M. bought the commercial organization founded by Hollerith in 1911. See the account of the history of mechanical punching and sorting devices given by Allen Kent and James W. Perry in their introduction to *Punched Cards*, ed. Casey *et al.* (New York: Reinhart, 1958). See also, Harold Borko, "History and Development of Computers," in *Computer Applications in the Behavioral Sciences*, ed. Harold Borko (Englewood Cliffs, N.J.: Prentice-Hall, 1962), pp. 36–38.

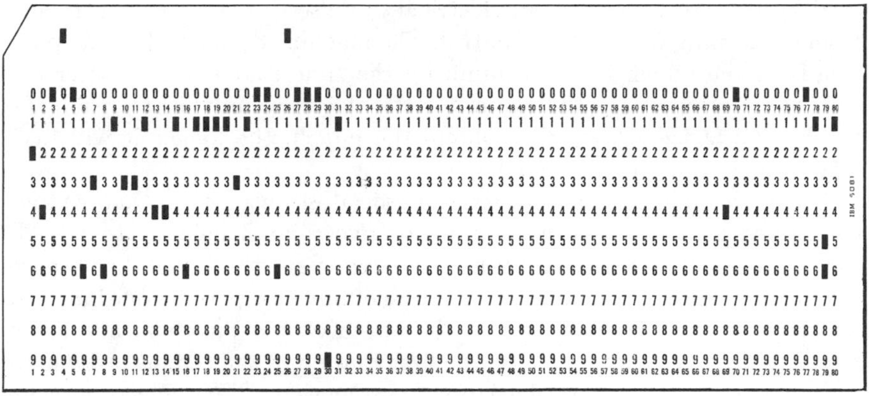

Figure 3.4 An I.B.M. card.

size and complexity, when the investigator wants to stay close to the analysis process and himself monitor what happens every step of the way. Yet computer development is moving so quickly that even this function of electromechanical equipment may soon be absorbed.

The I.B.M. system uses a card (Figure 3.4) that has eighty columns, each of which is a punch position analogous to the punch position in an edgepunch card, in which may be entered information about some quality of a studied unit.[2] In the edgepunch card, information was entered by punching or failing to punch the edge of a punch position. In the I.B.M. card, information is entered by punching a hole in one of twelve punch positions within each column. Whereas only two values can be indicated in an edgepunch card, thirteen can be indicated by the placement of a punch or by its absence in one column of an I.B.M. card.

The first ten rows of the I.B.M. card are given the numbers 0 to 9. The remaining two positions, which are conventionally identified as the top two positions in a column, are referred to sometimes as "11" and "12," sometimes as "X" and "Y," sometimes as "-" and "&." (Whereas manually sorted punched cards use a binary arithmetic, mechanically sorted punched cards use a duodecimal arithmetic.)

In most I.B.M. machines, cards are fed between an electrified drum and a metal brush. So long as there is no punch in the column along which the brush travels, the card functions as an insulator, preventing current from passing from the drum to the brush. A punch in the column being

[2] Remington Rand, I.B.M.'s closest competitor, uses a different layout for its punched card, and therefore produces cards that cannot be read by I.B.M. machines. There exist, however, translating machines that will read cards punched in the one system and produce from them cards punched in the other.

read by the brush permits an electrical impulse to reach the brush, and from it a sorting or counting control. The machine decides what the position is of the punch in the column by the time that it takes, after the card has been fed onto the drum, for the electrical impulse to reach the brush. The farther down the column the punch, the longer it will take before the impulse is registered.

There are few category systems in social science work that cannot be entered into either a one-column or two-column field in an I.B.M. card. A one-column field permits twelve categories—thirteen if the absence of a punch is given a meaning—and a two-column field permits one hundred and forty-four categories even if the absence of a punch is not given meaning. In a two-column code, the first column of the code is often used to indicate a more general basis for classification. Thus, if a code were dealing with reactions to a political candidate, the first column might indicate "positive," "negative," "mixed," and "neutral," and the second might give more specific codes. If all positive responses were given a two-digit number beginning with "1," a response such as "He is for the little guy" might be numbered "14." A response such as "I'm for him," which did not elaborate further, might be coded "11" together with other unelaborated responses.

Kinds of Electromechanical Equipment

There are a good many different machines that perform a wide variety of operations. The following list by no means includes them all.

The *key punch* enters information into the card. The cards are fed into the machine automatically. The operator reads a code sheet and punches holes into the proper columns by hitting keys on what looks very much like a typewriter keyboard.

The *verifier* is just like a keypunch except it checks on the punch already in the card rather than putting a new punch in the card.

The *sorter* drops cards into pockets according to their punch on a preselected column. A *counter* attachment can also use the electrical circuit completed when a punch is sensed by the wire brush. The counter will automatically record the number of "1" punches, "2" punches, and so on.

The *reproducer* can transfer to a new deck of cards information in one or more columns of an old deck. It can also be used to duplicate a deck of cards.

The four machines just described—key punch, verifier, sorter (with or without counter attachment), and reproducer—are frequently found as auxiliary equipment in computer installations where the computer uses a punched-card input (see below). Other equipment, with the possible exception of a machine for producing printed material from the information in punched cards, is more rarely associated with computers.

A machine that was, at one time, important in social research work was the I.B.M. No. 101 statistical machine—or its more recent version, the No. 108—which can sort cards by combinations of values in any number of columns, count the numbers of cards that had specific patterns of punches, and print out the results. Many a social research worker who was trained in the years between 1950 and 1960 became an expert at wiring this machine; but the skill seems to have had only a brief period of great usefulness. Today, the same research worker would learn to write a computer program.

There are few statistical tasks involving nothing more than sorting and counting which electromechanical equipment cannot accomplish if given enough time. Computers, however, can do most of these tasks better, and often more cheaply, and so are effective competitors to electromechanical equipment. Yet, if a computer is not easily available, and electromechanical equipment is, then there is no argument; the electromechanical equipment wins. Even if a computer is available, if the job is one that can be done fairly quickly by electromechanical equipment, use of this equipment may be preferable because of the possibility of serious time delays in learning to tell the computer what to do. At this writing, electromechanical equipment still has a place in social research, although it is not as large a place as it once was.

The question of availability is an important one in deciding what equipment to use. In any detailed analysis, questions are likely to arise halfway along which require further tabulations, and then it can be an enormous waste of time and energy to have to negotiate for access to equipment. There are levels of availability, ranging from immediately on hand, to available only after a phone call and a meeting; the first kind of availability can be a distinct advantage for a study.

The High-Speed Computer

The digital computer is of ever-increasing importance in the processing of social research data. It has made easy the kinds of statistical analysis that once required so much work that only the most determined investigator would embark on them. It has also made it possible to do more quickly and efficiently the basic tabulation work necessary in every large-scale quantitative study. Finally, it has raised the possibility of entirely new methods of data analysis, particularly in connection with developing pictures of structures from sociometric data—data having to do with relationships between pairs of individuals—and in simulating processes that are hypothesized as accounting for observed relationships.

A digital computer, as distinguished from an analog computer, may be thought of as an extremely quick and flexible counting and decision-making machine. Its operations are always in terms of units, which it can count and compare, whose totals it can remember, and about which it can report. The analog computer is not much used in social science work. Its principle is to represent the elements of a computation by physical variables that can take any values, and not just whole-number values. The slide rule, which represents the logarithms of numbers by distances, is an analog computer, albeit a very simple one.

Mechanical aids in computation have been known for centuries, but the development of electronic computers is entirely a post-war phenomenon. The first high-speed digital computer, the Mark I, was completed at Harvard in 1944. Since its development, computers have increased enormously in speed, capacity, and flexibility, and have also, because of developments in programming, become easier to use. To suggest the magnitude of improvement in this brief period, operations that on the Mark I were performed in tenths of seconds are performed on today's machines in millionths of seconds.

Because a computer can perform its operations with extreme rapidity and complete accuracy, and because it can also manage great amounts of data, it can perform in a reasonable time virtually any procedure that can be stated in terms of additions, subtractions, comparisons, or other simple operations. The task of analyzing a complex statistical procedure (for instance, Guttman scaling) into the simple operations that a computer can perform is called *programming*.

Programming in terms of the computer's operations is called using a machine language. Programming can be made much simpler if the programmer can use a more developed language, in which certain complex operations are set in motion in the machine by a single code word, such as "sqroot" for "take the square root of." A number of these higher-order languages have been developed, of which Fortran is among the best known.

Even when a higher-order language is being used, it requires experience and skill to work out the step-by-step instructions that will direct a computer through a procedure. The procedure must be broken down to its elementary parts, no step must be omitted, everything must be taken in order, and no error can be included. Any mistake and the computer, dutifully following instructions, will either run into a dead end or produce meaningless data.

The Components of Computers

A great many computers are in use today and we may expect even more varieties in the near future. From the point of view of the social science investigator, however, all computers can be discussed in terms of their input, internal features, and output.

Input refers to the introduction of instructions or data into the machine. It is almost always performed either by having the machine read a set of punched cards or by having the machine respond to properly prepared magnetic tape. The instructions section of the input is the *program*. This prepares the machine for the operations it is to conduct. The program cards or tape are generally fed into the machine first, then the data that are to be dealt with. The data have to be marked and organized so that the machine can recognize important subdivisions, and will know, for example, when it has come to the end of one group and is beginning another. There are various devices for doing this; this detail, as others, can be managed only by someone who understands the program, the computer, and the needs of the investigator.

The *internal features* of the machine are the fixed characteristics that together determine what types of programs are possible for the machine, how much data can be dealt with, and how fast the machine can do its work. Most important of the internal features is the capacity of the machine's memory. Machines today use as a memory (or "storage unit") a magnetic drum or magnetic core that has many discrete spots, each of which can be either magnetized or left unmagnetized. A sensing device can be directed to any of these spots and asked its condition; is it "magnetized" or "unmagnitized"? In this way, the sensing device can learn which alternative was introduced into the memory. A modern computer of very modest capacity will have 20,000 discrete positions in its magnetic core or drum, which means that information regarding 20,000 alternatives may be stored within its memory. This is not, in fact, a large enough capacity to permit all possible statistical analyses of the very large amount of data that may be gathered in a national survey. Such studies can do better with the larger capacity machines.

A second important internal characteristic of machines is the rapidity with which they work. The very fast computers of today may be able to produce results in one-tenth the time of computers only five or ten years old. What this means is that a factor analysis (a very common technique for multivariate analysis) that would take thirty minutes on an older machine can be done in two or three minutes on a newer one. Since computer time is extremely expensive, and sometimes hard to get, this saving in time may be of value, though there are few computations in social research—as there are in other fields—that would have taken unacceptable lengths of time before the advent of the newest generation of high-speed computers.

Other internal characteristics of the computer—whether it has a multiplication table built in or multiplies by repeated addition, how addresses have been associated with each other, and so on—are of much less importance to the social science user, although they may matter a great deal to the computer specialist.

Finally, the computer's *output* may be punched cards, or tape, as well as results that are typed directly onto tabulating sheets. If the results are not immediately given in the form of printed or typed tables, they should be brought to that form by running the cards or tapes through the appropriate auxiliary equipment. Computers can be programmed so that their results are carefully labelled, with the names of the variables examined, the nature of the analysis (if this is not clear from the form of the table), and even the headings of the categories, all printed in the proper places. This should always be done. There is so much output from computers that labelling by hand would be arduous and, here as elsewhere, what we do not label, we eventually shall be unable to identify.

Computers probably ought to be used whenever there is a quantitative analysis that can be planned from the very beginning and that will take two or three days or more of clerical time. This is a rough guide, but may be the proper order of magnitude. The cost of computer time, exclusive of programming, should not be any greater than the cost of the clerical assistance, and the work will be done more reliably and more quickly. As the size of the operation increases, computers become more efficient. For a small operation, of a type that could be done by a clerical person in a day, the use of the computer is likely to be inefficient.

As has already been suggested, programming can be expensive and time-consuming. Already developed programs should be used whenever possible. There now exist programs for almost every complex statistical procedure which is used with any frequency, but this does not mean that these programs can be obtained as soon as they are wanted, or that they can be used as soon as they are obtained. Exchange services for programs do exist—SHARE, run by I.B.M. is one—but specialists say that their files tend to be two years or so behind current developments. In addition, programs developed for one machine usually must be adapted before they can be run with another machine, and at times the adaptation is difficult.

Investigators who have not learned to write computer programs themselves are apt to find that they have a linguistic problem when they try to tell the operator of the computer what they want to have done. The social science investigator speaks one language, the computer operator another. Where the social science investigator thinks of his problem as developing tables in which the relationship between one dimension and another is displayed, the computer operator will want to know what information must be entered into the computer's memory, how it is to be combined, and in what format it is to be printed out. Often an investigator will find that the most difficult aspect of work with a computer is developing some shared understanding with its operator.

Fortunate, well-financed projects sometimes employ an individual who speaks both languages and can understand what the social science investigator wants, and also understand how the problem must be phrased for the computer. An individual with these skills can be invaluable to a project. Some younger social research people who intend specializing in quantitative research are themselves developing an understanding of computer language, so that they can do their own translating.

One of the problems frequently brought to a computer is that of preparing a collection of tables showing the relationship between some variable of interest (for instance, success in school) with a whole battery of other variables that might be associated with it. It may take weeks to work out just how these tables are to be produced, but once all the translating problems are solved, the computer seems to take a single deep breath and then in minutes produces a pile of tables a foot high. At that point, the investigator has a problem unlikely to be encountered with any other data-processing approach: to manage to read and make sense of all the output. One possible solution to the problem is not to try, but instead to organize the tables, put them into binders, prepare a table of contents that will permit any table to be located easily, and then treat the collection as a data repository, to which reference will be made as required. The investigator might search through his tables for initial answers to important questions, and then consult the tables again as need occurs. This may well not be the best system for every situation, but the alternative of trying to evaluate and account for each and every table is almost always unpromising.

New Developments

In recent years, there has been great progress in the development of programs for social research. One direction has been the development of omnibus programs that contain within them a whole set of specific procedures. One such omnibus program contains virtually all the analysis procedures in common use. Several have been written that contain a good many advanced procedures (procedures for multivariate analysis) and that allow the investigator to decide which procedures he will request, and in what order. There has been some experimental work with programs that would have the computer itself decide what sequence of analyses to pursue; if this line of development proves successful, an investigator may be able to feed his data into the machine and then do nothing more but wait, possibly with curiosity, to see the reports it will produce.

In recent years, there has also been amazing progress in solving the problem of access to a computer, by means of what are referred to as "on-line terminals." These are input-and-output devices that are in direct contact with a computer by telephone lines, even though physically they may be any number of miles away. A good many such input-and-output devices, each of which resembles an oversize typewriter, may be in contact with the same central computer, with almost no inconvenience to any user. With this development, it is now theoretically possible for every research worker to have in his office, along with desk, typewriter, calculating machine, and recording equipment, an on-line terminal in communication with a central computer. The day may not be far off when a research worker may be able to switch his terminal to "on," type in the code number or name of his project, type in the particular information he wants, and then, in seconds, have the computer type out the answers.

A system now being developed, using input-and-output terminals, would make it possible for investigators to request tables of the computer as they need them. This system, when it is perfected, will solve the problem of access to the computer which is the reason for mass data runs.

PROBLEMS

3.1. For the codes developed in response to the problems of Chapter 2, work out a numbering system appropriate for (a) handsort, (b) edge punch, and (c) I.B.M.

3.2. List coding categories for some characteristics listed in Appendix 2. You might work with age, marital status, and sex. You might also consider working out categories for region of residence (central city, urban residential area, and so on) and occupation (for example, professional or managerial). Develop a code book for each of the systems (hand sort, edge punch, I.B.M.). The code book should give the position or positions of the card where the code for the item appears, the numbers of letters which stand for the categories, and if necessary, a brief description of the categories. For example, the beginning of the code book, using I.B.M. as the system, might be as follows.

Column

1, 2, 3   Three-digit interview number

4   *Age*
                1. Under 20
                2. 21 to 30
                3. 31 to 40
                4. 41 to 50
                5. 51 to 60
                6. 61 and over
                7. Not ascertained

5   *Marital status*
                1. Single
                2. Married

Chapter 4

Tables

When we have finished collecting our data, we have all the information that we shall ever have about the population. Statistical treatment adds no information; if we have not gathered material from a particular sub-group, no amount of statistical work will remedy the failure. What statistical work does is to make evident implications in the data of which we could not otherwise be aware. Statistical treatment makes it possible for us to grasp the implications of our data, and to understand what they mean.

Tabulation is the first step in the statistical treatment of data. By tabulation we mean the presentation in an organized form of the measurements of one or more characteristics of a population. Consider the following array of what might be the ages of fourth-grade students in a certain class:

9, 10, 10, 9, 8, 9, 9, 9, 8, 9, 9, 8, 10, 10, 9, 8, 8, 9

Even though we can summarize these figures as we read them over, they are not presented to us in an organized form. Their tabular presentation would be as shown in Table 4.1.

Table 4.1

Ages of Fourth-Grade Students in Hypothetical Study

Age	Number of Students
Eight	5
Nine	9
Ten	4
Total	18

Notice how much easier the data are to grasp when presented this way. This table is the simplest form we shall have occasion to work with. Age is listed in terms of a few discrete categories, instead of a number of continuous categories, in which case we would have had to define where one category ended and the next began. The data deal only with age; there is no further division by sex or by class level. Nor does the table list percentages. The ways in which tables may become more complex are discussed in the remainder of the chapter.

REPOSITORY TABLES

Statistical tables are of two kinds, according to their function. The first is a table that is intended to display for the investigator, in a single compilation, all the data he has in his study that deal with specific attributes. These tables serve an inventory purpose; they tell the analyst what is available. Parten says:

. . . typically they present full summations of items from the schedules, classified according to the original categories. Usually they contain the original, unconverted, unrounded figures.[1]

The *repository* table is distinguished from a second kind of table which is intended to communicate to a reader some particular configuration of data: to *present* some fact or facts to a reader. Parten calls such tables "special purpose, analysis, or text tables." She notes:

The special purpose table, which is often developed from a general purpose table and is published in the body or text of most reports, usually presents selected or summary data in order to emphasize some significant relationships. The data in this table may be grouped, averaged, rounded, derived, or handled in any legitimate manner which will best serve the special functions of clarification and emphasis.[2]

The special purpose, or *presentation*, table is designed to make a few specific points. Its aim is effective communication. It is therefore as simple and clear as the investigator can make it.

Examples of repository tables abound. Most census tables are essentially of this kind. To suggest what these might look like, Table 4.2 presents an excerpt from a repository table of almost one hundred pages. Few repository tables are this large; most take up only a page or so.

Examination of the repository table may suggest the selection of attri-

[1] Mildred Parten, *Surveys, Polls, and Samples* (New York: Harper & Bros., 1950), p. 477.
[2] *Ibid.*

Table 4.2

A Section of a Repository Table

| City | Vital Statistics | | | Income in 1959 of Families, 1960 | | | |
	Live Births (1960)	Deaths (1959)	Number of Families (1960)	Median Income (Dollars)	Under $3000 (Percent)	$10,000 and Over (Percent)	Population 1960, Total
Boston	15,726	8914	162,215	5747	16.7	13.6	697,197
Brockton	1,802	909	18,595	5914	12.6	12.2	72,813
Cambridge	2,324	1249	24,490	5923	15.3	17.4	107,716
Chelsea	712	433	8,648	5298	19.0	9.1	33,749
Chicopee	1,350	452	15,287	6170	10.9	12.6	61,553
Everett	1,046	479	11,683	5983	10.3	12.8	43,544
Fall River	1,996	1225	27,026	4970	20.0	6.6	99,942
Fitchburg	1,014	511	11,279	5833	14.0	11.5	43,021
Gloucester	550	323	6,584	5285	17.2	8.8	25,789
Haverhill	982	670	12,266	6077	13.8	13.5	46,346

Source: United States Bureau of the Census. *County and City Data Book, 1962*, pp. 516–517.

butes and management of categories that will produce the best presentation table: the presentation table that makes its points most effectively and most simply. Some investigators prefer to study repository tables before developing a presentation table if this is at all possible. Others, however, are much more cautious in their use of repository tables. They believe that constant reference to these compendia takes a great deal of time. At the very least, it means studying two sets of tables instead of one; and if computers are being used, it means two computer runs instead of one. They may also believe, and this is a more serious objection, that constructing presentation tables only after study of repository tables comes very close to selecting and shaping evidence. They argue that any large collection of data will have its oddities, and that judicious organization of the data can make these oddities all the more striking.

To illustrate the dangers of overzealous prospecting in repository tables, suppose we were to examine a repository table like that from which Table 4.2 is taken, listing the median income, number of births, and so on, for a long array of cities. Suppose we separated out those cities that seemed to have few births, in view of the size of their populations. We might list these in another table and, along with them, list half-a-dozen other characteristics, copying them from the repository table or calculating them from data in the repository table; for instance, the ratio of deaths to population, median income, the size of the city, the percent of residents who moved in the preceding year, and the level of home ownership. We could examine our listing of data and discover that a low birthrate seemed to go together with a low listing on Attribute X, which might be a correlate as plausible as the percent of the population living within a family group, or as implausible as the number of letters in the city's name. We might find, with further study, that there were some exceptions to our generalization, but we might also be able to explain these away; they might be cities with a large population of older people, for example. Finally we might, by trial and error, hit on a way of grouping our cities that would make the relationship between birthrate and Attribute X seem absolutely regular, perhaps with a few easily explained exceptions. We might then propose that our data supported the proposition that low birthrate and Attribute X were associated, exceptional cases aside.

This procedure is, in truth, somewhere near the borderline of responsible practice. It is certainly desirable for an investigator to study the relationships between a phenomenon he wants to understand and the other, possibly explanatory, phenomena. He will naturally test ideas as they come to him, by referring to his data, and he will also naturally scan his data to see what he can find. But when a relationship is discovered in the data, the investigator must treat it cautiously. If the relationship is strong and also makes theoretical sense, well and good. If other findings support the line of thought suggested by the relationship, then even better. But if, in order for the relationship to seem a healthy one, he must drop "exceptional cases" or artfully revise categories, and if there is little corroboration in additional data, then he ought to be slow to accept the finding as generalizable.

In work with repository tables, it is important to keep in mind the danger of creating specious findings. Yet the analysis of survey data, or other forms of nonexperimental data, in contrast to the analysis of experimental data, tends to be a search for relationships, rather than a test of already developed hypotheses. We use the model of hypothesis testing as a way of evaluating the reliability of relationships in the survey, but we should be aware, when we do this, that this model may not be fully applicable, and that often we must have additional reasons for believing in our finding, even beyond statistical support. (The model of hypothesis testing is discussed at length in Chapter 13.)

In the experiment, we are concerned only with the test of one or, at most, a small number of hypotheses. We phrase these hypotheses before performing the experiment and the experimental evidence tells us what we ought to believe. In the survey, in contrast, because we are often concerned with *locating—discovering*—potentially explanatory linkages, or patterns among characteristics, we often do study repository tables, to see what we can turn up. When we do this, we must evaluate the trustworthiness of our findings not only on the basis of the apparent strength of the relationship, but also on the basis of substantive plausibility, relationship to other findings, and something only we can know, the extent to which we forced our data into its presentation form.

Rules to keep in mind when going from repository to presentation tables might include the following.

1. We ought to be skeptical of relationships that are not plausible, in view of existing theory and other findings in the study. The fact that a discovered relationship *is* plausible is not conclusive evidence in its favor, since an ingenious investigator can often supply rationales for a great many possible relationships. But if a relationship is theoretically inexplicable, if it does not tie in with what is known about the situation from other studies or experiences, and especially, if it does not tie in with other materials from the study at hand, then it ought to be held suspect. We cannot, however, use this principle as a basis for neglecting the embarrassing finding that fails to fit an otherwise satisfactory argument.

2. We ought to insist that a relationship be fairly strong. Any repository table will abound in weak relationships, the result of the chance intersection of factors.

3. The relationship should hold up with "natural" collapsing of categories. If thirty lines of a repository table are to be collapsed into three or four categories, then the collapsing should be done *either* in such a way that the population is divided roughly into thirds or quarters, *or else* the collapsing should be done into substantively meaningful groups. (As an example of a substantively meaningful categorization, survey analysts believe that the best way to categorize information on years of education is by segregating those who have finished high school from those who have not. They find that this separation corresponds to other differences: for example, in level of employment.) Under no circumstances should data in a repository table be recategorized in order to maximize a relationship, with no other justification for the recategorization.

4. We ought to be extremely wary of dropping categories that weaken our generalization, no matter how compelling our justification for dropping these categories seems to us. If we do believe it is theoretically justifiable to drop one or two categories, we must warn the reader that this has been done, and that the evidence in these categories went against us.

PRESENTATION TABLES

With these cautions in the use of repository tables stated, we may now turn to a discussion of presentation tables, beginning with the issue of dimensionality.

The Dimensionality of a Table

The entries of Table 4.1 are arranged according to only one characteristic: age. Students aged eight are all together, irrespective of their social class, their sex, their height or weight or political preference. Because entries are arranged according to only one attribute, Table 4.1 is called a *one-dimensional table*. Table 4.3 is an example of a *two-dimensional table*.

Table 4.3

Age and Sex of Fourth-Grade Students in Hypothetical School

	Sex	
Age	Male	Female
Eight	3	2
Nine	5	4
Ten	1	3
Total	9	9

Entries are arranged according to *two* attributes. Examples of layouts for three-dimensional and four-dimensional tables are given in Figure 4.1. Notice that an entry in the three-dimensional table is located by its value on three different attributes and, in the four-dimensional table, by its value on four different attributes. (For simplicity, each attribute is considered to have been measured dichotomously: that is, using only two categories.) It should be apparent that tables of higher dimensions can be constructed by further subdivisions. A four-dimensional table, however, is about as complicated a table as one can expect a reader to grasp. To illustrate this remark a four-dimensional table is given as Table 4.4. Even here the results, which are very striking, emerge only after study of the table. A four-dimensional table is often like a repository table in its lack of focus. Zeisel has this to say about what to do with multi-dimensional tables:

. . . in modern research, tables of four and more dimensions have ceased to be rare. . . . And if it is necessary to show all factors to the reader simultaneously . . . it is advisable to dismember the table, giving the story in its sections, one at a time. This process of dismemberment, however, must be carried on very systematically lest part of the story be lost. . . . The proper method is to present the story by starting with the more general results and gradually adding the details and modification.[3]

		Attribute A Category 1	Attribute A Category 2
Attribute B Category 1	Attribute C Category 1		
	Attribute C Category 2		
Attribute B Category 2	Attribute C Category 1		
	Attribute C Category 2		

Body of a 3-dimensional table

		Attribute A Category 1		Attribute A Category 2	
		Attribute B Category 1	Attribute B Category 2	Attribute B Category 1	Attribute B Category 2
Attribute C Category 1	Attribute D Category 1				
	Attribute D Category 2				
Attribute C Category 2	Attribute D Category 1				
	Attribute D Category 2				

Body of a 4-dimensional table

Figure 4.1 Layouts for bodies of tables of 3 dimensions and 4 dimensions.

[3] Zeisel, *Say It with Figures* (4th ed. rev.; New York: Harper & Row, 1957), p. 86.

Table 4.4

An Example of a Four-Dimensional Table: "Whose News Broadcast Do You Trust Most, American or Your Foreign Language One?"

		Germans		Poles		Italians	
		Generation		Generation		Generation	
		1	2	1	2	1	2
Teach children traditions of old country	Prefer Foreign	20	0	159	10	371	20
	Do Not Prefer Foreign	81	69	120	62	249	309
Do not teach children traditions of old country	Prefer Foreign	29	0	61	0	130	21
	Do Not Prefer Foreign	291	461	131	238	188	498
Total Total in Sample 1786		421	530	471	310	938	848

Adaptation of Table IV-20 in Hans Zeisel's, *Say It with Figures* (4th ed. rev.; New York: Harper & Row, 1957), p. 86.

Beginners in quantitative analysis sometimes want to examine data listed by five or more dimensions of classification. In a study of attitudes of college students, for example, they may argue that they cannot understand the responses unless they can take into account, simultaneously, the age, parental income, major, and sex of the respondent. There are differences of opinion among practiced investigators regarding the worth of these tables; some investigators believe that they are too cluttered and complicated to allow anyone to see what is going on, while others believe that some attention should be paid to possible interactions among determinants before dimensionality is reduced. In any event, for anyone of less than expert standing, it will be the better procedure to first determine whether age, parental income, major, and the like, independently make a difference in student attitude, before moving to a table that displays their joint influence. And certainly we should rarely, if ever, present to a nonprofessional reader a table of even four dimensions.

Table 4.2, incidentally, appears at first glance to be a very complicated table, but it is, in fact, five one-dimensional tables and one two-dimensional table placed side by side. In the first table, the entries are "live births," and to decide where a live birth is to be listed, it is necessary to know only one of its attributes: its city. In the second table, the entries are "deaths," and to know where a death is to be listed, again it is only necessary to know its city. The two-dimensional table is the one presenting income information.

What Goes into a Table

Tables should be constructed so that they most effectively realize these aims:

1. They communicate clearly the information they contain.
2. They make few demands on the reader. He is not required to follow complicated instructions in order to understand what is in the table.
3. They can stand alone. A reader need not turn to the text surrounding the table to understand the table.

The first two aims of tabular construction, which might be characterized as *clarity* and *considerateness*, are obviously desirable. The third aim rests on a couple of arguments: first, it is difficult for a reader to refer from text to table and back to text, in order to understand the entries in a given column; and second, a reader may want to refer to the table in work of his own, and the table should therefore be able to stand alone. In survey work, the practice of presenting as much of the study as possible both in tables and again in text is quite general. Some investigators insist that they prefer to read only tables in a report, and rarely look at the text. The implication here, exaggerated to be sure, is that all the information in a research report can be found in the tables, and these are free from the author's annoying interpretation.[4]

Figure 4.2 shows the elements of a typical two-dimensional table. The information presented by the table is listed according to two attributes, one represented by the row or "stub" categories, the other by the column categories. The number of instances observed in a given row and column

[4] A detailed discussion of methods for the construction of census-type tables is to be found in Bruce L. Jenkinson, *Bureau of the Census Manual of Tabular Presentation*, (United States Government Printing Office, Washington, D.C., 1949). A discussion more useful for those concerned with constructing presentation tables is that of Helen M. Walker and Walter N. Durost, *Statistical Tables, Their Structure and Use* (New York: Teachers College Press, 1936). There is a useful brief discussion based in good part on Walker and Durost in Mildred Parten, *op. cit.*, pp. 477–483, and a more elementary discussion in Lillian Cohen, *Statistical Methods for Social Scientists* (New York: Prentice-Hall, 1954), pp. 9–14. Hans Zeisel, *op. cit.*, deals with several problems of tabulation. Particularly useful are Chapters II, III, and IV.

Table Number

Title of Table

(Headnote, giving further information about contents of table—
but only if necessary)

		Spanner head[a]			
		Spanner subhead		Spanner subhead	
Stub head		Column Head	Column Head	Column Head	Column Head
Stub subhead					
Stub category		Cell	Cell	Cell	Cell
Stub category		Cell	Cell	Cell	Cell
Stub subhead		Cell	Cell	Cell	Cell
Stub category		Cell	Cell	Cell	Cell
Stub category		Cell	Cell	Cell	Cell
Total line		Cell	Cell	Cell	Cell

Boxhead, Field or body, Stub

[a] Footnote.

Figure 4.2   The anatomy of a typical two-dimensional table. (*Source:* adapted from Bruce L. Jenkinson, Tabular Presentation, *op. cit.,* pp. 10–11.)

category are listed in the cell associated with each. A totals line, table number, and title, and, if necessary, headnote, footnote, and source information complete the table.

The Title

"A table is a list of something, and the title should name that of which the table is a list."[5] Generally, this means that the title should state what measurements the table presents, and, unless this is obvious from the context of the table, the population that has been studied. Thus, a reasonable title for Table 4.3 would be: "Age and sex of fourth-grade students in a hypothetical school." If the table appeared in a research report devoted to discussion of these same students, it would not be necessary to refer to the population in the table's title. If the measurements presented in the table were for some reason unusual, this might be indicated in the title, as: "Age, measured in months, of students in the fourth grade."

[5] Helen M. Walker and Walter N. Durost, *Statistical Tables, Their Structure and Use, op. cit.,* p. 8

Headings

Obviously, every row and column in the table ought to have a heading. There should, in addition, be headings for the set of rows and set of columns that tell the reader what attributes are being presented. There are terms to refer to all these elements, which the research person might learn to recognize. The row headings together make up the *stub*. The column headings together make up the *boxhead* (see Figure 4.2). Advice regarding the proper formulation of these categories is given by Walker and Durost:

Decide upon the main headings and subheadings and the categories for the stub. Write these down and study them to be sure that the categories for the stub are logically consistent, parallel in meaning and in phrasing, mutually exclusive, all-inclusive, and clearly defined. Make sure that subclassifications are logically subsumed under their more inclusive headings. Make sure that box headings are used effectively to avoid repetition in column headings and that brevity in headings is secured without undue abbreviation and without confusion of meaning.[6]

Experimenting with Styles of Presentation

It is difficult, even when the investigator has much experience, immediately to hit on the most effective way of drawing up the table. Decisions to be made include choosing to present actual numbers or percentages or some combination of each; choosing to show more or fewer categories; assigning one or the other dimension to the stub and the remaining dimension to the columns; writing the various headings; and placing the "totals" line. The only way of deciding on the best form is to compare all those that seem plausible.

One-Dimensional Tables

Tables that report the numbers of different values of a single attribute (for example, the number of individuals of different ages, or the number of students who make A's, B's, and so on, or the number of cities in different categories of population) have a format similar to that in Figure 4.3.[7]

Most often, a table like that shown in Figure 4.3 presents either the percentage column or the number column, but not both. Both are shown in the "totals" line, however. When the total number is given, percentages

[6] Walker and Durost, *op. cit.*, p. 71. Reprinted with the permission of the publisher.
[7] Tables may report in their cells many other statistics, in addition to numbers of instances. They may report arithmetic means, correlation coefficients, significance levels, and the like.

Table Number	Title	
Stub Heading (Name of Attribute)	Number	Percent
Category	Cell entry	Cell entry
Category	Cell entry	Cell entry
. . . .	. . . .	. . . .
Category	Cell entry	Cell entry
Total	Cell entry	100%

Figure 4.3 Format for a table displaying distribution of values of a single attribute.

in a category can be deduced from the number in that category, and vice versa. These tables are often called *marginal* or *straight-run* tables. The first of these terms draws attention to the fact that a one-dimensional distribution appears in the "totals" column or row of a two-dimensional distribution. The second term refers to the mechanical process by which such a table is constructed when the basic data are coded into cards. A one-dimensional distribution is found by a single pass of the cards; that is, a "straight run." A two-dimensional distribution requires first separating—"breaking"—the deck into categories on the one dimension, and then again separating—"spreading" or "cross-breaking"—the deck on a second dimension. Two-dimensional tables are in consequence often referred to as *cross-breaks*.

Definition of Categories

The first problem faced in making up a table is that of the number and definition of categories. Should age be separated into five categories or twelve? If occupation is the attribute being described, how narrow should the categories be? There are no hard and fast rules, but some rough guides may be proposed.

1. It is difficult for a reader to grasp more than fifteen or twenty categories. Going beyond this often turns a table from a presentation table, which communicates directly, to a repository table, which must be worked with before it can be understood. There are exceptions to this rule, but generally it is desirable to keep the number of categories under twenty.

2. The distribution itself may help determine the number of categories that are necessary. There is a sense of futility in a table that presents cell entries of 0, 1, 2, and 3. Unless some of the entries are larger than this, the investigator ought to collapse categories into more general groupings.

3. Collapsing categories always loses information, although it does so in the interest of gaining communicability. If the information that would be lost by collapsing categories is potentially of interest to a reader, then this is a weighty argument for presenting narrow, uncollapsed categories, perhaps grouping them to make the total picture easier to understand.

4. It is always desirable to categorize and to collapse categories in ways that are *natural:* that is, which reflect either theoretically meaningful divisions in the data, or else convenient ways of thinking about the data. Thus, if the investigator begins with a list of states as his categories (in a table presenting numbers of auto registrations, for example), then it might be natural to collapse by region, or by amount of industry in the state, or by density of the state's population. It would be unnatural to set up categories by the population of the largest city in the state, or by alphabetical order among the states. What determines "naturalness" here is the assessment of which groupings would be meaningful. In another situation, where the investigator is setting up age categories for a population whose range in age extended from twenty at the youngest to sixty at the oldest, it might be natural to break the population into five-year intervals; 20 to 24, 25 to 29, and so on. Here "naturalness" depends on this being a convenient way to think about the data.

5. It is often desirable, when working with metric data, to set up class intervals that are of the same size. In setting up age divisions, for example, it is preferable to have the divisions run 20 to 24, 25 to 29, 30 to 34, 35 to 39, and so on, rather than to have them run 20 to 29, 30 to 34, 35 to 39, 40 to 49. In the second case, it is more difficult for a reader to compare entries in the different categories with each other.

When the investigator is working with nominal data (for instance, ethnic background, or region of the country), then a problem that is likely to arise is that of the *order* in which the categories are to be presented. Here almost any logical order, even alphabetical, will do. One possibility is to list groupings in order of decreasing frequency. Another is to try to follow through some theoretical connection in the listing—but here it is important that the theoretical substructure be as apparent to a reader as it is to the investigator.

When the investigator is working with interval or ratio scale data, a problem may be posed by the need to define *class boundaries*. Suppose a population is being listed according to height. And suppose the categories (in inches) go: 57 to 60, 61 to 64, 65 to 68, 69 to 72, and so on. Should someone 68.6 inches tall be grouped within the category 65 to 68 inches, or within the category 69 to 72 inches? This must be decided in advance, in the definition of class boundaries. The category 65 to 68 inches can be defined to include all those cases, in the intervals 64 to 65 inches and 68 to 69 inches, that are closer to this category than to any other category; the *true* class limits will then be 64.5 to 68.49999. On the other hand, the category 65 to 68 inches can be defined to include only those measurements that have a whole number value of at least 65 and no more than 68; the *true* class limits will then be 65.0 to 68.9999.

Class boundaries are important not only when assigning cases to categories, but also when calculating certain statistics—the mean, the standard deviation, and the correlation coefficient—from grouped data. Then it is necessary to know where the midpoint of a class interval is, and this depends on knowing the true limits, rather than the specified limits, of the categories.[8]

When the intention in presenting a one-dimensional distribution is to suggest the way in which frequencies pile up in some categories and are small in others, or, more generally, to compare the frequencies in different categories, then it is useful to report percentages rather than actual numbers of observations. It is not necessary to give numbers of observations for each cell, along with the percentage, as long as the total number of observations is given.

Two-Dimensional Tables

A two-dimensional distribution is determined by the frequencies of conjunction of given values of two attributes. Tables presenting these distributions are also called *contingency tables*, because it is possible to read them as the number of instances in which attribute A is found to have a given value, contingent on attribute B having some given value.

The problems of definition of categories in two-dimensional tables are identical to the problems met with in one-dimensional tables, except that there may be even more reason here to try to keep down the number of categories. The problem of percentaging in two-dimensional tables is, however, a good deal more complicated than the same problem in a one-dimensional situation. The question now may be asked· "Which way to percentage?" The answer is often not obvious.

Table 4.5*a* presents the average incidence of four chronic conditions in the United States. The absolute frequencies of Table 4.5*a* are translated into percentages three different ways in Table 4.5*b*, Table 4.5*c*, and Table 4.5*d*. Notice, in Table 4.5*a*, that it is difficult to tell at a glance that high blood pressure is more than twice as common among

---

[8] The question of setting up class boundaries when working with metric data is dealt with in several textbooks on statistics in social science work. See John H. Mueller and Karl F. Schuessler, *Statistical Reasoning in Sociology* (Boston: Houghton-Mifflin, 1961), pp. 39–42, and Hubert M. Blalock, Jr., *Social Statistics* (New York: McGraw-Hill, 1960), pp. 33–39.

women as among men, while the opposite is true of peptic ulcer. Proper percentaging can make the table easier to read.

Many beginners consider trying the idea of Table 4.5b. It never is correct. Table 4.5b shows cell frequencies as a percentage of the grand total. The entry in the male heart-condition cell would have to be read: "Among all those individuals in the country who have some one of these four conditions, 12% are males who have heart conditions." But we never are interested, when studying a two-dimensional table, in the question of

Table 4.5a

Average Prevalence of Selected Chronic Conditions by Sex: 1957 to 1959, Listed by Absolute Frequency (Numbers in Thousands)[a]

| Chronic Condition | Sex | | Total |
	Male	Female	
Heart conditions	2,529	2,484	5,013
High blood pressure	1,498	3,736	5,234
Peptic ulcer	1,771	669	2,440
Asthma—hay fever	4,556	4,669	9,225
Total having listed conditions	10,354	11,558	21,912

[a] Adapted from Statistical Abstract of the United States, 1961, Bureau of the Census, Washington, 25, D.C., p. 82.

Table 4.5b

Average Prevalence of Selected Chronic Conditions by Sex: 1957 to 1959, Shown as Percentages of Total Suffering from Selected Conditions

| Chronic Condition | Sex | | Total |
	Male	Female	
Heart conditions	12%	11%	23%
High blood pressure	7	17	24
Peptic ulcer	8	3	11
Asthma—hay fever	21	21	42
Total	47%	53%	100% (21,912)

Table 4.5c

Average Prevalence of Selected Chronic Conditions by Sex: 1957 to 1959, Shown as Percentages of Same-Sex Groups Suffering from Selected Conditions

Chronic Condition	Sex		Total
	Male	Female	
Heart conditions	24%	22%	23%
High blood pressure	14	32	24
Peptic ulcer	17	6	11
Asthma—hay fever	44	40	42
Total	100%	100%	100%
	(10,354)	(11,558)	(21,912)

Table 4.5d

Average Prevalence of Selected Chronic Conditions by Sex: 1957 to 1959, Shown as Percentages of Those Having Conditions Who are of One or the Other Sex

Chronic Condition	Sex		Total	
	Male	Female	Percent	Number
Heart conditions	50%	50%	100%	5013
High blood pressure	29	71	100	5234
Peptic ulcer	73	27	100	2440
Asthma—hay fever	49	51	100	9225
Total	47%	53%	100%	21912

the proportion of the total to be found in a given cell. Instead, we want to know about the relative compositions of the rows or columns; for example, we want to compare the incidence of different conditions among males and females. Percentaging like that in Table 4.5b obscures the two-dimensional nature of the information.

Table 4.5c presents as cell entries percentages of the column total. It would be read: "Twenty-four percent of men having one of the four listed conditions have heart conditions." The incidence among males of each condition, *within the population defined as those having some one of the four conditions,* may now be compared. So may the incidence of each condition, among females. But these comparisons are pointless, because the populations are arbitrary. There is no reason for not adding a fifth condition (for instance, arthritic difficulties, or winter colds.) If this were done, percentages within the male and female population would change greatly. The problem is that we have calculated percentages in a direction in which our category system is not bounded, and the percentages therefore have little meaning.

Still another approach is shown in Table 4.5d. Here the entries are percentages of the row totals. This table *does* yield immediately meaningful statements. It is obvious, for example, that high blood pressure is, at this date, much more often found among women; of those having the disease, 71% are women.

Rules for Percentaging Two-Dimensional Tables

Four rules will help in the construction of two-dimensional percentage tables. The first two have to do with the nature of the data in the table and, when they are applicable, take precedence over the latter two, which have to do with the way the investigator thinks about the relationship.

1: When groups have been sampled at different rates. Let us call one of the attributes in our table A and the other B. Attribute A might be income, for example, and B educational attainment. It sometimes happens that we will sample the different levels of A at different rates. We might have interviewed everyone in a community who was wealthy, but only one in one hundred at other income levels. The rule is: *When the categories of attribute A have been sampled at different rates, then the category totals of A must be used as the bases for calculating percentages.*

Suppose we were concerned with the political beliefs of individuals who have been long-time residents of a hospital (perhaps to test the idea that exposure to an institutional setting develops an acceptance of strong central government) and we wanted to compare their beliefs with those of a sample of the larger population, matched for social class. We might decide to sample 50 individuals from the hospital, which could be 10% of the hospital population, and 100 individuals from the community in which the hospital is lodged, which might be 1/10 of 1% of the community population. Our table might look like Table 4.6a.

To construct a percentage table from this table of absolute frequencies, we percentage along the "population" dimension because the hospital population has been sampled at a different rate from the community population. The percentage table would then be as shown in Table 4.6b.

2: Incomplete set of categories. When the categories of attribute A are not bounded—when more categories could be added to those which appear in the table—percentaging must be within the categories of A. An undergraduate

Table 4.6*a*

Attitudes Toward Increased Centralization among Individuals in Two Populations

	Population	
Political Belief	Hospital Population	Community Population
In favor of increased centralization	30	45
Not in favor of increased centralization	20	55
Total	50	100

Source: Fictitious.

Table 4.6*b*

Percentage of Those in Each of Two Populations in Favor of and Opposed to Increased Centralization

	Population	
Political Belief	Hospital Population	Community Population
In favor of increased centralization	60%	45%
Not in favor of increased centralization	40	55
Total	100%	100%
	(50)	(100)

at a small liberal arts college recently compared a sample of students in his school with a sample of students at a state university in terms of the ranking they gave several possible aims of college students. Table 4.7*a* is based on his study.

Even though the student may have drawn samples from the college and the state university at the same rate, still, he *must* percentage within his school categories. If he does not, he may say something like: "Twenty-five percent of the students in the study who felt that social development was the most important aim of a college student were at the liberal arts

Table 4.7*a*

Beliefs Regarding Most Important Aims among Students at Two Schools

Most Important Aim as a College Student	School	
	College	State University
Social development	10	30
Intellectual development	45	10
Other	20	20
Total	75	60

Source: Student paper. Cell entries are approximate.

college." This is misleading: if another college were added to the study, this percentage would change. Table 4.7*b* is the correct percentage table:

Table 4.7*b*

Percentage among Students at Two Schools Believing Social Development or Intellectual Development Most Important

Most Important Aim as a College Student	School	
	College	State University
Social development	13%	50%
Intellectual development	60	17
Other	27	33
Total	100%	100%
	(75)	(60)

3: One attribute identified as independent, one as dependent. Tables are often made up to present evidence for or against a proposition of the form, "When A changes, then B changes also": for example, "Smoking is a cause of cancer"; "Increasing aspiration when there is no possibility of mobility increases frustration"; or "Propinquity is one of the factors determining with whom one falls in love." In these propositions the attribute that is believed to affect the other attribute is called the independent variable. The attribute that is believed to be affected by changes in the independent variable is called the dependent variable.

The rule is: *Percentage along the independent variable.* Percentaging the

Table 4.8a

Attitudes Toward Unsupervised Play among Mothers of Different Socioeconomic Classes

Attitude Toward Unsupervised Play	Mother's Socioeconomic Class Level			
	I or II (highest)	III	IV or V (lowest)	Total
Generally positive	10	15	10	35
Mixed or uncertain	5	5	15	25
Generally negative	5	20	15	40
Total	20	40	40	100

Source: Fictitious.

other way makes it more difficult for the reader to grasp the intended message of the table.

Suppose we were interested in whether working-class mothers and middle-class mothers differ in their willingness to let children engage in unsupervised play. Our data might appear as shown in Table 4.8a.

We want to examine the extent to which the evidence supports a proposition such as "'Socioeconomic level affects attitude toward unsupervised play." In this proposition, "socioeconomic level" is the independent variable, "attitude toward unsupervised play" the dependent variable. Let us consider the tables formed by percentaging each way. First we shall percentage along the independent variable, as the rule would have us do (Table 4.8b).

Table 4.8b

Percentage of Mothers in Different Social Classes Having Various Attitudes Toward Unsupervised Play

Attitude Toward Unsupervised Play	Mother's Socioeconomic Class Level			
	I or II	III	IV or V	Total
Generally positive	50%	38%	25%	35%
Mixed or uncertain	25	13	38	25
Generally negative	25	50	38	40
Total	100%	100%	100%	100%
	(20)	(40)	(40)	(100)

Table 4.8c

Percentage of Mothers Having Various Attitudes Toward Unsupervised Play Who Belong to Various Socioeconomic Classes

Attitude Toward Unsupervised Play	Mother's Socioeconomic Class Level			
	I or II	III	IV or V	
Generally positive	29%	43%	29%	100% (35)
Mixed or uncertain	20	20	60	100 (25)
Generally negative	12	50	38	100 (40)
Total	20%	40%	40%	100% (100)

We might read the table by beginning with the first column and saying: "Among mothers in Class I or Class II, 50% are generally positive toward unsupervised play, 25% are mixed or uncertain, while 25% are generally negative. Among mothers in Class III, 38% are generally positive, 13% mixed or uncertain, while 50% are generally negative." This tells us that Class I and II combined seem to have a higher proportion of positive mothers than does Class III. The "Class IV or V" column would be compared with other columns in a like fashion.

Now let us look at the same table, percentaged along the dependent variable (Table 4.8c).

We should read this table by saying: "Of those generally positive toward unsupervised play, 29% were in Class I or II, 43% were in Class III, and 29% in Class IV or V. Of those mixed or uncertain in their attitude, 20% were in Class I or II, 20% in Class III, and 60% in Class IV or V." Remember that our question is whether the evidence supports the proposition that class level affects attitude. From the first table, percentaged along the independent variable, we can say immediately that it seems that 50% of the higher-class group is favorable, 38% of the middle-class group is favorable, and 25% of the lower-class group is favorable. From the second table, percentaged along the dependent variable, we can say that a greater percentage of those who are generally positive are in the middle class, and the same is true of those who are generally negative. But this is not what we want to know. We do not want to know the class composition of those with positive, mixed, or negative attitudes. Rather, we want to know the effects on attitude of class membership. Percentaging along the independent variable permits us to see this immediately.

4: We are concerned about comparative composition of two groups. When the intent of the table is to communicate the comparative composition of the

Table 4.9a

Composition by Ranks of Two Different Military Units

	Military Unit		
	Unit A	Unit B	Total
Senior Officers	20	25	45
Junior Officers	30	35	65
Enlisted Men	150	60	210
Total	200	120	320

Source: Fictitious.

categories of attribute A, then the category totals of A should be used as the bases for calculating percentages. Had we wanted to compare the compositions of two military units, we might have gathered the data in Table 4.9a.

The proper percentage table would direct attention to the composition of the two military units, by percentaging within the unit categories. Table 4.9b shows the percentage composition of the two units.

Table 4.9b

Percent at Various Ranks in Two Different Military Units

	Military Unit	
	Unit A	Unit B
Senior Officers	10%	21%
Junior Officers	15	29
Enlisted Men	75	50
Total	100%	100%
	(200)	(120)

Tables in Three Dimensions

It is not difficult to devise a format for presenting tables in three, four, or more dimensions; the general approach is described in an earlier section of this chapter. It is, however, extremely difficult to find a way of making

Table 4.10*a*

Size of Family, Income Level, and Size of Home, among 285 Families

	Size of Family							
	Large			Total of Large Families	Small			Total of Small Families
Income Level	Small Home	Medium Home	Large Home		Small Home	Medium Home	Large Home	
High	9	22	10	41	10	14	14	38
Medium	11	33	20	64	27	29	5	61
Low	30	20	10	60	13	7	1	21
Total	50	75	40	165	50	50	20	120
Grand total								285

Source: Problem is adapted from that presented by Goode and Hatt, p. 351. Data are fictitious.

tables of four or more dimensions easy to understand. Three-dimensional tables can sometimes be simplified by the device described below, but there are no devices of this kind for a table in four or more dimensions. As noted earlier, it is usually best to break these higher-order tables down into simpler components, and present the components separately, especially if a lay audience is being addressed.[9]

Three-dimensional tables often show how two independent variables jointly affect a dependent variable. Table 4.10*a*, which presents what might have resulted from a study of the joint operation of income and family size in determining size of home, is of this type.

To read Table 4.10*a*, it is necessary to refer to all three dimensions in each statement. We might say, for example, about the upper left-hand row, "In large families, with high incomes, of which there were 41, 9 lived in a small house, 22 in a medium-sized house, and 10 in a large-sized house." Or, alternatively, we might prefer to read the left-hand column, "Among those living in small houses who come from large families, of whom there were 50, 9 were from high-income backgrounds, 11 from medium-income backgrounds, and 30 from low-income backgrounds."

[9] We have already noted the discussion of the problem of presenting tables of three and four dimensions in Hans Zeisel, *Say It With Figures, op. cit.,* pp. 67–90. A more compact treatment is given by William J. Goode and Paul K. Hatt, *Methods in Social Research* (New York: McGraw-Hill, 1952), pp. 351–353.

But no matter how we approach the table, it is difficult to keep everything in mind, and to get an overall view.

The device for simplifying a three-dimensional table is to replace one dimension by a summarizing statistic, one that can represent an important characteristic of all the information about that dimension. If the table can be interpreted as showing the joint effect of two independent variables on one dependent variable, then the dependent variable should be the one summarized.

In Table 4.10*a*, we show the joint effect of income level and size of family on size of house. How can we summarize the distribution of house sizes for a particular size of family and income level? There are a number of possibilities. Perhaps the simplest is to calculate the percentage of individuals who have homes in the large category, or medium plus large category combined: in other words, the percentage of individuals to be found on one end of the distribution. If it were possible to work out a measure of average house size—perhaps average number of rooms might do—then this too would serve the purpose.

In Table 4.10*b* the third dimension is summarized by means of the percentage of individuals in medium-sized or large houses.

This table would be read: "Of the large families with high income in our population, 76% lived in medium or large houses," and so on. Note how much easier it is to grasp the overall import of the data here, compared with the original table. Here, for example, it is clear that with high income, size of family hardly matters; most families live in medium or large houses. But with low income, size does matter; few small families live in medium or large houses, while half the large families live in medium or large houses.

Table 4.10*b*

Percentage of Families in Medium or Large Houses, by Size of Family and Income Level

	Size of Family	
Income Level	Large	Small
High	76%	74%
	($N = 41$)	($N = 38$)
Medium	82%	56%
	($N = 64$)	($N = 61$)
Low	50%	38%
	($N = 60$)	($N = 21$)

PROBLEMS

4.1. Present the data of Table 4.11 in another form which will make clear the extent to which women are among the recipients of the various degrees.

Table 4.11

Earned Degrees Conferred, by Field of Study, Level of Degree, and Sex, for Selected Fields, 1963

	Bachelor's and First Professional		Master's Except First Professional		Doctor's (Ph.D., Ed.D., etc.)	
	Male	Female	Male	Female	Male	Female
Agriculture	4,478	109	1,048	28	400	8
Architecture	1,940	88	344	12	3	—
Biological sciences	13,827	5,391	2,153	768	1279	176
Business and commerce	49,463	4,221	5,633	214	244	6
Education	26,175	76,621	20,439	17,083	1672	403
Engineering	33,328	130	9,603	32	1667	11
English and journalism	10,916	19,441	2,110	2,197	415	112
Foreign languages and literature	3,240	6,621	983	978	214	61
Health Professions (dentistry, medicine, nursing, etc.)	16,011	9,903	1,161	863	147	10
Home economics	69	4,394	118	534	4	41
Law	9,824	327	594	21	29	—
Mathematical subjects	11,163	4,958	2,665	658	454	36
Philosophy	3,545	540	392	54	117	17
Physical sciences	14,048	2,248	3,704	428	2285	95
Psychology	6,505	4,557	1,345	573	700	144
Sociology	3,785	5,270	487	197	177	31
Social work	1,160	1,915	144	174	26	14

Source: United States Bureau of the Census, *Statistical Abstracts of the United States, 1965* (86th edition), p. 136.

4.2. Consider Table 4.12.

Table 4.12

	Attribute A			
	Category 1	Category 2	Category 3	Total
Attribute B				
Category 1	50	50	100	200
Category 2	25	20	55	100
Category 3	25	30	145	200
Total	100	100	300	500

Develop a percentage table under each of the following set of assumptions:

(a) Attribute A is occupation
    Category 1 is airline pilot
    Category 2 is steelworker
    Category 3 is office worker
  Attribute B is incidence of colds during the winter
    Category 1 is no colds
    Category 2 is one cold
    Category 3 is more than one cold
(b) Attribute A is plans to move
    Category 1 plans to move within the next year
    Category 2 plans to move, but not within the next year
    Category 3 has no plans to move
  Attribute B is region of residence
    Category 1 is a 1/1000 sample from an expensive district
    Category 2 is 1/1000 sample from a less expensive district, excluding
      the most run-down areas
    Category 3 is a 1/100 sample from the most run-down area in the city
(c) Attribute A is occupation of father
    Category 1 is professional or managerial
    Category 2 is white collar, but not professional or managerial
    Category 3 is blue collar
  Attribute B is attitude toward education
    Category 1 ranks education higher than any other immediate goal
    Category 2 ranks education among most important goals
    Category 3 does not rank education among most important goals

(d) Attribute A is region of residence within a state
    Category 1 is the largest city
    Category 2 is all other cities
    Category 3 is all other regions
  Attribute B is education
    Category 1 is less than high school graduate
    Category 2 is high school graduate
    Category 3 is at least some college

4.3. Invent a percentage table that will illustrate each of the four rules for percentaging in two-dimensional tables.

Chapter 5

Pictorial Representation of Data

A picture of the relative frequencies in a table usually is less precise, and contains less information, than a presentation of the same data in a table, but we may accept this loss because of the picture's ability to make its point loud and clear. Especially when we are addressing a nontechnical audience, there is nothing like a good picture for getting a message across. Many government reports rely heavily on pictorial representations. When individuals in commercial research are required to make a verbal presentation to a general audience, they are apt to accompany their talk with charts and graphs. Even when reporting to a technical audience, we may choose to make some of our points through pictures, if we want to maximize the likelihood that they will be grasped and remembered. One statistician puts it this way:

> Diagrams help us to see the *pattern and shape* of any complex situation. Just as a map gives us a bird's eye view of a wide stretch of country, so diagrams help us to visualize the *whole meaning* of a numerical complex *at a single glance*. Give me a diagram and I am positively encouraged to forget detail until I have a real grasp of the overall picture. Diagrams register a meaningful impression almost before we think.[1]

If the chart is effectively done, the data are seen, rather than studied, and grasped as a totality rather than by careful comparison of magnitudes in cells. For this reason, pictorial representation is useful when presenting a talk that involves a statistical argument. It is difficult to grasp the meaning of a table, in the time the speaker can allow, while a picture can communicate it almost immediately. It is true that pictorial representations are easily modified to produce misleading statements.[2] But

[1] M. J. Moroney, *Facts from Figures* (Baltimore: Penguin Books, 1958), p. 20.
[2] See, for many examples, Darrell Huff, *How to Lie With Statistics* (New York: W. W. Norton, 1954).

72

this should only alert, not discourage, an investigator contemplating their use. The fact that diagrams *can* be slanted does not mean they have to be.

In sum, pictorial representation sacrifices detail and accuracy in order to improve communication. The sacrifice is justifiable if the point at issue is important; if the point is one that can be effectively captured in pictures; if the audience is not technically trained and would be unlikely to get as much from a table as from a pictorial representation; or if it is important to get a point across quickly, either because the point is embedded in a speech, or because it is anticipated that the audience will be impatient or uninterested.

TYPES OF PICTORIAL REPRESENTATIONS

The ideas most often used in picturing data are the following:

1. The magnitude of a given cell may be represented by a column or bar. This is the *bar chart*, and is perhaps the simplest way of picturing magnitudes.

2. The rise and fall of a line as one moves from value to value may be used to represent the change of magnitudes from point to point. This is the *line chart*, some forms of which are referred to as *frequency polygons*.

3. A single area may be broken up in a way that shows the proportion of a total represented by each of several subcategories. These are *segmental representations*. When the single area is a circle, we have the *pie chart*. Sometimes the area is given some other shape; for example, a milk container may be subdivided to show how much of its cost goes to the farmer, how much to the distributor, and how much in taxes. Bars in bar charts may be subdivided to show components.

4. A unit of magnitude may be represented by a pictorial symbol. The number of such symbols then represents the total magnitude of a category.

These are by no means a complete inventory of devices available, although they are the ideas most often used. (As an example of another, more specialized approach: if we have data grouped by geographical regions, like the number of social welfare clients in various counties, it is possible to suggest frequencies in regions by different cross-hatchings of the regions.) Even when no new idea is involved, there are many variations possible in the use of those devices given here. The material of this chapter should be taken only as a preparation for ingenuity.[3]

[3] For detail beyond that presented here, the following may be consulted. Calvin F. Schmid, *Handbook of Graphic Presentation* (New York: Ronald Press, 1954), and by the same author, in Pauline Young, *Scientific Social Surveys and Research* (Englewood

Most often the individual responsible for a research report will have to decide himself on the representation that best communicates his point. Although he can seek advice from a statistician, only he will know what he wants to get across, and he will usually have to draw a rough sketch of his idea himself. He then might do well to take the sketch to a draftsman, since the design of good pictorial representations demands a fairly high level of skill. It is worth keeping in mind that an uninterpretable picture is worse than a difficult table; the picture has no reason for being, other than communication. If there is any doubt about whether a picture gets its message across, it should be tested by having a few individuals whose technical competence is similar to that of the intended audience attempt to interpret the picture.

The Bar Chart

A bar chart associates the magnitude of a quality with the length of a bar of standard width. The chart is inherently comparative: if a bar of one length represents so much of a quality, a bar of twice the length represents twice as much. A chart consisting of a single bar makes no sense at all. Neither does a bar chart in which lengths are not proportional to magnitude.[4]

A bar chart may be used to compare the frequencies of nominal scale measurements; for example, numbers of bushels of *different kinds of grain* harvested in a given year; numbers of *automobiles of different makes* manufactured in a given year; and numbers of *different majors* among undergraduates. However, there is some evidence that the bar chart is the most easily grasped of all pictorial devices,[5] and so might be considered, no matter what the level of measurement is. Ordinal information can be pictured effectively with the bar-chart techniques, since the order among categories can be represented by an order among bars. Metric data cannot be pictured in a bar chart without a more serious loss of information.

Figure 5.1 presents an example of a simple bar chart. Because nominal data is pictured, there is no necessary order among the bars. In the ab-

---

Cliffs, N.J.: Prentice-Hall, 1949), Chapter XIII, "Graphic Presentation." Also Rudolph Nadley and Dyno Lowenstein, *Pictographs and Graphs* (New York: Harper & Bros., 1952). A good general discussion is given by William A. Nyswander in *Elementary Statistical Methods as Applied to Business and Economic Data* (revised New York: MacMillan, 1956). Darrell Huff's *How to Lie With Statistics, op. cit.* presents a useful collection of cautionary tales.

[4] In some special circumstances, it may be necessary to picture a bar in which a part has been removed so that the bar will fit on the page. Huff, *op. cit.*, gives illustrations of the use and abuse of this tactic.

[5] L. E. Sarbaugh, Richard Powers, Hugh Culbertson, and Thomas Flores, *Comprehension of Graphs*, Bulletin 31, Department of Agriculture Journal, University of Wisconsin.

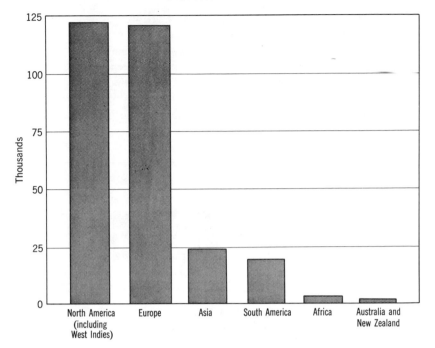

Figure 5.1 Immigrants to the United States, 1962, by continent on which born. [*Source:* United States Bureau of the Census, *Statistical Abstract of the United States: 1963* (eighty-fourth edition, Washington, D.C., 1963), p. 101.]

sence of other guides, we put the category with the largest magnitude first. The actual numbers of immigrants represented by the bars might have been introduced into Figure 5.1, either within the base of the bars, or beside the bars. This is one way of retaining the information of a tabulation while gaining the increased communication value of a picture. It is bad practice to increase the apparent length of the bars by setting captions or numbers at their tips; each bar would then seem longer, by the length of the caption.

There are many ways more information might be brought into the chart. We could subdivide the bars to show the numbers of each sex. We could add bars to represent what had been the situation ten years ago. In fact there are so many ways of adding to a bar chart that we must guard against the temptation of producing a cluttered and ineffective picture.

Figure 5.2 shows that, while the population in at least a number of other central cities has been declining over the past ten years, the population of the cities of Los Angeles and Long Beach has increased considerably. This suggests that a process is at work in Los Angeles which is different from that in some other large cities of our country.

Figure 5.3, a paired bar chart, presents two-dimensional data: information is classified by year and by occupational category. The same information could also have been presented by means of two segmented bars. The technique of Figure 5.3 makes a number of points: the labor force has more than doubled in the first half of the present century; it

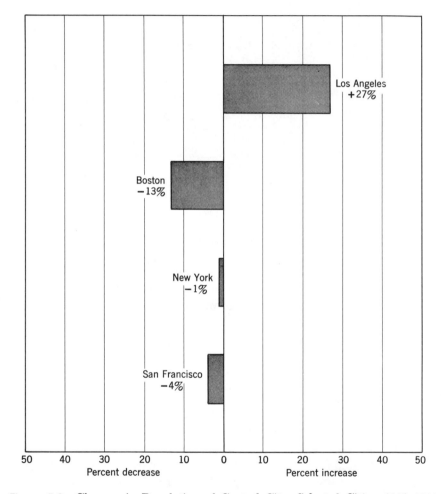

Figure 5.2 Changes in Population of Central City, Selected Cities, 1950–1960. [*Source:* United States Bureau of the Census, *Statistical Abstract of the United States: 1963* (eighty-fourth edition), Washington, D.C., 1963, pp. 13–18.]

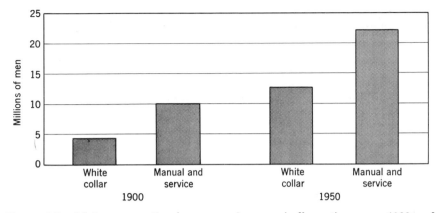

Figure 5.3 Major occupational groups of economically active man, 1900 and 1950. (*Source:* United States Bureau of the Census, *Historical Statistics of the United States, Colonial Times to 1957*, Washington, D.C., 1960, p. 74.)

has also changed so that a greater proportion of the labor force is now "middle class"; the first change is greater than the second.[6]

The Line Graph

A line graph represents the frequencies of successive values of a quality by a line of varying height. The line graph, in contrast to most bar charts, suggests an underlying continuum of ordered values. It is not possible to construct a line graph if we are working with nominal data; measurements must be at least ordinal, and preferably interval scale.

A simple line graph involves only a baseline, along which the values of the quality are listed, a vertical line marked off to indicate the heights that will represent different frequencies, and the graph itself, whose rise and fall traces the changes of frequencies observed for different values. An example of a line graph is given as Figure 5.4.

In Figure 5.4, the underlying dimension is time, the values of which are given in years. The values are continuous; there exists a value between any two values we can name. The heights of the line above the base represent the frequency of births per thousand population. The graph communicates the existence of large-scale changes in the birth rate, such as the trough during the Depression, and the post-World War II baby boom, and also smaller, difficult to explain, fluctuations of the birth rate. Notice how effective the graph is in communicating overall trends.

[6] A variety of bar chart, the *histogram*, is discussed in the next section, since it is based on an assumption of an underlying frequency polygon.

78   STATISTICS IN SOCIAL RESEARCH

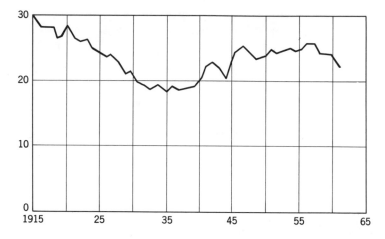

Figure 5.4 Birth rates, United States, 1915–1962. (*Source:* United States Bureau of the Census, *Statistical Abstract, op cit.,* adapted from chart, p. 51.)

The data of Figure 5.4 are interval scale. It is possible to plot a line graph for ordinal data, but it must be remembered that the distances between ordinal measurements are indeterminate. To show the problem this introduces, consider how we should picture the information in Table 5.1.

Table 5.1

Grades of Students at X College, in English Composition

Grades	Numbers
A	15
B	25
C	60
D	10
F	2
Total	112

If it is assumed that each letter grade is about the same distance from the next higher or lower letter grade, then Figure 5.5*a* would result. If it is assumed, on the other hand, that the grade of A is about twice as far from a B as a B is from a C, and that the F is virtually off the continuum in the level of performance it indicates, then Figure 5.5*b* would result. In such situations, it may be preferable to use a bar chart, which does not suggest interval relationships, to represent the data.

Line Graphs from Grouped Data

When we attempt to draw a line graph from data that have been grouped into categories, we must decide where to place the magnitudes of the categories. We may also have to work out some way of dealing with categories of unequal width, or with "open-ended" categories.

Consider the grouped data presented in the first two columns of Table 5.2. On the left are categories of incomes, each given in terms of an interval of a certain width. The first interval is \$1000 in width, as is the

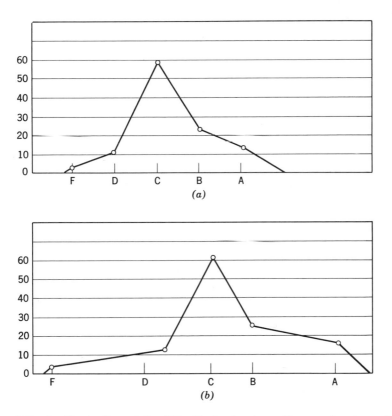

Figure 5.5   An illustration of the difficulty in drawing a line graph using ordinal data. Grades of students at X College, in English Composition. Both *a* and *b* represent the same information.

Table 5.2

Distribution of Families by Income, United States, 1955

Family Income (Dollars)	Number (in Thousands)	Midpoints	Relative Widths of Interval
Under 1000	3,300	500	1000
1000–1999	4,200	1,500	1000
2000–2999	4,700	2,500	1000
3000–3999	6,300	3,500	1000
4000–4999	6,600	4,500	1000
5000–5999	5,400	5,500	1000
6000–6999	4,100	6,500	1000
7000–9999	5,500	8,500	3000
10,000–14,999	2,100	12,500	5000
15,000 and over	600	—	Open-ended
Total	42,800		

Source: United States Bureau of the Census, *Current Population Reports, Consumer Income,* Series P-60, No. 24, United States Government Printing Office, Washington, D.C., April, 1957, as it appears in John H. Mueller and Karl F. Schuessler, *Statistical Reasoning in Sociology* (Boston: Houghton Mifflin Co., 1961), p. 50.

second, third, and so on, until we reach the interval $7000 to $9999. This is $3000 in width. The next interval is $5000 in width. The final category, "$15,000 and over," is open-ended: there is no way of telling where it ends. There might be an income of $100,000 or even $1,000,000 in it.

Where on the graph will the frequencies (3300, 4200, 4700, and so on) within these categories be placed? One approach is to distribute the frequency over the category: to give every value within the category an average frequency. This would produce a set of bars. Alternatively, we could assume that, within any category, the incomes closer to those most frequent for the total population should occur more frequently.

We can develop a line graph that assigns greater frequencies to the side of the category closer to the population mode by following these rules.

1. Decide the width of interval to be taken as "standard" within the tabulation. This should be the most frequently used width. In the case of the data presented in Table 5.2, it is $1000.

2. Plot the frequencies of the standard categories in the tabulation, at the midpoints of these categories (see Figure 5.6).

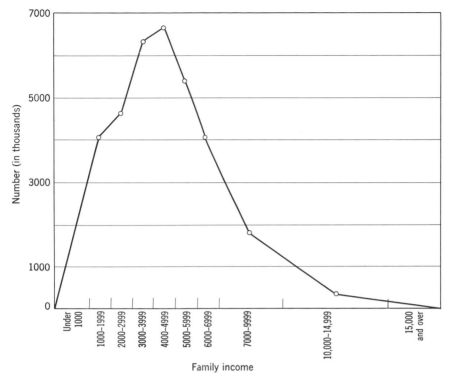

Figure 5.6 Distribution of families by income, United States, 1955. (*Source:* Drawn from Table 3.1.11, in John H. Mueller and Karl F. Schuessler, *Statistical Reasoning in Sociology, op. cit.*, p. 50.)

3. For categories different from the "standard" width, but nevertheless bounded, calculate the relationship of their width to the standard width. Are they twice as wide, half as wide, three times as wide? Divide the frequency by the number of standard categories represented in the non-standard category. If the category is three times the standard, divide the frequency for that category by three. If it is half of the standard, divide it by 1/2 (which means multiply it by two). Plot this new frequency above the midpoint of the category.

4. When a category is open-ended, it is necessary to guess where the arithmetic average of incomes *within the category* would be. One way of deciding this is to continue the curve already drawn through the open-ended interval. Graphing an open-ended interval is, however, guesswork. The fact that the interval is open-ended may be suggested by carrying the curve out along the base, not touching it, for some distance.

5. Connect all midpoints. The curve should be brought to the base both at its beginning and its end at points where it is clear that there are no more cases.

A histogram is a bar chart that is based on a line graph. The *histogram* that would be associated with the line graph of Figure 5.6 is shown in Figure 5.7. The histogram is intended to suggest an underlying frequency distribution, just as would a line graph. The width of the bars of a histogram are given by the intervals of the original table. The height of the bars is determined by the same distributing of frequencies in nonstandard categories which is necessary when drawing a line graph from grouped data. In the histogram, it is not the length of the bar that is proportional to (or representative of) the frequency in a category, but rather the area of the bar.

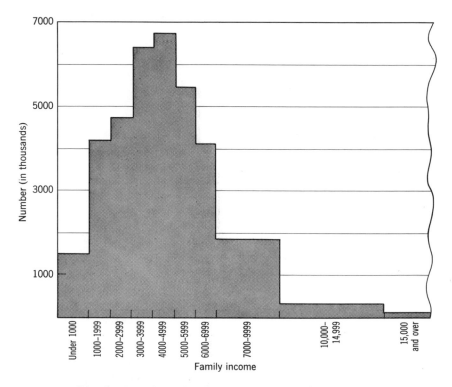

Figure 5.7 Distribution of families by income, United States, 1955 (histogram). (*Source:* See Figure 5.6.)

Further Developments Based on Line Graphs

It is not possible to describe in detail the varieties of ways in which charts involving line graphs may be constructed. There are too many, and the ideas involved are sometimes complex. We might, however, mention a few of the most frequently encountered ideas.

1. The placement of several graphs on a single chart. When we plot several graphs on a single chart, we can easily decide whether rises and falls in the one are accompanied by rises and falls in the other. This becomes a way of suggesting that phenomena are associated with each other. We might, for example, plot for the years 1950 to 1965 the levels of unemployment, the levels of public assistance, and the levels of petty theft in a particular community.

2. Graphs of relative frequencies. We might plot on our chart not the frequencies of some occurrence, nor the amount of some characteristic, but rather the relative frequencies, or relative amounts. To do this, we should plot the ratio between the observed values and the values in some base year. We might choose this as a way of communicating the rise and fall of stock prices. We could choose 1950 as a base year, and then plot the ratio of prices to 1950 prices, for every month thereafter.

3. Graphs of cumulative frequencies. We might want to represent not the percentage of cases that would be found at a particular value, but, instead, the percentage of cases that would be found at that value or anything less than that value. A graph of this sort will begin at 0%, at the extreme left, and move steadily upward until it reaches 100% at the extreme right. We might use such a graph as a device for communicating the range of life spans of a "cohort" of individuals; that is, of a group of individuals born at a certain time. Few of them will die in their early years, but as we move to later and later ages there will be an increasing percentage who will have died.

4. Graphs representing two dimensions of data. To this point, we have assumed that the line graph represents the frequency of values of only one dimension of data. We can also design a chart on which we can plot the cases that exhibit particular conjunctions of values of two dimensions. A way of doing this is suggested in Chapter 11, in the discussion of the Pearson product-moment correlation coefficient. When this is done, it sometimes appears as though a smooth curve can be drawn through most of the plotted points, or at least can be drawn in such a way as to suggest that the plotted points are not too far from it. This curve may be interpreted as "describing" the relationship between values of the one characteristic and values of the other. The product-moment correlation coefficient described in Chapter 11 states the extent to which a straight line relationship actually holds. Some investigators believe it to be a desirable practice to sketch a two-dimensional graph of data before working out a product-moment correlation coefficient, just to be sure that some curve other than a straight line is not suggested by the plottings.

5. Graphs of logarithms of frequencies. We might decide that what ought to be charted is not the observed frequencies, but rather some other value that depends on the observed frequencies. For example, if we were to try to plot the numbers of people in the world since the beginning of the Modern Age, we should find that we could get a graph that showed a much more even rise if we were to plot, not the estimated populations themselves, but rather the logarithms of the estimates. This would not be the only reason for using logarithms; they would also be advisable because of our understanding of the process of population growth. To go further into the question would take us too far afield, but in general, when we believe that a process of increase is a process that involves multiplication of the existent population by a constant amount, rather than addition to the existent population by a constant amount, we might find it desirable to picture the growth of the population by plotting the logarithms of frequencies.

6. Theoretical distribution curves. The graph we obtain when we plot our observations is a graph of *an empirical distribution.* Because we connect the plots of frequencies of adjacent points by straight lines, we sometimes call the resulting graph a *frequency polygon.* Sometimes we want to interpret a frequency polygon as representing an underlying *theoretical distribution.* This is discussed at greater length in Chapter 8, but we may say here that what we mean by a theoretical distribution is the frequencies that would result if a particular mathematical (actually probabilistic) process were at work. When we want to suggest what might be the form of this theoretical distribution, which we believe the empirical distribution to approximate, we may round off the angles of the frequency polygon to obtain a smooth curve.

Segmental Representation

At times, when it is desirable to emphasize that the various categories in which data are gathered together add up to a single whole, the categories may be pictured as segments of a whole. If we were showing how a family budget was divided up into sums for food, shelter, clothing, and recreation, we should want to show the budget as the whole—by showing it as a circle, or even as a bag of money—and food, clothing, and the like,

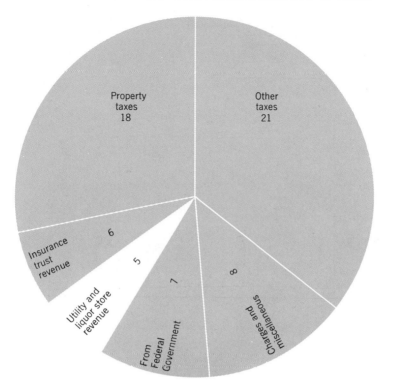

Figure 5.8 State and local government sources of income (in billions of dollars). (*Source:* Bureau of the Census, *Statistical Abstract: 1963, op. cit.*, p. 412.)

as a part of this whole. When we represent the whole by a circle, and the segments by wedges, the result is termed a "pie chart." An example of a pie chart is given as Figure 5.8.

In a segmental representation, each category is given an area proportional to its size. A category that represents 50% of the total would have twice the area of a category that represents 25% of the total.

Segmental charts are hard to compare with each other. Actually, segmenting a bar permits somewhat more accurate comparisons than does segmenting a circle. Bars can also be used to show changing sizes of the whole, something which would be much more difficult to interpret in pie charts. Figure 5.9 shows a set of segmented bars that permit comparison of relative composition and also of relative total magnitude of tax revenues in the United States in the years 1959, 1960, and 1961.

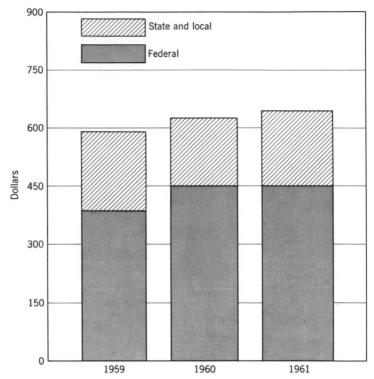

Figure 5.9 Government per capita tax revenue, by level of government: 1959–1961. (*Source:* Bureau of the Census, *Statistical Abstract: 1963, op. cit.,* p. 412.)

Pictographs

The pictograph is a pictorial representation in which the magnitude of a category is conveyed by the number of symbols that stand for the individuals in the category. If the table shows the relative number of men in the armed forces, categorized Army, Navy, Marine Corps, then a pictograph would indicate the size of the Army by a number of soldiers, the size of the Navy by a number of sailors, and so on. If one symbol were to represent 10,000 men, a 100,000-man force would be represented by 10 symbols.

A good pictograph has great dramatic value. Even more than other forms of pictorial representation, it communicates with immediacy the idea of different magnitudes of different sorts of elements. Done properly, it is not much more imprecise than a bar chart, and more precise than a pie chart.[7] The very vividness of the pictograph may, however, suggest meanings that are not intended. In a pictograph of the armed forces, for example, it might be necessary to crowd the symbols representing soldiers to get the proper number on the page. The unintended message that the Army is overcrowded might thereby be suggested.

One kind of pictograph *ought* to be avoided: that is, the approach in which a single symbol represents the magnitude of a category, and the symbol is increased in size or decreased in size as we move from category to category. The problem is that it is impossible for a reader to guess whether the researcher intends the relative heights or the relative areas of the symbols, or even what might be imagined to be relative volumes, to represent the frequencies of the different categories. In addition, unintended meanings are particularly difficult to avoid. There is always a tendency to interpret a large symbol as suggesting a large actuality; if the size of the Army is represented by a large soldier and the size of the Marine Corps by a small marine, there is an implicit suggestion that men in the Army are bigger than men in the Marines.[8] Good practice avoids this kind of chart.

PROBLEMS

5.1. Decide what type of pictorial representation would communicate the main features of Tables 5.3, 5.4, and 5.5 and present each. (You might want to consider using different types of line for the graph of Table 5.3.)

[7] For further discussion of how to draw pictographs, together with examples, see Calvin F. Schmid, *Handbook of Graphic Presentation, op. cit.*
[8] See, in this connection, some of Darrell Huff's examples, *How to Lie With Statistics, op. cit.,* pp 67–73.

Table 5.3

Income in 1959 of Families of Husband, Wife, and Two Children under 18, Living in Urban Areas of the United States, by Color[a]

	Thousands of Persons	
Income (Dollars)	White	Nonwhite
Under 1000	21.5	6.3
1000 to 1999	53.5	16.1
2000 to 2999	125.9	34.8
3000 to 3999	272.5	42.7
4000 to 4999	479.6	39.1
5000 to 5999	711.1	32.5
6000 to 6999	668.7	21.6
7000 to 7999	532.1	14.1
8000 to 8999	383.5	10.0
9000 to 9999	259.3	6.7
10,000 to 14,999	500.5	10.1
15,000 to 24,999	159.0	1.7
25,000 and over	68.5	0.6

[a] For definition of "urban areas" see Source, p. 485.
Source: United States Census, 1960, as reproduced in Ben J. Wattenberg and Richard M. Scammon, *This U.S.A.* (Garden City, N.Y.: Doubleday, 1965), p. 439.

Table 5.4

Numbers of Men in Civilian Labor Force and Armed Forces, by 1960

	Thousands of Men	
	White	Nonwhite
Civilian labor force	60,885	7259
Employed	58,010	6629
Unemployed	2,875	630
Armed forces	1,593	131

Source: United States Census, 1960, as reproduced in Wattenberg and Scammon, *op. cit.*, p. 422.

Table 5.5

Occupation Groups of Employed Persons, by Sex, for the United States, 1960

	Thousands of Persons	
	Male	Female
Professional, technical, and kindred	4479	2753
Farmers and farm managers	2387	118
Managers, officials, and proprietors	4629	780
Clerical and kindred workers	3015	6291
Sales workers	2977	1661
Craftsmen, foremen, and kindred workers	8488	253
Operatives and kindred workers	8641	3256
Private household workers	61	1665
Service workers other than private households	2599	2946
Farm laborers and farm foremen	1201	243
Laborers	2998	110
Occupation not reported	1987	1197

Source: United States Census, 1960, as reproduced in Wattenberg and Scammon, *op. cit.*, p. 423.

5.2. Consider the data of Tables 5.6 and 5.7 together. List some pictorial representations that could be developed from these data which you think might be interesting. Present a free-hand sketch of two of these.

Table 5.6

Major Occupation Groups of Men, by Color, 1960

	Thousands of Men	
	White	Nonwhite
Professional, technical, and kindred	4324	155
Farmers and farm managers	2212	176
Managers, officials, and proprietors	4539	91
Clerical and kindred workers	2815	201
Sales workers	2918	60
Craftsmen, foremen, and kindred workers	8082	407
Operatives and kindred workers	7702	939
Private household workers	32	29
Service workers other than private households	2050	549
Farm laborers and farm foremen	916	286
Laborers	2221	776
Occupations not reported	1652	335

Source: United States Census, 1960, as reproduced in Wattenberg and Scammon, *op. cit.,* p. 423.

Table 5.7

Major Occupation Groups of Experienced, Unemployed Men, by Color, 1960

	Thousands of Persons	
	White	Nonwhite
Professional, technical, and kindred	59.6	3.7
Farmers and farm managers	15.5	3.0
Managers, officials, and proprietors	62.6	2.7
Clerical and kindred workers	92.8	11.9
Sales workers	73.5	3.6
Craftsmen, foremen, and kindred workers	447.3	36.6
Operatives and kindred workers	507.8	84.3
Private household workers	1.9	2.0
Service workers other than private households	104.5	42.1
Farm laborers and farm foremen	65.0	22.9
Laborers	296.2	111.0
Occupation not reported	126.0	42.6

5.3. Develop graphs for presenting some of the leading characteristics of the population of Appendix 2.

Chapter 6

A Representative Value

Tables and graphs can tell a reader what our findings look like. There will be times, however, when we shall want to go beyond displaying the data, and shall want to direct a reader's attention to some specific characteristic of our data. In particular, we may want to deal with the following four issues.

1. *What is a single value that in some sense can represent the entire distribution of values,* a value that is "typical," "central," or "average"?

2. *How much variation is there in the data,* as we go from case to case? At times, we deal with distributions where the values are pretty much the same, at other times with distributions in which the values fluctuate more or less.

3. *How can we describe the "shape" of the distribution, taken as a whole?* We might try to describe the distribution of incomes by saying there are some, but not many, people at the lowest end, a great many people bunched around an average value, and then a trailing off into the higher values. Is this kind of verbal description the best we can do? We need a conceptual equivalent of the line graph: a way of saying in words or through a mathematical description what the line graph says in a picture.

4. If we are working with two dimensions of the data, we may want to be able to describe the extent to which the two qualities go together. *We need a measure of the extent to which specific values of the one are associated with specific values of the other.*

This chapter will discuss techniques for deciding on a single value that can be interpreted as "central," or "typical," or in some other sense representative of all values in the distribution. The five chapters that follow will continue the discussion of descriptive statistics.

Three different measures can be used to state a "representative" value:

the mode, the median, and the mean. These measures are not mathematical synonyms. Each captures a different feature of the data. Each, too, depends on a different level of measurement.[1] The mode views data as sorted into bins, and names the bin that is fullest. It uses only a nominal level of measurement. The median views data as lined up, ranked, in terms of the level of some quality, and selects the middle individual in the ranking. It requires an ordinal level of measurement. The mean supposes that we can aggregate all our values into one large pile, and states the amount everyone would have if the pile were then redistributed equally. It requires that our measurements be at least interval.

THE MODE

The mode is the value which occurs most frequently in a distribution. If in a class of 30 students, 15 are brunettes, 10 blondes, and 5 are redheads or unclassifiable, then the modal hair color is brunette.

When we are working with nominal data, the mode is the only value

Table 6.1

Fields of Concentration among Residents of a College Dormitory

	Number
Anthropology	4
Biology	2
Chemistry	2
Economics	6
English Literature	5
French	1
Geography	1
Geology	2
German	0
History	4
Linguistics	2
Mathematics	3
Physics	5
Politics	4
Psychology	10
Sociology	2
Total	55

[1] These measures are referred to in many texts as "measures of central tendency." However, this characterization fits the median well, the mean slightly less well, and the mode not at all.

Table 6.2

Fields of Concentration among Residents of a College Dormitory

Fields	Number	Percent
1. Social Sciences (includes anthropology, economics, geography, history, politics, psychology, and sociology)	33	60
2. Natural Sciences (includes biology, chemistry, geology, mathematics, and physics)	14	25
3. Humanities (includes English Literature, French, German and linguistics)	8	15
Total	55	100

that can justifiably be called "representative." Yet sometimes the modal value, even though it occurs more frequently than any other value, still is a small percentage of all cases. An example is given in Table 6.1. Among the fields of concentration listed there, psychology is clearly the modal category. The problem is that there are so many fields listed, and each has so small a percentage of the total number of students, that even psychology has only 18% of all those in the dormitory.

A solution is to combine the categories into more general groupings: into the social sciences, the physical sciences, and so on. This produces Table 6.2. It is now possible to say that the typical student in the dormitory is a social science major. We might want to add that in this way we refer to 60% of the students within the dormitory.

Suppose that two of the categories contained very nearly equal percentages. Suppose, for example, that social sciences contained 45% of the residents of the hall and natural sciences contained 40%. Then the best way of communicating what is a typical major in this residence hall might be to note the two nearly equal categories, perhaps in this way: "The typical resident of North Hall is a major in either the social sciences or the natural sciences. About 85% of all residents have elected majors in one of these two fields." It would be easy, here, to describe the rest of the distribution as well: "The remaining 15% of residents are majors in the humanities."

Which category turns out to be modal clearly depends on the way categories are defined. It is possible, in many situations, to shift the modal category by judicious recategorizations. In going from Table 6.1 to Table 6.2, for example, we could make natural sciences the modal category by pulling history and politics out of the social sciences, labeling them "social history," and shifting psychology and geography into the natural sciences. This is hardly fair, of course, although if the researcher were a natural science representative arguing for special privilege on the grounds that more students in the dormitory were in natural sciences than in any other field, he might be seriously tempted to recategorize along these lines. Recategorization ought to follow careful definition of the nature of the new, more abstract, categories, rather than the impression that it "seems all right."

When ought categories to be collapsed before identifying a mode? There is no hard and fast rule, but a useful guide might be that the description of the modal case should not lead the reader to form a distorted picture of the situation. Describing as modal a category that includes only 10% of the population may be technically correct, but is nevertheless misleading. On the other hand, it would seem satisfactory to describe as modal a category that includes 40% of the population, if the remaining 60% is spread over a number of other categories.

The mode is the only way of defining a representative value in nominally measured data. It may also be used to describe data of other kinds, if the data are being treated as though they are nominal, each category an entity in itself, and different in quality rather than in quantity from other categories. If a housing administrator wanted to know the size of family of a set of applicants for housing—including two-child families, three-child families, four-child families, and so on—it would be reasonable for him to ask first for the modal value, since each family size might be thought to have different spatial requirements. Even though he can work out a median and a mean from the data, he may want to treat the data as though they were nominal measurements.

THE MEDIAN

We can identify a median case only when we have a ranking. Then, if there is an odd number of cases, the median is the middle case in the ranking. In Table 6.3, the median individual, in terms of height, is E.F., whose height is 5 ft 9 in.

Table 6.3

Members of Class, Ordered by Height

Member	Height
A.B.	6 ft 10 in.
C.D.	5 ft 10 in.
E.F.	5 ft 9 in.
G.H.	5 ft 8 in.
I.J.	5 ft 5 in.

If there were an even number of class members, no one individual would be in the median position. Suppose there were a sixth member of the class, whose height was 5 ft 8 1/2 in. Now the median members of the class are E.F. and the new member—or so, at least, strict logic would require. It would seem proper now not to name a single median height, but instead to name two median heights, or to name the heights of the two median individuals, and say "The median heights in this array are 5 ft 8 1/2 in. and 5 ft 9 in.," or "The heights of the median individuals are 5 ft 8 1/2 in. and 5 ft 9 in." The problem is that this way of reporting the median is almost never used. Instead, investigators almost always hold that the median must be a single value, and in a situation of this type, they will shift uncomfortably before announcing that the median is midway between 5 ft 8 1/2 in. and 5 ft 9 in. The convention and the logic of the situation are at odds. Actually, we rarely identify the median value if we have a small array, such as this one, and with much larger arrays the problem is unlikely to come up in this insoluble form.

Our data may not come to us as an ordered array. In Table 6.4, there are 50 cases altogether, grouped in four categories. The median cases will be the 25th and 26th. The first 12 cases fell into Category 1. The next 20 cases, which include cases 25 and 26, are in Category 2. We can therefore say the median degree of care within our population (in terms of our criteria) is "generally shows care, but with some relaxation." Actually we might prefer the mode as a representative measure, feeling that even though these are ranked categories, they are different enough from each other qualitatively to make the median inappropriate.

Table 6.4

Care of Home among Survey Respondents

Categories	Number	Percent
1. Great care (completely neat, everything in place, absence of dust, carefully furnished)	12	24
2. Generally shows care, but with some relaxation (generally neat, but a few things out of place; informal feeling, although generally neat)	20	40
3. Some care (some attempt at neatness, but with a number of things out of place; books, magazines, newspapers, may be just dropped; may be dust)	10	20
4. Little care (no attempt at neatness; few things seem to have a place; sense of things being strewn about)	8	16
Total	50	100

There is no need to learn a formula for finding the median. However, it may be helpful to treat the following as compact definitions. If cases are in an ordered array, from smallest to largest, then the number of the median case is:

$$\text{For an odd number of cases: } \frac{\text{number of cases} + 1}{2}$$

$$\text{For an even number of cases: } \frac{\text{number of cases}}{2} \text{ and } \frac{\text{number of cases} + 2}{2}$$

The convention is, as noted, to report only a single value for the median if this is at all possible, which leads many investigators to report as the median of a series of an even number of cases the point halfway between the two observed median values. This is defensible if this halfway value is a *possible* observation. For example, a height of 5 ft 8 3/4 in. is a possible observation, but a family size of 3 1/2 children is not; we could report the first as a median value, but not the second.

The necessity that the median be a value that might have been observed determines in which cases we can *interpolate* for the median. (To interpolate means to estimate a likely intermediate value on the basis of observed values that bracket it.) In Table 6.5 interpolation is justified, because the resulting estimate is a possible observation.

In Table 6.5 we can find the median either by working with the column of number of families, or with the percent column. Let us work with the frequencies; the technique is the same in either case. There are 42,800 families in the table. The median families will be numbers 21,400 and 21,401, but with so many families listed, and with frequencies rounded off to the nearest hundred in any event, it makes no sense to try to maintain the precision suggested by naming the two cases that, together, define the median value. Here it is sufficient just to identify what might be Case No. 21,400. Counting from the top, we find that we reach Case No. 18,500 when we come to the end of the $3000 to 3999 category. When we get to the end of the next category, we have come to Case No. 25,100. We passed the median case in traversing the $4000 to 4999 category.

We can estimate just where in the $4000 to 4999 category the median case will be found if we assume that cases are spread evenly throughout the category. There are 6600 cases within the category. The case we want to find is 2900 cases beyond the beginning of the category, and so we must pass 2900/6600 of the people in the category to come to it. If the cases are not all bunched up at one end or another of the category, we shall also then have traversed 2900/6600 of the width of the category. We

Table 6.5

Distribution of Families, by Income, United States, 1955

Family Income (Dollars)	Number of Families (in Thousands)	Percent
Under 1000	3,300	7.7
1000–1999	4,200	9.8
2000–2999	4,700	11.0
3000–3999	6,300	14.6
4000–4999	6,600	15.6
5000–5999	5,400	12.7
6000–6999	4,100	9.5
7000–9999	5,500	12.9
10,000–14,999	2,100	4.8
15,000 and over	600	1.4
Total	42,800	100.0

Source: United States Bureau of the Census, *Current Population Reports*, Series P-60, *Consumer Income*, No. 24, United States Government Printing Office, Washington, D.C., April 1957, adapted from presentation in John H. Mueller and Karl F. Schuessler, *Statistical Reasoning in Sociology* (Boston: Houghton-Mifflin Co., 1961), p. 50.

therefore work out how far 2900/6600 of the width of the category brings us.

$$\text{Proportion of category} \rightarrow = \frac{2900}{6600} (4999.999 - 4000)$$

$$= \frac{2900}{6600} (1000)$$

$$= 440 \text{ (approximately)}$$

We should thus have traversed \$440 worth of the thousand dollars represented by the category. (Notice that we used the real limits, rather than the stated limits, in deciding how wide the category was, although it would not have made much difference in this case.) We can therefore say that we should estimate the median family income to be \$4440. We *know for sure* that the median family income falls in the bracket \$4000 to \$4999. We *estimate* that it is \$4440, on the assumption that cases are distributed evenly within the category.

A formula for interpolation is easily written, although it is better practice to learn the technique of interpolation than to memorize the formula. To find the point M, which is n cases within a category whose lower limit is l_1, whose upper limit is l_2, and whose frequency is f:

$$M = l_1 + \frac{n}{f}(l_2 - l_1)$$

When interpolating for the median, consider M in the above formula to be the median, l_1 to be the first point in the category within which the median lies, n to be the number of cases within the category which must be passed in order to come to the median, f to be the total number of cases in the category, and l_2 to be the last point in the category.

In the above example, we would make substitutions as follows:

$$M = l_1 + \frac{n}{f}(l_2 - l_1)$$

$$M = 4000 + \frac{2900}{6600}(5000 - 4000) = 4440$$

As an example of data in which we should not interpolate for the median, we may take Table 6.6. There it would be a mistake to interpolate

Table 6.6

Median Family Size, Indiana, 1950

Size of Family	Frequency	Percent
1	64,045	7.6
2	222,047	26.4
3	185,340	22.0
4	146,519	17.5
5	95,757	11.4
6	57,914	6.9
7	32,916	3.9
8	18,500	2.1
9	10,285	1.2
10	5,219	.6
11	2,469	.2
12	1,855	.2
Total	842,000	100.0

Source: Mueller and Schuessler, *op. cit.,* Table 5.2.3, p. 126.

within the category of three people and say that the median family size is "3.23 persons," because there could be no such observation. The family that stands midway in an array of families, beginning with the smallest, and going on to the largest, is a family of size 3.

THE ARITHMETIC MEAN

The arithmetic mean is the value that every member of the distribution would have if the aggregate of the distribution were spread evenly among the members. To calculate it, we simply sum up all individual values and divide by the number of individuals. This is the "average" we are familiar with from daily life, to which we refer when we discuss, for example, grade point average. We can calculate a mean of a set of measurements only when the measurements are in terms of some unit that we can aggregate, which means that the mean presupposes metric data.

A characteristic of the mean worth noting is that it is a balance point. The sums of the distances from the mean of all units to the right of the mean and of all units to the left of the mean exactly cancel each other. Figure 6.1 illustrates this. There are three cases at 1, one case at 3, two cases at 9, and three cases at 10. The mean value (spreading the total of 54 units distance from the origin over 9 cases) is 6. Cases to the left total 18 units of deviation. So do cases to the right. The mean is the point where the distribution as a whole is balanced.

One way in which we might write our definition of the arithmetic mean in mathematical symbols is the following:

$$\text{Mean} = \frac{x_1 + x_2 + x_3 + \cdots + x_N}{N}$$

However, it is awkward to have to represent a sum by writing out $x_1 + x_2 + x_3$, etc. We avoid this by using a single symbol, Σ, called "sigma,"

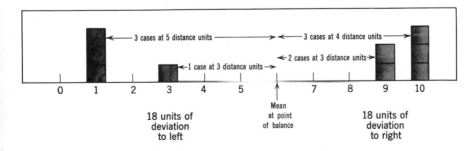

Figure 6.1

to mean "sum of." Subscripts and superscripts are used when necessary to indicate which terms are being summed.

$$\sum_{i=1}^{N} (x_i) = x_1 + x_2 + x_3 + \cdots + x_N$$

This symbol means this

We would read the above, "sum of x-sub-i from i equals one to i equals N."

Similarly,

$$\sum_{i=1}^{3} (x_i)$$

would mean

$$x_1 + x_2 + x_3$$

and would be read, "sum of x-sub-i from i equals one to i equals three."

Often it is so clear from the context that we are adding up all values that we do not need the subscript and superscript. The formula for the mean can be written compactly as:

$$\text{Mean} = \frac{\Sigma(x)}{N}$$

The above formula should be read, "the mean is given by the sum of the x's" (which means the sum of the observations), "divided by N" (the number of observations).

As a symbol for the mean, it is conventional to use $\bar{x}$, read "x-bar." Then the formula for the mean can be written

$$\bar{x} = \frac{\Sigma(x)}{N}$$

The calculation of the mean should, in most cases, be straightforward. If the problem of addition is difficult because the numbers are large, or because there are many values, a desk calculator should be used. Occasionally, we shall want to calculate the mean of a series of values which are awkward to deal with because they are very large or because they involve decimals, or for some similar reason. In such a case, we can often take advantage of the following two rules.

(a) If we add a constant amount to each value in a set of observations, this has the effect of adding that constant amount to the mean value. If we subtract a constant amount from each value in a set of observations, this has the effect of subtracting that amount from the mean value.

(b) If we multiply each value in a set of observations by a constant amount, this has the effect of multiplying the mean value by that constant amount. If we divide each value in a set of observations by a constant amount, this has the effect of dividing the mean value by that amount.

Table 6.7a illustrates the first rule, and Table 6.7b illustrates the second.

An application of the change-of-scale idea to the calculation of the mean of a more sizable array of cases is illustrated in Table 6.8. Twenty temperature readings are presented in Table 6.8, and the problem is to work out the mean temperature. Since all the readings are close to 60 degrees, it is reasonable to subtract 60 from every observation and work with the remainder. The values of remainders are shown in the second column, headed $x' = (x - 60)$. Some of the remainders involve half degrees, however, and since these are awkward computationally, we double the values to produce whole numbers. These are shown in the third column, headed $x'' = 2(x - 60)$. The sum of the x'' values is easy to calculate, and turns out to be -35; the mean of the x'' values, $\bar{x}''$, is then -1.75. We then take half of this to get the mean of the x' values, and add 60 to get the mean of the original values.

We may use the layout of Table 6.8 as a model for the calculation of the mean from ungrouped data, when a change of scale is involved. We list the new values of observations formed from the old observations by

Tables 6.7a and 6.7b

Illustrations of Rules for Simplifying Computations by Changing Values of Observations by a Constant Amount

6.7a—Illustration of Rule (a)			6.7b—Illustration of Rule (b)		
Values	Change	New Values	Values	Change	New Values
18	-20	-2	.25	$\times 4$	1.00
21	-20	1	.50	$\times 4$	2.00
23	-20	3	2.25	$\times 4$	9.00
14	-20	-6	.75	$\times 4$	3.00
25	-20	5	.25	$\times 4$	1.00
		1			16.00

Mean of new values: 1/5

Mean of old values:

$$20\ 1/5 = 20.2$$

Mean of new values: 3 1/5

Mean of old values:

$$\frac{3\ 1/5}{4} = \frac{3.2}{4} = .8$$

Table 6.8

Measurements of Temperature in a Twenty-Hour Period to Nearest Half Degree

Measurements	$x' = (x - 60)$	$x'' = 2(x - 60)$
57.5	-2.5	-5
57.5	-2.5	-5
58.0	-2.0	-4
58.5	-1.5	-3
58.5	-1.5	-3
59.0	-1.0	-2
59.0	-1.0	-2
59.0	-1.0	-2
59.0	-1.0	-2
59.5	-0.5	-1
60.6	0.0	—
61.0	1.0	2
61.5	1.5	3
61.0	1.0	2
60.5	0.5	1
59.0	-1.0	-2
59.0	-1.0	-2
58.5	-1.5	-3
58.5	-1.5	-3
58.0	-2.0	-4
		$\Sigma x'' = -35$

$$\Sigma x'' = -35$$

$$\bar{x}'' = \frac{\Sigma x''}{N} = \frac{-35}{20} = -1.75$$

$$\bar{x}' = \frac{1}{2}\bar{x}''$$

$$\bar{x}' = -.875$$

$$\bar{x} = \bar{x}' + 60 = -.875 + 60$$

$$\bar{x} = 59.125$$

or

$$\bar{x} = 59.1 \text{ (to nearest tenth)}$$

subtracting, adding, multiplying, or dividing a constant. We may change scale twice or even three times if we see that our work will be substantially reduced by doing so. We record the scale changes in the heading of the new values. When we have worked out the mean of our final values, we then reverse operations, adding a constant to the mean where we subtracted it from the values before, multiplying by a constant where we divided by it before. We must, of course, remember to reverse the order of the operations as well as the operations themselves. In Table 6.8, we subtracted and then multiplied. When we work out the mean of the x'' values, we must divide and then add, in that order, to get the mean of the original values.

Grouped Data

Table 6.9 lists the same values as are listed in Table 6.8, but this time groups them. Instead of listing 57.5 twice, because it occurs twice, or 59.0 six times, because it occurs that many times, Table 6.9 lists each value just once, but then indicates that the frequency of the first is two, and the frequency of the second is six. The method of computing the mean is the same, except that we must remember, in Table 6.9, that there is apt to be more than one observation at a scale value. We must therefore multiply the scale values by the frequency with which they occur, to get their contribution to the aggregate. This requires us to add just one column to those shown in Table 6.8, for the $f(x'')$ values.

Some students find it helpful to have a formula for the mean which is phrased in terms of the entries in a table of grouped data. In the following, x stands for the values of the observations, and f for the frequency of observations of a specific value.

$$\bar{x} = \frac{\Sigma fx}{\Sigma f} \text{ (Formula for the arithmetic mean of grouped data)}$$

Grouping within categories. It may happen that data is grouped not by specific values, as in Table 6.9, but rather within categories, as in Table 6.10, which presents ages of men in the labor force. When we have data in this form, we can only work out an estimated mean for the data; too much information is lost in the process of categorization to allow us to be certain of the precise value of the mean.

To arrive at an estimate of the mean, we use three rules. They are stated below, and illustrated by reference to the problem of calculating the average age of men in the labor force, Table 6.10.

1. In the absence of good reason for believing otherwise, we assume that *the midpoint of a category* is the average observed value within that category, and so use the midpoint to represent all values in the category.

Table 6.9

Grouped Measurements of Temperature in a Twenty-Hour Period to Nearest Half Degree

Measurement	Frequency	$x' = (x - 60)$	$x'' = 2(x' - 60)$	$f(x')$
57.5	2	-2.5	-5	-10
58.0	2	-2.0	-4	-8
58.5	4	-1.5	-3	-12
59.0	6	-1.0	-2	-12
59.5	1	-0.5	-1	-1
60.0	1	0.0	0	0
60.5	1	0.5	1	1
61.0	2	1.0	2	4
61.5	1	1.5	3	3
	$N = 20$			-35

$$\Sigma f(x'') = -35$$

$$\bar{x}'' = \frac{-35}{20} = -1.75$$

$$\bar{x}' = \frac{1}{2}\bar{x}'' + 60$$

$$= \frac{1}{2}(-1.75) + 60$$

$$= -0.875 + 60$$

$$= 59.125,$$

$$\text{or } 59.1$$

There is no reason for believing that the midpoint of the category 25 to 34 is not a reasonable average for all values within the category; we therefore use it to represent all values. In calculating the midpoint, incidentally, notice that the stated limits are not the true limits of the category. Actually the category extends from 25 through 34.999 . . . ; in other words, from 25 to 35. The midpoint is at 30.

2. Where there is good reason to believe that the midpoint of a category is *not* a good estimate of the average value within the category, then we may prefer to use some other value as our estimate. We should select some other value in preference to the midpoint when the rate of increase or decrease within a category must be assumed to be changing; i.e., when the curve within the category can with confidence be asserted to look

Table 6.10

Males in the Labor Force, by Age, 1960

Age	Number (in Thousands)
14–17	1,952
18–19	1,840
20–24	4,939
25–34	10,940
35–44	11,454
45–54	9,568
55–64	6,445
65 and over	2,425

Source: Department of Labor, Bureau of Labor Statistics: Reprinted in United States Bureau of the Census, Statistical Abstract of the United States, 1963, p. 220.

like Figure 6.2,

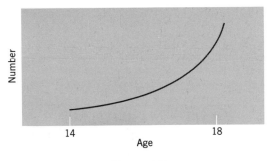

Figure 6.2

rather than like Figure 6.3.

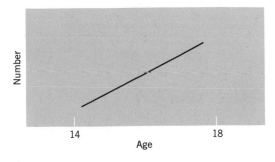

Figure 6.3

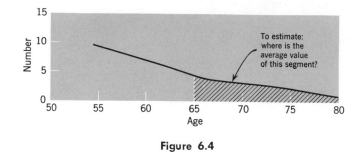

Figure 6.4

In Figure 6.2 the midpoint is *not* a good estimate of the average value within the category, while in Figure 6.3 it is. In Table 6.10, if we believe entrance into the labor force in the age groups 14 to 18 is likely to be an upward curving phenomenon, rather than a straight line increase—if we believe that Figure 6.2 is the better estimate of the situation—then we

Table 6.11

Males in the Labor Force, by Age, 1960

Age	x = Estimated Category Averages	f = number
14–17	17	1,952
18–19	19	1,840
20–24	22.5	4,939
25–34	30	10,940
35–44	40	11,454
45–54	50	9,568
55–64	60	6,445
65 and over	70	2,425

$$\Sigma f = 49,563$$

$$\Sigma fx = 2,000,481.5$$

$$\bar{x} = \frac{\Sigma fx}{\Sigma f} = 40.36$$

Source: U.S. Statistical Abstract, 1963, *loc. cit.*

ought to choose 17 or some similar value to represent all the observations in the category, rather than the midpoint 16. Notice that this argument depends entirely on knowledge that we bring to the data, and not on analysis of the data.

3. When we are given an open-ended category, such as "65 and over," we must estimate what we believe to be the average value within the category. This situation is similar to that described in Rule 2, except that we do not have the option of choosing a midpoint as an average value. We might take, as a guide, an extrapolation of the trend set by the preceding categories. To do this, we can draw a rough sketch of the right half of the frequency polygon associated with Table 6.10 (Figure 6.4).

On this basis, we might estimate the average at age 70, but it could be anywhere between 68 and 73 or 74.

These rules permit us to assign values to the frequencies given for the various categories. But notice that all these rules are guides to estimation, and that, as a result, the arithmetic mean based on categorized data *is an estimate*. It should be reported as such.

Table 6.11 shows the details of computation. We could have introduced changes of scale, but here it was much simpler to find the quantities Σfx and Σf directly, using a calculating machine.

PROBLEMS

6.1. Consider the data of Table 5.3.
   (a) If you were interested in comparing the relative success of whites as a group and nonwhites as a group in drawing income from our economy, would you prefer the mean or the median? Why?
   (b) If you were interested in comparing the financial well-being of a representative white family and a representative nonwhite family, would you prefer the mean or the median? Why?
   (c) Calculate means and medians for the data of Table 5.3.
6.2. Consider the data of Table 6.12.
   (a) Is it possible to calculate a mean? If you believe not, explain why not. If you believe it is, describe how you would do it. (What would be the midpoints of categories?)
   (b) What are the median values for both men and their fathers?
   (c) Which of the three kinds of representative value noted in this chapter (mean, median, mode) would you think best to use, given such data? Explain. What arguments might be made against using the mode with these data?

Table 6.12

Percent Distribution, by Educational Level, of Men 20 to 64 Years Old and Their Fathers, March, 1962[a]

Educational Level	Men	Fathers
Less than 5 years	4.9	18.8
Elementary 5 to 7 years	8.8	20.1
Elementary 8 to high school 3 years	31.0	37.5
High school 4 years	29.4	13.8
College 1 to 3 years	12.6	4.6
College 4 years or more	13.3	5.2
	100.0	100.0

[a] Excludes cases with no report on education of the fathers.
Source: United States Census, Current Population Survey, as reproduced in Ben J. Wattenberg and Richard M. Scammon, *This U.S.A.* (Garden City, Doubleday, 1965), p. 475.

6.3. Consider the data of Table 6.13.

    (a) Under what circumstances might you prefer to identify the modal value rather than the median or mean value, in describing these data? What would you identify as the modal category or categories? (See (b) for one approach.)

Table 6.13

Size of Households, by Type, United States, March, 1962

Size of Household	Husband-Wife Household (in Thousands)	All Other with Male Head	All Other with Female Head
1 person	—	2512	4,946
2 persons	12,055	999	2,375
3 persons	8,376	369	1,311
4 persons	8,501	177	650
5 persons	5,540	67	397
6 persons	3,126	39	196
7 persons or more	2,741	29	246
All households	40,339	4192	10,121
			54,652

Source: United States Census, as reproduced in Wattenberg and Scammon, *op. cit.*, p. 475.

(b) Summarize in words the import of Table 6.13, referring as appropriate to the modal values in each of the columns. (For example, after noting that households are described by whether they are headed by a married couple, by an unmarried man, or by an unmarried woman, you might go on to note that among those headed by a married couple, almost two-thirds have others living with them, presumably children, while among those headed by a single man. . . .)

(c) Calculate the mean number of persons living in households headed by a single male and in households headed by a single female. Are these meaningful figures? Explain.

(d) Calculate the medians for the two columns noted in (c). Are these meaningful figures? Explain.

6.4. Refer to the data of Appendix 2. Note a characteristic for which the mean is the best descriptive measure. Note a characteristic for which the median is the best descriptive measure. Note a characteristic for which the mode is best. Work out the appropriate mean, median, and mode.

Chapter 7

Measures of Variation

In addition to characterizing a set of measurements by stating a typical, central, or average value, we shall often also want to describe another feature of the set of measurements: how closely the measurements are bunched together—whether the distribution is homogeneous or heterogeneous in respect to the measured quality. We require for this techniques for describing variation.

It has already been noted that each of the techniques for identifying a representative value is associated with a definite level of measurement: naming the modal category suggests that the data are being treated as though they were nominal; noting the median encourages the reader to think in terms of an ordered array; and noting the arithmetic mean suggests units of measurement that may be aggregated for the total group. With each of these techniques for finding a representative value, we may associate a definite approach to stating how much variation there is, in the distribution of measurements, from the representative value. If we focused our attention on the nominal characteristics of our data, we could tell the reader how much of our distribution is concentrated in a modal category (or categories) and how many other categories are necessary in order to account for all or almost all of the remaining members of our distribution. If we treated our data as an ordered array, we could communicate the extent to which the array is "strung out" by naming the values between which a given percentage of the cases can be found. And, finally, if we interpreted our measurements as interval or ratio scale, we could use, in our estimate of variation, the difference in units between each of our measurements and the arithmetic mean of the measurements.

COMMUNICATING VARIATION WITHIN NOMINAL DATA

In Table 7.1 is presented a tabulation of nominal data, the place of home residence of members of a university dormitory. Our problem is to

110

Table 7.1

Place of Home Residence, Members of X Dormitory

	Number	Percent
New York	22	28
Massachusetts	18	22
Pennsylvania	12	15
Maine	6	8
Vermont	4	5
Illinois	4	5
New Jersey	3	4
Other States	6	8
Foreign Countries	5	6
Total	80	100

describe, for this collection of measurements, what is typical and how much variation there is from the typical.

More students come from New York State than from any other state, but the New York State group accounts for only 28% of the total. We should mislead the reader if we were to characterize the typical student as from New York State. We can do better by saying, "Just 50% of students in this dormitory come from either New York or Massachusetts." Perhaps we could do still better by saying, "65% of students come from one of the three states: New York, Massachusetts, or Pennsylvania." This characterization may be preferable because it communicates to the reader that this is a dormitory that draws, for some reason, from the populous Northeast states; naming only New York and Massachusetts within the modal category suggests a dormitory more New England in quality than is the case. The investigator must be guided, in his decision of which and how many categories to include in a statement of the typical case, by his sense of what such a statement communicates to a reader, together with a sense of what would accurately describe his data.

The variability of the data would be communicated by naming the categories that contain the remaining data. If the category "other states" did not appear in Table 7.1—in other words, if we had only four other states from which students came—we could say, simply, "The remaining students come from four other states: Maine, Vermont, Illinois, and New Jersey." If there were ten other states, we could say, "The remaining students hail from ten different states," perhaps adding a descriptive note about where the states are located. In this situation, because of the category "other states," we do not know how many states in all the students come from. The best we can do is say, "The remaining students come from a number of states, including Maine, Vermont, Illinois, and New Jersey."

There are some students who do not hail from one of the United States at all, but are from foreign countries. This fact has to be noted; it is, in a way, another order of variation. Since the category is so different from other categories, we may want to state the number or the percent of the population of the dormitory within it. We might, therefore, add to our other statements, "Five individuals within the dormitory, 6% of the total number, are from foreign countries."

There are no rules for describing variation in nominal data. Our aim should be to present a description that is at once compact, vivid, and communicative of the main features of the data.

MEASURES OF VARIATION IN ORDINAL DATA

When we are working with data that are measured within at least an ordinal system, and when we want to draw attention to a ranking of the measurements, the representative measure used would be the median and the measure of variation, the breadth of an appropriate range. The total range of a distribution is the set of values over which the distribution extends. We can specify the breadth of the total range by specifying the highest and lowest values in a distribution. Often, however, it is more useful to specify the extreme values of an *intermediate range*, such as the middle 80% or the middle 60%, because we can then neglect the truly aberrant measure far from the rest of the distribution, which may make the total range misleading. Just as the total range is the set of values over which an entire distribution extends, an intermediate range is the set of values over which an intermediate portion of the distribution, such as the middle 80%, extends.

We make our choice of which range we shall use to communicate variability by asking ourselves how to best represent the data, accepting that there could well be disagreement between investigators in their choice. Consider the data of Table 7.2. These are data that might have been obtained had we measured and recorded the class memberships of members of five different social clubs in a large community (or, for that matter, five different churches, or five different patient loads, or five different high schools). The class ranking system, let us say, is some modification of that used by Warner, which yields six different classes, arranged in a prestige hierarchy. Clearly the social clubs listed have different membership compositions, both in terms of the class membership of a representative member and of the heterogeneity of the members.

Table 7.2

Class Ranking of Members of Various Social Clubs

	Social Club				
Class Ranking	A	B	C	D	E
I (Highest)	19	0	30	40	5
II	20	20	40	35	15
III	45	60	30	25	15
IV	10	20	0	0	25
V	5	0	0	0	25
VI (Lowest)	1	0	0	0	15
Total	100%	100%	100%	100%	100%
	85	20	60	120	115

The problem of identifying a representative member in each of these clubs is easily solved. The class ranking of the median member is class IV in club E, class III in clubs A and B, and class II in clubs C and D.

Now let us consider what is the appropriate range for best communicating variation in the data. If we selected the total range, we should say something like the following: "In social clubs A and E there are members in all six of the social classes. Membership within these clubs extends from highest class ranking through lowest. In social clubs B, C, and D, on the other hand, the class ranking of members extends over only three categories. In social club B members are within class ranks II through IV, and in social clubs C and D, in class ranks I through III." The total range seems to do reasonably well, except that we might feel it obscures a difference in relative homogeneity of membership between club A and club E. Club E has at least 15% of its membership in each of the social class categories, with the exception of the very highest, while club A has its membership clustered within the middle and upper categories.

Suppose we examine where we find the middle 50% in the social clubs in Table 7.2. This particular intermediate range is named *the interquartile range*. The interquartile range in social club E extends from class III to class V, a breadth of three class categories. In social club A it extends only from class II to class III. Clearly this way of stating variation does distinguish between the variabilities of class membership in clubs A and E. What about the other clubs? In social club B, the middle 50% is entirely within class ranking III. In club D the middle 50% is contained within two categories; in club C, within three. This approach to stating variability identifies social clubs C and E as having the greatest variability, and social club B the least. On examining the data, this seems a reasonably good description. Social club B is clearly the most homogeneous; in fact it is a contribution of the interquartile range to draw this to our attention. But it seems mistaken to characterize social clubs C and E as having the same amount of variation. We might feel that there is a distinction here which is obscured by use of the interquartile range. Let us try the middle 80%, which extends from the 10% value to the 90% value. This covers classes I through IV in A, classes II through IV in B, classes I through III in C, classes I through III in D, classes II through VI in E. The difference between social clubs A and E is brought out, as is the great difference between social clubs C and E. B is no longer identifiable as the most homogeneous club, but one may argue there is less difference among B, C, and D, than between any one of the set and A or E. On these grounds we might prefer the middle 80% to the middle 50% as our measure of variation.

The method for finding the values of the extreme members of an intermediate range should be obvious. If we are interested in the intermediate $x\%$, where x stands for 50 or 80 or whatever the breadth of the range, we can find the first and last point in this range by means of the following formulas:

$$(a) \quad \text{First point} = \frac{100 - x}{2}$$

$$(b) \quad \text{Last point} = 100 - \left(\frac{100 - x}{2}\right)$$

We may have to interpolate within a category to estimate the value of one or both of these points, in which case the method of interpolation described in connection with finding the median value can be used. The caution that the estimate arrived at by interpolation must be a possible value of the distribution applies here too. In the example of Table 7.2 it would be wrong to interpolate for an 80% range and say it extended from "class 2.2 to class 4.8."

MEASURES OF VARIATION IN INTERVAL DATA

Neither the total range nor any of the intermediate ranges are sufficiently sensitive as measures of variation to respond consistently to a shifting of cases from one category to another. Because every range measure is insensitive to some degree, we prefer more sensitive measures of variation when the data permit them to be used. When the data are at least interval, we can use a measure of variation based on the distance between each case and the mean. Almost any shift of a case from one point to another affects this measure.

How ought we to construct a measure of variability based on the distance of each case from the mean? A plausible idea that unfortunately turns out to have important drawbacks is simply to sum up the absolute distance of each observation from the arithmetic mean, and then calculate the average absolute distance. Such a measure, because it is so plausible as a way of capturing variation in interval or ratio data, has occasionally been used in the past, and is called the "mean deviation." It is very infrequently used today, however, because statisticians have found that this measure is not easily related to formulas for theoretical distributions, and so has no clear meaning in theoretical statistics. Indeed, it makes a number of statistical tasks difficult, such as comparing amounts of variation in different sized samples. In consequence, the measure, although simple to compute, has been discarded almost completely.

The measure of variation that is universally used in work with interval or ratio scale data goes by two names, a technical name that is highly descriptive but rarely used today, and a common name by which it is now generally known. The older technical term for the measure of variation is "the root mean squared deviation." The common name is "the standard deviation."

We will refer to this measure by the symbol σ, which is called "sigma," and is the lower case of the symbol Σ, also "sigma," which we use to stand for "sum of."[1]

The standard deviation is defined by this formula:

$$\sigma = \sqrt{\frac{\Sigma(x - \bar{x})^2}{N}}$$

In the above formula, $(x - \bar{x})$ stands for the deviation of any particular observation from the arithmetic mean of all observations. $\Sigma(x - \bar{x})^2$ is the sum of the square of the deviations of all observations. To find it, we would take each deviation in turn and square it, and then add all the squares. When we divide this quantity by N (the total number of observations), we have computed the "mean-squared deviation," the arithmetic average of all the squared deviations. The formula requires

[1] Other symbols for the standard deviation are also in common use. Some texts refer to this measure by the symbol s. Many texts use σ to refer to a standard deviation of a theoretical distribution and s to refer to a standard deviation of a distribution of observed data. There are arguments for such complications, but in this presentation σ will be the symbol used to refer to the standard deviation in every situation. When it becomes important to distinguish between the standard deviation of a sample and the standard deviation of a population, subscripts will be used.

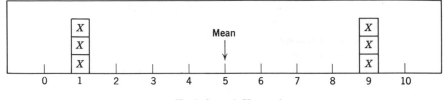

Figure 7.1   Each boxed X equals one case.

that we find the square root of this quantity, whereupon we have computed "the root-mean-squared deviation." This name for the measure describes accurately its definitional formula.

We demonstrated how the mean could be visualized as the point of balance of an array of observations. It is more difficult to visualize the standard deviation, but the following examples should help.

Consider the distribution in Figure 7.1.

There are three observations at scale point 1, and three observations at scale point 9. The arithmetic mean of these six observations is 5. Now let us compute the standard deviation.

x (*Observations*)	$(x - \bar{x})$ (*Deviations from Mean*)	$(x - \bar{x})^2$ (*Squared Deviations*)
1	-4	16
1	-4	16
1	-4	16
9	4	16
9	4	16
9	4	16
$\Sigma x = 30$		$\Sigma = 96$

$$\bar{x} = 5$$

$$\Sigma(x - \bar{x})^2 = 96$$

$$\frac{\Sigma(x - \bar{x})^2}{N} = \frac{96}{6} = 16$$

$$\sigma = \sqrt{\frac{\Sigma(x - \bar{x})^2}{N}} = \sqrt{16} = 4$$

We see that, in the above distribution, the standard deviation is 4 units. This happens to be the distance between the mean and each of the points at which the observations are concentrated. This will be true in general. Where there is an even number of observations, half at one point in the distribution, and half at another point, then the mean is halfway between the two groups of observations, and the standard deviation is the distance between the mean and either of the two values at which the observations are concentrated.

Now let us complicate the situation as shown in Figure 7.2.

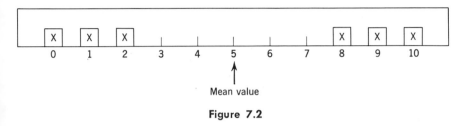

Figure 7.2

In Figure 7.2, instead of all three cases on the left of the mean being concentrated at value 1 and all three on the right of the mean being concentrated at value 9, the cases are spread a little about their points of concentration. This does not affect the mean. Let us calculate the new standard deviation.

x	$x - \bar{x}$	$(x - \bar{x})^2$
0	−5	25
1	−4	16
2	−3	9
8	3	9
9	4	16
10	5	25
		$\Sigma = 100$

$$\Sigma(x - \bar{x})^2 = 100$$

$$\frac{\Sigma(x - \bar{x})^2}{N} = 16.67$$

$$\sigma = \sqrt{\frac{\Sigma(x - \bar{x})^2}{N}} = \sqrt{16.67} = 4.08$$

Spreading the cases on either side of the point at which they were concentrated did not affect the mean, but did affect the standard deviation, although only slightly. What it did was to slightly *increase* the standard deviation.

Figure 7.3 shows a set of distributions, their means, and their standard deviations. The student should first attempt to estimate mean and standard deviation without doing any computation at all, simply from examination of the distribution. It should be easy to estimate where the mean is,

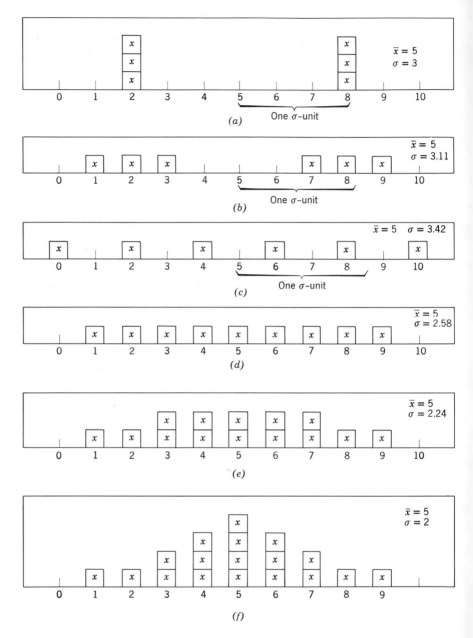

Figure 7.3 Some distributions, their means, and their standard deviations (each boxed X equals one case).

118

since this is the point at which the distribution would balance. To estimate how many units in length the standard deviation is, we might look at one side of the distribution (all the examples are symmetric), and ask at which point the observations on that side of the distribution, taken by themselves, would balance. If all the observations were concentrated at this one point, the distance between this point and the mean would be the length of the standard deviation. However, as the observations are spread out around this point, the standard deviation increases, although not greatly. Observations that have exactly the value of the mean can be thought of as half belonging to one side of the distribution, half to the other.

The Calculation of the Standard Deviation

The formula that was given for the standard deviation is straightforward enough, as a definition of what we mean by the term "standard deviation," but it is inconvenient to use when making calculations. It requires that we first calculate the mean, which may be an awkward figure, perhaps with decimals; and then calculate the deviation of each observation from the mean, an equally awkward figure; then square this figure; then add the squares; and so on. Because this is so likely to be an arduous exercise, statisticians have sought a revision of the formula that will make calculation simpler. Just a little algebraic manipulation allows us to restate the formula in a way that avoids basing it on the deviation of each observation. The formula which results is:

$$\sigma = \frac{1}{N} \sqrt{N\Sigma x^2 - (\Sigma x)^2}$$

(The calculating formula for the standard deviation)

The above would be read, "the standard deviation equals one-over-N times the square root of N-sum-of-the-x-squared minus sum-of-the-x-quantity-squared." An application of the formula is given as Table 7.3. The data in Table 7.3 are grouped as were the data in Table 6.9. There were 31 subjects in all, and thus, if the data were to be presented in ungrouped form, there would be 31 observations listed one under the other. Grouping the data permits us to present them in a more compact form. Instead of listing the 6 different subjects who made no errors, we show the frequency 6 opposite the value 0. When we want to aggregate the number of errors made by all students in the class, we first multiply each value by the frequency with which that value was observed. We therefore have a column for the frequency of the value times the value itself, the

Table 7.3

Distribution of Number of Errors Made in Experimental Situation[a]

Number of Errors (x)	Frequency (f)	$(f)(x)$	$(f)(x^2)$
0	6	0	0
1	7	7	7
2	6	12	24
3	4	12	36
4	4	16	64
5	1	5	25
6	1	6	36
7	2	14	98
	$N = \Sigma f = 31$	$\Sigma x = 72$	$\Sigma x^2 = 290$

$$\sigma = \frac{1}{N} \sqrt{N\Sigma x^2 - (\Sigma x)^2} = \frac{1}{31} \sqrt{31(290) - (72)^2} = \frac{1}{31} \sqrt{8990 - 5184}$$

$$= \frac{1}{31} \sqrt{3806} = \frac{1}{31} (61.7)$$

$\sigma = 1.99$,   or 2.0 to one decimal place

[a] Adapted from Solomon Asch, *Social Psychology* (Englewood Cliffs, N.J.: Prentice-Hall, 1952), p. 482.

$(f)(x)$ column. Similarly, we have a column for the frequency times the square of the value, the $(f)(x^2)$ column. It may be helpful to notice that the entry in the column $(f)(x^2)$ is the product of the entry in the column $(f)(x)$ and the entry in the column (x).

Some students find it helpful to have a special formula for calculating the standard deviation from grouped data. In this formula f stands for frequency.

$$\sigma = \frac{1}{\Sigma f} \sqrt{\Sigma f \Sigma f x^2 - (\Sigma f x)^2}$$

The work shown here can be done on a desk calculator. The formula is so designed that the quantity under the square root sign can be calculated entirely on the machine. We first compute the products of N and Σx^2 and then negative multiply the quantity Σx by itself. ("Negative multiplication" is a machine operation which subtracts a product from a quantity already listed in the machine.) Probably the best way of finding the square root of a quantity is to consult a table of square roots, such as Appendix Table 1.1.

Change of Scale

The work involved in calculating a standard deviation can sometimes be simplified by adding or subtracting a quantity to each observation, or by multiplying or dividing each observation by a constant amount. Just as was the case in calculating the arithmetic mean, there are two rules to have in mind when changing the observed values in calculating the standard deviation, although one of the rules is different.

1. If we add or subtract a constant amount to each observation in a distribution, the standard deviation is unchanged. (This is the different rule.)

2. If we multiply or divide by a constant amount each observation in a distribution, the standard deviation is multiplied or divided by that amount.

The first rule means that we can add or subtract any quantity we like to the observed values, so long as we add or subtract the same quantity to each, without changing the standard deviation. This follows from the fact that the standard deviation is a measure not of location on a scale (as is the mean), but of the dispersion of the values in a distribution. Obviously, we can often simplify our work greatly by finding an amount which, when added or subtracted to our observations, makes them smaller numbers. Table 7.4 illustrates the procedure, using the data of Table 7.3. In Table 7.4, three units have been subtracted from each of the observations.

If, instead of number of errors, we had been working with something like number of dollars earned in the previous year, to the nearest thousand, our observations would have increased in units of 1000 rather than in single units. We might then have divided each observation by 1000 to change to a scale easier to work with arithmetically. We should then have had to multiply the standard deviation based on these new values by 1000 to obtain the standard deviation of the original values.

The data in Tables 7.3 and 7.4 are grouped, but grouped at a set of definite points, rather than within broad categories. If we are calculating a standard deviation for categorized observations, all the questions raised in connection with calculation of the arithmetic mean from such data, in Chapter 6, are appropriate. A standard deviation calculated from categorized data is always an estimate. (As a matter of fact, it is apt to be a biased estimate, almost always overstating the value of the standard deviation, although generally by a negligible amount.)[2] It should not be

[2] A discussion of a technique for producing a better estimate of the standard deviation of categorized data, is given in M. G. Kendall, *The Advanced Theory of Statistics* (London: Charles Griffen and Co., 1948), Vol. I, p. 41.

Table 7.4

Distribution of Number of Errors Made in Experimental Situation[a]

Number of Errors (x)	x' Translated Scale Values	Frequency (f)	(f)(x')	(f)(x'²)
0	−3	6	−18	54
1	−2	7	−14	28
2	−1	6	− 6	6
3	0	4	0	0
4	1	4	4	4
5	2	1	2	4
6	3	1	3	9
7	4	2	8	32
		$N = \Sigma f = 31$	$\Sigma x' = -21$	$\Sigma x'^2 = 137$

$$\sigma = \frac{1}{N} \sqrt{N\Sigma x^2 - (\Sigma x)^2}$$

$$= \frac{1}{31} \sqrt{(31)(137) - (21)^2}$$

$$= \frac{1}{31} \sqrt{4247 - 441}$$

$$= \frac{1}{31} \sqrt{3806}$$

$$= \frac{1}{31} (61.7)$$

$$\sigma = 1.99, \quad \text{or 2.0 to one decimal place}$$

[a] Adapted from Solomon Asch, *Social Psychology*, loc. cit.

forgotten that, when we work with categorized data, too much information has been lost to permit precise calculation of arithmetic mean and
standard deviation.

Table 7.5 will illustrate the procedure that ought to be followed in calculating a standard deviation from categorized data. The data are the
labor force statistics for which the mean age of men was calculated in
Chapter 6.

Table 7.5

Number of Men in the Labor Force, by Age

Age	x = Estimated Average	$x' = \dfrac{x - 30}{10}$	f = Number	x'^2
14–17	17	−1.3	1,952	1.69
18–19	19	−1.1	1,840	1.21
20–24	22.5	−0.75	4,939	0.5625
25–34	30	0	10,940	0
35–44	40	1	11,454	1
45–54	50	2	9,568	4
55–64	60	3	6,445	9
65 and over	70	4	2,425	16

$$N = 49,563$$

$$\Sigma x = 51,359.15^a$$

$$\Sigma x^2 = 154,834.4675^a$$

$$\sigma_{x'} = \frac{1}{N} \sqrt{N\Sigma x^2 - (\Sigma x)^2}$$

$$= \frac{1}{49,563} \sqrt{(49,563)(154,834.4675) - (51,359.15)^2}$$

$$= \frac{1}{49,563} \sqrt{7,647,683,166.8540}$$

$$= \frac{1}{49,563} (87,451.03)$$

$$\sigma_{x'} = 1.764$$

To translate back to original scale

$$\sigma_x = 10(\sigma_{x'}) = 17.64 \text{ to two decimal places.}$$

Since this is in any event an estimate, we should not try to be too precise. Say, estimated σ is 17.6 years.

[a] Decimals should be disregarded, since they will not affect the answer when it is calculated to only two decimal places.

Source: U.S. Statistical Abstract, 1963, *loc. cit.*

Variance

In some statistical work, such as that described in Chapter 15, we find that the square of the standard deviation, which is called the *variance*, is more useful than the standard deviation itself. When we are interested in the amount of variation in one factor that seems to result from the influence of another, for example, we find the variance to be the more useful measure of variation. The formulas for the variance are, of course, just the formulas for the standard deviation, except that we do not take the square root.

PROBLEMS

7.1. Referring to the data of Table 5.3.
  (*a*) If you were interested in comparing the relative success of whites as a group and nonwhites as a group in drawing income from our economy, would you prefer the standard deviation or an intermediate range as a measure of variation? Why?
  (*b*) If you were interested in comparing the financial well-being of representative white families and representative nonwhite families, would you prefer the standard deviation or an intermediate range as a measure of variation? Why?
  (*c*) Calculate the standard deviation for the data.
  (*d*) Decide which intermediate range would be appropriate for use with the data, and calculate it.
7.2. Referring to Tables 5.3 through 5.7, how would you communicate the variability within the data in each case? What measure would you use?
7.3. Referring to Table 6.13, discuss variation.
7.4. Suppose you were told that men in the armed forces averaged 69 inches in height, with a standard deviation of three inches. Sketch a distribution of heights which would be compatible with this information.
7.5. Suppose you were told that the median scholastic aptitude score at a particular college was 625 and that the interquartile range was 50 points. Make up a table of a distribution of aptitude scores which is compatible with the information.
7.6. For an appropriate distribution of data presented in Appendix 2, calculate an intermediate range, and the standard deviation.

Chapter 8

Frequency Distributions:
Observed and Theoretical

In this chapter we continue our discussion of communicating to an audience the nature of a collection of data. We have thus far discussed how to identify just one value which might "represent," "stand for," or "locate" the collection as a whole, and how to develop a measure of the amount of variation within the collection. We now turn to a third problem: how to describe the *distribution* of the data.

The term "distribution" means the entire collection of measurements, taken as a whole. When our data are nominal in level, the best we can do to communicate the nature of the distribution is to name the categories and report the frequencies in each, as was indicated in some of the earlier examples. When our data are ordinal in level, we can go beyond this and, within the limits noted below, say something about the "shape" of the distribution. When our data are metric in level, we can often go still further and characterize the distribution by finding a mathematical expression for it, or by comparing it with some well-known theoretical prototype.

First, let us consider some nonmathematical terms we might use to describe the shape of a distribution. Let us assume our data are metric in level. One dimension on which we might contrast distributions is that of *flatness-peakedness*. A distribution in which there are about the same frequencies at all values is flat; where the frequencies mount toward the center, the distribution is peaked. The distribution pictured in Figure 8.1 actually is not completely flat, but it is close enough, given the range of imprecision allowed these essentially suggestive terms, to be referred to in this way.

An income curve, on the other hand, is peaked (Figure 8.2).

Some curves are *symmetrical* in the sense that a line may be drawn down

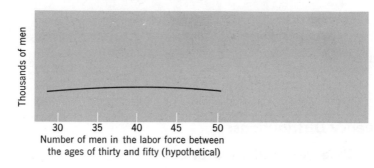

Number of men in the labor force between
the ages of thirty and fifty (hypothetical)

Figure 8.1

their middle and then the curve on one side of the line is the mirror image
of the curve on the other side of the line (Figure 8.3).

Other curves are *skewed:* that is, they are asymmetric, with one side
longer than the other. A curve is skewed to the right if it has what appears
to be a central mass of cases, but the cases extend much farther to the
right of this central mass than they do to the left. An income curve is
likely to be skewed to the right, as shown in Figure 8.4. A distribution of
grades is apt to be skewed to the left (Figure 8.5).

Occasionally, we may have a distribution that is *bimodal* (Figure 8.6).

As can be seen, descriptive terms like "flat," "peaked," "skewed," and
"bimodal" give only a rough idea of the shape of the curve. When it is
important to characterize the precise nature of a distribution, we search
for an equation which connects a value with its frequency. For example,
the equation $y = x$ could be such an equation, if y were to stand for the

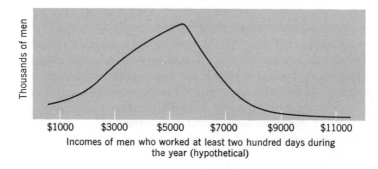

Incomes of men who worked at least two hundred days during
the year (hypothetical)

Figure 8.2

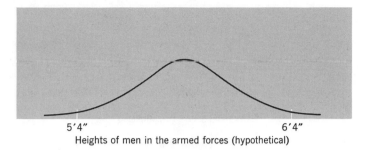

5'4"   6'4"
Heights of men in the armed forces (hypothetical)

Figure 8.3

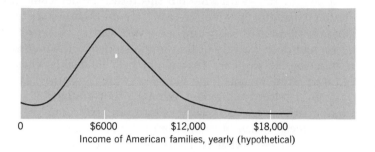

0              $6000 $12,000 $18,000
Income of American families, yearly (hypothetical)

Figure 8.4

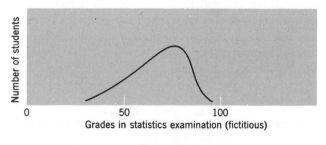

0   50   100
Grades in statistics examination (fictitious)

Figure 8.5

frequency, and x for the value. The equation would then say that the frequency is the same as the value.

We may develop equations for distributions by "fitting"—mathematically tailoring—a curve to observed data, or we may develop equations from a theory we have about how the distribution came to be. Generally,

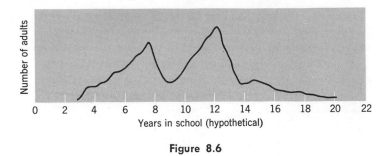

Figure 8.6

when we do the second, we also examine the observed distribution to check on whether it agrees with what our theoretical model would predict.

Let us take an example in which we compare an observed distribution with the distribution a theoretical model would lead us to expect.

Suppose we had done a study of first-grade students in which we were interested in gathering evidence that might help us decide whether the preference for other members of the same sex, which is found in the later years of latency, is already in evidence among first-graders. We select a class in which there are as many boys as girls, and we count the number of times during recess when boys are seen talking with other boys, girls with other girls, and boys with girls. We restrict our attention to pairs. We observe one thousand cases. In 260 of them—a relative frequency of 260/1000, or 0.26—boys talked to boys. The complete data would be as shown in Table 8.1.

The model with whose results we want to compare these observations is one which assumes that the sex of the youngsters has no effect on their choice of a conversational partner. Assuming this model to be true, we can work out the relative frequency with which each of the three types of pairs ought to be observed. For example, we should expect a boy-girl pair

Table 8.1

One Thousand Cases in Which Two Students Were Talking with Each Other (Fictitious)

Type of Pair	Number of Cases	Relative Frequency
Boy-boy	260	0.26
Boy-girl	480	0.48
Girl-girl	260	0.26
	1000	1.00

about half the time. We give below an equation showing the relative frequency to be expected for pairs containing no boys, one boy, and two boys, on the assumption that sex is irrelevant in choice. This equation describes a theoretical distribution; it is based on theory.

We let y stand for relative frequency, and x stand for the number of boys in a pair. Then the equation which connects y and x on the assumption of neither affinity nor repulsion between the sexes, is:

$$y = \frac{1}{2}\left[\frac{1}{(2-x)!\,x!}\right]$$

In this equation,

$$x!\ \text{means}\ (x)(x-1)\ \cdots\ (1)$$

$$\text{therefore}\ 2! = 2$$

$$\text{and}\ 1! = 1$$

$$0!\ \text{is defined as}\ 1$$

(The symbol !, in the above equations, is called "factorial." It means that the number is multiplied by the next smaller number and then by the next smaller after that, and so on, until 1 is reached. Zero factorial is defined as equal to 1.)

To show how the formula works, let us calculate the relative frequency of the pair boy-boy. We make x in the formula equal to 2. Then

$$y = \frac{1}{2}\left(\frac{1}{0!\,2!}\right)$$

$$y = \frac{1}{4} = 0.25$$

By use of this formula, we find that the expected relative frequency of two boys talking with each other is 0.25; of a boy and a girl talking, it is 0.50; and of two girls talking, it is 0.25. This is very close to our observed frequencies, and so we may say that the data are consistent with our model. (Chapter 14 describes a way of answering the question of how discrepant data must be from the model in order to be ruled "inconsistent.")

In this example, an observation could have one of only three possible values: there might be 0, 1, or 2 boys in a pair. If we had been concerned not with the number of boys in a pair, but with the ages of the children, we could have observed any number of values between, for instance 5 and 7, if we assume that these are the limits of the age range of first-graders. One of the children could, conceivably, have been 5.89136 years old. Our observations might have been any of a *continuous* series of possible values. (Actually our measurement is never precise enough to produce a really continuous series, but this is not an important point.) When every conceivable value between two end points is a possible observation, we have *a continuous distribution:* otherwise we have *a discrete distribution.* In work with a discrete distribution, as in the example above, we are able to say what proportion of the population may be found at a point. But when working with a continuous distribution, as in the next example, we have to say rather what proportion of the population may be found in an interval between two points.

The use of theoretical distributions. There are two different reasons why theoretical distributions are important in statistics. The first is that, by reference to the appropriate theoretical distribution, we can often judge whether a particular empirical distribution is compatible with a hypothesized underlying process. We very often know the theoretical distribution that will result if a particular process is at work, and this knowledge enables us to judge whether a particular empirical distribution could have occurred as a result of that process. An example of this use of theoretical distributions has already been given, in our comparison of the observed distribution of boy-boy, boy-girl, and girl-girl conversational pairs with the distribution we would have expected if children were as likely to talk with others of the opposite sex as with others of the same sex.

The second reason why theoretical distributions are important in statistics is that they describe the way measures may be expected to vary as we go from sample to sample. For example, we would not expect the average of one sample to be the same as the average of another sample drawn from the same population; they should be close to each other, but not identical. The average of a third sample would probably be different from either of these, and so on. It turns out that we can deduce mathematically the theoretical distribution of these sample means. When we know this distribution, we can then decide whether two different sample means can reasonably be thought to belong to the same distribution of sample means, even though they are different from each other. In that case the samples can reasonably be thought to come from the same population. Much more is said about this use of theoretical distributions in Chapter 12 and the chapters that follow it.

Let us look at another example of the way a particular process may be represented by a theoretical distribution. Imagine a carnival wheel marked off into twenty divisions (Figure 8.7). A pointer spins freely around the wheel, and can stop anywhere at all.

If every point on the wheel had the same chance of being the place where the pointer stopped, we would expect that a very large number of spins would produce a line graph like that shown in Figure 8.8.

Figure 8.7 A carnival wheel.

The line graph is simply a horizontal line, because the relative frequency of any point is the same as the relative frequency of every other point. We might think of a distribution of this type as an honest wheel distribution, since it is the distribution that results if a wheel is honest. It is called *the horizontal distribution* in mathematical statistics. Its equation is $y = C$, where y is the relative frequency, and C is a constant. It is a continuous distribution, which means that we are not able to talk about the proportion of cases that will occur at a particular point, but rather have to talk about the proportion of cases that will occur within a particular interval.

We can use this distribution as a model against which to judge an observed distribution. If the observed distribution were very different, we should decide that the honest wheel process, which gives rise to a

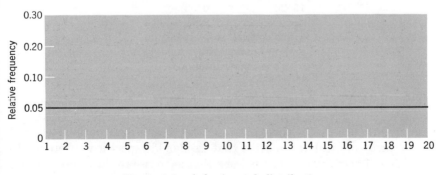

Figure 8.8 A horizontal distribution.

horizontal distribution, is not the process responsible for the observed distribution. For example, suppose we observed one thousand turns of a carnival wheel, and found the results shown in Table 8.2. The results are given in "relative frequency," which is the proportion of all observations that have a given value.

Table 8.2

Relative Frequency of Results of One Thousand Turns of a Carnival Wheel

Value	Relative Frequency
0 –1[a]	0.03
1 –2	0.04
2 –3	0.03
3 –4	0.05
4 –5	0.04
5 –6	0.05
6 –7	0.04
7 –8	0.04
8 –9	0.05
9 –10	0.04
10–11	0.05
11–12	0.06
12–13	0.06
13–14	0.17
14–15	0.06
15–16	0.05
16–17	0.04
17–18	0.04
18–19	0.03
19–20	0.03

[a] If the pointer stops exactly on a whole number, this is counted with the higher interval.

These data do not look compatible with the horizontal distribution we should expect to result from an honest wheel. Values between 13 and 14 seem to do much better than the rest. The actual distribution does not match the theoretical distribution that we should expect if we were working with an honest wheel. The process that gave rise to these data cannot be the honest wheel process.

In addition to the horizontal distribution, there are many theoretical distributions of use in statistical work. Two of these, the binomial and the normal, are of such pervasive importance that we must give them special attention. But before turning to them, we shall make a brief exploration of the theory of probability.

All of the processes that give rise to statistical distributions are *probabilistic*. The result of a spin of an honest carnival wheel cannot be predicted. It may be a 3, or a 4, or anything else. However, the *probability* of a 3 or a 4 or anything else can be stated, and consequently the approximate number of times that any of these numbers will come up in a long series of trials *can* be predicted. It is the operation of probabilities, over a long series of trials, which gives us the honest wheel distribution, and every other statistical distribution. We must, therefore, turn to the questions of what we mean by probability and how probabilities operate, before returning to the discussion of theoretical distributions.

SOME THEORY OF PROBABILITY

Let us begin by defining what we might mean by the probability of an event. Actually, we might mean any one of three things.

First, by the probability of an event, we might mean simply its relative frequency. If our experience has told us that out of every one hundred men who celebrate their thirty-fourth birthday, ninety-nine live to celebrate their thirty-fifth, then we would say that the probability of someone who is just thirty-four living to be thirty-five is 99/100. If out of every thousand students coming to college, four hundred drop out before receiving their B.A., then the chance of any particular entering student staying to receive his B.A. is 600/1000. The essence of the relative frequency approach to probability is that, for any particular case, we find a relevant class; then the probability of an event occurring is the relative frequency of the event within the relevant class.

Objections have been raised to the "relative frequency" approach to probability because there is an unsettling absence of rules for finding the right class to which to refer a given case. Suppose we wanted to decide the probability of a given student completing graduate school. We know that 50% of entering students do not complete their work, and so we could say about this student, knowing only that he is about to enter a graduate program, that he has a 1-in-2 chance of finishing. However, suppose we are now told that this student has gotten his B.A. with Honors, and 75% of entering students who received Honors in their undergraduate work manage to complete the graduate program. We must now assign a different probability to the student's finishing his work. Yet the student has not changed; what has changed is our information about him. If we had still further information which suggested that this particular student, although an Honors B.A., was totally unmotivated in his graduate training, we would change our probability estimate again. We begin to suspect that the "relative frequency" idea of probability is not meaningful in relation to single events, but only in relation to classes of events. We can assign probabilities to single events only by considering them members of classes about which we know something.

The relative frequency idea, for all its difficulties, seems to work in practice. All insurance companies evaluate risks in terms of relative frequencies, and they are doing very well indeed. In addition, relative frequency over a long series of trials is probably our intuitive notion of the meaning of probability. However, it is an idea difficult to apply to events with which we do not have a great deal of experience.

Mathematicians—and gamblers—have developed a second approach to the meaning of probability which permits calculation of the probability of occurrence of certain kinds of events even though no one has taken the trouble to record their relative frequency. This approach, which can be termed the *mathematical* or *á priori* approach to probability, depends on being able to analyze the event being studied into a compound of simpler, equally likely events. For example, if a mathematician or gambler wanted to decide what the odds were of drawing a "five" from a pack of playing cards, he might proceed by this analysis: "Every playing card has the same chance of being drawn, to begin with. There are fifty-two playing cards, so any particular playing card has one chance in fifty-two of being drawn." (These are the equally likely events.) "There are four playing cards which are 'fives,' and every one of them has one chance in fifty-two of being drawn. The chance of the five of spades being drawn is one in fifty-two; of the five of hearts is one in fifty-two; therefore the chance of *any* 'five' being drawn is four in fifty-two."

The rules for the combination of probabilities, described in the next section, are fairly easy to understand. Complex problems in probability theory may be very difficult to solve, however, even though, basically, all that is involved is the application of simple rules. Usually the essential difficulty is in analyzing the problem into its simpler components. Certain problems in probability admit of a number of different solutions, because of the possibility of different decisions regarding what will be taken to be the fundamental equally probable events. In short, the application of the mathematical theory, like the application of the frequency view, is not without its uncertainties.

The mathematical theory of probability and the frequency theory are, of course, entirely compatible with each other. Indeed, one way mathematicians check on some of the conclusions of the mathematical theory is by actually developing frequency information. In this way we could, for example, check that the probability of observing two heads in a flip of two coins is 1/4.

There is a third view of probability, which is also compatible with the mathematical theory, which is called the *subjectivist*. Here the probability of an event is identified with an individual's degree of belief in it. On first acquaintance, such an approach seems to permit arbitrariness and an absence of consistency from individual to individual. Yet, as Abraham Kaplan says, it describes our actual behavior:

> In making decisions outside of actual gambling games we seldom do proceed, as a matter of fact, after the fashion of the a priori theories. The choice of a wife, a public policy, or a church may well entail assignments of probabilities to antici-pated futures, but it is doubtful at best whether in matters of sex, politics, or religion we proceed by determining a set of equiprobable outcomes and then counting the proportion of favorable ones. . . . Instead of treating psychological probabilities as our personal estimates of a magnitude, the subjectivist theories take them to constitute the magnitude itself.[1]

The subjectivist view of probability is closely connected to a new direction in statistical inference, sometimes referred to as Bayes' methods. It is therefore taking on increased prominence in advanced work, but for the level of work discussed in this text, it is not yet necessary to be able to deal with it. An understanding of the frequentist view and the mathe-matical view is sufficient foundation for a grasp of elementary ideas.[2]

Some Elements of Probability Theory

Let us return to the definition of probability as "relative frequency over the long run," and note that the following assertions are designed to be compatable with it.

1. All probabilities lie between 0 and 1, inclusive.
2. An event that is certain has a probability equal to 1.
3. An impossible event has a probability equal to 0.

Let us now work out rules for assigning probabilities to events, when the events are compounds of constituent events whose probabilities are known.

[1] Abraham Kaplan, *The Conduct of Inquiry* (San Francisco: Chandler, 1964), p. 229. Copyright 1964 by Chandler Publishing Company. Reprinted by permission.
[2] An excellent presentation of the ideas of probability on an elementary level is given by Frederick Mosteller, Robert E. K. Rourke, and George B. Thomas, Jr., in *Proba-bility and Statistics* (Reading, Mass.: Addison-Wesley, 1961). A briefer statement is contained in Morris Cohen and Ernest Nagel, *An Introduction to Logic and Scientific Method* (New York: Harcourt-Brace, 1934), pp. 151–172. See also Bertrand Russell, *Human Knowledge* (New York: Simon and Schuster, 1962), pp. 335–420.

First, we introduce two important terms. We call two events *mutually exclusive* if it is impossible for both to happen; if when one happens, the other cannot. Getting a head and getting a tail on any one flip of a coin are mutually exclusive events. We call a set of events *exhaustive* if one of them has to happen. In a flip of a coin, the events "getting a head" and "getting a tail" are both mutually exclusive and exhaustive.

As already noted, the mathematical analysis of a probability situation is likely to require the identification of component events that are *equally probable*. (An exception occurs when we are informed of the probability of a component event, as derived from experience, or already calculated mathematically.) Often, *the identification of events that are equally probable is part of the definition of the situation.* The example of the carnival wheel, given early in this chapter, is a case in point. For the wheel to be honest, each spot on the edge of the wheel must be an equally probable result of a spin.

If a compound event is made up of a number of mutually exclusive, exhaustive, equally probable events, then we can immediately calculate the probability of each of the component events. The outcome of a flip of a coin consists of two equally probable events, head and tail, which are mutually exclusive and exhaustive. Given that there are just two such events, the probability of each is 1/2. If there are 6 equally probable, mutually exclusive, exhaustive events, as there are when we are rolling an honest die, then the probability of each is 1/6. If there are 52 such events, as when we are selecting a card from a well-shuffled deck, then the probability of any one is 1/52.

We now need rules for combining probabilities, so that we can work out the probability of compound events when we have information about their components. The rules for combining probabilities are simple, but it is useful to be able to refer to Venn diagrams, which are ways of pic-

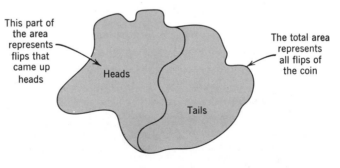

Figure 8.9

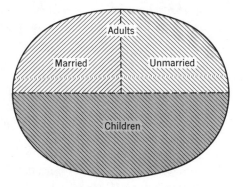

Figure 8.10 *Areas:* 25% married, 75% unmarried, 50% adults, and 50% children.

turing probability situations to help us grasp them. The idea of a Venn diagram is to represent a probability by an area. Suppose that a certain outcome had a probability of occurrence of about 0.5. We might represent the situation with a figure like Figure 8.9.

Or we might be dealing, not with a population of events, but with a population of people or things. We could represent that population by a similar diagram. Suppose that our population is half adults and half children, and half the adults are married. Our diagram would be as shown in Figure 8.10.

We can introduce here the concept of a *conditional probability*. This is the probability of one thing happening on the assumption that something else has already happened. For example, the probability of our selecting at random an individual from this population and having him turn out to be a married adult is one-fourth. However, the conditional probability of someone being married, given that he is an adult, is 1/2. We should write this conditional probability as $P(M/A)$, which we would interpret as "the probability of a member of this population being married, given that he is an adult."

What is the conditional probability of someone being married, given that he is a child? No children are married. Therefore,

$$P(M/C) = 0$$

When the probability of occurrence of an event is not affected by the fact that another event has occurred, we say the two events are *independent* of each other. In fact we define independence in just this way: an event is independent of a second event if the conditional probability of the first, given that the second event has occurred, is the same as the initial probability of the first. In other words, event A is independent of event B if

$P(A) = P(A/B)$ *(Definition of independence between events A and B)*

Being married is not independent of being adult in the situation just described because the initial probability of someone in the population being married is 1/4 while the conditional probability of someone being married, given that he is an adult, is 1/2.

Now we may give rules for combining probabilities.

Rule 1, for the probability of either or both. The probability of either A or B or both, which is written $P(A + B)$, is equal to the probability of A plus the probability of B, minus the probability of A and B occurring together.

$$P(A + B) = P(A) + P(B) - P(AB)$$

[The probability of two events occurring together is indicated by $P(AB)$.]

In the above example, the probability that someone is unmarried or an adult is equal to the probability that he is unmarried, which is 3/4, plus the probability that he is an adult, which is 1/2, minus the probability that he is both unmarried and an adult, which is 1/4. The probability is 1, which means that everyone in the population is either unmarried or an adult or both.

The reason the formula works is made clear by a Venn diagram (Figure 8.11).

The area occupied by either A or B or both together is made up of three parts. The first part is A, but not B. The second part is B, but not A.

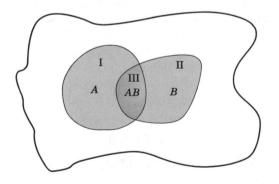

Figure 8.11

The third part is both A and B together. If we take all of A, it will include both the first part and the third part. If we add all of B, we add the second part and again the third part. So when we add together A and B, we wind up with the first part, the second part, and twice the third part. We must subtract the third part once, in order to end with what we want.

Rule 2, for the probability of joint occurrence. The probability of both A and B occurring, which is written $P(AB)$, is equal to the product of the probability that A occurs and the conditional probability that B occurs, given A.

$$P(AB) = P(A) \cdot P(B/A)$$

For example, the probability of being both adult and married is equal to the probability of being adult times the conditional probability of being married, given that a person is an adult.

Of course, if event A and event B are independent, and the conditional probability of B, given A, is the same as the initial probability of B, then the joint probability of A and B is

$$P(AB) = P(A) \cdot P(B) \quad (\textit{If } A \textit{ and } B \textit{ are independent})$$

Some Applications

The following examples show how the rules are applied in situations that have some research interest.

Someone claims he can distinguish brands of cigarettes simply by their taste. We arrange the following test. We take two brands of cigarettes, Brand A and Brand X. We arrange three pairs of these cigarettes, each pair containing one of Brand A and one of Brand X. We blindfold the claimant. We give him one pair of cigarettes at a time and require him to correctly identify, in each pair, which is Brand A and which is Brand X. What is the chance that the claimant can successfully pass the test just by guessing?

If the claimant cannot tell the difference between the cigarettes, what is his chance of guessing right in the first pair? If he cannot distinguish between the two cigarettes, then picking the right one and picking the wrong one are equally probable, and his chance of picking the right one is one in two. He also has one chance in two of being right in the second and the third pair. What is the chance of all these outcomes occurring together?

We need the following equation:

$$P(A_1 A_2 A_3) = P(A_1) \cdot P(A_2/A_1) \cdot P(A_3/A_1 A_2)$$

$P(A_1)$ is the probability of correctly identifying Brand A in the first trial, and so on.

Let us note that, as we have set up this problem, the conditional probability of A_2, given A_1, is no different from the initial probability of A_2: the accuracy of the guess on the second pair is *independent* of the accuracy of the guess on the first. Since this is so, we can simply note that:

$$P(A_2/A_1) = P(A_2)$$

$$P(A_3/A_1A_2) = P(A_3)$$

And,

$$P(A_1A_2A_3) = P(A_1) \cdot P(A_2) \cdot P(A_3)$$

We can rewrite the formula this way only because A_1, A_2, and A_3 are independent of each other.

Since $P(A_1) = P(A_2) = P(A_3) = 1/2$, we have

$$P(A_1A_2A_3) = \frac{1}{2} \cdot \frac{1}{2} \cdot \frac{1}{2} = \frac{1}{8}$$

This means that even if the claimant could not do more than guess, he still has a one-in-eight chance of correctly identifying the brands in each of three trials.

Let us set up a different test. We begin with five different brands of cigarettes, and give the claimant, while he is blindfolded, one cigarette of each brand. We require him to identify correctly three of the five brands, and we do not permit him to name the same brand twice. What is his chance of passing the test if he is totally unable to distinguish between the cigarettes and must guess?

To answer this question, we must first recognize that the claimant can pass the test in a number of ways. He can be correct on the first three cigarettes and wrong on the last two; or he can be correct on the first two, wrong on the next two, and correct on the last; or he can be correct on just three of the cigarettes in eight other ways. There are ten ways altogether in which the claimant can be right on just three cigarettes. What is the probability of any one of these ways occurring? Let us take the case where the claimant is right on the first three cigarettes and wrong on the next two. The formula to apply is the formula for the joint occurrence of events:

$$P(R_1, R_2, R_3, W_4, W_5)$$
$$= P(R_1)P(R_2/R_1)P(R_3/R_1R_2)P(W_4/R_1R_2R_3)P(W_5/R_1R_2R_3W_4)$$

This says that the probability of being right on the first trial, right on the second trial, right on the third trial, wrong on the fourth trial, and wrong on the fifth trial, is given by the probability of being right the first time, times the probability of being right the second time (assuming that we have been right the first time), times the probability of being right the third time (assuming that we have been right the first and second time), times the probability of being wrong the fourth time (assuming that we have been right the first three times), times the probability of being wrong the fifth time, given all the preceding. This is easier to calculate than to say. The proper values are:

$$P(R,R,R,W,W) = \left(\frac{1}{5}\right)\left(\frac{1}{4}\right)\left(\frac{1}{3}\right)\left(\frac{1}{2}\right)\left(\frac{1}{1}\right) = \frac{1}{120}$$

It turns out that each of the ten different mutually exclusive ways in which this result of three right, two wrong, might come about, has a probability of 1/120. The probability of getting just three right is 10/120. But we have not yet accounted for all the conditions under which we should accept that our claimant could identify cigarettes by taste. Suppose he got all five of the cigarettes right. There is not much chance of this if he is going on luck—only one chance in one hundred and twenty—but, nevertheless, let us count it in. (It is impossible to get four cigarettes right and one wrong, so we do not have to worry about that.) Taking everything into account, we have the following:

$$P(\text{at least 3 right}) = \frac{11}{120}$$

The claimant has eleven chances in one hundred and twenty of getting three or more cigarettes right, on the assumption that he is unable to tell one cigarette from another. This test is slightly more difficult to pass than was the first one, but it still is not as stringent as we might want.

The Binomial Distribution

The first distribution discussed in this chapter was the horizontal distribution. We can now discuss a second theoretical distribution, the *binomial distribution*.

A great many apparently diverse processes lead to binomial distributions:

1. We flip ten coins together and count the number of heads. We again flip the ten coins and count the number of heads. We repeat this many times. The distribution of numbers of heads is a binomial distribution.

2. From a large population of voters, we select a sample of ten and list the number who are Democrats. We then select a second sample and

again list the number who are Democrats. We repeat this many times. The distribution of the number who are Democrats is a binomial distribution.

3. From a large population of true-false questions, we sample ten items, answer them, and then list the number we answered correctly. We take another sample of ten items and again list the number we answered correctly. We repeat this many times. The distribution of numbers of correct responses is binomial.

Any process that has the following characteristics will result in a binomial distribution.

1. *There is an event which has two, and only two, possible outcomes.* Flipping a coin is such an event. It can come up heads or it can come up tails. Asking a man his political preference is such an event, if we agree to exclude anyone who says anything other than Republican or Democratic. We shall call such an event a *trial*.

2. A particular outcome has a *constant probability* of happening in every trial. Every time we flip a coin, there is just one chance in two that it will come down heads. If we choose a voter at random within a population where we know that sixty percent are Democratic, then there are just sixty chances in one hundred that the voter will be a Democrat. These are, therefore, trials in which the outcomes have a constant probability.

3. The probability of the outcome of any particular trial is *independent* of the outcomes of other trials. A coin always has a one-in-two chance of landing heads, no matter what happened on previous flips. The chance of selecting a second Democrat in a large population is not affected, for practical purposes, by the fact that we already have selected someone else who is a Democrat.

4. *We are concerned, not with the outcome of a single trial but rather with the number of "successful" outcomes in a number of trials.* We are concerned with the number of coins that come up heads, when ten are flipped, or with the number of voters who are Democrats, when ten are interviewed, or with the number of correct responses, when ten questions are answered.

To summarize: a binomial distribution is the theoretical frequency distribution of the numbers of times a particular outcome occurs in samples of repeated trials of mutually independent events of constant probability.

Suppose we were interested in how many times we should get zero heads, one head, or two heads, when flipping two coins. Let us calculate the theoretical probabilities of these different outcomes:

$P(0 \text{ heads}) = P(\text{tail}_1 \text{ and } \text{tail}_2) = P(\text{tail}_1)P(\text{tail}_2)$

[Formula for joint occurrence of independent events.]

$$P(0 \text{ heads}) = \left(\frac{1}{2}\right)\left(\frac{1}{2}\right) = \frac{1}{4}$$

(*Note:* tail$_1$ means "tail on the first coin.")

The answer is obvious, but it is useful to see the application of our rules for working out the probabilities of complex events. The probability of getting no heads at all is the probability of not getting a head on the first coin *and* the probability of also not getting a head on the second coin. This is equal to the probability of not getting a head on the first coin times the conditional probability of not getting a head on the second coin (assuming that we have not gotten a head on the first.) This conditional probability is the same as the initial probability, since the two events are independent.

Similarly, the probability of two heads is 1/4. What about the probability of one head and one tail? This would be:

$$P(H \text{ and } T) = P(H_1 \text{ and } T_2) + P(H_2 \text{ and } T_1) = \frac{1}{4} + \frac{1}{4} = \frac{1}{2}$$

We now see that the theoretical probabilities of 0 heads, 1 head, and 2 heads are, respectively: 1/4, 1/2, and 1/4. Since theoretical probabilities are statements of expected relative frequencies, we can assert that if we flipped two coins many, many times, we should have the following results.

Number of Heads	Expected Relative Frequency
0 heads	0.25
1 head	0.50
2 heads	0.25
	1.00

What would happen had we flipped three coins? Then the number of heads might be 0 heads, 1, 2, or 3. With what relative frequency might we expect these different results?

$P(0 \text{ heads}) = P(T_1)P(T_2)P(T_3) = \dfrac{1}{8}$

$P(1 \text{ head}) = P(H_1)P(T_2)P(T_3) + P(T_1)P(H_2)P(T_3)$

$$+ P(T_1)P(T_2)P(H_3) = \frac{3}{8}$$

$P(2 \text{ heads}) = P(H_1)P(H_2)P(T_3) + P(H_1)P(T_2)P(H_3)$

$$+ P(T_1)P(H_2)P(H_3) = \frac{3}{8}$$

$$P(3 \text{ heads}) = P(H_1)P(H_2)P(H_3) = \frac{1}{8}$$

Number of Heads	Expected Relative Frequency
0 heads	0.125
1 head	0.375
2 heads	0.375
3 heads	0.125
	1.000

Table 8.3

Expected Relative Frequencies of Heads for Four, Five, Six, and Ten Coins

	Four Coins			Five Coins	
Number	Percentage of All Coins	Expected Relative Frequency	Number	Percentage of All Coins	Expected Relative Frequency
0	0	0.0625	0	0	0.031
1	25	0.25	1	20	0.156
2	50	0.375	2	40	0.313
3	75	0.25	3	60	0.313
4	100	0.0625	4	80	0.156
		1.000	5	100	0.031
					1.000

	Six Coins			Ten Coins	
Number	Percentage of All Coins	Expected Relative Frequency	Number	Percentage of All Coins	Expected Relative Frequency
0	0	0.016	0	0	0.001
1	17	0.094	1	10	0.010
2	33	0.234	2	20	0.045
3	50	0.312	3	30	0.117
4	67	0.234	4	40	0.205
5	83	0.094	5	50	0.246
6	100	0.016	6	60	0.205
		1.000	7	70	0.117
			8	80	0.045
			9	90	0.010
			10	100	0.001
					1.000

By similar reasoning, we can make up tables of expected relative frequencies for 4 coins, 5 coins, 6 coins, or 10 coins (Table 8.3). Notice how the expected relative frequency piles up around a central value (in this case 0.50 heads) and how, as we get farther from this result, the relative frequency becomes progressively smaller. Notice, too, that the distribution is more and more concentrated around the central value as we increase the number of trials in a series or sample. These points may be clearer if we draw a graph. Histograms representing the 4-coin situation and the 10-coin situation are shown in Figure 8.12. The two histograms have been drawn so that their total areas are identical. In the 10-coin situation more of the distribution is concentrated near the 50% point than in the 4-coin distribution.

It should be possible to see that the mean value in both histograms falls at 50%, or, to state this as a fraction, at 1/2. This is just the probability of getting a single head in a single trial. In general, in any binomial distribution, the mean of the distribution falls at p, the probability of a successful outcome in a single trial.

The formula for the standard deviation of the binomial distribution cannot be so easily seen. However, we ought to notice that the standard deviation becomes smaller and smaller as the number of trials in a sample increases; the expected relative frequencies of "successful outcomes"

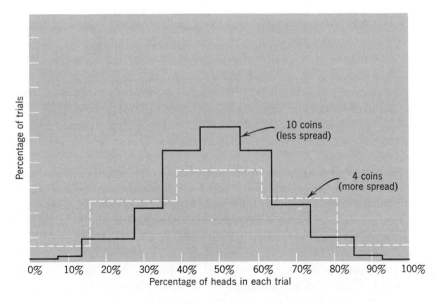

Figure 8.12 Two binomial distributions.

increasingly bunch around the central value. The formula for the standard deviation should involve a term for the number of trials in a sample in a way which reduces the standard deviation as the sample size increases. The formula is the following:

$$\sigma_p = \sqrt{\frac{p(1 - p)}{n}}$$

where σ_p is the standard deviation of the observed relative frequency; p is the probability of success in a single trial; n is the number of trials in a sample.

The standard deviation of a binomial distribution can be calculated by taking the square root of the product of the probability of success in any trial and the probability of failure in the trial, divided by the total number of trials in a sample.

An Example of the Application of the Binomial Distribution

A political scientist suspects that women are more conservative than men, and that when a married couple disagree on which party to vote for, it is usually the man who votes Democratic and his wife who votes Republican. To test this idea, the political scientist takes, at random, a sample of one hundred couples. Only ten of this one hundred report a difference of opinion between husband and wife. Within this group of ten couples, seven are as predicted by his hypothesis; that is, in seven couples, it is the wife who voted Republican, the husband who voted Democratic. The question he now asks is, "Suppose that there is really no more likelihood that the wife will be more conservative than that the husband will be more conservative. What was the chance on this assumption of nevertheless getting evidence this strong in support of the assertion that wives are more conservative than husbands?" Clearly, this is asking the question, "What is the relative frequency of seven or more 'successes' in samples of ten trials, when the true probability of a 'success' in any one trial is 0.5?" We have already worked this out in Table 8.3. The chance of getting 7, 8, 9, or 10 successes when the true probability of success is 0.5 is $11.7\% + 4.5\% + 1.0\% + 0.1\%$; or 17.3%. We could therefore say that the probability of evidence as strongly in favor of the hypothesis as has actually been found, even if the hypothesis is not correct, is 0.173, or about one in six. Ordinarily, we should not consider a test that could support a false hypothesis one-sixth of the time to be stringent enough. The political scientist might decide to increase the size of his sample so that he could develop a more stringent test.

The Normal Distribution

The process that gives rise to a *binomial distribution* is one in which each datum represents the relative frequency of "successful" outcomes within a sample containing a number of independent trials of constant probability. The more trials we have in a sample, the less important any specific trial will be. If we are flipping only two coins, what happens to the first will be very important to the overall result, but if we are flipping a thousand, what happens to the first will hardly matter at all in terms of the relative frequency of heads in the sample. Let us now suppose that we have a very large sample in which there are a great many separate trials, each independent of the others, each with a constant probability of contributing to the relative frequency of a certain outcome, none of very great importance in the total result. This process is just a binomial process involving a great many trials. Now let us suppose we examine sample after sample, each of this sort. As the number of our samples increases, the observed frequency of successes will yield a very nearly *continuous frequency distribution*. It will no longer be the discrete binomial distribution; or, better, it will be a smoothed binomial, the limit of a binomial distribution where there are many samples and the number of trials in a sample has increased indefinitely. This is *the normal distribution*.

The general appearance of the normal distribution is shown in Figure 8.13. It is bell-shaped: bulky at its center and trailing off to zero at its edges, although never becoming absolutely zero at any point. It is symmetric, and each of its sides has an *inflection point*, a place where the curve stops turning inward and starts turning outward. Its mean is at its center, which is also the point of its maximum height. Its standard deviation happens to be the same as the distance from the mean to the inflection point. Two standard deviations, on both sides of the mean, will cover

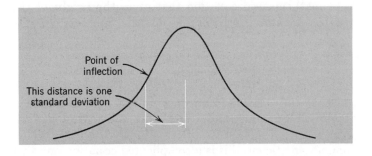

Figure 8.13 A normal curve.

close to 95 % of the area of the curve. (It should be recalled that "standard deviation" is a measure of distance, like an inch or a mile.)

There are a number of qualities in the real world which seem to be nearly normally distributed: heights of men, to name one. Can we develop a model that would "explain" the fact that, in a large population, height tends to be normally distributed?

One model we might try would be as follows. Assume that the actual level a man's height comes to is the sum of a single factor of major importance which we might call "species height," which is the basic height below which no adult man can be found, and a whole host of factors, each of minor importance, which would include what had been inherited from the man's forebears, elements of his diet over his early years, whatever accidental factors controlled his endocrine balance during that period, aspects of climate, of habit, of nutrition, and much more. Suppose each factor beyond the basic "species height," if it is positive, contributes a small amount to the increased height of the man. For example, if a man has a certain mineral in his diet as a child, he will be taller by a certain amount; and so on, for hundreds and thousands of factors. According to this model, the height of a given man beyond "species height" is the sum of the number of positive outcomes among thousands of independent trials. The heights of a very large population of men would then be normally distributed.

Of course, because this model explains the normal distribution of heights does not demonstrate that the model is true. Other explanatory models could also be developed. There are a number of ways in which this model is not even plausible: the assumption of the independence of outcomes of trials, for one; it is likely that where diet is weak in one respect, it will be weak in others as well. Yet this model at least suggests the kind of process that might underlie the nearly normal distribution of heights.

The normal distribution, like any theoretical distribution, can be described by a mathematical equation that gives the height of the curve for any particular value. For a normal distribution this equation is as follows.

$$y = \frac{1}{\sqrt{2\pi\sigma^2}} e^{-\frac{(x-\bar{x})^2}{2\sigma^2}}$$

where: y = expected relative frequency; x = any given value; e and π are mathematical constants; and $\bar{x}$ and σ are constants for a given distribution.

To a nonmathematician, this is a complicated equation and there is no getting around it. Let us analyze it more closely. π, called "pi," is the constant that, in geometry courses, is defined as the ratio between the cir-

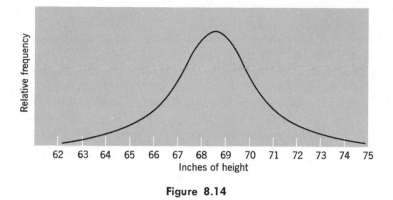

Figure 8.14

cumference of a circle and its diameter, and *e*, called "epsilon," is another mathematical constant, which is defined as the sum of a certain infinite series. Each of these quantities is fixed. Every normal curve will use exactly the same values for each of these quantities—they have no other values. Different normal curves may, however, use different values for σ and for $\bar{x}$. These two values represent, respectively, the standard deviation and the mean of the normal curve. What this means is: *normal curves may differ from each other in their mean and in their standard deviation, but in no other way.*

To illustrate, suppose we had drawn the frequency distribution of the heights of American men, and used inches as our unit of measure. Our result might look like Figure 8.14.

If we had used feet as our unit of measure, instead of inches, our curve would look like that shown in Figure 8.15.

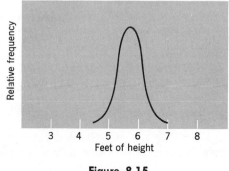

Figure 8.15

These two normal curves differ from each other in the *scales* on which height was measured. Because one scale (inches) is finer than the other, the normal curve is spread out more. The standard deviation is about three when we are talking about inches, but only about 1/4 when we are talking about feet. Also, it takes fewer units to go from zero to the mean value when we talk about "feet of height" than when we talk about "inches of height." But *we can translate the one normal curve* into the other just by making *a change in scale*. Suppose we want to bring the curve based on measurements in terms of feet to the form of the curve based on measurements in terms of inches. We need only use the following formula.

$$x' = 12x$$

where: x' = observation measured in inches; x = observation measured in feet.

In just this way—by making the proper change in scale—any normal curve can be superimposed on any other normal curve. Here we multiplied every observation by a constant. Sometimes we shall have to subtract or add a constant, as well.

Tables of the Normal Distribution

What we have just pointed out is that every normal distribution is like every other normal distribution except for its unit of measure. We can make any normal distribution exactly like any other by the proper *linear transformation* of measurements. (A linear transformation is one that involves only multiplication, division, addition, or subtraction, in each case of a constant amount.) Because this is true, statisticians have been able to decide on a *standard normal distribution* and make up tables for it. When we need to use the tables, we simply transform whatever distribution we are working with into standard form. What is taken as our standard normal distribution is one in which the standard deviation is equal to one unit and the mean is at zero. This is purely a convention, but it is a useful one. The standard normal distribution looks like Figure 8.16.

To transform any particular normal distribution into standard form, we subtract from each observation the mean of the distribution and divide the result by the standard deviation of the distribution. This accomplishes the proper change in scale. The formula is:

$$z = \frac{x - \bar{x}}{\sigma}$$

This is the transformation formula for bringing a normal distribution to standard form, where x is the original value, $\bar{x}$ is the mean of the original

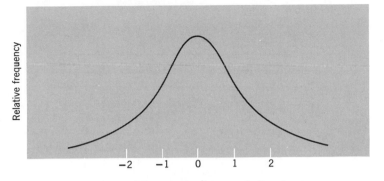

Figure 8.16   The standard normal distribution.

distribution, σ is the standard deviation of the original distribution, and z is the new value.

No matter what the mean and sigma of the original distribution are, mean and sigma of the distribution of z are zero and one, respectively. Another way of stating the matter is that the z measures are in terms of "sigma-units." One unit in the z scale is equal to one standard deviation in the original scale. But if this becomes too complicated to keep in mind, it is really only necessary to recognize that the normal distribution in standard form has its mean at zero and its standard deviation at one, and that any normal distribution may be brought to standard form by use of the transformation formula given above.

To show how one may use this formula for changing scale to that of a standard normal distribution, suppose we have the observation of 62 inches in height, and are told that the mean height is 70 inches and that the standard deviation is 4 inches. Then our calculation would be:

$$z = \frac{62 - 70}{4} = -2$$

The value of the observation 62 inches in the standard normal units is -2. This is sometimes referred to as the observation's "z-score," or "standard score."

As was stated earlier, the reason that the standard form of the normal distribution is important is that it has been tabled. We have tables telling us just what proportion of the normal distribution lies between the mean and other values of the standard normal distribution. A portion of such a table is given as Table 8.4 and a fuller table is included in Appendix 1.

Table 8.4

Portion of a Table Showing Areas under the Normal Curve, for Selected z Values

Distance from Mean: z	Area between Mean and z
0.0	0.0000
0.5	0.1915
0.8	0.2881
1.0	0.3413
1.5	0.4332
1.96	0.4750
2.0	0.4772
2.5	0.4938
2.58	0.4951
3.0	0.4987

Table 8.4 shows that 34% of the population of a normal distribution will fall between the mean and one standard deviation beyond the mean. Since the normal curve is symmetric, this means that 68% of the population will fall between minus one standard deviation and plus one standard deviation. Ninety-five percent of the population will fall between plus and minus 1.96 standard deviation units.

The Normal Approximation to the Binomial Distribution

Some statistical problems that involve the binomial distribution can be solved more easily if we work with the normal distribution that approximates the binomial, rather than with the binomial itself, since tables of the normal distribution are more accessible. The nomal approximation to the binomial takes as its mean p, the mean of the binomial, and as its standard deviation $\sqrt{[p(1-p)]/n}$, the standard deviation of the binomial. This is a good approximation if n is 10 or greater, so long as p is not too far from 0.5. Where n is smaller than 10, or p very different from 1/2, there are tables of the binomial which may be consulted, or it is possible to work out the probabilities directly, although it must be said that the computations can become tedious. If the normal approximation is used when the number of trials in a sample is small, it must be remembered that the binomial distribution is discrete, while the normal distribution is continuous, and we therefore will have to correct for this difference in our approximation. How this is done is illustrated in the second example below.

As our first example, let us take a sampling situation. Suppose that a polling concern is trying to predict who will win an election for sheriff. Contestants are Smith and Brown. The polling concern selects more than one hundred voters' names from the list of registered voters in the county. They call each of these voters on the phone and ask him if he intends to vote in the next day's election. If the voter says that he does not, they thank him and drop his name from their sample. If he says that he does intend to vote, they ask him whether he will vote for Smith or Brown for sheriff. The polling concern winds up with exactly one hundred voters saying they intend to cast a ballot, and reporting for whom they will cast it.

Let us suppose that everyone who intended to vote actually did so, that no one who said he would not vote changed his mind, that every respondent answered the questions honestly, and that there were no switches of loyalty between election eve and election day. Let us also assume that, at the time of the poll, Smith was favored by 54% of those who had a preference and intended to vote. *What was the polling outfit's chance of predicting, incorrectly, that Brown would win the election?*

We can answer this question by recognizing that the problem is one involving a binomial process in which there were one hundred trials. Each answer by a member of the sample that he was for Smith or for Brown constituted a trial. There was a probability of 0.54 that the outcome of each trial would be the response, "Smith" (assuming honesty in response, and so on). The question posed above therefore boils down to: "In repeated samples of one hundred trials each, with probability of success in a given trial of 0.54, what percentage of samples will have relative frequencies of success of less than 0.50?"

What we are suggesting in our rephrasing of the question about the likelihood that the polling concern may be wrong is a situation in which we repeatedly take samples of one hundred voters each, and in each sample calculate the percentage for Smith. We would not actually do this, of course. But it is useful to have this model in mind as a way of understanding the approach. We should expect most of these imaginary samples of one hundred to have about 54% in favor of Smith. But some would have 56% or 59% or even 60% in favor of Smith. And some would have 50% or 52% in favor of Brown. Whenever the percentage in favor of Brown became greater than 50%, the polling concern would make an incorrect prediction. They would say that Brown would be the winner, on the basis of their sample, and when the election results were counted, their faces would be red.

To work out the proportion of samples that will yield 50% or more for Brown, we take the normal approximation to the binomial distribution.

$$\text{Mean of normal approximation} = p = 0.54$$

$$\text{Standard deviation of normal approximation} = \sigma_p = \sqrt{\frac{p(1-p)}{n}}$$

$$\sigma_p = \sqrt{\frac{(0.54)(0.46)}{100}}$$

$$\sigma_p = 0.05$$

We now ask: What proportion of the population of a normal distribution, with mean 0.54 and standard deviation 0.05, will be found to be less than 0.50? We must consult a table of the normal curve for the answer, but before we can do this, we must first transform our distribution into standard form.

When we take our distribution to standard form, its mean will be 0 (instead of 0.54) and its standard deviation will be 1. What will the point, 0.50, be? We apply the following formula.

$$z = \frac{x - \bar{x}}{\sigma}$$

$$z = \frac{0.50 - 0.54}{0.05} = \frac{-0.04}{0.05}$$

$$z = -0.8$$

Our question now is, "What proportion of the standard normal curve lies to the left of $z = -0.8$?" Table 8.4 tells us that between the mean and 0.8, there lies 28.8% of the curve. Since the normal curve is symmetric, the same amount lies between the mean and -0.8. This leaves (50% − 28.81%), or 21.19% of the curve to the left of -0.8 (Figure 8.17).

This means that 21% of the samples would show Brown, not Smith, as having more than 50% of the vote. The polling concern's chance of error in predicting the election, if they interview one hundred intended voters, with everything working for them, is still 0.21, or about one in five. Of course, taking a larger sample will cut the risk greatly, but even so it should be clear that election predicting is a risky business.

Let us turn to a second example. Suppose that we are interested in comparing the effectiveness of group therapy and individual therapy and one of the things we wonder about is which is more attractive to the patient. We have the opportunity to conduct a study in a large hospital for the treatment of the mentally ill. Many patients in this hospital are

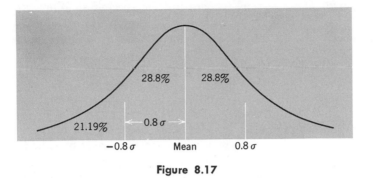

Figure 8.17

involved in both types of therapy. We select a sample of ten patients from this population, and ask each of them "If you could only continue with group therapy or with individual therapy, which would you choose to continue with?"

Suppose this is a matter of complete indifference to the population of patients as a whole. A few like group therapy, a few like individual therapy, but most do not care. Taking it all together, it is a fifty-fifty chance that any particular patient will say "individual," or that he will say "group." What is the chance that, within our sample of ten, we shall nevertheless get 80% or better saying either group or individual? If we got eight out of ten, even in this tiny sample, we might let this fact influence our judgment. We should say, wrongly, that one was definitely preferred. What is our chance of being thus misled?

Again we take the normal approximation to the binomial:

$$\text{Mean} = p = 0.50$$

$$\text{Standard deviation} = \sqrt{\frac{p(1 - p)}{n}} = \sqrt{\frac{(0.50)(0.50)}{10}} = 0.025$$

$$\sigma = 0.158$$

Our question is, "What proportion of this curve is to the right of 0.8 and to the left of 0.2?" Here we have to pause to remember that the normal is a continuous distribution and the binomial a discrete distribution. The binomial distribution has frequencies only at 0, 0.2, 0.4, 0.6, 0.8, and 1.0. The normal distribution has frequencies everywhere between 0 and 1. Therefore, we shall say that the binomial value of 0.8 actually stands for all normal distribution values between 0.75 and 0.85. The binomial value of 0.2 stands for all normal distribution values between

0.15 and 0.25. Our question, recognizing this, becomes "What proportion of the normal curve is to the right of 0.75 and to the left of 0.25?"

To answer this, we translate 0.75 and 0.25 into standard scores:

$$z_1 = \frac{0.75 - 0.50}{0.158} = \frac{0.25}{0.158} \qquad z_2 = \frac{0.25 - 0.50}{0.158} = \frac{-0.25}{0.158}$$

$$z_1 = 1.58 \qquad\qquad\qquad z_2 = -1.58$$

Reference to the complete table of areas under the normal curve, in the Appendix, will disclose that areas more extreme than 1.58 sigmas beyond the mean, in both directions, include about 11% of the distribution. This means that our investigator has about 11 chances in 100 of getting a sample of 10 in which 8, 9, or all 10 of the members are in agreement in their preference for one therapeutic setting rather than the other, even though there is no genuine preference within the hospital.

We might check on how close this value, based on the normal approximation to the binomial, comes to the true value. Table 8.3 lists the probabilities of various numbers of successes in samples of 10 trials of probability 1/2. If we add together the probabilities of 0, 1, 2, 8, 9, and 10 successes we see they sum to 0.11, which is what we found by use of the normal approximation.

PROBLEMS

8.1. Consider the distributions pictured in response to the problems for Chapter 5. Describe each of these distributions in words.

8.2. Picture by bar graphs both the expected and the observed for the following fictitious data dealing with conversation pairs among teen-agers.

Type of Pair	Observed Relative Frequency	Expected Relative Frequency
Boy-girl	0.20	0.50
Boy-boy	0.36	0.25
Girl-girl	0.44	0.25

What inference might your draw from the discrepancies between observed and expected relative frequencies?

8.3. Describe situations other than those noted in the text which might give rise to the following:
 (a) A horizontal distribution.
 (b) A binomial distribution.
 (c) A normal distribution.

8.4. An investigator sets up four experiments to test four independent hypotheses; that is, the results of any of the experiments have no bearing on the results of any of the others. *Assume that all four of his hypotheses are false.* Nevertheless, there is the possibility that the evidence will appear to support at least one of the hypotheses. *Assume that the chance that the evidence will appear to support any one of the hypotheses, even though it is false, is* 1/10.

(a) What is the probability that *at least one* hypothesis will appear to be supported by the evidence? (Hint: the easiest way of doing this is to work out the probability of no hypothesis being supported and subtract from one. The answer is 0.34.)

(b) What is the probability that *no more than one* hypothesis will be supported by the evidence? (Answer: 0.95.)

8.5. An undergraduate class in methods of research decides to conduct a survey of fellow students. It decides to send 50% of the student body, selected randomly, a questionnaire by mail, and also to conduct personal interviews with a randomly selected 10% of the student body.

(a) What percentage of the student body may be expected to both receive a questionnaire and be asked to participate in an interview?

(b) What percentage of the student body may be expected either to receive a questionnaire or be contacted for an interview? (Answer: 55%.)

8.6. Assume that heights of American men of draft age are distributed by a normal distribution with mean of 70 inches and standard deviation of 4 inches. Suppose the Armed Forces decide to exclude the smallest 0.005 and the tallest 0.005 of the population. Between what limits in height will men still be draftable?

(a) Those responsible for furnishing clothing to the Armed Forces would like to know the height of the men in the Armed Forces who are at the 20th percentile, the 50th percentile, and the 80th percentile. What is the answer?

8.7. A test in Sanskrit is made up with 100 true-false items. It is administered to a large number of men, many of whom know nothing of the language.

(a) Within what range of scores would you expect 95% of the scores of men who knew no Sanskrit? (Answer: between 40 and 60 correct responses.)

(b) Suppose that a man scored only 20 correct responses. Suggest explanations.

(c) Suppose that responses were not independent of each other. For example, if an individual responded "true" to item 1, then he would be required also to answer "true" to the next 10 items. This would be bad test construction, but how might it affect the distribution of scores?

Chapter 9

Association

The preceding chapters have dealt with the problems of description of a distribution of measurements of a *single* quality. However, almost any quantitative study involves measurements of *many* qualities. In a study of political attitudes, for example, we should collect information not only about the attitudes, but also about sex, age, income, voting history and perhaps also some more general values of respondents. Then, after describing the distribution of political attitudes within the population, we should be able to describe the extent to which one or another political attitude went together with being male, or being in a certain age group, or having a certain income, or holding a certain value. Is the belief that we ought to have a strong central government, for example, associated with the income of the respondent or with his region of residence? Locating such associations may help us to understand the factors that determine political attitudes.

Much of the effort in the analysis of quantitative data is directed toward evaluating and interpreting *associations* among qualities. There are many ways of defining this term, as is noted below, but perhaps the best initial definition is: *Two qualities are associated when the distribution of values of the one differs for different values of the other*. Another form of this definition is: two factors are associated if, for either factor, the proportions in subgroups are different from the marginal proportions.

In Table 9.1, occupation and job satisfaction are associated because the distribution of scores on the satisfaction measure is different for different occupations. The distribution of satisfaction with job is: 90% satisfied, 10% to some extent dissatisfied, for professionals; only 64% satisfied, 36% dissatisfied, for managers.

If a change in the value of the one quality does not result in a change in the distribution of values of the other, *the qualities are independent of each other*. An example is shown in Table 9.2. These two qualities are inde-

Table 9.1

Satisfaction with Job Within Middle-Class Occupations[a]

Occupation	Very Satisfied and Satisfied		Pro-Con or Dissatisfied		Total	
	Percent	Number	Percent	Number	Percent	Number
Professionals	90	25	10	3	100	28
Managers	64	14	36	8	100	22
Salesmen	82	18	18	4	100	22
Total	79	57	21	15	100	72

[a] Adapted from N. Morse and R. S. Weiss, "Function and Meaning of Work and the Job," *American Sociological Review*, **20** (April, 1955), p. 198.

pendent because the distribution of values of the one is the same for every value of the other. Another way of saying this is: *subgroups do not differ.* The same proportion of students have I.Q.'s above 100 in the one group as in the other. *Whenever subgroups do not differ, we have independence. Whenever subgroups do differ, we have association.*

Notice the similarity between the idea of absence of association between factors and the idea of independence of events. We say that there is an absence of association when the subgroup percentages are all the same and, incidentally, also the same as the total percentage. We say that there is independence when the conditional probability of an event, given another event, is the same as the initial probability of the event. We can

Table 9.2

I.Q. Scores Among Students Identifying Themselves as Members of Different Ethnic Groups in a Certain School (Fictitious)

Ethnicity	Below 100		Above 100		Number
	Percent	Number	Percent	Number	
Irish	45	18	55	22	40
Italian	45	27	55	33	60
Jewish	45	9	55	11	20
Total					120

translate these statements into one another by associating the percentage in a subgroup with a conditional probability and associating the percentage in the total group with an initial probability. This is entirely plausible. The percentage of a subgroup is the relative frequency of a particular attribute, assuming that we are told that another attribute is present. This can be thought of as a conditional probability. Similarly, the percentage of the total group is the relative frequency of a particular attribute in the population as a whole, and this can be thought of as an initial probability.

It is worth noting before going further that every discussion of association implies a comparison of subgroups. It makes no sense to ask whether one quality is associated with another unless we can compare people who have the quality with people who do not have it, or people who have much of the quality with those who have less. Suppose, for example, you were told that at a certain school 86% of the students on the honor roll were girls. Would this convince you that being a girl was associated with being on the honor roll? If so, look at Table 9.3.

To decide whether sex and honor roll status are associated, we must compare the percentage of girls within the honor roll group with the percentage of girls within the not-honor-roll group. Incidentally, this table has been percentaged to direct the reader's attention to the composition of the honor roll group and of the not-honor-roll group, rather than percentaged to direct the reader's attention to a possible causal relationship. To accomplish the latter purpose it would have been percentaged the other way: along the possibly independent variable. So far as the demonstration of independence or association goes, it doesn't matter which way one percentages. If subgroups within the one quality differ, then subgroups within the other quality also differ.

Table 9.3

Honor Roll Status and Sex of Students at a Certain School (Fictitious)

Honor Roll Status	Sex of Students (Percent)		Number
	Male	Female	
On honor roll	14	86	50
Not on honor roll	14	86	250
Total student body			300

Alternative Ways of Viewing Association

The definition of association suggested to this point is, in terms of table proportions, that two factors, A and B, are associated if the proportions in the subgroups of either factor are different from the marginal proportions. (The term "marginal proportion" is another way of referring to the proportion of the total.) We find, when we come to construct measures of how much association exists between factors, that there are many facets of the concept of association which can be emphasized, and that measures differ in this respect. The following may each be taken as representing what is meant by "degree of association":

1. Departure from independence between two factors. We imagine what the data would look like if there were no association. Then we say that there is association to the extent that the observed data depart from this. Of the measures discussed in the next chapters, those dased on chi-square represent this point of view.

2. Magnitude of subgroup differences. Assuming that there is some association, its degree may be measured by direct comparison of subgroup proportions with each other. Of the measures discussed in the next chapters, the percentage difference reflects this point of view.

3. Summary of pair-by-pair comparisons. Another approach would be to think of forming all possible comparisons of one member of the population with another. In each of these comparisons, we should decide whether the two factors under study occurred together or did not. We should then summarize the results of all these pair-by-pair comparisons, and association would be measured by the preponderance of one type of pair. This idea underlies Q, γ, and τ among the measures discussed in the next chapters.

4. Proportional reduction of probable error. We might imagine that we are called on to predict whether factor A exists or not, first without information regarding B, and then with information regarding B. The more we are helped by information regarding B, the more association we are willing to admit. This approach underlies the various g-measures described in the next chapter.

5. Extent to which increments in the one factor occur together with increments in the other factor. We might take as our meaning of association the extent to which increase in the one factor is accompanied by increase in the other, or decrease in the one by decrease in the other. This idea, perhaps more aptly termed "correlation" than "association," underlies Pearson's r, the product-moment correlation coefficient, discussed in the chapter after the next.

All the approaches listed above represent different specifications of just what we mean by the general idea of association. Each leads to different measures of association and it can be shown, by suitably constructed cases, that one measure can be a very low value, or zero, when another measure suggests quite a reasonable amount of association. The investigator, before choosing a measure of association, must think through his problem and ask himself just what it is he wants to measure. The task is the same as that encountered in deciding among ways of identifying a representative case or value; the concept of association is broad enough to encompass a number of specifications. The list given above, although it presents those most likely to be encountered, is by no means complete.[1]

Why Are We Interested in Identifying Associations?

Why do we want to know whether qualities "go together"; whether a member of the population who has a great deal of one quality is also likely to have much of another?

The first reason is that it is easier to grasp data if they have been organized, and stating the way in which qualities are associated contributes to the organization of the data. In fact, it might be argued that knowing how qualities relate to each other is essentially what we mean by the phrase "understanding the way data are organized." But we search for association in our data not only because we are trying to make the data more orderly and easier to grasp, but also because we believe that by finding this organization in the data, we come closer to understanding the organization of qualities in the real world. We begin our research with the assumption that there is an organization of qualities in nature; that certain events or qualities or states are regularly related to other events or qualities or states. We also believe that we can develop informed theories about the nature of this organization by collecting relevant data and then searching for the associations within the data which must reflect the organization of events or qualities or states in nature.[2]

---

[1] Of particular value in making clear the implications of alternative specifications of "association" is William H. Kruskal, "Ordinal Measures of Association," *Journal of the American Statistical Association*, **53** (December, 1958). See also Robert H. Somers, "A New Asymmetric Measure of Association for Ordinal Variables," *American Sociological Review* (December, 1962), and Leo A. Goodman and William H. Kruskal, "Measures of Association for Cross-classification," *Journal of the American Statistical Association* (December, 1954).

[2] In this discussion, the terms "events," "qualities," and "states" may all be used. To an extent, these terms can be used interchangeably, but they suggest different ways of thinking about what is being observed or measured. "Quality" suggests an aspect of an entity. "State" suggests the overall condition or character of an entity. "Event" suggests something happening which may involve a number of entities, or may involve a change in state of an entity.

If we should find associations within our data, we should still not be satisfied if we could only say, "People who smoke seem to have more respiratory complaints than people who do not smoke," or "Workers whose performance is less satisfactory seem more closely supervised than workers whose performance is more satisfactory." We almost always want not only to know that two factors are associated, but also to have some idea of why the association exists. Most often, we look for a cause-effect relationship (or a series of cause-effect relationships) which will explain the observed association. There are other ways of "explaining" associations besides having it that one factor is the cause of the other, but in much quantitative work in social science the causal mode of thought is the most appropriate.[3] For one thing, if we can successfully demonstrate that one factor is the cause of a second, we have a basis for control. The demonstration that smoking is a cause of lung cancer makes clear how to go about avoiding lung cancer, where the weaker assertion that the two were associated did not. (It might, possibly, have been the case that high-strung individuals were particularly likely to smoke and also particularly likely to develop lung cancer, as was in fact argued, although not persuasively, by one scientist.) If it could be demonstrated that absence of access to social goals is a cause of delinquency, we should have available a guide to at least one route to the abolition of delinquency. There are other reasons, too, why causal explanations are desirable if they are available: they are neat, easily testable, make possible prediction as well as control, and are likely to lead to further investigation and further understanding.

[3] For a list of other categories of explanation see Mario Bunge, *Causality* (Cleveland: World Publishing, 1963), pp. 255–262. Another listing is given by Abraham Kaplan, *Conduct of Inquiry* (New York: Chandler, 1964), pp. 109–113. See also Ernest Nagel, *The Structure of Science* (New York: Harcourt, Brace, and World, 1961), Chapters 2, 3, and 4. Two examples of other ways in which association might be "explained" are the following. First, we might take associated factors as each properties of the same entity, in the way that wetness, a blue-green color, and tastelessness are each properties of water. Thus, crowded conditions, a high proportion of recent immigrants to the region, and a high delinquency rate may be seen as elements within the syndrome, "slum." See, in this connection, Bertrand Russell's discussion of "natural kinds," in *Human Knowledge, Its Scope and Limits* (New York: Simon and Schuster, 1948), pp. 317–318. Second, we might hold that two associated factors are each necessary to the maintenance of some system and that while neither causes the other, both must exist together or neither can exist at all. Thus, teachers and students are each necessary for the existence of schools, and where we find one we shall find the other, although neither causes the other. An excellent, although advanced, treatment of the idea of system is given by W. Ross Ashby in *Design for a Brain* (New York: John Wiley, 1960). There is an extensive literature on the closely related functional approach to explanation. Perhaps most relevant to the concerns of this chapter is Ronald R. Dore, "Function and Cause," *American Sociological Review*, **26**(6) (December, 1961), pp. 843–853.

What Do We Mean by "Cause"?

The idea of causation has been given a great deal of critical attention by scientists and philosophers. It has variously been held a phenomenon that cannot possibly be doubted, and an illusion; the essential element of all scientific law, and a category of thought that an advanced science will discard. The concept has been associated with attempts to understand the world about us, at least since Aristotle, who offered an analysis of the nature of causation. The concept was refined and reformulated through the Middle Ages and although its substance at times appeared elusive, few doubted that causal processes existed. With Hume's famous critique, the reality of the concept came into question. Bertrand Russell has written:

> We must ask ourselves: When we assume causation do we assume a specific relation, cause-and-effect, or do we merely assume invariable sequence? That is to say, when I assert "Every event of Class A causes an event of Class B," do I mean merely "Every event of Class A is followed by an event of Class B," or do I mean something more? Before Hume, the latter view was always taken; since Hume, more empiricists have taken the former.[4]

Before Hume's analysis, there was little question that we could identify situations in which one event, such as throwing a rock at a window, carried an "agency" sufficient to determine a subsequent event, such as a shattered pane. Hume pointed out that all we observe is invariable association, and that any concept of "agency" is contributed by our own minds. We can never see it, isolate it, sense it in any way. Since this is the case, he continued, why should we believe it actually exists?

We need not follow the shifting fortunes of the concept of cause since Hume's time, although it makes an interesting story. Many physicists, as the science of physics became more analytic, found that they could forego use of the concept entirely, and some philosophers of science began to believe that the concept was a relic from "ordinary" thought which ought to be discarded in scientific work as soon as sufficient progress was made.[5] Yet in some fields of study the search for causal linkages between factors is the heart of the endeavor; we have only to think of the development of the germ theory of disease, or, to keep closer to social science concerns, the search for the determinants of marriages that will work. In

[4] Bertrand Russell, *Human Knowledge, op. cit.* p. 454. Reprinted by permission of the publisher.
[5] See Bertrand Russell, *A History of Western Philosophy* (New York: Simon and Schuster, 1945), for articles on Hume and Kant. The very best discussion of causality that I have encountered is Mario Bunge, *Causality, op. cit.*, an erudite, closely reasoned, wide-ranging book.

these examples, we have in mind a kind of determination of one event or state by another that we can only call causal. Since the concept is important to us here and in many other instances, let us not discard it because it is philosophically controversial. Instead, let us be clear about what we mean by it, and under what circumstances we can propose that evidence supports a belief that it exists.

Bunge suggests that we think of a cause as an external producing agent. His statement of a causal relation is: "If C happens, then (and only then) E is always produced by it."[6] What we mean by the term "production" here is the bringing forth of something new. How this happens is a matter for theory. That we cannot see the production take place is not the insoluble difficulty it has been supposed to be by radical empiricists. If we have adequate reason for the belief, that is enough. "Causation" in Bunge's view, is one process of production (that involving an external agent) but not the only process of production. There are many others: for example, maturation, the production of something new as a result of growth, as when an adolescent boy finds it necessary to begin to shave. (This is not to say that the event cannot be explained causally, but rather that there are other styles of explanation as well.) Notice, in the definition of causation offered above, that invariable association is necessary for causation, but not itself enough. The weather in two neighboring cities may invariably be the same, but neither produces—brings forth—the other.

When we identify a series of events in which we believe one causes the next, we may speak of a causal line, causal process, or causal sequence. Russell has the following to say about "causal lines."

A "causal line," as I wish to define the term, is a temporal series of events so related that, given some of them, something can be inferred about the others whatever may be happening elsewhere. . . . That there are such more or less self-determined causal processes is in no degree logically necessary, but is, I think, one of the fundamental postulates of science. . . . That the universe is a system of interconnected parts may be true, but can only be discovered if some parts can, in some degree, be known independently of other parts. It is this that our postulate makes possible.[7]

"Causal line" is a useful concept for a number of reasons. First, it may identify the limit to which causal analysis may be pushed, since beyond some final event in a causal process it may be impossible—and unnecessary—to predict what will happen. For example, adequate communication may lead to (cause) shared understanding in a group, which may

---

[6] *Ibid*, p. 47.
[7] Bertrand Russell, *Human Knowledge, op. cit.*, p. 459. Reprinted by permission of the publisher.

lead to (cause) effective action, but what effective action leads to may be outside the sphere of the study, and difficult to guess. It is useful to consider the causal sequence as thereby limited. Second, the concept of causal line allows us to make explicit what we mean by a "chance event"; it is the intersection of unrelated causal lines. In addition the concept helps us understand the possible roles of third factors, as is indicated in a later section.

We almost never find invariable association in quantitative work, and yet we may nevertheless sometimes believe that two variables are causally related. We are able to maintain this belief by recognizing, implicitly, that (a) we never work with closed systems from which have been excluded other factors that might intersect the causal process we are studying; and (b) our measurements are subject to countless sources of imprecision. A causal rule can be required to hold invariably only so long as other things are equal, but in real situations other things are never equal.

It must be recognized that when we move from observation of an association to assertion of a causal connection we are inferring a good deal from the observation.[8] Showing that close supervision and poor productivity are *associated* does not demonstrate that one *produced* the other. Only an experiment can do this. Furthermore, even if an association between attributes leads us to accept that they are causally related, we are told nothing about the direction of causation. Nevertheless, when we observe a strong relationship between factors, it is natural to speculate about their possible causal connection, and sometimes we may introduce theory and argument enough to build a convincing case.

When involved in the analysis of quantitative data, we often reason that any causal connection would show itself by an association between variables in the data, and so if we search for associations, then even though we may pick up some that do not indicate underlying causal connections, we shall also pick up all those that do. It would then be our problem to examine the associations of interest and, with the help of theory and whatever internal evidence we can locate, decide which can be justified as the result of underlying causal connections.

This is essentially the approach advocated by John Stuart Mill when he proposed what he referred to as "experimental methods." We may use his suggested methods to make clear some frameworks for arguing that A causes B, although we must recognize that Mill's methods were not experimental methods as we understand the word "experiment" today,

[8] A discussion of possible bases for the imputation of causal significance to associations is given by Patricia L. Kendall and Paul F. Lazarsfeld in *Continuities in Social Research*, eds. Robert K. Merton and Paul F. Lazarsfeld (Glencoe: Free Press, 1950). See also Leo Srole *et al.*, *Mental Health in the Metropolis* (New York: McGraw-Hill, 1962), Chapter 2.

because they did not involve control of an independent variable. Instead, they were rules for locating possible causal relations.

Four of Mill's rules are the following (see Figure 9.1).

Rule 1 (The Method of Agreement). If two or more instances of the phenomenon under investigation have only one circumstance in common, the circumstance in which alone all the instances agree is the cause (or effect) of the given phenomenon.

Rule 2 (The Method of Difference). If an instance in which the phenomenon under investigation occurs, and an instance in which it does not occur, have every circumstance in common save one, that one occurring in the former; the circumstances in which alone the two instances differ is the effect, or the cause, or an indispensable part of the cause, of the phenomenon.

Rule 3 (Joint Method of Agreement and Difference). If two or more instances in which the phenomenon occurs have only one circumstance in common, while two or more instances in which it does not occur have nothing in common save the absence of that circumstance; the circumstance in which alone the two sets of instances differ is the effect of the cause or an indispensable part of the cause, of the phenomenon.

Rule 4 (Method of Concomitant Variation). Whatever phenomenon varies in any manner whenever another phenomenon varies in some particular manner, is either a cause or an effect of that phenomenon or it is connected with it through some fact of causation.[9]

An application of the Method of Agreement might be the assertion, which has sometimes been made, that smoking marijuana is causal to heroin addiction, because almost all heroin addicts at some previous time smoked marijuana. Mill's first rule would have it that this was an adequate demonstration of a causal relationship *if* it was also true that there was *no other factor* that the heroin addicts had in common. Is this true? Undoubtedly not. To point out the absurdity of the proposal that heroin addicts might have nothing more in common than their addiction and a history of smoking marijuana, it might be noted that, at some time, they had undoubtedly all taken aspirin. Of course, aspirin is not relevant to heroin addiction; but why believe that marijuana smoking is? It should be clear that the method of agreement will always break down because "instances of the phenomenon" will never have "only one circumstance in common."

An example of the Method of Difference might be offered by the appearance of character change in a patient under psychiatric treatment. Pre-

[9] John Stuart Mill, *System of Logic*, 1875, 2 Vols., published 1843. I am basing this discussion on quotations given by Morris R. Cohen and Ernest Nagel in *An Introduction to Logic and Scientific Method* (New York: Harcourt, Brace, and Co., 1934). I have omitted the "method of residues" since its examination would add little to the discussion of association.

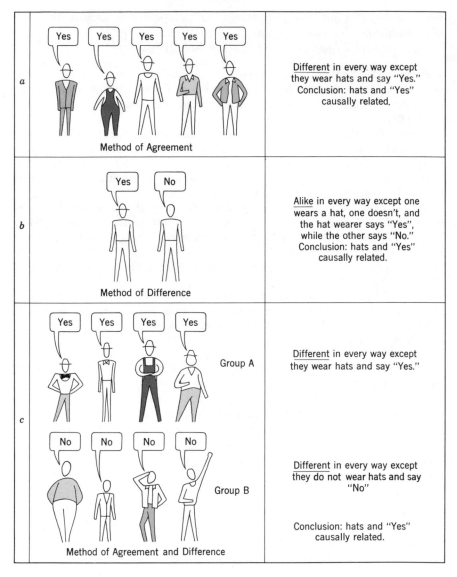

Figure 9.1 Diagramatic presentation of Mill's methods.

sumably his character did not change before he entered treatment; therefore, if his character changed after treatment, then treatment, as the only circumstance not common to the before and after situation, must be the cause of the change. The problem with this demonstration is, of course, the assumption that nothing else changed in the individual except his exposure to psychiatry. Yet the situation is not as grim here as it is in the former case. We can devise tests to check on whether other things have changed. Better yet, we can find a comparison case in which we will *not* introduce the presumed cause, and see whether the effect nevertheless occurs. Yet we would probably want many cases in both our "experimental" and our "comparison" group, to rule out chance factors. This brings us to Mill's next method.

The Joint Method of Agreement and Difference requires that we have two different groups, in each of which we have heterogeneity in every circumstance, except that the phenomenon of interest is always present in the first, while in the other the phenomenon of interest is always absent. If, despite our striving after heterogeneity, there is nevertheless some second factor, in addition to the phenomenon of interest, which is always present in the first group, and always absent in the second group, then this other factor is causally related to the phenomenon of interest. This method presents an idea we use again and again in quantitative work. When we control the introduction of the phenomenon of interest into the first group, we have the modern experiment.

We may modify this third method so that it is open to neither the objections directed at the first method nor those directed at the second. We need make no impossible demands regarding "different in all other ways," as we do in the first method, since ways in which *all* cases are alike occur in both the phenomenon-present and phenomenon-absent groups, and we may consider them irrelevant to the issue. (Another way of looking at the matter is that the groups are matched on these factors.) We may also amend this method so that it does not require that there be no other changes besides those in the phenomena of interest, as does the method of difference, since again we can consider changes which take place in both groups to be irrelevant.

A schematic table, Table 9.4, illustrates what is sought by Mill's third method, as amended.

Table 9.4 is the kind of table we look for when asking whether qualities are associated. If we should find association, we might still want to take one more step before we asserted that the qualities were causally connected: we might want to test that the cases in which factor and phenomenon are jointly present or in which factor and phenomenon are jointly absent are not alike in still other ways not common to all cases.

Table 9.4

A Schematic Table Reflecting the Presence of a Causal Relationship, According to the Joint Method of Agreement and Difference (Amended)

	Phenomenon Present	Phenomenon Absent
Factor present	Many cases, nothing else in common[a]	Few cases
Factor absent	Few cases	Many cases, nothing else in common[a]

[a] Except what is common to all cases.

Incidentally, Mill's rule requires that *whenever* the phenomenon is present, the factor is also present, and *whenever* the phenomenon is absent, the factor is also absent, but Table 9.4 has in its cells, "Many Cases" and "Few Cases," which is different from Mill's all-or-none stand. The justification for this is that Mill is presenting an idealized model, which may be approached, but will never be realized, by reality. There are always errors of measurement, incomplete control, and the like.

The fourth of Mill's rules, the Method of Concomitant Variation, is really a stronger statement of the third rule for the case of qualities that permit metric or ordinal measurement, and so can vary through a number of levels. The application of this rule is exactly like that of the third rule, except that, instead of setting up a four-cell table like that in Table 9.4, we set up correlations. For more on this, see Chapter 11.

Testing for the Presence of Third Factors

We have at least established the plausibility of a causal connection if we can demonstrate a strong, if not invariable, association and can argue the existence of a linkage. We need also to show that no other factors are held in common by cases in which factor and phenomenon are also present, which might account for the relationship observed between factor and phenomenon.

The technique for testing for a third factor is to hold constant a suspected factor and see whether the association between the two original factors remains. If it disappears, the original association may possibly, although not necessarily, have been spurious. As an example of a spurious association, it has been shown that towns that pay higher salaries to schoolteachers also have higher levels of alcohol sales. The conclusion that it is the teachers who buy the alcohol can be disproven by holding constant the wealth of the town, as indicated by average annual income of its residents. Then it will be found that within wealthy towns there is no association between teacher's pay and alcohol sales and also in poor towns there is no association.

A statistical example: a certain candidate has just won an election in a rural county, with 52% of the vote. A student of the election finds that the candidate actually lost the one city in the county, where he received only 44% of the vote, but won the election when he received 62% of the vote in the rural farms and towns. "Ah," he says. "It was the candidate's stand on issues important to farmers which gave him the election." But it is also the case that the candidate was identified with an ethnic group that was heavily represented in the rural areas, and more lightly represented in the city. Could it have been ethnic loyalty that was responsible for the apparent association between rural residence and vote for the candidate? The answer to this question is to be found by holding ethnicity constant, and seeing whether there then continues to be an association between region of residence and vote.

The original data are given in Table 9.5a; the results when ethnicity is held constant are in Table 9.5b.

Table 9.5a

Region of Residence and Vote, X County[a]

	Vote		
Residence	Supported Candidate	Against Candidate	Total
Urban	12,000 (44%)	15,000 (56%)	27,000
Rural	13,000 (62%)	8,000 (38%)	21,000
Total	25,000 (52%)	23,000 (48%)	48,000

[a] Fictitious.

Table 9.5b

Region of Residence and Vote, X County, Candidate's Ethnic Group Separated Out[a]

	Candidate's Ethnic Group				Population, Candidate's Ethnic Group Excepted		
Residence	Supported Candidate	Against Candidate	Total	Residence	Supported Candidate	Against Candidate	Total
Urban	5,000 (83%)	1000 (17%)	6,000	Urban	7,000 (33%)	14,000 (67%)	21,000
Rural	10,000 (83%)	2000 (17%)	12,000	Rural	3,000 (33%)	6,000 (67%)	9,000
Total	15,000	3000	18,000		10,000	20,000	30,000

[a] Fictitious.

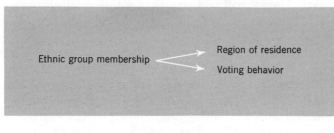

Figure 9.2

We see that when we hold ethnicity constant, in Table 9.5*b*, there is no longer any association between region of residence and vote. Eighty-three percent of members of the candidate's ethnic group vote for him, no matter where they live, and 67% of those not of the candidate's ethnic group vote against him, no matter where they live.

In this fictitious example, we have *explained* an association by finding a third factor that reduced the association to zero, and which also suggested that the original association was due to the existence of two causal lines branching off from the same fact of ethnicity (see Figure 9.2).

It is when we can assert that there are branching causal lines, as in Figure 9.2, that we describe the original association as spurious. We shall not always treat such situations in this way. In fact, there are three different ways in which we can imagine a third factor affecting an association found between two factors.[10] This is the first way, *where the third factor explains what is in fact a spurious association between factors or events that are not on the same causal line.*

Notice that even though the great majority of individuals who shared the candidate's ethnic background voted for him, still there was a minority who did not vote for him. We might surmise that the reason for this was that despite their similarity in background, they felt no sense of identification with the candidate. Suppose that we were able somehow to measure "sense of identification with the candidate," and that we proceeded to hold this constant, and then examined the relationship between ethnicity and vote. We might find that where there was an absence of sense of identification, neither those with the same ethnic background nor those of different ethnic backgrounds were likely to vote for the can-

[10] See "Problems of Survey Analysis," by Patricia L. Kendall and Paul F. Lazarsfeld, in *Continuities in Social Research*, Robert K. Merton and Paul F. Lazarsfeld, editors (Glencoe, Ill.: Free Press, 1950). The terms "explanation," "interpretation," and "specification" are theirs. See also, for an introduction to the problem of third factors, Hans Zeisel, *Say It with Figures, op. cit.*

didate, and those few votes he got were equally likely to come from either group. And we might also find that where there was identification with the candidate, there was an excellent chance that the individual would vote for him, but again there was no particular association between tendency to vote for the candidate and ethnicity. But here we should *not* say that the relationship between ethnicity and vote is spurious, and we have explained it by introducing the factor of identification with the candidate. Instead, we should say that likeness of ethnic membership is one factor among a number which seem to create a sense of identification with the candidate, and the sense of identification with the candidate is an important factor in disposing an individual to vote for him. We should, in other words, say that a causal line exists connecting ethnicity to identification with the candidate to voting. We might picture it in this way:

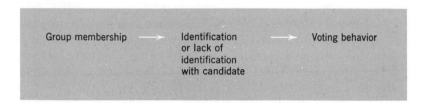

When we find a third factor which intervenes between a possible cause and a possible effect, we say that we have *interpreted* the cause-effect relationship. We have made clear the intervening states between presumed cause and effect, and have thus furnished a rationale—an interpretation— for the association. *A third factor interprets an association when it is shown to be an intervening factor or event on a causal line connecting the associated factors.*

Of course, a third factor that is offered as an interpretation of an association must have been able to occur between the time of occurrence of the cause and the time of occurrence of the effect. Ethnicity could not be an interpretive factor in the association connecting region of residence and voting since it could not have occurred between the time of occurrence of these other two factors.

Finally, in a situation called *specification*, we may find that the association between two factors seems to be affected by the value of a third factor as a catalyst affects the reaction between chemicals. When the third factor is present, or at a certain level, there is an association between the first and second factor. When it is absent, or at another level, the association changes. For example, we might find that when times are bad, members of labor unions vote for candidates endorsed by the union, while when times are good, members of labor unions do not pay attention to union endorsement when they vote. The nature of the economic situation might not be causally related to either union endorsement or to the vote of the individual member. Rather, the economic situation might be related to the existence of the relationship. The third variable here *specifies the conditions under which the relationship will exist.*

In specification, *the investigator shows that a causal link connecting the factors exists only under certain circumstances.* The demonstration is the same as is used in explanation or interpretation: the third factor is held constant. But here we should not expect that when the third factor was held constant there would no longer be association in our tables, but instead that the associations would be different, depending on the value of the third factor. This is, in fact, the hallmark of specification: *the nature of the association is different for different levels of the specifying factor.* For example, it has been found that individuals who have had first-hand contact with computers are slightly less likely than others to feel negatively toward computers: to believe, for example, that they are mechanical monsters who will one day turn on man. However, among those individuals who have long had technical interests, first-hand acquaintance is strongly associated with positive reaction to computers, while among individuals whose interests are primarily humanistic, in contrast, first-hand acquaintance may even make them slightly more antagonistic to the computer. The pervading interests of the individual *specify* the effect exposure to the computer will have.[10]

Let us put together the ideas of this section. We begin by recognizing that the demonstration that an association exists between two phenomena is necessary but not sufficient for the assertion that they are causally related. Their association might result from a causal connection that would take one of these forms: A produces B; B produces A; the two reciprocally produce each other, as the anger of one spouse may produce the anger of the other. We should diagram these possibilities in this way:

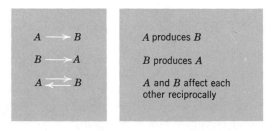

$A \longrightarrow B$ — A produces B

$B \longrightarrow A$ — B produces A

$A \rightleftarrows B$ — A and B affect each other reciprocally

[10] This example was suggested by Dr. Robert S. Lee on the basis of research conducted for a manufacturer of computers.

However, a third factor might be involved in the causal picture. It might have produced both A and B, in which case, because A and B are not on the same causal line, we say the association is spurious.

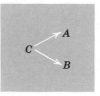

Or the third factor might come between A and B; A might produce C, which in turn produces B. In this case, we say the association between A and B is genuine, but is "interpreted" by the intervening variable, C.

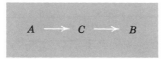

We can discover whether a third factor is associated with A and B in one of these two ways—either as a cause of each, or as an intervening variable—by holding the third factor constant. When we try out a suspected third factor by holding it constant to see whether this affects the association between A and B, we may call the suspected third factor a *test variable*. If a test variable *is* related to the associated variables in either of the above two ways, the association between A and B will disappear when the test variable is held constant.

Examination of survey data alone will not allow us to distinguish between a spurious association and an interpreted association. This is because associations in survey data do not tell us in which direction a causal process takes place; and if we reverse the direction of one arrow in the spurious association diagram, we shall get the interpreted association diagram. We can only decide which case we have at hand by considering the relationship of the three phenomena, A, B, and C, in time; or by in some other way applying understanding based on something beyond the data themselves.

There is a third way in which a third factor can affect the association between the two phenomena, which will look different in the data from the two described above. Here the association seems to change, depending on the value of the third factor. This we call specification. One form of it may be diagrammed in this way:

C present : $A \longrightarrow B$

C absent : A not related to B

PROBLEMS

9.1. In the following table, introduce numbers in the cells which would:
  (a) Indicate an absence of association.
  (b) Suggest that mobility is associated with a low level of tension.
  (c) Suggest that mobility is associated with a high level of tension.

		Tension Level		
		Low	High	Number
Mobility	Present			50
	Absent			150
	Number	100	100	200

9.2. Assume that you actually found the table you invented in response to 9.1(c). What further evidence might support each of the following:
  (a) The argument that a high level of tension is causal to mobility.
  (b) The argument that mobility is causal to a high level of tension.
  (c) The argument that mobility and tension level, although associated, are not causally related.

9.3. Suppose the following table were to turn up in a study of attitudes of high school students toward attending football games:

	Enjoy Football	Do Not Enjoy Football	Total
Boys	54 (57%)	41 (43%)	95 (100%)
Girls	25 (45%)	30 (55%)	55 (100%)
	79	71	150

This table suggests that a greater percentage of boys than of girls enjoy football. Suppose, however, that the boys and girls come from two kinds of high schools, academic and art, and if kind of high school is held constant, it no longer is the case that there is any association between sex and attitudes toward football. Assume there are 75 boys and 30 girls in the academic high school and 25 of the boys do not enjoy football. What would the complete tables, kind of high school held constant, look like?

9.4. Give examples different from those in the text for each of the three different reasons for introduction of a third factor changing a level of association.

Added in proof. The holding constant technique described in pages 170–176 will entirely remove the contribution of a third factor only if the subgroups of the third factor do not contain residual variation. This is pointed out by Travis Hirschi and Hanan C. Selvin in *Delinquency Research*, (New York, Free Press, 1967), pp. 50–51. The condition is met only if the third factor is inherently nominal and each of its subgroups contains only one of its values.

Chapter 10

Measures of Association:
Nominal Level Data

In Chapter 9 it was asserted that our intuitive idea of association is best represented by holding that two factors are not associated if subgroups of the one factor do not differ in their proportion in various categories of the other factor, and that two factors are associated if subgroups of the one factor do differ in their proportion in various categories of the other factor. But association may be strong or weak, and in addition to knowing whether association is present, we need some device for describing just how much association is present.

Literally dozens of different measures have been used for stating the amount of association in cross-classifications of nominal level data. Some of these represent different ways of specifying association; as was indicated in Chapter 9, association can be taken to mean a number of things that are generally, but not necessarily, to be found together.

Some measures of association have been in use for so long, and are so widely known, that they have assumed the status of "traditional" measures. Measures based on chi-square, and the measure Q, are of this sort. Measures based on chi-square have been criticized because their values are difficult to interpret. Nevertheless, we present them in this chapter because of their wide currency, and because they may yet have uses when an investigator wants to measure the extent to which a table departs from independence. This chapter will also present other measures that may be preferable to the traditional measures in some circumstances: the percentage difference, and measures of proportional reduction of probable error.[1]

---

[1] This chapter is indebted to the important articles on cross-classification by Leo A. Goodman and William H. Kruskal which appeared in the *Journal of the American Statistical Association:* "Measures of Association for Cross-Classifications" in Decem-

Criteria for a Measure of Association

A measure of association is a device designed to capture and communicate the level of association in a cross-classification. The following is a list of some properties we might reasonably expect this invention to have. As we shall see, no measure possesses all of them.

1. *Conceptualizability*. We would like any value of the measure to have an interpretation outside itself: to be something more than simply a number. If the value is 0.45, we should like to be able to say that this indicates a 0.45 reduction of probable error, or something like this, instead of being forced to say the 0.45 cannot be interpreted further. Some measures, however, permit no interpretation except that a higher value shows more association than a lower value. The traditional measures based on the chi-square statistic are notably lacking in this respect.

2. *Norming*. It is convenient to ask that our measure cover the same range that the measure of probability covers. A probability is zero if the event is impossible, one if the event is certain, and somewhere between zero and one if the event is neither of these. We may ask that the measure of association vary between zero, when there is no association, and one, when there is perfect association. If it is meaningful to speak of inverse association (which suggests order within the categories of each attribute), then we may want minus one to represent perfect inverse association. Not all measures satisfy these requirements. Measures based on chi-square sometimes do not have one as an upper bound. Measures of proportional reduction of probable error can be zero even when attributes are not independent of each other.

3. We want a measure that will *increase in response to increasing degrees of association:* that is, which will tend to give different values to tables that display different degrees of what we might intuitively call "association." The measures of proportional reduction of probable error are at least dubious in this respect.

4. *Invariance of the measure under proportional change in row or column frequencies.* We may want a measure that will not change if we increase the sample of cases in any row or column. For example, we should want a measure of the association between smoking and cancer to be the same whether we had one hundred smokers in our table or one thousand, even if the number of nonsmokers remained the same, so long as the proportion

---

ber, 1954; "Measures of Association for Cross-Classifications, II: Further Discussion and References" in March, 1959; "Measures of Association for Cross-Classifications, III: Approximate Sampling Theory," in June, 1963.

of afflicted smokers remained constant. (Another way of stating this criterion is to say that we want the measure to be independent of the marginal frequencies.) Some of the measures presented here (the percentage difference and Q) have this property; others do not. It is closely connected to the idea of one-way association, discussed below.

5. *Invariance under change in number of categories.* This may be a more debatable requirement than the others listed. Suppose that the data were originally given with many categories in each of the cross-classified attributes. We should want a measure that would be relatively constant whether the degree of association were calculated with the data in its original many-categoried classification or whether the degree of association were calculated with the data reclassified into just two large inclusive categories. It has been argued (by Pearson, the inventor of the measure,) that C, one of the measures based on the chi-square statistic, has this property under certain circumstances.

Different Types of Association: Asymmetric versus Symmetric; Mutual Implication versus One-Way Implication

One-way association refers to the extent to which one phenomenon implies the other, but not vice versa. Mutual association refers to the extent to which two phenomena imply each other. For example, innoculation against polio implies later freedom from polio, but the converse is not the case. The one-way association of innoculation and immunity is high; the mutual association may be rather low, depending on the population studied. If we want our measure to tell us the extent to which all A is B, but we do not care about the extent to which all B is also A, we want a measure of one-way association. If we want to know to what extent the two phenomena go together, we want a measure of mutual association.

Some measures of association give us different values depending on which phenomenon we start with. For example, if we ask the percentage difference of the incidence of B among different groups of A, the answer will be different, usually, from the percentage difference of the incidence of A among different groups of B. Measures that act this way are called *asymmetric*, because they may yield different values depending on how the table is looked at. Measures that give only a single value for a table are called *symmetric*.

All asymmetric measures are measures of one-way association. Some symmetric measures are measures of one-way association, too, however. Then it is up to the investigator to decide just which direction of implication is responsible, if the measure takes a high value.

In the following example, the one-way association of counselling with the absence of delinquency is complete. The first implies the second, in all cases. Mutual association is much weaker; the second does not at all imply the first.

	Delinquency	No Delinquency	Total
With counselling	0	10	10
Without counselling	50	40	90
	50	50	100

The following is complete mutual association:

	Delinquent	Not Delinquent	Total
Gang member	40	0	40
Not a gang member	0	40	40
	40	40	80

The Percentage Difference

A very simple asymmetric measure of association is the comparison of the percentages in different columns of the same row category, or in different rows of the same column category. Consider Table 10.1 which shows that when people talk politics, Republicans tend to talk to Republicans and Democrats to Democrats. We could simply note that there is a 41% difference between Republicans and Democrats in the party affiliation of the person last talked to about politics. This would be an example of the use of the percentage difference. (Note that we percentage along one variable and compare along the other.)

Table 10.1

Person Last Talked to about Politics—by Party Affiliation of the Respondent

Person Last Talked to about Politics	Affiliation of Respondent			
	Republican		Democrat	
Republican	118	75%	26	34%
Democrat	39	25	51	66
	157	100%	77	100%

Source: Berelson, Lazarsfeld and McPhee, *Voting* (Chicago: University of Chicago Press, 1964), p. 105. Reprinted by permission of The University of Chicago Press. Quoted by Morris Zelditch, Jr., in *A Basic Course in Sociological Statistics* (New York: Henry Holt, 1959), p. 132.

The percentage difference goes from 0% when there is complete independence to 100% when there is complete association in the direction under consideration. This 0 to 100 range can be changed to a 0 to 1 range easily by dividing the results by 100, but this usually is not done. Because the percentage difference has a clear conceptual meaning, communicated in the name for the technique, and because it is so easily calculated, it is a most useful measure of one-way association. However, the percentage difference is uniquely defined only when there are only two categories in the variable along which we percentage and only two categories in the variable within which we compare.[2]

When working with a table in which there are only two categories in each of the two variables of classification, and when concerned with one-way implications, there is much to recommend the percentage difference. It is easy to calculate and easy to understand, sensitive, norms properly, and captures directly an important, if not fundamental, intuitive idea of the nature of association.

Measures Based on the Chi-Square Statistic

Instead of comparing the subgroups within a table with each other, we might develop a measure by comparing the cells of the table with what would have been found had there been no association at all. Our concern would be with the extent of departure from independence rather than with the size of subgroup differences. Let us assume, in Table 10.1, that the number of Republicans, number of Democrats, number of Republicans talked to by respondents, and number of Democrats talked to by respondents, all remain the same. (Let us, in other words, assume that the marginals remain fixed.) Then, if there were no relation at all between the affiliation of the respondent and the affiliation of the last person he talked to about politics, we would have Table 10.2.

We can check that subgroups do not differ, in Table 10.2, by calculating the percentage differences. We shall find them to be zero.

Table 10.2 was constructed by *requiring* that the proportion of Republicans talked to by the Republican group be the same as the proportion of Republicans talked to by the Democratic group; which means that each would be the same as the proportion talked to by the population as a whole. In the population as a whole, 144/234 talked with Republicans. Therefore, it was necessary to have 144/234 of the Republican subgroup talk with Republicans, and 144/234 of the Democratic subgroup talk

---

[2] A generalization of the percentage difference which may be used with *ordinal* data of any number of categories is presented by Robert H. Somers, in "A New Asymmetric Measure of Association for Ordinal Variables," *American Sociological Review*, **27**(6) (December, 1962), pp. 799–811.

Table 10.2

Person Last Talked to about Politics, by Party Affiliation of the Respondent, on Assumption of Independence of These Characteristics

Person Last Talked to about Politics	Affiliation of Respondent		Total
	Republican	Democrat	
Republican	97	47	144
Democrat	60	30	90
Total	157	77	234

with Republicans, for the table to illustrate independence. We accomplished this by multiplying the number of Republicans (157) by 144/234, and the number of Democrats (77) by 144/234. The result is the top line of Table 10.2.

We now compare Table 10.1 and Table 10.2. In Table 10.1, the table of observed data, there is a surplus of 21 Republican-Republican conversations over the number in the corresponding cell in the expected table. Let us work with the squares of differences between the observed and expected rather than with the surpluses themselves; it turns out that the resulting measure has superior mathematical properties. Then we might imagine that the average of the 97 individuals in the Republican-Republican cell of the expected table would contribute 441/97 of a squared deviation to the final summary statement of discrepancies between observed and expected. (This is 21^2 divided by the number expected in the cell.) The average individual in the Republican-Democrat cell brought with him 441/60 of a squared deviation. Similarly, in the other cells, the average squared deviation would be 441/47 and 441/30. The sum of these average squared discrepancies is called chi-square. It will be zero when there is no discrepancy at all between observed and expected; that is, when the observed table displays no association at all. It will reach its maximum of $(r - 1)N$, where there are r rows and columns in the table, and there is complete mutual association. In a table of two rows and two columns, its maximum is just N, the total number in the table. In this table, chi-square is $441/97 + 441/60 + 441/47 + 441/30 = 35.9$.

The formula for chi-square, the sum of the mean squared deviations, is usually written:

$$\chi^2 = \sum \frac{(o - e)^2}{e}$$

The above formula should be read: chi-square equals the sum, over all cells, of the quotient of the squared difference between observed and expected, divided by expected.

Various suggestions have been made for developing a measure of association from the chi-square statistic. In a two-by-two table, a measure sometimes used is the "mean-square contingency," usually referred to as "phi-squared."

$$\phi^2 = \frac{\chi^2}{N}$$

The square root of this measure, phi ($\phi = \sqrt{\chi^2/N}$) is more commonly employed. Phi is a symmetric measure of the extent to which a table displays mutual association, as are all measures based on chi-square. It can be seen that it norms properly, since it will be zero when the observed table is identical to that expected on the assumption of independence, and one when chi-square reaches its maximum value, which is N. In distinction from other measures based on chi-square, ϕ does have an accessible meaning beyond itself, although it is not a clear one. This stems from the fact that tau$_b$ (τ_b) becomes ϕ in the 2-by-2 case. (The measure τ_b is described and an interpretation of it is given in the next chapter.) In addition, ϕ may be interpreted as the Pearson r (Chapter 14) for dichotomized variables.

There is another formula for ϕ which is mathematically identical to the definitional formula given above, but which may be more convenient computationally. The formula refers to the following schematic table:

	A Present	A Absent	
B Present	a	b	r_1
B Absent	c	d	r_2
	c_1	c_2	N

where a, b, c, and d are cell entries; r_1 and r_2 are row totals; c_1 and c_2 are column totals; and N is the grand total.

The formula is:

$$\phi = \frac{ad - bc}{\sqrt{r_1 r_2 c_1 c_2}}$$

It requires only simple algebra, although a lot of it, to show that this is identical to:

$$\phi = \sqrt{\frac{\chi^2}{N}}$$

A generalization of ϕ not limited to the 2-by-2 case is referred to as "T." This measure has the upper limit one when the table has as many rows as columns, but something less than one otherwise.[3] Its formula is:

$$T = \sqrt{\frac{\chi^2}{\sqrt{(r-1)(c-1)}N}}$$

where: r = number of rows; c = number of columns; and N = total in the table.

The oldest of the measures based on the chi-square statistic is due to Pearson and referred to as C, the Contingency coefficient. Its formula is:

$$C = \sqrt{\frac{\chi^2}{\chi^2 + N}}$$

This measure has as its upper limit something less than 1, although as the number of rows and columns increases, the upper limit approaches 1. For the 2-by-2 table, the upper limit of C is 0.71. This follows from the fact that the maximum value of χ^2 in a 2-by-2 table is N. Some investigators consider this a serious difficulty, although, since we can only judge Cs by comparison with other Cs in any event, the defect is hardly fatal. As we noted earlier, the measure has the interesting property that if the underlying distribution of the attributes being related to each other is of a certain sort,[4] then no matter how many categories are used to slice up the distribution into discrete portions, it will remain relatively constant. That is, given the proper underlying distribution, the same C may be expected if the distribution is divided up into a 2-by-2 table, into a 3-by-6 table, or into a 10-by-20 table. When the measure was first developed, this property was considered important. Now opinion is not so sure, because so few tables are encountered in which the underlying distribution is likely to be the required one.

To summarize: the measures based on chi-square are well known, but have in common (with the possible exception of ϕ) the defect of an absence of clear conceptual meaning. The upper bound of C varies depending on the number of rows and columns, and so does the upper bound of T

---

[3] A similar measure, due to Cramèr, replaces $\sqrt{(r-1)(c-1)}$ in the denominator by either $(r-1)$ or $(c-1)$, whichever is smaller.

[4] Bivariate normal.

unless the table is a square one. Otherwise the range of these measures is zero to one; they are zero if, and only if, there is complete independence and reach their maximum if, and only if, there is complete mutual association.

The Calculation of Chi-Square

Chi-square requires the cell-by-cell comparison of the observed frequencies with the frequencies that would have been expected if there had

Table 10.3

Reading of Comic Books, by Sex of Child, in San Francisco Tenth Grade Class

	Reading Habits			
Sex	Does Not Read Comics	Reads 1–8 per Month	Reads 9 or More per Month	Total
Boys	21	39	25	85
Girls	45	51	20	116
Total	66	90	45	201

Adapted from Wilbur Schramm, Jack Lyle, and Edwin B. Parker, *Television in the Lives of Our Children* (Stanford University Press, 1961), Table VII-24, p. 262. Reprinted by permission of Stanford University Press.

Table 10.4

Cell Entries for Expected Table

					Totals
	a	b			Row 1 total
					Row 2 total
					Row 3 total
Totals	Column 1 total	Column 2 total	Column 3 total	Column 4 total	Grand total

[a] The number in this cell is obtained by multiplying the Row 1 total times the Column 1 total and dividing by the Grand total.
[b] The number in this cell is obtained by multiplying the Row 1 total by the Column 2 total and dividing by the Grand total.

been no association between the attributes. Consider the data of Table 10.3.

Inspection of Table 10.3 suggests that the qualities are associated because the marginal proportionality of 85 boys to 116 girls is not maintained in the subgroups. Instead, there is slightly less than 1 boy to every 2 girls in the "does not read" subgroup and more boys than girls in the "reads 9 or more" subgroup.

The expected value in a cell is worked out by multiplying together the row and column totals for that cell and dividing the result by the grand total. This is shown schematically in Table 10.4.

The expected table would be as shown in Table 10.5.

Table 10.5

Expected Values Given Marginals of Table 10.3

	Did Not Read	Reads 1–8	Reads 9+	Total
Boys	28	38	19	85
Girls	38	52	26	116
Total	66	90	45	201

The entry in the "boys-did not read" cell is $(85)(66)/201$, and so on. Notice that the cell entries in the expected table add up to the original row and column totals.

Now list the observed and expected values, calculate the difference between them, square, divide by the expected values, and sum (see Table 10.6).

Table 10.6

Calculation of Chi-square for Data of Table 10.3

Cell	Observed	Expected	Difference	(Difference)^2	$\dfrac{(\text{Difference})^2}{\text{Expected}}$
Row 1, Column 1	21	28	7	49	1.75
Row 1, Column 2	39	38	1	1	0.03
Row 1, Column 3	25	19	6	36	1.89
Row 2, Column 1	45	38	7	49	1.29
Row 2, Column 2	51	52	1	1	0.02
Row 2, Column 3	20	26	6	36	1.38
				$\chi^2 =$	6.36

Q: A Measure Based on the Number of "Positive" and Number of "Negative" Pairs

All the traditional measures based on the chi-square statistic reflect the extent to which mutual association exists. Another widely used traditional measure, Q, although symmetric, reflects the extent to which one-way association exists in *either* direction; that is, it reflects the extent to which all A is B *or* the extent to which all B is A, whichever is the greater. In this respect, it differs from the other symmetric measures discussed in this chapter.

The idea behind Q is to summarize the results of a pairwise comparison of all entries in the table with all other entries. In this approach to measuring the extent to which attribute A is associated with attribute B, we examine every possible pair in our sample. If one member of a pair possesses both attribute A and attribute B, while the other possesses neither, we count it as one pair in which there is association. If one possesses attribute A but not attribute B, and the other possesses attribute B but not attribute A, we count the pair as one in which there is inverse association. If both possess either attribute A or attribute B, we say that the pair can shed no light on whether the attributes are associated, and we do not count it at all. (Of course, another measure could be devised in which we did count such pairs, perhaps considering them negative cases.) Finally, we subtract the number of pairs that indicate inverse association from the number of pairs that indicate positive association, and we divide the difference by the number of pairs considered relevant; that is, the number of pairs in which there was either positive or negative association. The result is Q. The formula for Q is a simple one. Consider the schematic 2-by-2 table, repeated below.

	A Present	A Absent	
B Present	a	b	r_1
B Absent	c	d	r_2
	c_1	c_2	N

All the pairs in which one member is from the a cell and one member from the d cell will show positive association between A and B. All the pairs in which one member is from the b cell and one member from the c cell will show inverse association between A and B. Pairs formed from

Table 10.7

Individuals Who Contracted Polio among Those Who Were and Those Who Were Not Innoculated, Community X (Fictitious)

Contracted Polio	Innoculated		
	Yes	No	Total
Yes	1	11	12
No	399	389	788
Total	400	400	800

other combinations of cells will be alike in possession of one or both attributes, and so will be irrelevant. The formula for the measure follows:

$$Q = \frac{ad - bc}{ad + bc}$$

This measure turns out to meet a number of criteria for a good measure in addition to the important one of clear conceptual meaning. It is unchanged by change in marginal frequencies, so long as the proportions within either the rows or the columns are unchanged. It varies between -1 and $+1$, although the negative values should be used only if ordering has more than a conventional meaning.

The data in Table 10.7 would best be represented by a measure that, like Q, reflects one-way association.

We are interested in the extent to which innoculation safeguards a person against contracting polio, but not in the converse; therefore, we want a measure of one-way association.

$$Q = \frac{389(1) - 399(11)}{389(1) + 399(11)} = 0.84$$

The value 0.84 has a clear conceptual meaning; it is the proportionate preponderance of relevant instances that support the idea that innoculation and freedom from polio are associated over relevant instances that support the idea that innoculation and the contracting of polio are associated. Note that Q, although it reflects one-way association, does not require that we treat the variables differently, as would the percentage difference; it gives a single figure for the table, as contrasted with the two figures that can be developed with the percentage difference. Note also that, as with any measure, Q may not capture the aspect of the table to which we want to direct attention. In this case, we might not be interested in the preponderance of evidence that innoculation helps over evidence that it *hurts*, but rather in the preponderance of evidence that innocu-lation helps over evidence that it fails to help. If this is the case, we might want to use the percentage difference, or we might want to devise still another measure that would exactly represent what we think to be important in the table.[5]

Measures Based on Reduction of Probable Error

Goodman and Kruskal have reintroduced a set of measures devised originally by Louis Guttman which propose to interpret the association between A and B in terms of the extent to which information about B helps in the prediction of A.[6] If A and B are independent, then knowing about B can have no value for making guesses about A. But if A and B are closely connected—if, for example, A is liberal political opinion, and B is a professional concern with social problems—then knowing B may help greatly in guessing A. Goodman and Kruskal propose that we take the extent to which knowing B helps as our measure of association. Clearly this would then be still another way of specifying what we mean by association, different from those previously discussed in the chapter. We shall call the various measures that result p.r.e. measures, for "pro-portional reduction of error."

1. *The asymmetric case.* Consider the data of Table 10.8. They deal with the relationship between becoming a partner or a permanent asso-ciate in a legal firm and having attended a public or a private secondary school. Both partners and permanent associates are permanent members of a firm, but partners share in the direction of the firm, and permanent associates, although guaranteed continuation of their jobs, do not have the authority or standing of partners.

Suppose we knew only that a man was a permanent member of a law firm. Should we guess that he is a partner or a permanent associate? Twenty-four of the 46 men listed in Table 10.8 are partners, and 22 are associates. If the individual about whom we are guessing is one of those listed in Table 10.8 (or if the table is a representative sample of the population of which the individual is a member), then we are

---

[5] One possibility is the ratio between the percentage difference along the innoculation dimension, and the percentage of those without innoculation who contracted polio. We might call this measure the percentage reduction. Another possibility, as is sug-gested in the text, is a variation of Q in which we consider as relevant all of the pairs that do not show positive association. Undoubtedly, still other measures, perhaps better than either of these, can be devised.

[6] See the articles by Goodman and Kruskal cited earlier. See also Herbert L. Costner, "Criteria for Measures of Association," *American Sociological Review*, **30(3)** (June, 1965), pp. 341–353.

Table 10.8

Type of Secondary School Attended, and Present Position, Members of Comparison Firm II

Secondary School	Partner	Permanent Associate	Total
Private	15	10	25
Public	9	12	21
Total	24	22	46

Adapted from Erwin Smigel, *The Wall Street Lawyer* (New York: The Free Press, 1964), Table V-3, p. 133. Reprinted with permission of The Free Press, A Division of The Macmillan Company. Copyright © The Free Press, 1964.

better off, although not much, in guessing that he is a partner. Suppose, however, that we were told that the individual we must guess about was a graduate of a public secondary school. Now the better guess is that he is a permanent associate rather than a partner, because of the 21 graduates of public secondary schools, the majority are permanent associates. The additional information about the individual's background helps us make a better guess about his present status.

How *much* better is our guess, knowing the school background of the individual? Without this knowledge, we should be mistaken 22/46 of the time; slightly less than half the time. With this knowledge, we shall be mistaken in 9 of the 21 cases of individuals with public school background and in 10 of the 25 cases of individuals with private school background; a total of 19 of the 46 cases. Our error has been reduced from 22 cases in 46 to 19 in 46; a reduction of probable error of 3 cases from the original 22. We take the proportional reduction of probable error as the measure of association in the table. Let us call the measure g. In this example, we have calculated the reduction of probable error in predicting present status when past schooling is given, which might be referred to as $g_{(position/schooling)}$; in words, "g of position, given schooling."

The formula for g when we are given the row variable and predicting the column variable is

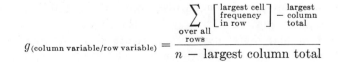

$$g_{(\text{column variable/row variable})} = \frac{\sum_{\substack{\text{over all} \\ \text{rows}}} \left[\begin{array}{c} \text{largest cell} \\ \text{frequency} \\ \text{in row} \end{array} \right] - \begin{array}{c} \text{largest} \\ \text{column} \\ \text{total} \end{array}}{n - \text{largest column total}}$$

In this case,

$$g_{(position/schooling)} = \frac{(15 + 12) - 24}{46 - 24} = \frac{3}{22}$$

$$g_{(position/schooling)} = 0.14$$

The value of g has the meaning that there is a 0.14 reduction in probable error in guessing position, when we are told about the individual's schooling. The value of g in the converse situation—guessing schooling when we are told about the individual's position—will be a different value. Asymmetric p.r.e. measures, like percentage differences, produce a different value for a table depending on the direction of association in which we are interested.

Of course the formula for $g_{(row/column)}$ is:

$$g_{(row/column)} = \frac{\sum_{\substack{over\ all \\ columns}} \left[\begin{array}{c} \text{largest cell} \\ \text{frequency} \\ \text{in column} \end{array}\right] - \begin{array}{c} \text{largest} \\ \text{row} \\ \text{total} \end{array}}{n - \text{largest row total}}$$

2. The symmetric case. The idea behind p.r.e. measures fits most naturally with an interpretation of Table 10.5 in terms of one-way association; how much does knowing A help us in predicting B. It is possible, however, to develop a symmetric measure of mutual association by assuming that half the time we are predicting in the one direction and half the time in the other. The formula that results is

$$g_{(symmetric)} = \frac{\sum_{rows} \left[\begin{array}{c} \text{largest} \\ \text{frequency} \\ \text{in row} \end{array}\right] + \sum_{columns} \left[\begin{array}{c} \text{largest} \\ \text{frequency} \\ \text{in columns} \end{array}\right] - \begin{array}{c} \text{largest} \\ \text{row} \\ \text{total} \end{array} - \begin{array}{c} \text{largest} \\ \text{column} \\ \text{total} \end{array}}{2n - \text{largest row total} - \text{largest column total}}$$

For the data of Table 10.4, we should calculate

$$g_{(symmetric)} = \frac{15 + 12 + 15 + 12 - 25 - 24}{92 - 25 - 24} = \frac{5}{43}$$

$$g_{(symmetric)} = 0.12$$

The symmetric measure is not quite as easy to interpret as the asymmetric p.r.e. measures. Here, for example, to give 0.12 meaning, we must say that it represents the reduction in probable error of prediction when we are given information about schooling half the time, and information about position the other half the time.

3. Adjusting marginals, asymmetric measure. P.r.e. measures have certain drawbacks that can sometimes be remedied by adjusting marginal frequencies. The measures are not very sensitive; it may take a shift in a good many cases to change the value of the measure. As a special case of this, there can be a good deal of association in the sense that the data may be far from exhibiting statistical independence, and yet the p.r.e. measure will be zero. In addition, p.r.e. measures have the characteristic, sometimes a drawback, of being affected severely by changes in marginal frequencies.

There does not seem to be any device for making p.r.e. measures more sensitive in general, but there is a useful device for reducing the importance of marginal frequencies. Consider again the data of Table 10.7:

| | Inoculated | | |
Contracted Polio	Yes	No	Total
Yes	1	11	12
No	399	389	788
	400	400	800

For the above data, we should have the following asymmetric measures:

$$g_{(\text{inoculated/polio})} = \frac{11 + 399 - 400}{800 - 400} = \frac{10}{400} = 0.025$$

$$g_{(\text{polio/inoculated})} = \frac{399 + 389 - 788}{800 - 788} = \frac{0}{12} = 0$$

These measures express the fact that knowing whether someone has polio helps us slightly in deciding whether he was inoculated, while knowing that he was inoculated does not in any way help us decide whether he had contracted polio. There is clearly an association between inoculation and not getting polio, but we cannot see it because the nonpolio group is so very large.

We can make clear that there is one proposition for which Table 10.7 offers strong support by an adjustment of the marginal values, but first let us attempt a logical analysis of the table. There are two different, although related, propositions that the table supports. The first proposition, on which we shall focus in this example, is that those inoculated against polio have a better chance of not contracting it than those not inoculated against it. This does not show up in the measure, since contracting polio happens so infrequently. Inoculation helps, but the disease occurs so rarely that it can hardly help much. The second proposition is that those who have contracted polio are much more likely not to have been inoculated than those who have not contracted polio. Here the relation appears stronger, since only one of the twelve of those who contracted polio was inoculated, while over half of those who did

Table 10.9

*Percentages of Individuals Who Contracted Polio,
among Those Who Were and Those Who Were Not
Inoculated,   Community X*

| | Inoculated | | |
Contracted Polio	Yes	No	
Yes	8	92	100
No	51	49	100
Total	59	141	200

$$g_{\text{(adjusted polio/inoculation)}} = \frac{92 + 51 - 100}{200 - 100} = .43$$

$$= \frac{43}{59}$$

$$= 0.43$$

not contract polio were inoculated.   Thus, knowing whether someone contracted polio should be of definite assistance in assessing whether he was inoculated.   We do not find this reflected in our $g_{\text{(inoculated / polio)}}$ because there are so few who contracted polio. But if we imagine that we have taken one sample of polio victims and a separate sample of individuals who did not contract polio, and that each sample represents 100% of some group, then we can calculate a new g that *will* reflect the connection between inoculation   and relative invulnerability to polio. Essentially, we develop a percentage table (Table 10.9), and recalculate g, now treating the percentages as though they were absolute numbers. In this way, we construct equal-sized samples.

We must be careful in the interpretation of g when it is based on a table in which we have adjusted the marginals. The value 0.43 is the reduction in probable error of prediction regarding adjusted polio when we are given information about having been inoculated,   when we assume that there are as many individuals in the population who have contracted polio as individuals who have not contracted polio, and when we assume that within each group the ratios of inoculated   to not inoculated   are the same as those observed in our original data. Thus, 0.43 is not a measure of association in the original table so much as it is a measure of the strength of support offered by our original table for a specific proposition. It would seem prudent not to calculate this new g if one of the marginal totals in the original table is very small—less than ten, for instance. Of course, the measure should be used only if the investigator is satisfied that it reflects what he considers the main feature of the data.

What Measure to Use?

Goodman and Kruskal conclude their first paper with this comment:

> The aim of this paper has been to argue that measures of association should not be taken blindly from the handiest statistics textbook, but rather should be carefully constructed in a manner appropriate to the problem at hand. . . . (Yet) this methodogically neutral position should not be carried to an extreme. . . . The artist cannot paint many pictures if he must spend most of his time mixing pigments.[7]

Certainly the most desirable course, if the time and skill are available, is to design for each study that measure which exactly reflects the aspect of the data with which the investigator is concerned. But, as the authors note, this is impractical in most cases; the investigator must work with what is available to him. The measures presented in this chapter hardly exhaust the list of measures available, but they do have some claim to being among the most frequently encountered for use with nominal data. Comparing them with each other, what can we say about them?

The percentage difference has the advantage of being easy to calculate, easy to talk about, easy to understand. When more than two categories are involved in the percentaging, there is a certain arbitrariness in how we calculate the measure. When only two categories are involved, and when we are interested in one-way association, there is much to recommend the percentage difference as a measure.

Traditional measures based on the chi-square statistic have had long years of use and as a result have developed about them an aura of legitimacy. They reflect only mutual association and if the investigator intends assessing one-way association, there is no point in using them. Even in relation to mutual association they have no easily grasped meaning, so that a C, for example, of 0.40 is simply a C of 0.40 and nothing more. (The measure ϕ is an exception to this statement.) However, it is possible to compare among Cs or among Ts, and the chi-square statistic that is their central component is often calculated for another purpose anyway (see Chapter 14).

The traditional measure Q does have a clear conceptual meaning and is a useful symmetric measure of one-way association. However, Q cannot be generalized to a table in which there are more than two rows and two

[7] Goodman and Kruskal, "Measures of Association for Cross-Classifications," p. 763.

columns unless the data are of ordinal level, and so for nominal level data the measure is available only for the 2-by-2 table.

The measures of proportional reduction of probable error, the various gs, are newer developments than any of the preceding, and it is difficult to judge whether they will prove useful only in special situations, or will have a broader range of applicability. One of the deficiencies of these measures is that they may remain zero even when there is some association, in the sense of nonindependence, in the data. Yet the measures have many arguments in their favor. They have, first of all, a clear conceptual meaning (although some of the clarity is lost when marginals are adjusted). In addition, unlike Q, they can be used with tables of any number of rows and columns. If an investigator wants to assess the degree of one-way association in tables greater than 2-by-2, he has available to him, of the measures discussed here, only some form of g and some adaptation of the percentage difference. In this circumstance, it would seem that unless there is a special reason for wanting to draw attention to a percentage difference, g would be the measure to choose.

PROBLEMS

10.1. For each of the cross-classification tables presented in Chapter 4, decide which measure of association you would use with the table. Defend your decision.

10.2. Calculate, for a table of Chapter 4, for which it is appropriate:
   (a) A percentage difference   (e) T
   (b) C (f) $g_{(column/row)}$
   (c) ϕ (g) $g_{(column/adjusted\ row)}$
   (d) Q

10.3. What characteristic of the data in Table 10.10 would you want to reflect in a measure of association?

Table 10.10

Occupations of Fathers and Sons in Fifty Families

Occupation of Son	Occupation of Father		
	Blue Collar	White Collar	Farming
Blue collar	8	5	4
White collar	7	20	1
Farming	0	0	5
	15	25	10

(a) What measure of association would you use? Why?

(b) Calculate the measure you decide on.

10.4. In describing Table 10.10 of Problem 3, how many different percentage differences could you report?

(a) Give two different percentage difference statements.

(b) Can you devise a measure that could summarize several or all of the percentage differences contained within Table 10.10? (This is a difficult problem, although there are many ways the task may be accomplished. You are being asked, of course, to develop a new measure.)

10.5. Consider how Table 10.10 of Problem 3 might be collapsed so that the use of Q would be appropriate. Is there a better way than the following?

Son	Father Urban Blue Collar or White Collar	Farming
Urban Blue Collar or White Collar	40	5
Farming	0	5

(a) Discuss why you believe the above is or is not the best way of collapsing the table.

(b) Discuss why you believe Q is or is not an appropriate measure.

Chapter 11

Measures of Association
in Ordinal and Metric Data

If ordinal and metric data are interpreted as nominal data, there is a loss of information. Although we always have the option of measuring association between qualities measured in ordinal or metric systems by first categorizing the data, and then applying the techniques described in Chapter 10, the loss of information this procedure entails will outweigh whatever increase in convenience it affords.

When working with ordinal or metric data, we more often speak of "correlation" than of "association." Correlation suggests two factors increasing or decreasing together, while association suggests two factors occurring together. A second modification of viewpoint in our discussion of these measures will deal with norming. When considering relationships between factors measured in ordinal and metric systems, the idea of inverse association has meaning; thus, a desirable range for a measure would be from -1, when there is complete inverse association, through 0, when there is no association, to $+1$, when there is complete positive association.

The Idea of Positive Pairs and Negative Pairs

Several measures of association in ordinal data depend on working out the number of pairs in which attributes are positively associated and the number of pairs in which attributes are negatively associated. One of these measures, Q, has already been discussed. Because the idea of counting positive and negative pairs is so important in ordinal measures, we here return to give it additional attention.[1]

---

[1] Measures based on the counting of positive and negative pairs are discussed by Maurice G. Kendall, *Rank Correlation Methods* (London: Drury Lane, 1948); Robert H. Somers, "A New Asymmetric Measure of Association for Ordinal Variables,"

Table 11.1

Pairings of Three Individuals Ranked on Two Qualities

Pairs		Rank in Math	Rank in Chess	Relationship of Abilities in Pairs
(1)	Andrew	1	2	Inversely related
	Burton	2	1	
(2)	Andrew	1	2	Directly related
	Chester	3	3	
(3)	Burton	2	1	Directly related
	Chester	3	3	

Suppose we have rankings of three high-school boys—call them Andrew, Burton, and Chester—on both ability in mathematics and ability in chess. The ranking on mathematics ability might be based on the order of grades on an examination; let us say that this order is Andrew, Burton, Chester. On the other hand, Burton is the best chess-player and Andrew is next best. We can form three pairs of the three boys and ask of each pair whether chess playing and mathematical abilities are associated.

The ranking, to repeat, is the following:

	Rank in Math	*Rank in Chess*
Andrew	1	2
Burton	2	1
Chester	3	3

The pairs are as shown in Table 11.1. Let us call the number of positive pairs where there is a direct relationship, P, and the number of negative pairs, where there is an inverse relationship, Q. Here $P = 2$; $Q = 1$. There is one more positive than negative pair.

Now let us suppose that we have not three, but thirty, boys ranked on both mathematical ability and chess-playing ability, and that they are classified into three groupings on each: high, medium, and low. Let us suppose that the data are as shown in Table 11.2.

American Sociological Review, **27** (December, 1962), pp. 799–811; Leo A. Goodman and William H. Kruskal, "Measures of Association for Cross-Classifications," *Journal of the American Statistical Association*, **49** (December, 1954), pp. 732–764; Herbert L. Costner, "Criteria for Measures of Association," *American Sociological Review*, **30(3)** (June, 1965), pp. 341–353.

Table 11.2

Thirty Individuals Ranked on Two Qualities

		Chess-Playing Ability			
		High	Medium	Low	Total
Mathematical ability	High	6	3	1	10
	Medium	4	5	1	10
	Low	0	2	8	10
	Total	10	10	10	30

Now we have $[(30 \times 29)/2] = 435$ different pairs. Listing and counting is impractical. How can we now work out the number of positive and negative pairs? Notice that if we take *any* boy from the high-high cell and *any* boy from the medium-medium cell, the result will be a positive pair. There are 6 boys in the high-high cell and 5 boys in the medium-medium cell and so we can make 30 different pairs, all positive, of boys from these two cells. Similarly, we can make only positive pairs if we take one boy from the high-high cell, and one boy from the medium-low cell, and so these two cells together form six positive pairs. In general, so long as the second member of a pair comes from a cell to the right of, and below, the cell of the first member of the pair, the result is a positive pair.

Similarly, if the second member of a pair comes from a cell to the left of, and below, the cell of the first member of a pair, the result is a negative pair. We can systematize the computation of the number of positive and number of negative pairs by developing a P-table and a Q-table to accompany the original table. In the cells, the P-table will list the number of *positive* pairs of which members of the corresponding cell of the original table are the first member. The Q table will list in the cells the number of *negative* pairs of which members of the corresponding cell of the original table are the first member. The cell values for the P table are found by multiplying the number of cases in the corresponding cell of the original table by the sum of all cases in cells to the right of and below its cell. The cell values for the Q table are found by multiplying the number of cases in the corresponding cell of the original table by the sum of all cells to the left of and below its cell. The system is pictured in Table 11.3.

There are a total of 203 positive pairs and 25 negative pairs, or a preponderance of 178 positive pairs. The preponderance of positive pairs, $P - Q$, is referred to as S: "sum of all pairs." If there are more negative than positive pairs, S will be negative.

Table 11.3

Thirty Individuals Ranked on Two Qualities: Calculation of P and Q

	Original Table				P Table		Q Table	
	High	Medium	Low					
High	6	3	1	10	96[a]	27	12	11[b]
Medium	4	5	1	10	40	40	0	2
Low	0	2	8	10	$P = 203$		$Q = 25$	
	10	10	10	30				

[a] This is $6 \times (5 + 1 + 2 + 8)$.
[b] This is $1 \times (4 + 5 + 0 + 2)$.

Measures of Association Involving S: the Goodman-Kruskal Gamma, and Kendall's Taus

A number of measures of association involving S have been suggested, all of which involve a ratio between S and a quantity which may stand for "maximum possible value of S" (the value of S which would be obtained if there were complete association between the attributes). The measures differ in what they understand as complete association. We shall consider three of the measures: the Goodman-Kruskal γ; the Kendall τ_a and the Kendall τ_b.[2] Only γ and τ_b seem to be in common use in social investigation; situations that would make τ_a the appropriate measure apparently are rarely encountered.

1. The Goodman-Kruskal γ takes as its maximum value the total number of pairs that may be assessed as positive or negative. It treats pairs in which there is the same value on either attribute (ties on either attribute) as irrelevant. Its denominator is therefore $P + Q$, and its formula:

$$\gamma = \frac{P - Q}{P + Q} \quad \text{or} \quad \frac{S}{P + Q}$$

It should be obvious that the measure Q, discussed in Chapter 10, is a special case of γ. The characteristics of γ are like those of Q: it is responsive to one-way association, but is symmetric; it varies between -1 and $+1$; it has a clear conceptual meaning: the proportion of positive pairs less the proportion of negative pairs.

[2] Others are suggested by Robert Somers in his "A New Asymmetric Measure of Association for Ordinal Variables," *loc. cit.*

2. Kendall's τ_a takes as its maximum value the total number of pairs that could be formed, given the number in the table. It implicitly compares S with the maximum value S could take, either in a positive or negative direction, if there were no ties and every pair formed from instances in the table were positive or negative. If there are n instances in the table, a total of $[n(n-1)]/2$ pairs might be formed, and so the formula for τ_a is:

$$\tau_a = \frac{P - Q}{1/2[n(n-1)]} \quad \text{or} \quad \frac{S}{1/2[n(n-1)]}$$

In most contingency tables, the limits of τ_a are fairly low, because the denominator will be much larger than $P + Q$.

3. Kendall's τ_b takes as its maximum value what would be the total number of pairs if there were complete mutual association, and the ties were discounted as irrelevant. For complete mutual association to be possible, the marginals of the table must be the same, as in Table 11.4.

Table 11.4

An Example of a Table in which Marginal Values are Identical in Rows and Columns

	B_1	B_2	B_3	
A_1	5	0	0	5
A_2	0	12	0	12
A_3	0	0	8	8
	5	12	8	25

In this table, there are not $[25(24)]/2 = 300$ distinct pairs because there are ties on both dimensions among, respectively, five, twelve, and eight pairs. Each set of ties reduces the total number of positive or negative pairs by $[t(t-1)]/2$, where t is the length of a tie. There are, as a result,

$$300 - \frac{5(4)}{2} - \frac{12(11)}{2} - \frac{8(7)}{2} = 300 - 10 - 66 - 28$$

$$= 196 \text{ positive or negative pairs}$$

We can corroborate this easily enough. There are no negative pairs, and the number of positive pairs is $5(12 + 8) + 12(8) = 196$.

Let us refer to the marginal values in the row variables as r_1, r_2, and so on, and to the marginal values in the column variables as c_1, c_2, and so on.

In the very special case where the row marginals and column marginals are the same, the denominator of τ_b (for the case of three rows and columns) is

$$\frac{1}{2}n(n-1) \qquad \frac{r_1(r_1-1)}{2} - \frac{r_2(r_2-1)}{2} - \frac{r_3(r_3-1)}{2}$$

since this is the total number of untied pairs, assuming complete mutual association. Ordinarily, however, we shall not have the same numbers in both the row marginals and the column marginals. We must, therefore, take as our denominator an estimate of what would be the total number of pairs if there *were* the same marginal values both in rows and columns, and also complete mutual association between the attributes. A reasonable estimate is the square root of the product of the value we should give the denominator if the row marginals were the same as the column marginals, and the value we should give the denominator if the column marginals were the same as the row marginals.[3]

Imagine that the marginals of the table are represented as follows:

			r_1
			r_2
			r_3
			r_4
c_1	c_2	c_3	n

Let
$$C = \frac{c_1(c_1-1)}{2} + \frac{c_2(c_2-1)}{2} + \frac{c_3(c_3-1)}{2}$$

and
$$R = \frac{r_1(r_1-1)}{2} + \frac{r_2(r_2-1)}{2} + \frac{r_3(r_3-1)}{2} + \frac{r_4(r_4-1)}{2}$$

Then
$$\tau_b = \frac{P-Q}{\sqrt{[1/2n(n-1)-C][1/2n(n-1)-R]}}$$

or
$$\tau_b = \frac{S}{\sqrt{[1/2n(n-1)-C][1/2n(n-1)-R]}}$$

There is a simpler formula for τ_b which is algebraically equivalent to the above. Let us use Σc^2 to mean the sum of the squares of the column

[3] Kendall's rationale for the denominator for τ_b is different. See his *Rank Correlation Methods, op. cit.*, pp. 25–26.

totals, and Σr^2 to mean the sum of the squares of the row totals. Then τ_b can be written in this way:

$$\tau_b = \frac{2S}{\sqrt{(n^2 - \Sigma c^2)(n^2 - \Sigma r^2)}}$$

Both τ_a and τ_b reflect the extent to which the table exhibits mutual association between the attributes. In some ways, they resemble the measures based on the chi-square statistic, which also reflect the extent to which there is mutual association. The maximum value of τ_b is less than 1 except when there are the same number of rows and columns and when the marginal values of the rows and columns are the same. In the 2-by-2 table, τ_b and ϕ are identical.

When should each measure be used? All the measures discussed in this section are symmetric, but the Goodman-Kruskal γ reflects the extent to which one-way association exists, and the Kendall τ measures reflect the extent to which mutual association exists. The nature of the question being asked of the data should decide between gamma and one of the taus.

It would seem that τ_a should be used in preference to τ_b only when the investigator has some reason to believe that ties are relevant cases against the interpretation of association. Such a case might occur if the investigator were assessing the extent to which there was association between some attribute that he knew to be untied—as, for example, ranking in a prestige hierarchy—and some other attribute. Except in these special

Table 11.5

Ordinal Position and Fighter Pilot Effectiveness, Men Whose Families Included Four or More Children[a]

Ordinal Position in Family	Fighter Pilot Effectiveness			Total
	Ace	Near-Ace	Non-Ace	
First-born	1	1	3	5
Second-born	1	4	1	6
Third-born	4	4	2	10
Fourth-born	4	2	2	8
Total	10	11	8	29

[a] Adapted from Stanley Schachter, *The Psychology of Affiliation,* (Stanford University Press, 1959), Table 26, p. 75. Reprinted by permission of Stanford University Press.

cases, the assumptions of τ_b are much closer than those of τ_a to the questions we bring to contingency tables.

A study of the incidence of anxiety conditions within individuals who were first-born, second-born, third-born, and so on, examined, in passing, the relationship between ordinal position in the family and success as a fighter pilot in the Korean War. The data, for men who came from families of four or more children, are given in Table 11.5.

The P table and Q table are as follows.

P Table Q Table

15	5		9	57
10	16		32	14
16	8		16	12

$P = 70$ $Q = 140$

$$S = P - Q = -70$$

$$\gamma = \frac{S}{P + Q} = \frac{-70}{210} = -0.33$$

$$\tau_a = \frac{S}{1/2n(n-1)} = \frac{-70}{406} = -0.17$$

$$\tau_b = \frac{2S}{\sqrt{(n^2 - \Sigma c^2)(n^2 - \Sigma r^2)}}$$

$$= \frac{-140}{\sqrt{[29^2 - (10^2 + 11^2 + 8^2)][29^2 - (5^2 + 6^2 + 10^2 + 8^2)]}}$$

$$= \frac{-140}{\sqrt{(556)(616)}}$$

$$= -0.24$$

The γ of -0.33 indicates that among pairs where there was difference both in ordinal position and combat achievement, the proportion in which low ordinal position went with high achievement was 0.33 greater than the proportion in which high ordinal position went with high achievement.

The τ_a of -0.17 indicates that the proportion of all pairs, tied as well as untied, in which there was an inverse relationship, is 0.17 greater than the proportion of all pairs in which there was a direct relationship.

The τ_b of -0.24 may be interpreted as the proportion of an estimate of all untied pairs that could be formed (if there were complete mutual association) in which there was a direct relationship, less the analogous proportion in which there was an inverse relationship.

ASSOCIATION OF METRIC MEASUREMENTS: THE PEARSON PRODUCT-MOMENT CORRELATION COEFFICIENT

When we are working with interval or ratio data we can ask not only the ordinal question, "To what extent is it true that the more you have of the one quality, the more you have of the other?", but also the metric question, "To what extent is it true that an increase *of a certain number of units* in the one quality produces an increase *of a related number of units* in the other?" Generally, when we ask this question, we want to know the extent to which there is a *linear relationship* between the qualities, a situation in which a change of a certain number of units in the one quality results in a proportionate change in the other quality. When qualities are linearly related, a graph of observations showing the values of the one quality for specific values of the other would be a straight line. For example, suppose there were a linear relationship between the number of crimes committed in a city and the amount of alcohol sold in that city, with one crime committed for every ten barrels of alcohol. If one hundred barrels of alcohol were sold, there would be ten crimes; if a thousand

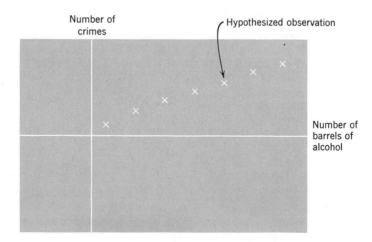

Figure 11.1

barrels were sold, there would be one hundred crimes; and so on. If we were to graph our observations, we should have the picture in Figure 11.1.

All the observations would lie along a straight line, whose equation would be:

$$\text{Number of crimes} = k \text{ number of barrels}$$

$$(k = \text{a constant})$$

Or, because we are representing the number of crimes along what is conventionally called "the y axis," and the number of barrels of alcohol along what is conventionally called "the x axis," we could write:

$$y = kx \quad \text{or} \quad \text{if } k = \frac{1}{10}$$

$$y = \frac{1}{10} x$$

So long as the association between number of crimes and barrels of alcohol is perfect, all the observations will lie on the line defined by the above equation. If the association is strong, but less than perfect, some observations would lie near the line but not on it. Actually, when we plot observations on a graph there is no "line." The line is something we imagine, a representation of what would exist if we had perfect association, and a model in terms of which we evaluate the degree of association that actually exists. If we have no association, or only very weak association in our data, our observations will not suggest a line at all.

We can make these ideas more precise by adopting a standard way for graphing observations. We draw two axes at right angles to each other, the one representing one of the qualities, the other representing the other quality. We mark off values on the two axes in such a way that the mean values of each quality will fall at the point where the axes cross. We then mark off each of the axes in units whose size is determined by the values of the observations, so that the length of the range of observations of the one quality is about the same as the length of the range of observations of the other quality.

This is done in Figure 11.2, where four possible graphings of observations of the relationship between income and age are shown. The markings of the x and y axes are shown only in Figure 11.2a, and are to be understood as the same in Figures 11.2b, c, and d.

We can characterize those observations that have values greater than the average on either quality as deviating in a positive direction on that quality, and those that have values less than the average value as deviating in a negative direction. In Figure 11.3, the character of different deviations is indicated.

A plausible way of summarizing the degree of association between qualities is to add together *the products of the deviations from the mean on the one quality and deviations from the mean on the other quality.*

If the deviations are in the same direction, as is true for observations that are graphed into the upper right quadrant and the lower left quadrant, then the product of the deviations will be positive. If the deviations are in different directions, as is true in the upper left quadrant and the

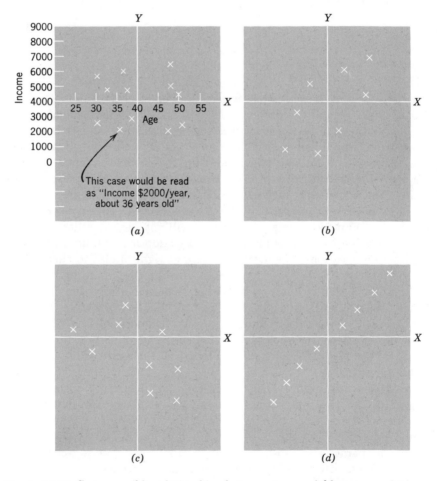

Figure 11.2 Some possible relationships between two variables: age and income (fictitious). Cases are indicated by an *X*. (*a*) No association. (*b*) Positive association. (*c*) Negative association. (*d*) Perfect positive association.

y Axis

In this quadrant $(x - \bar{x})$ is negative while $(y - \bar{y})$ is positive.	Observations in this quadrant are greater than average on both qualities: $(x - \bar{x})$ and $(y - \bar{y})$ are positive.
Observations in this quadrant are less than average on both qualities: $(x - \bar{x})$ and $(y - \bar{y})$ are negative.	In this quadrant $(x - \bar{x})$ is positive while $(y - \bar{y})$ is negative.

x Axis

Figure 11.3 Character of deviations which fall in each of four quadrants. (Axes are assumed to cross at mean value of each quality.)

lower right quadrant, then the product of the deviations will be negative. If all the products of the deviations are positive, then their sum will be positive and large. If all the products of the deviations are negative, then their sum will be negative and large. If some of the products are positive and some of the products are negative, as is true in Figure 11.2a, then the sum of the products will be close to zero.

We may form a measure of association by dividing the sum of the cross-products by the maximum value this sum can take.

It may be intuitively apparent that the sum of the cross-products of the deviations will be a maximum when all the observations lie along a straight line, as is true in Figure 11.2d. If the observations lie along a straight line, then there is a simple equation that connects the y-deviations and the x-deviations:

$$(y - \bar{y}) = k(x - \bar{x})$$

where k is a constant.

When this is true—when the sum of the products is at its maximum, and a straight line connects all observations—then the sum of the deviation products can be written two different ways, the first resulting when we substitute for $(y - \bar{y})$ and the second when we substitute for $(x - \bar{x})$.

(1) $\max \Sigma(x - \bar{x})(y - \bar{y}) = \Sigma(x - \bar{x})k(x - \bar{x}) = k\Sigma(x - \bar{x})^2$

or

$$(2) \quad \max \Sigma(x - \bar{x})(y - \bar{y}) = \Sigma \frac{1}{k}(y - \bar{y})(y - \bar{y}) = \frac{1}{k}\Sigma(y - \bar{y})^2$$

We can eliminate the constant of proportionality, k, by multiplying equations (1) and (2) together. Then we have:

$$\max [\Sigma(x - \bar{x})(y - \bar{y})]^2 = \Sigma(x - \bar{x})^2\Sigma(y - \bar{y})^2$$

Taking the square root

$$\max \Sigma(x - \bar{x})(y - \bar{y}) = \sqrt{\Sigma(x - \bar{x})^2\Sigma(y - \bar{y})^2}$$

We can form a measure of correlation by taking the ratio between the observed sum of the deviation products and the maximum value that the sum of the deviation products can take. This correlation coefficient is symbolized as r and is referred to as "the Pearson product-moment correlation coefficient."[4] Its formula is:

$$r = \frac{\Sigma(x - \bar{x})(y - \bar{y})}{\sqrt{\Sigma(x - \bar{x})^2\Sigma(y - \bar{y})^2}} \qquad \text{(definitional formula)}$$

The definitional formula of the correlation coefficient is not the formula used for computation. It may be instructive, nevertheless, to apply it to

Table 11.6

Physician	Years of Postgraduate Medical Education	Income (in Thousands)
A	0	30
B	2	20
C	5	10
D	3	50
E	0	40

[4] The coefficient is due to Karl Pearson, who developed many of the basic ideas of statistical work. The name "product-moment" refers to a concept important in theoretical statistics. Many of the important characteristics of a distribution can be diecussed as "moments" of the distribution. In a univariate distribution, the mean is ths first moment, and the variance—the squared standard deviation—the second moment. In a bivariate distribution, the moment given by the mean of the product of the deviations is known as the "first product-moment." More on this topic can be found in G. Udny Yule and M. G. Kendall, *An Introduction to the Theory of Statistics*, (14th ed.; New York: Hafner, 1950).

a simple example. Suppose that we have the figures in Table 11.6, on income and education, for a group of physicians.

To apply the *definitional* formula, we first calculate the mean value of the group on each of the two qualities. We then calculate differences from the mean, form the products and the squares of these, sum, and introduce the sums into the formula. The process is shown below.

Ind	x (first quality)	y (second quality)	$(x - \bar{x})$	$(x - \bar{x})^2$	$(y - \bar{y})$	$(y - \bar{y})^2$	$(x - \bar{x})(y - \bar{y})$
A	0	30	−2	4	0	0	0
B	2	20	0	0	−10	100	0
C	5	10	3	9	−20	400	−60
D	3	50	1	1	20	400	20
E	0	40	−2	4	10	100	−20
	$\Sigma x = 10$	$\Sigma y = 150$		$\Sigma(x - x)^2 = 18$		$\Sigma(y - y)^2 = 1000$	$\Sigma(x - x)(y - y) = -60$
	$\bar{x} = 2$	$\bar{y} = 30$					

$$r = \frac{\Sigma(x - \bar{x})(y - \bar{y})}{\sqrt{\Sigma(x - \bar{x})^2 \Sigma(y - \bar{y})^2}}$$

$$r = \frac{-60}{\sqrt{(18)(1000)}}$$

$$r = -\frac{60}{\sqrt{18,000}}$$

$$r = -\frac{60}{134.2}$$

$$r = -0.45$$

The problem with using the definitional formula in computation is that it requires us to calculate differences from the mean for each of our cases; if the mean is an awkward figure, this results in a concentration of awkwardness. We might recall the difficulty encountered in using the definitional formula for the standard deviation. We there stated that some simple algebra would take the standard deviation to a form that made calculations more nearly straightforward. The same can be done here. In fact, there is a relationship between the standard deviations of the two qualities that are being correlated and their correlation coefficient which it is useful to examine.

Consider the definitional formula for the correlation coefficient:

$$r = \frac{\Sigma(x - \bar{x})(y - \bar{y})}{\sqrt{\Sigma(x - \bar{x})^2 \Sigma(y - \bar{y})^2}}$$

Divide numerator and denominator by N:

$$r = \frac{\dfrac{\Sigma(x - \bar{x})(y - \bar{y})}{N}}{\sqrt{\dfrac{\Sigma(x - \bar{x})^2}{N}\dfrac{\Sigma(y - \bar{y})^2}{N}}}$$

$$r = \frac{\dfrac{\Sigma(x - \bar{x})(y - \bar{y})}{N}}{\sqrt{\dfrac{\Sigma(x - \bar{x})^2}{N}}\sqrt{\dfrac{\Sigma(y - \bar{y})^2}{N}}}$$

$$r = \frac{\dfrac{\Sigma(x - \bar{x})(y - \bar{y})}{N}}{\sigma_x \sigma_y}$$

(Note that

$$\sqrt{\frac{\Sigma(x - \bar{x})^2}{N}} = \sigma_x$$

And

$$\sqrt{\frac{\Sigma(y - \bar{y})^2}{N}} = \sigma_y \Bigg)$$

The correlation coefficient can thus be seen as a ratio of the quantity $[\Sigma(x - \bar{x})(y - \bar{y})]/N$ to the product of standard deviations. Computing forms for the standard deviations were presented in Chapter 7 and can be adopted here. A computing form for the numerator of the correlation coefficient can be developed by noting that it is like a standard deviation in which we have multiplied $(x - \bar{x})$ by $(y - \bar{y})$ instead of multiplying $(x - \bar{x})$ by $(x - \bar{x})$ or $(y - \bar{y})$ by $(y - \bar{y})$.

When we substitute appropriate computing forms we get:

$$r = \frac{N\Sigma xy - (\Sigma x)(\Sigma y)}{\sqrt{N\Sigma x^2 - (\Sigma x)^2}\sqrt{N\Sigma y^2 - (\Sigma y)^2}} \qquad (\textit{Computing formula})$$

Let us apply this to the simple example worked out above. Notice that we need six quantities for the formula: N, Σx, Σx^2, Σy, Σy^2, and Σxy. We can get these best on a calculating machine. This example, however, is simple enough to do easily without a machine.

Ind	x	y	x^2	y^2	xy
A	0	30	0	900	0
B	2	20	4	400	40
C	5	10	25	100	50
D	3	50	9	2500	150
E	0	40	0	1600	0
$N = 5$	$\Sigma x = 10$	$\Sigma y = 150$	$\Sigma x^2 = 38$	$\Sigma y^2 = 5500$	$\Sigma xy = 240$

$$r = \frac{N\Sigma xy - (\Sigma x)(\Sigma y)}{\sqrt{N\Sigma x^2 - (\Sigma x)^2}\sqrt{N\Sigma y^2 - (\Sigma y)^2}}$$

$$r = \frac{5(240) - (10)(150)}{\sqrt{5(38) - (10)^2}\sqrt{5(5500) - (150)^2}}$$

$$r = \frac{1200 - 1500}{\sqrt{190 - 100}\sqrt{27,500 - 22,500}}$$

$$r = \frac{-300}{\sqrt{90}\sqrt{5000}}$$

$$r = \frac{-300}{\sqrt{450,000}}$$

$$r = \frac{-300}{100\sqrt{45}}$$

$$r = \frac{-3}{6.71}$$

$$r = -0.45$$

Using the computing formula and a calculating machine, there is not much more work in computing a correlation coefficient based on many cases, involving awkward figures, than there was in computing this correlation coefficient.

As in calculation of mean and of standard deviation, there are rules for changing scale when calculating the correlation coefficient which may sometimes be helpful. The rules here are the simplest possible. *No change in scale of the kind we have previously considered* (that is, addition, subtraction, multiplication, or division of each of the observations by a constant) *will affect the correlation coefficient.* Specifically:

(1) We can change each observation by adding or subtracting a constant amount without changing the correlation coefficient.

(2) We can change each observation by multiplying or dividing by a constant amount without changing the correlation coefficient.

Calculation of the Product-Moment Correlation
Coefficient when Working with Grouped Data

The product-moment correlation coefficient is somewhat awkward to calculate when working with data that are in the form of a contingency table. The general procedure is to give each cell of the contingency table an x value, y value, x^2 value, y^2 value, and xy value; then to multiply the frequency within the cell by each of these values; and finally, to sum the products over the entire table. An illustration of the procedure is given below.

Burgess and Cottrell[5] have attempted to correlate a "prediction score" based on background factors and an "adjustment score" relating current marital happiness, for 519 couples. Each of the couples filled in a questionnaire giving the investigators information on many aspects of their background and also of their current adjustment. The background factors (which included such things as health, education, earnings, friendships, length of courtship, and happiness of parents' marriage) were each rated on an appropriate scale, and the ratings added to make up the prediction score. A similar procedure was used in making up the adjustment score. The final adjustment scores were divided into four roughly equal groups, and labelled "very low," "low," "high," and "very high." For purposes of this example, these groups will be treated as though they had been rated 1, 2, 3, and 4: in other words, the ordinal information about quality of information will be treated as though it were metric. This is not a procedure we endorse, even though it is sometimes used by expert investigators. We do it here partly because it is so difficult to find metric data in the research literature that would be of interest to sociologists. The results obtained in Burgess and Cottrell are presented in Table 11.7.

In calculating the correlation coefficient for the data in Table 11.7, we shall treat the marital adjustment scores as the x scores and the prediction scores as the y scores. As they presently stand, the prediction scores pose two problems. First, each category represents a range of scores, rather than a single score, and we shall have to choose some one score to represent the entire range. Second, the numbers are large and we should prefer smaller, easier to work with, numbers. The first problem is easily settled. We shall use the midpoint of the range as our estimate of a

---

[5] See Ernest W. Burgess and Leonard S. Cottrell, Jr., "The Prediction of Adjustment in Marriage," in Paul F. Lazarsfeld and Morris Rosenberg (eds.), *The Language of Social Research* (Glencoe: Free Press, 1955), pp. 268–276. Reprinted with permission of the Free Press, a division of the Macmillan Company.

Table 11.7

Prediction Scores and Marriage Adjustment Scores for 519 Couples

| Prediction Score | Marriage Adjustment Scores | | | | Total |
	(Very Low) 1	(Low) 2	(High) 3	(Very High) 4	Number
700–779	0	1	1	8	10
620–699	1	8	17	40	66
540–619	8	30	40	59	137
460–539	47	50	44	29	170
380–459	37	29	14	13	93
300–379	20	9	4	2	35
220–299	6	2	0	0	8
Total	119	129	120	151	519

single value that can stand for all the values in the category. The mid-point of the 700 to 779 category will be 740, and so on. Actually, however, we do not even have to calculate the midpoints. Notice that each category covers a range of 80 points. Whatever the specific values of midpoints of the categories, each midpoint will be just 80 points away from the next midpoint. Let us change the scale, remembering that any change of scale that involves only addition, subtraction, multiplication, and division will not affect the correlation coefficient at all. Since this is true, let us choose a change of scale that will divide each midpoint by 80, and then subtract enough from each of them to bring the resulting series down to 3, 2, 1, 0, −1, −2, and −3. *Whenever there is a constant difference between the original midpoints, a change of scale can produce a new series of values with constant difference, such as 1, 2, 3, 4, 5, and so on, or −2, −1, 0, 1, 2, and so on, which will make calculations simpler.* While we are changing scales, we can save some work by changing the other scale, too, from 1, 2, 3, 4 to −1, 0, 1, 2.

Now let us make up a new contingency table, with new x values, x^2 values, and new y values, representing our changes in scale. Let us also give the appropriate xy values to each cell, and add a column for y^2 values and a row for x^2 values. The result is Table 11.8. Observations have been omitted for clarity's sake. The total, or f row and column are therefore blank.

Now let us enter the observations. We shall have to add to the table two more columns and two more rows for the frequencies times the y and

Table 11.8

Layout for Calculating Product-Moment Correlation Coefficient from Grouped Data

					Total = f	y Value	y^2 Value
	-3[a]	0	3	6		3	9
	-2[a]	0	2	4		2	4
	-1[a]	0	1	2		1	1
	0	0	0	0		0	0
	1	0	-1	-2		-1	1
	2	0	-2	-4		-2	4
	3	0	-3	-6		-3	9
Total = f							
x Value	-1	0	1	2			
x^2 Value	1	0	1	4			

[a] These are the xy values of the cells. The x value in this column is -1. The y values are, respectively, 3, 2, 1. The xy values are, therefore, -3, -2, -1.

y^2 values and the frequencies times the x and x^2 values, respectively. We shall also need one more column or row to keep track of the frequencies times the xy values.

We need six quantities for the formula for r: N, Σx, Σy, Σx^2, Σy^2, Σxy. We find these by totalling the appropriate rows or columns.

A computing formula for the correlation coefficient for grouped data is presented now. The formula presented earlier can also be used with grouped data if it is kept in mind that its components are sums of the frequencies times row and column values. The two forms for r are these:

The general computing formula is

$$r = \frac{N\Sigma xy - \Sigma x \Sigma y}{\sqrt{[N\Sigma x^2 - (\Sigma x)^2][N\Sigma y^2 - (\Sigma y)^2]}}$$

The computing formula for the case of grouped data is

$$r = \frac{\Sigma f \Sigma fxy - \Sigma fx \Sigma fy}{\sqrt{[\Sigma f \Sigma fx^2 - (\Sigma fx)^2][\Sigma f \Sigma fy^2 - (\Sigma fy)^2]}}$$

The computation of r is presented as Table 11.9. We might note that r is a symmetric measure of the extent to which mutual association exists. It varies from -1 to $+1$, but will reach these extremes only if all the cells except those along some diagonal (not necessarily the main diagonals) are zero. It does not itself have a clear interpretation, but it can

Table 11.9

Calculation of Product-Moment Correlation Coefficient for Data of Table 11.7

				f	y	y^2	fy	fy^2	fxy
-3	0	3	6						
0	1	1	8	10	3	9	30	90	51
-2	0	2	4						
1	8	17	40	66	2	4	132	264	192
-1	0	1	2						
8	30	40	59	137	1	1	137	137	150
0	0	0	0						
47	50	44	29	170	0	0	0	0	0
1	0	-1	-2						
37	29	14	13	93	-1	1	-93	93	-3
2	0	-2	-4						
20	9	4	2	35	-2	4	-70	140	24
3	0	-3	-6						
6	2	0	0	8	-3	9	-24	72	18
f 119	129	120	151	519			$\Sigma fy =$ 112	$\Sigma fy^2 =$ 796	$\Sigma fxy =$ 432

x	-1	0	1	2
x^2	1	0	1	4
fx	-119	0	120	302 $\Sigma fx = 303$
fx^2	119	0	120	604 $\Sigma fx^2 = 843$

$$\Sigma f \text{ or } N = 519$$

$$\Sigma fx \text{ or } \Sigma x = 303$$

$$\Sigma fx^2 \text{ or } \Sigma x^2 = 843$$

$$\Sigma fy \text{ or } \Sigma y = 112$$

$$\Sigma fy^2 \text{ or } \Sigma y^2 = 796$$

$$\Sigma fxy \text{ or } \Sigma xy = 432$$

$$r = \frac{N\Sigma xy - \Sigma x \Sigma y}{\sqrt{[N\Sigma x^2 - (\Sigma x)^2][N\Sigma y^2 - (\Sigma y)^2]}}$$

$$r = \frac{(519)(432) - (303)(112)}{\sqrt{[(519)(843) - (303)^2][(519)(796) - (112)^2]}}$$

$$r = 0.51$$

be shown that r^2 is a measure of the reduction of the variance (the square of the standard deviation) of assessments of either attribute when we predict it from the other by use of the linear equation which connects the two.

PROBLEMS

11.1. For each of the following fictitious examples (Tables 11.10, 11.11, and 11.12) decide what measure of correlation is appropriate, calculate it, and give some interpretation for it.

(a) Physicists and musical interests (Table 11.10).

Table 11.10

Musical Proficiency	Physics Degree			
	BA	MA	PhD	Totals
Expert	1	3	4	8
Amateur	3	5	6	14
None	14	4	2	20
Totals	18	12	12	42

(b) Entrance exam scores and later performance (Table 11.11).

Table 11.11

Entrance Scores	Grades in College					
	I	II	III	IV	V	Totals
I	8	7	7	1	2	25
II	7	9	6	2	1	25
III	7	5	6	3	4	25
IV	1	2	2	12	8	25
V	2	2	4	7	10	25
Totals	25	25	25	25	25	125

(c) Absenteeism and length of service (Table 11.12).

Table 11.12

Years of Service	Days Missed This Year					
	0–5	6–11	12–17	18–23	24 or more	Totals
0–2	5	4	9	10	2	30
3–5	18	20	4	2	1	45
6–8	34	13	2	1	0	50
9–11	9	8	4	3	1	25
12 or more	14	5	1	2	0	22
Totals	80	50	20	18	4	172

11.2. Are there arguments both for and against calculating a product-moment correlation coefficient for 11.1(b), above? What are they? What would your position be?

11.3. Invent a research problem, leading to a contingency table, for which each of the following would be an appropriate measure of correlation: (a) γ, (b) τ_a, (c) τ_b, and (d) r.

11.4. Calculate the product-moment correlation between age and income, using the data of Appendix 2.

Chapter 12

Sampling

This chapter first discusses probability sampling, then the rationales for some variations in probability sample design, and, finally, alternatives to probability designs. It should be recognized that, although the basic ideas of sampling are not obscure, designs may be modified in many ways to suit particular situations. Both experience and training are necessary to choose the best possible design: that is, a design that will produce the most information for the least cost. Unless an investigator is himself an expert sampling statistician, or unless he is doing his study on a shoestring—and even then, if he can manage it—he should call in a consultant if he has sampling problems. Nevertheless, the investigator will need some knowledge of sampling in order to be an intelligent client.

Samples and Populations

A sampling problem is raised when we want to learn something about the frequency of an attribute or combination of attributes within a population, through a study of some part of the population. *A population is any collection of individuals (or organizations or communities) whose boundaries can be stated;* that is, for which rules can be given for deciding whether a particular individual should be included or not. The boundaries may not be easy to specify; the "population of the United States," for instance, is not defined to the satisfaction of the Census Bureau until two pages have been filled with the conditions under which American citizens living abroad or foreign nationals living here should be counted, how this country's territories and possessions should be treated, and the like. *A sample is a subset of the population.* The aim in sampling is to choose the subset in a way that maximizes the likelihood that it will serve as an adequate representative of the population as a whole.[1]

[1] Useful references on sampling, which are, however, quite mathematical, include: W. G. Cochran, *Sampling Techniques* (New York: John Wiley, 1963); W. E. Deming,

If we are very much concerned about the accuracy of our estimates, we might insist that the only acceptable sample is one that includes every member of the population: a census. We do not sample voters when we want to know who won an election, nor do we draw a sample in any other situation where it is essential to know with something approaching certainty precisely how many individuals did what. Often, however, we do not really need this degree of precision, and then a census is a waste of money, energy, and time, which, together with insight, are the raw materials of research.

Some statisticians have argued that a properly drawn sample is likely to be more precise than a census, because the biasing effect of poor case finding or interviewing procedures can be more effectively controlled in the smaller sample than they can in a census, while the variability of sampling can be reduced to an unimportant amount. Indeed, it may be argued that errors of estimation are as likely to come from poor data gathering as from sampling variation, and there is no point in decreasing sampling variation when the result is inadequate control of data gathering. However, it is not necessary to accept this argument that samples are really better than censuses in order to justify a concern for sampling. In a great many situations, a properly drawn sample can produce enough precision for the purpose at hand, while a census would be prohibitively expensive.

Our aim, in sampling, is almost always to construct a sample that can represent the entire population. Sometimes the sample is a smaller replica of the population; sometimes weighting of some section of the sample is necessary to achieve representativeness. As a first example of sampling, consider a chef preparing a stew. He wants to know whether the mixture of ingredients throughout the stew is palatable. He tests a small sample: a spoonful. He will decide that if the spoonful is hot, the stew as a whole is hot; if the spoonful is salty, the stew as a whole is salty; and so on. He must first be sure, however, that the stew has been well mixed. If he had just added a fair amount of salt to one region in the stew, his sampling might lead him astray. He might overcome this problem by taking several samples from different parts of the pot, or he might overcome it by mixing the stew. Representativeness can be

Some Theory of Sampling (New York: John Wiley, 1950); M. H. Hansen, W. N. Hurwitz, and W. G. Madow, *Sample Survey Methods and Theory* (New York: John Wiley, 1953); and L. Kish, *Survey Sampling* (New York: John Wiley, 1965). A good introductory treatment is given by Russell L. Ackoff in *The Design of Social Research* (University of Chicago Press, 1953), Chapter IV, pp. 83–130. Also useful is the brief discussion by William Goode and Paul Hatt in their *Methods in Social Research* (New York: McGraw-Hill, 1952), Chapter XIV, pp. 209–231.

achieved either by drawing the sample from different regions of the population (in other words, mixing the sample) or by mixing the population. In sampling from human populations, we choose the first method, by use of *random selection*. The idea of random selection is so important in sampling that it should be looked at more closely.

The Idea of Random Selection

A selection process is random if it favors no member of the population over any other member; that is, if every member of the population has the same chance of being selected. We may define *random selection* as *any process that gives each member of a population an equal chance of falling in the sample.*[2]

This is not quite our intuitive idea of randomness, which has to do with the absence of pattern, the sense that choice is haphazard. "Haphazard," however, turns out to be a poor synonym for random, whereas if we examine the matter closely, "equal probability process" captures the idea exactly. Suppose an instructor needed four members of a class of one hundred to help him with a demonstration. He might, with no particular thought, point to a group of four sitting in the second row and ask them to serve. Despite his having given the matter no thought, this is not random selection, because the process by which the choice was made did not give everyone in the class an equal chance of being called. Those in the back of the room, particularly if they were hidden from the instructor's view, were relatively safe; those in the front of the room, especially vulnerable. From the instructor's point of view, the process may have appeared to be pure chance; but the structure of the situation, like a loaded roulette wheel, gave some people a greater probability of selection than others.

Random selection produces a representative sample by the continued operation of probabilities. Suppose that men with beards make up 1/20 of our population. Random sampling in which each member of the sample has the same chance of selection gives bearded men, as a group, one chance in twenty of having one of their members selected. If we repeat the selection over and over again—take a large enough sample—then 1/20 of our sample, just the same proportion as the proportion in the population, will be bearded. The same will hold true for every other characteristic. We can be sure that if we only take a large enough sample, the proportion in our sample of individuals with any given characteristic will be virtually identical to the proportion in the population.

[2] In some kinds of sampling—stratified sampling—the population of interest is segmented into smaller populations which may be sampled at different rates. Within these smaller populations everyone has an equal chance of falling in the sample.

Whether a sample is random depends on the process by which it is chosen. A sample is random if and only if it is the result of a random process. We do not know whether a set of individuals make up a random sample unless we know that they were selected in such a way that everyone in the population had an equal chance of falling in the sample. A group of individuals walking by a downtown street corner at high noon is not a random sample of the population of that city, because not everyone in the city is equally likely to walk by that corner at that time. It *may* be a *representative* sample—although this is unlikely—but it is not a *random* sample.

The notion of randomness can sometimes be elusive. It might be asked, in reference to the selection of students for a demonstration, whether the instructor's ignorance of which students were going to sit in the front rows did not result in random selection even though front-row students were more likely to be selected. The answer is that the instructor's ignorance of the identity of the students who would fill those seats is irrelevant to the issue; as irrelevant as would be anyone else's ignorance. Some students, for some reason, have a tendency to sit toward the front of the classroom, while others are more retiring in nature, and the selection process was biased toward the former even before anyone entered the room. If seats were assigned randomly, then the situation would be different.

Most often, when we want to make up a random sample, we have recourse to a table of random numbers. A table of random numbers may be made in a number of ways, one of which is to program a computer to produce a table in which any number between 0 and 9 has the same probability of appearing at every place. In a table of random numbers, there is no connection whatsoever between a number that appears in one place and any number that appears in any other place in the table. A section of a table of random numbers is given as Table 12.1.

Table 12.1

Table of Random Numbers—Excerpt[a]

24066	59885	93188	99399	16009	51281	52542	77511	18106	62483
03443	40382	33485	46907	80006	19092	10590	40823	26566	34580
17699	88138	22670	30391	25437	09440	56138	13114	09068	85328

[a] Taken from The RAND Corporation, *A Million Digits with 100,000 Normal Deviates* (Glencoe, Ill.: The Free Press, 1955), p. 363. Reprinted by permission of The RAND Corporation.

It is not likely that an individual would be able to write a table of random numbers, no matter how hard he tried or how practiced he was. Notice the group of five numbers in the first line, fourth column: 99399. Someone trying to make up a table of random numbers himself might well say, "Too many nines" and change one of them to a six and another to a two. But this would mean that he allowed the number that came up in one place to affect the number that came up in another place, which is not supposed to happen in a table of random numbers. The resulting nonrandomness in his constructed table could be detected by comparing the number of times he allowed consecutive pairs of numbers to be "doubles"—11, 22, 33, and so on—with what would be expected if the table were truly random. It is because we cannot function randomly ourselves, without the assistance of some device, that a table of random numbers is so useful.

In the discussion so far, the point has been made that we can trust a sample to stand for a population if we have selected the sample by means of a random process. It was also noted that if the population is itself well mixed—homogeneous—we can forego random sampling. Not many populations are. People who live in particular neighborhoods are apt to be more like each other than like people who live in other neighborhoods, and thus unrepresentative of the wider community. Faculty at one college or delinquents in one city are apt to differ from their counterparts elsewhere, and so to be unrepresentative of the category as a whole. Yet this does not mean that we can *never* generalize to a population from a nonrandom sample. Sometimes we can assume that the characteristic in which we are interested is homogeneous enough, given the range of accuracy within which we are willing to work, for us to generalize even though the sample is a nonrandom sample. For example, we might study child-raising practices in a middle-income district of a Northern city and propose that, by and large, the same attitudes should be found in other middle-income groups, at least in the North. We might be wrong; there could be greater regional or local variation than we suppose. Sometimes, too, we are interested not so much in the incidence of some characteristic in the population, as in the connection between two characteristics, and we may assert that any demonstrated connection would have to hold good in any setting. This would be the case if we wanted to show that susceptibility to illness was associated with few green vegetables in the diet, in which case we could demonstrate this connection (if it, indeed, exists), anywhere at all, and expect that it would remain good everywhere else. This last assumption is frequently made, but it is not always correct. Sometimes the context affects the strength of a connection, as when the superior student in a middle-class, college-oriented high school is also likely to be a member of the leading group, but in a working-class school is not. (See the discussion of specification in Chapter 9.)

Confidence Intervals

The special feature of probability sampling is that it permits use of the theory of probability for the computation, from the sample itself, of probability limits of sampling variation in the estimates that come from repeated application of the prescribed sampling procedure to the same . . . system.[3]

The quotation above, from a book by the man who coined the term, "probability sampling," focuses attention on an essential advantage of sampling based on random selection. *When we sample randomly, we can state the population values that are compatible with our sample at specific probability levels.* When we want to focus attention on this aspect, we refer to random samples as "probability samples."

Suppose we have selected a random sample of one hundred voters from a larger population. We find in our sample that 60% are Republican. We can then infer that the proportion of Republicans in the larger population lies between 50% and 69%, and be sure that the chances are 95 in 100 that we are right. The steps by which this is done are outlined in the next section of this chapter.[4] Here we need only note that, on the basis of information in the sample, we can construct an interval within which we can assert that a population value lies, and that we can also say what the likelihood is of our assertion being correct. This is the essential contribution of probability sampling; it allows us to state the likelihood that we are correct when we assert that a population value—generally a mean or a proportion—lies within a certain range.

A confidence interval is a range within which we assert that a population value lies. To show more clearly just what is the relation between sample value, population value, confidence interval, and confidence level, let us take a near-trivial example. Suppose that we have a population of ten voters, all either Republicans or Democrats. We sample four of them. On the basis of this sample of four, we shall infer the percentage of Republicans in the population of ten.

[3] W. Edwards Deming, *Sampling Design in Business Research* (New York: John Wiley, 1960), p. 24.
[4] A note that anticipates the material later in the chapter: the sampling error of a proportion is $\sqrt{[p(1 - p)]/n}$ where p is the population proportion. We calculate the 95% confidence interval by determining from what parent populations the value 0.60 is two sampling errors away. We are required to solve the quadratic equation,

$$p - 2\sqrt{\frac{p(1 - p)}{100}} = 0.60$$

The roots of this equation are $p = 0.50$ and $p = 0.69$.

In our sample, we can have only five different results. These are:

Possible Sample Value 1: 0% Republican, if we find 0 Republicans and 4 Democrats.

Possible Sample Value 2: 25% Republican, if we find 1 Republican and 3 Democrats.

Possible Sample Value 3: 50% Republican, if we find 2 Republicans and 2 Democrats.

Possible Sample Value 4: 75% Republican, if we find 3 Republicans and 1 Democrat.

Possible Sample Value 5: 100% Republican, if we find 4 Republicans and 0 Democrats.

Suppose we decide that *we shall assert that the population is within 25% of our sample value, no matter what the sample value.* In other words, if the sample is 0% Republican, we shall assert that the population is no more than 25% Republican; if the sample is 50% Republican, we shall assert that the population is somewhere between 25% Republican and 75% Republican. Each of these ranges within which the population value will be asserted to lie will form a confidence interval.

We shall now assess the level of confidence at which we may propose these intervals. We consider all possible conditions of the population and for each see what the probability is of our being in error.

Population condition 1. Suppose that the population includes no Republicans at all. Then, of necessity, the sample will include no Republicans at all. When we assert that the population is between 0% and 25% Republican, we shall certainly be right. So, if the population includes no Republicans at all, we shall always be correct in our statement that the confidence interval that we construct contains the population value.

By exactly the same reasoning, if the population is 100% Republican, our way of developing confidence intervals will also always result in intervals that include the population value. If the population is 100% Republican, so will the sample be, and we shall assert that the population value is between 75% and 100%, and be correct.

Population condition 2. If the population value is 10% Republican, there is only one Republican in the population, and our samples contain either no Republicans, or just the one. In the first case, we assert the percentage of Republicans in the population to be between 0% and 25%; in the second case we assert that it is between 0% and 50%. In either case we are right. By the same reasoning, if the population value is 90% Republican, our confidence interval will always include the population value.

Population condition 3. If the population is 20% Republican, it is possible to be misled by our sample. Our sample can have the values 0% Republican, 25% Republican, and 50% Republican. If the sample should be 50% Republican, we should say that the population value is in the interval between 25% and 75%, and we should be mistaken. Otherwise, our asserted interval would contain the population value. We must ask what the probability is that we should have a sample value of 50% if the population value is 20%. The question is how often would a random sample of four have within it two Republicans and two Democrats, if the population from which it is drawn includes two Republicans and eight Democrats. The answer is 13% of the time. There are six distinct ways in which a two-Republican sample can be drawn—RRDD, RDRD, RDDR, DRRD, DRDR, and DDRR—and each has a 1/45 chance of occurring; all together, these have a 13% chance of appearing. Thus, if the population value is 20%, our procedure will cause us to make incorrect assertions 13% of the time. The same is true if the population value is 80% Republican.

Population condition 4. If the population value is 30% Republican, (or 70% Republican), a sample in which we have 0% Republicans or a sample in which we have 75% Republicans will mislead us. One of these two samples is likely to result 20% of the time.

Population condition 5. If the population value is 40% Republican (or 60% Republican), we shall be misled by samples which include no Republicans, three Republicans, or four Republicans. One of these samples would appear 18% of the time.

Population condition 6. Finally, if the population value is 50%, we shall be misled by samples which include no Republicans or four Republicans. Samples of one of these kinds would appear only 5% of the time.

These results are collected in Table 12.2.

What can we now conclude? If we take as our policy to set up a confidence interval which is the sample value plus or minus 25%, we shall never have more than a 0.20 chance of failing to include the population value in the interval, *no matter what the population value is.* (Only if the population value were 30% or 70% would we have even this much chance of missing.) This means that irrespective of the population value, we can have a level of confidence in our procedure appropriate to a certainty of being right at least 80% of the time. We may call our procedure an 80% confidence procedure, and our intervals 80% confidence intervals.

There is one aspect in which this example may be misleading. In this example, we fixed the width of the confidence interval, then calculated the level of confidence we might have in it. In any real situation, we proceed in the other way; we fix the level of confidence, and then calculate the width of the interval. Also, in this example, the level of confidence or, had this been fixed, the width of the interval, is different for different presumed population values. In more life-like sampling situations this would not be so. The width of the confidence interval, for a fixed level of con-

Table 12.2

Probabilities that Confidence Interval Will Not Include Population Value (Population of Ten, Sample of Four, Interval Boundaries at Sample Value Plus or Minus 25%)

Population	Probability of Error
0%	0
10%	0
20%	0.13
30%	0.20
40%	0.18
50%	0.05
60%	0.18
70%	0.20
80%	0.13
90%	0
100%	0

fidence, would be either independent of the presumed population value or would not vary so markedly. If we are attempting to estimate a population mean, it does not matter if we place the true population mean at 52.8 or 152.8; we work out the width of our confidence interval without paying any attention to this. The width of a confidence interval when we are trying to estimate a population mean depends only on (1) the level of confidence; (2) the variability of the population; and (3) the size of the sample. If we are sampling proportions, as we were in this example, and our sample size is small, it is not true that the width of a confidence interval is independent of the presumed true population proportion.

Another sampling exercise. Appendix 2 lists, together with other information, age data for a population of one hundred women. Again, we can "take a census," and calculate the true average age of this population. Let us also see how we should approach the problem of estimating this average age by sampling.

To draw the sample, we first assign each case an identification number. Since there are one hundred cases, we can assign two-digit numbers beginning with 01 and going on up to 99, and every case will have a number and no two will have the same number. (The hundredth case will have to be given the number 00.) We can then go to a table of random numbers and draw the sample, selecting the cases whose identification numbers appear when we read off a series of two-digit numbers from the table.

Refer to Table 12.1, the excerpt from the table of random numbers. The first case to be drawn is case number 24. The age of case 24 is 70 years. The age of the next case, number 06, is 52 years. A sample of ten cases would give the values, and the average age, shown by the first line of Table 12.3. The average age of the ten women identified by the first ten random numbers is 43.9.

If we had to choose a single number as our guess of the population mean, we should do best to use our sample mean, 43.9. The sample mean is the best estimate we can make of the population mean, although there is very little chance that the sample mean will coincide exactly with the population mean.

In the previous example, we were concerned with the probability that a given procedure for designing confidence intervals would contain within it the actual population value, no matter what the population value happened to be. Here we will begin with a fixed level of probability and calculate the width of the interval. Let us take a 95% level.

Imagine that we select sample after sample, each of ten members, from the population. The means of different samples are almost always different. Four such samples are listed in Table 12.3. If we drew not just four, but hundreds of samples, we would be able to plot a distribution of

Table 12.3

Samples of Ten, Age Data

Samples					Case Number						
	1	2	3	4	5	6	7	8	9	10	$\bar{x}$[a]
First	70	52	46	29	43	36	38	53	36	36	43.9
Second	49	50	30	50	46	25	36	49	42	31	40.8
Third	28	28	36	38	70	61	58	42	62	36	45.9
Fourth	31	51	26	25	47	24	25	26	59	31	34.5

[a] Mean, four samples = 41.3 years.

the sample means. We can state, based on mathematical analysis, what such a distribution will be like. If the parent population is normal, then even if the sample size is only ten, the distribution of sample means will be normal. Even if the population is *not* normal, the distribution of sample means will be normal if the samples are large enough. (How large they have to be depends on how far from normal the parent population is. Investigators generally accept samples of size 30 as "large enough.") The *mean* of the distribution of sample means is the mean of the population: the true value. The standard deviation of the sample means may be expressed as a simple function of the standard deviation and the sample size, but for the moment let us simply refer to it as the "standard error of the mean." To repeat, the "standard error of the mean" is the standard deviation of the distribution of sample means. We refer to the standard error of a population of sample means by the symbol $\sigma_{\bar{x}}$.

If we can take the distribution of sample means as normal with mean at the population mean, and a definite standard error, $\sigma_{\bar{x}}$, we can work out a 95% confidence interval. We simply ask "For what population values would the observed sample value fall within a range that includes 95% of the samples from that population?"

Suppose that the sample value is 38, and the standard error of the mean is 4. Since the distribution of sample means is normal, we can say that the range extending from $2\sigma_{\bar{x}}$ below the population value to $2\sigma_{\bar{x}}$ above the population value includes 95% of the samples from the population. We may consider various possibilities as population values. Suppose that the population value is 42. Then we should have the distribution of sample means shown in Figure 12.1.

Suppose that the population value is 35. Then we should have the sampling distribution shown in Figure 12.2.

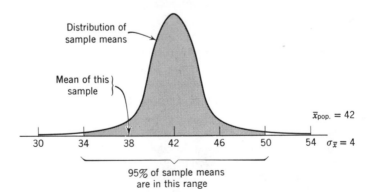

Figure 12.1

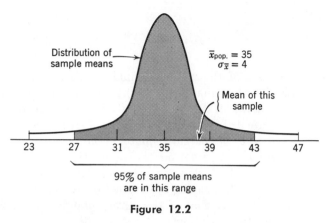

Distribution of
sample means

$\bar{x}_{pop.} = 35$
$\sigma_{\bar{x}} = 4$

Mean of this
sample

23   27   31   35   39   43   47

95% of sample means
are in this range

Figure 12.2

Now suppose that the population value is 50. Then we should have the sampling distribution shown in Figure 12.3.

In this case, our sample is extremely unusual; less than 5% of the time would a sample mean be this far from the true mean. If *we are willing to discount the possibility* of samples so far from the true mean that they could occur 5% of the time or less, then we can assert that the only population values from which a given sample could have come will lie within plus or minus $2\sigma_{\bar{x}}$ of the sample value. This assertion will lead us into error 5% of the time, since 5% of the time we may expect samples farther from the true mean than $2\sigma_{\bar{x}}$.

Now let us state the relationship between the standard deviation of a population and the standard error of the mean. If the population from which the sample is drawn is normal, or if the sample is large, then it can

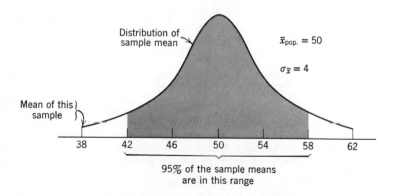

Distribution of
sample mean

$\bar{x}_{pop.} = 50$

$\sigma_{\bar{x}} = 4$

Mean of this
sample

38   42   46   50   54   58   62

95% of the sample means
are in this range

Figure 12.3

be shown that:

$$\sigma_{\bar{x}} = \frac{\sigma_{x\,\text{population}}}{\sqrt{n}}$$

The standard error of the mean is equal to the population standard deviation divided by the square root of the number in the sample.

Ordinarily, we shall not know the population standard deviation and shall have to estimate it. In the great majority of studies, *we must estimate the standard deviation of the parent population on the basis of the standard deviation in the sample.* Estimating the population standard deviation from the sample standard deviation is possible because the sample standard deviation, with a negligible correction factor, in the long run will average out to exactly that of the parent population. If the sample size is large enough, the variation in the standard deviation among samples may be neglected. As a rule of thumb, we may take samples of 30 or more as "large enough."[5]

If we took sample after sample, calculated the standard deviation of each and averaged out all these calculations, the result would not be the population standard deviation. What we should get would be slightly *less* than the standard deviation of the population. Often statisticians "correct" this by multiplying the standard deviation by the proper factor, $\sqrt{n/(n-1)}$ (where n is sample size), to make the result an unbiased estimate. The correction factor, however, changes things very little, if our sample is of size 30 or better. It amounts to replacing the n in the denominator of the formula for the standard deviation by $n - 1$.

$$\text{Estimated } \sigma_{\text{pop.}} = \sqrt{\frac{n}{n-1}\left(\frac{\sum\limits_{\text{sample}}(x-\bar{x})^2}{\sqrt{n}}\right)}$$

$$\text{Estimated } \sigma_{\text{pop.}} = \frac{\sum\limits_{\text{sample}}(x-\bar{x})^2}{\sqrt{n-1}}$$

[5] A technical note: if our sample is small, we must modify the discussion of the text by recognizing that the estimate of the population standard deviation itself has a range of error. If the parent population is normally distributed, then the quantity $(\bar{x}_{\text{sample}} - \bar{x}_{\text{pop.}})/(\text{est. } \sigma_{\bar{x}})$ is distributed by the t distribution, with $n-1$ degrees of freedom, where n is the number in the sample. When n is thirty, the difference between the size of the confidence interval based on the t distribution and the confidence interval based on the normal distribution is less than 3%. It rapidly approaches zero as the sample size increases. When samples are small and the parent population is not normal, the distribution of the statistic $(\bar{x}_{\text{sample}} - \bar{x}_{\text{pop.}})/(\text{est. } \sigma_{\bar{x}})$ may be quite different from a t distribution, and the proper size of confidence intervals may, as a result, be difficult to judge. For some further discussion of the t distribution, see Chapter 15.

In other words, the best estimate of a population standard deviation, given that all we have to work with is a sample, is:

$$\frac{\Sigma(x - \bar{x})^2}{\sqrt{n - 1}}$$

Let us return to our example, but to avoid the problems of work with small samples, shift to consideration of the mean of the combined sample of 40 cases, 41.3. To set up a confidence interval, we first need an estimate of the population standard deviation. We get this by calculating the standard deviation of the sample, which, it turns out, is 14.7. We now calculate the standard error:

$$\sigma_{\bar{x}} = \frac{\text{est. } \sigma_{\text{pop.}}}{\sqrt{n}} = \frac{14.7}{\sqrt{40}} = 2.3$$

The 95% confidence interval is given by the sample mean plus and minus two standard errors, or, to be accurate to two decimal places, plus and minus 1.96 standard errors. We therefore assert that the population mean, M, lies in the interval

$$[\bar{x} - 1.96\sigma_{\bar{x}}] \leq M \leq [\bar{x} + 1.96\sigma_{\bar{x}}]$$

(The symbol $\leq$ means "less than or equal to")

or $41.3 - 1.96(2.3) \leq M \leq 41.3 + 1.96(2.3)$

or $41.3 - 4.5 \leq M \leq 41.3 + 4.5$

or $36.8 \leq M \leq 45.8$

We thus assert, at the 95% level of confidence, that the population value lies between 36.8 and 45.8. As it happens, the population value is 40.5, so that we should be correct in this particular assertion. If we were not able to calculate the population mean, we could not know that our confidence interval definitely included the population mean; but what we *would* know is that, given the procedure we used, 95 times out of 100 it would.

The correction for finite sampling. The standard error depends only on the standard deviation in the parent population and the size of the sample. It goes up as the first goes up, down as the second goes up. But to many students this does not seem right. They wonder why it does not matter how large or small is the population being sampled. Surely, they say, a sample of one hundred taken from a school of two thousand, is much better as a basis for estimation than is a sample of one hundred taken from a country of two hundred million. They are right, but not nearly to the extent that they think.

The size of the population can be of importance only if we are sampling without replacement; only if, once an individual has fallen in our sample, he is ineligible for selection again. If we are sampling from a table of random numbers, we are sampling *without* replacement if we will not call the same number twice, and *with* replacement if we will. If we sample with replacement, our population may be treated as infinite whatever its actual size; it is as though we were in a supermarket and every time we took a can off a shelf another can of exactly the same kind was pushed forward to fill the empty place on the shelf, and we could never exhaust the supply. If we are sampling without replacement, however, we can exhaust the supply; our population is finite.

Almost all sampling from human populations is without replacement. Formulas we have presented so far all refer to sampling *with* replacement, which is mathematically a simpler model, and so the easier one with which to begin the discussion. To adapt the formula for the standard error to a situation of finite sampling, we multiply the sampling-with-replacement standard error by a correction for finite sampling. Unless our sample is at least one-fifth the total population, the effect of this correction is very small and we can neglect it.

Correction for finite sampling:

$$n = \text{sample size}$$

$$N = \text{population size}$$

$$\text{Correction} = \sqrt{1 - \frac{n}{N}}$$

$$\sigma_{\bar{x}} = \sqrt{1 - \frac{n}{N}} \frac{\sigma_{\text{pop.}}}{\sqrt{n}} \qquad \text{(standard error, finite sampling)}$$

Symbols. We have introduced an array of standard deviations—population, sample, and sample means—and a matching array of symbols. All these are summarized in Table 12.4, together with a listing of some of the symbols used by other authors. There is no uniform symbolic system, but many authors use Greek letters to stand for population values: mu, μ, for the mean, and sigma, σ, for the standard deviation. They then use Roman letters for sample values: M or $\bar{x}$, to stand for the sample mean, and s to stand for the sample standard deviation. An estimated value is, by some authors, indicated by a tilde, $\sim$, placed over the symbol: $\tilde{\sigma}$, for example, would be an estimated standard deviation. The symbols used in this chapter are too awkward for extensive algebraic work, but are used because they seem to be easier to interpret than more compact symbols.

Table 12.4

Concepts and Symbols Used in the Discussion of Sampling

Concept	Formula	Symbol in This Chapter	Other Symbols Sometimes Used
Mean of population	$\dfrac{\sum\limits_{\text{pop.}} x}{N}$	$\bar{x},\ \bar{x}_{\text{pop.}},\ M$	μ
Mean of sample	$\dfrac{\sum\limits_{\text{sample}} x}{n}$	$\bar{x},\ \bar{x}_{\text{sample}}$	M
Standard deviation of population	$\sqrt{\dfrac{\sum\limits_{\text{pop.}} (x - \bar{x})^2}{N}}$	$\sigma,\ \sigma_{\text{pop.}}$	
Standard deviation of sample	$\sqrt{\dfrac{\sum\limits_{\text{sample}} (x - \bar{x})^2}{n}}$	σ_{sample}	$s,\ s_x$
Estimated standard deviation of population, based on sample	$\sqrt{\dfrac{\sum\limits_{\text{sample}} (x - \bar{x})^2}{n - 1}}$	est. $\sigma_{\text{pop.}}$	$\tilde{\sigma}$
Standard error, sampling with replacement	$\dfrac{\text{est. } \sigma_{\text{pop.}}}{\sqrt{n}}$ or $\dfrac{\sigma_{\text{pop.}}}{\sqrt{n}}$	$\sigma_{\bar{x}}$	$s_{\bar{x}},\ \sigma_M$
Standard error, sampling without replacement	$\sqrt{1 - \dfrac{n}{N}}\ \dfrac{\sigma_{\text{pop.}}}{\sqrt{n}}$	$\sigma_{\bar{x}}$	$s_{\bar{x}},\ \sigma_M$

A confidence interval bounded on only one side: example involving proportions. The 95% confidence interval given by the range between the sample mean minus 1.96 standard errors and the sample mean plus 1.96 standard errors is the shortest 95% confidence interval we can construct, but it is not the only one. One alternative, in particular, is sometimes of value.

Suppose that we were concerned with predicting an election between, say, Brown and Smith. We drew a random sample of 400 voters, interviewed them, found that they were 53% for Brown. With what level of confidence could we assert that Brown, who is ahead in the sample, is also ahead in the voting population as a whole? What, in other words, is the confidence level at which we may state that the actual proportion of voters for a given candidate is greater than our sample value minus 3%?

Responses of voters in our sample may take only two values, for or against Brown, and we may treat each voter as a trial with, for practical purposes, constant probability. (Actually, unless we sample with replacement, the probabilities will vary a tiny amount from trial to trial.) As is discussed in Chapter 8, these are the conditions for a binomial process. If we took sample after sample, the proportion for Brown would be binomially distributed with the mean value of the distribution at p, the true proportion for Brown, and the standard deviation of the distribution at $\sqrt{[p(1 - p)]/n}$. Now suppose that the true value is 0.50; that half the voters are for Brown, and half against. What proportion of samples would then be 0.53 or more for Brown? Notice that we are not concerned with the proportion of samples 0.53 or more *for the opponent*, because such samples, although they are equally far from the true value, do not cause us to assert that Brown is ahead when he is not.

We calculate how many standard deviations away the point 0.53 is from the mean value, 0.50:

$$\frac{0.53 - p}{\sigma_p} = \frac{0.53 - 0.50}{\sqrt{\dfrac{(0.50)(0.50)}{400}}} = \frac{0.03}{\dfrac{0.50}{20}} = 1.20$$

The illustration of the normal curve (Figure 12.4), which we can use as an approximation to the binomial, tells us that 12% of samples are 1.20 standard deviations or more greater than the mean.

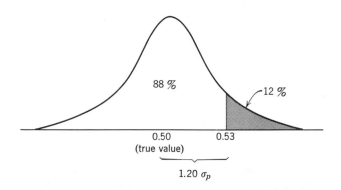

Figure 12.4 Distribution of proportions in samples of 400 from a population where the true value is 0.50. The symbol σ_p stands for the standard deviation of sample proportions.

When we assert that "Brown is ahead in the population," we are stating a confidence interval for the true proportion which runs from a shade better than 0.50, to 1.00. We have shown that population values just outside this interval could have given rise to our sample proportion 12% of the time. If we took as a repeated policy the construction of intervals beginning 1.2 sigmas to the left of the sample value, we should not have the true value in our interval 12% of the time. This follows from the demonstration that 12% of the time the sample value is more than 1.2 sigmas to the right of the true value. Therefore, a statement that Brown is winning can be made at only the 88% level of confidence.

The confidence interval in this example is different from the confidence intervals that we have discussed before in that it is bounded on only one side. Here we are only concerned with the level of confidence we may have in an interval bounded below at 0.50; we do not set any upper bound, except the logical upper bound of 1.00. The reason for this is that we shall only be mistaken if the population value is below a certain value—0.50—while any larger value will be all right. An interval of this sort is called one-sided or, sometimes, one-tailed. It is related to the one-sided tests of hypotheses discussed in the next chapter.

Variations in the Design of Probability Samples

The ideas of simple random sampling are fundamental to all sampling designs. However, in most practical applications, the sampling design incorporates some modification of the simple random sampling idea, because the latter model would be too difficult to carry through (imagine choosing a simple random sample from the population of the United States), or because other designs can achieve equal precision at less cost. What follows are very brief descriptions of other sample designs.[6]

Systematic Sampling

Suppose that we want to sample case records of clients of a social agency who were first seen by the agency in 1965. The records are all numbered, beginning with 15,236 (the number given to the first new client to appear in 1965) and ending with 17,286 (the number given to the last new client to appear). We want a one in ten sample, which will give us a sample size of 205. Random sampling would require us to select two hundred and five random numbers, each four digits in length, since we can neglect the first digit of the case numbers, which is one in all cases. Selecting the sample is straightforward, but tedious. It is simpler to pick at random a number between zero and nine, inclusive, and then

[6] For further discussion, the reader is referred to *Survey Sampling* by Leslie Kish (New York: John Wiley, 1965).

select every case that ends in the number we pick. For example, if our number turned out to be 3, we would select cases 15,243, 15,253, 15,263, etc. The selection of the cases would proceed systematically; hence the name for this design, *systematic* sampling.

There are two arguments sometimes made against systematic sampling. The first is that there may be periodicity in the list; for example, every tenth case may be one that is especially complicated. This is not often true, although it can happen. If we had a list of married couples with the husband's name listed first and the wife's name listed second, all through the list, and if we took a systematic sample with an even interval, then our sample would contain only men or only women. However, if our list exhibited this sort of internal arrangement, we should be likely to notice it, and choose our interval more wisely.

The second argument against systematic sampling is that it is likely to result in a good deal of error if there is some trend that runs all through the list. Suppose that we are interested in new clients in a social agency over a ten-year period rather than a one-year period. There are about 20,000 cases in this ten-year population, and we take a systematic sample with a sampling rate of one in one hundred. Now suppose that there has been a steady decrease in unemployment over this ten-year period. Then let us compare two possible systematic samples, one that begins with the very first case in the ten-year period—call these cases No. 1, No. 101, No. 201, and so on—and a sample that begins with the ninety-ninth case in the ten-year period, and includes cases No. 99, No. 199, and so on. The second systematic sample is displaced to a later part of the ten-year period, compared with the first. It will have no representative for the very first cases in the ten-year period, who are most likely to have been unemployed, but will have instead a representative for the very last cases in the ten-year period, where unemployment is least likely. Thus, the second sample is likely to underestimate unemployment; the first sample to overestimate it. The point at which we make our random start will be of some importance. Yet a strong trend is rarely found, and even if it should be, will matter only if the sample is quite small.

There is much to be said for systematic sampling. It can greatly reduce the work involved in drawing samples, and it is a rare list that will cause a systematic sample to be less trustworthy than a simple random sample.

Cluster Sampling

Most of the cost of interviewing, in most probability samples of general populations, is spent locating the respondent. It takes an interviewer only an hour to complete an interview, but it may take four or five hours spread over two or three callbacks to find the respondent at home. If the interviewer has other assignments in the neighborhood, then travel time per interview, which contributes to locating cost, will be reduced, sometimes drastically.

Cluster sampling means selecting respondents in bunches. A sample of individuals selected in this way is almost always less costly to interview than the same number of individuals selected as a simple random sample. However, there is a loss in cluster sampling; the bunched interviews do not give as much representativeness as would interviews that were more widely distributed, and so some of their information must be considered overlapping. Yet a cluster sample large enough to give as much information as a simple random sample may still cost less than the simple random sample, even though it includes more respondents.

Cluster sampling can make simpler the process of selecting the members of the sample. Suppose that in an underdeveloped area there is no list of inhabitants, but there do exist for tax purposes lists of larger units, such as village territories. Then a reasonable sample design might first select village territories and then within selected territories develop a list from which to sample, or sample systematically every fourth dwelling, or use some similar scheme. The design in any event will be a cluster sample.

Multistage Sampling

Some cluster samples, including the last example, use a multistage sampling design. The general idea of multistage sampling is first to sample inclusive units, then to sample within selected units at a lower level, and so on. For a sample of a state, we might first sample census tracts, then blocks within census tracts, then households within blocks. This would be a three-stage sample.

Multistage sampling introduces certain flexibilities into sampling procedure which can be of great value. Suppose that we are drawing a sample of a city. We know that most blocks have from forty to one hundred families to the block, but that some blocks have large apartment buildings on them, with two hundred families in a building, and well over a thousand families on the block. It is good practice to have two collections of blocks, with the blocks that are densely settled in one of them. Then we may select blocks in the sparsely settled collection at a sampling rate of, for example, one in one hundred, and sample people living on the block with a rate of one in ten, to give everybody in the collection a chance of one in one thousand of falling in the sample. In the collection of densely settled blocks, on the other hand, we might select blocks with a sampling rate of one in two, to make sure we did not miss many of them, but sample within blocks at a rate of one in five hundred, so that we do not have too many from one apartment house. This gives the individual living in a densely settled block the same one in one thousand chance of falling in the sample, and insures that the apartment dwellers are represented, without overwhelming the sample.

The flexibility of the multistage idea for studies of larger populations, such as the population of a nation, makes the approach invaluable. With it, it is possible to have some important areas—like the New York metropolitan region—sampled with certainty, while at the same time, by reducing the sampling rate for individuals within these areas, insure that they do not overwhelm the sample.

Nonprobability Samples

Unless we have a probability sample, we cannot develop a confidence interval; we cannot say that the population value lies between certain limits, with a probability of 95% or 99% that the statement is correct. But that does not mean that we can never draw inferences from samples that are not probability samples; sociologists at work, as well as men in everyday life, do it all the time. We might consider the rationale for the procedure.

Suppose that we are curious about whether college teachers believe in God, and we lack the resources for a national sample study. We have a leading university in the area, and we send questionnaires to its faculty. Suppose that they all are returned, although this is most unlikely. Can we generalize our results to college teachers across the country? Few would argue that we can; faculty at a leading university are apt to be different *in the phenomenon of interest* from faculty at, say, a small church-supported college. If, however, we could learn the blood types of the local college faculty, we might well argue that we could generalize from our results. If we found that 50% of the local faculty had Type O blood, we might argue that we should expect about 50% of the population of college teachers across the country, and, for that matter, of the entire population, to have Type O blood.

Why are we unwilling to generalize from our results in the first case, but willing to generalize from them in the second? Belief in God is related to clusters of attitudes, values, and beliefs, which will have much to do with whether individuals join particular faculties. The basis for selection into the sample, in this case, is related to the issue about which we want to learn, making bias likely. In contrast, possessors of Type O blood might reasonably be expected to be as likely to join one faculty as another; this characteristic, we may believe, is unrelated to our selection criteria. We believe that the population is not well mixed in the first respect—that faculty at one school are different from faculty at another—but is well mixed in the second. If the population is well mixed, then we can forego careful sampling. Any sample is as good as any other.

In the final analysis, we must rely on our judgment to decide whether generalization is advisable when we have a sample of this sort. We shall not be able to express our decision in the form of a probability statement; no confidence interval can be constructed. And, of course, one person's judgment may lead to a decision different from the one to which another person's judgment would lead. Samples such as this one might be termed *haphazard.*

Quota Samples

In quota sampling, we decide that there are three or four characteristics in the population which are closely connected to the variable we are interested in, and we try to make our sample representative of the population in these three or four respects. We actually *construct* a sample that is representative in these respects. If we were interested in studying attitudes of people in this country to the United Nations, we might consider that occupation, sex, age, and political preference were crucial variables. We should, therefore, require our interviewers to select, for every hundred cases in the sample, fifty Republicans and fifty Democrats, fifty men and fifty women, forty blue collar workers and sixty white collar workers, sixty individuals under thirty and forty individuals over thirty. Aside from meeting these quotas, our interviewers would be permitted to select anybody at all. One problem with quota sampling is that it puts great strain on interviewers who might need to find as their last respondent, for instance, a Democratic woman whose husband is a white collar worker and who is herself under thirty. Interviewers, faced with a demand of this sort, sometimes fudge their respondent's characteristics. The key problem of quota sampling, however, is that for *every variable except those controlled or closely related to those controlled, the quota sample is a haphazard sample,* chosen on the basis of availability. The cautions regarding haphazard samples listed above apply to the quota sample, except for the controlled variables.

There are many critics of quota sampling, as we might imagine. Yet some of the most noted triumphs of sampling method have been due not to probability sampling but to quota sampling. When the *Literary Digest,* relying only on numbers of returns, forecast a Landon victory in 1936, and the Gallup Poll, relying on sampling methods, forecast a Roosevelt victory, the Gallup Poll was not basing its prediction on probability sampling at all, but rather on quota sampling. Social class turned out to be both a major determinant of selection (and self-selection) into the *Literary Digest* study, and something very closely connected to the way an individual voted in that 1936 election. The Gallup sample was a quota sample in which social class was controlled. As a result, the *Literary Digest* was wrong and Gallup was right. It may happen some day that a determinant of voting behavior that is uncontrolled by the quota samplers will also determine selection into the sample. In that event, the quota samplers will sustain a black eye. But this has not happened in any very dramatic way so far, and perhaps the odds are with the quota samplers.

PROBLEMS

12.1. Discuss whether a sample or a census would be advisable in the following situations. If a sample would be advisable, discuss its general design.

(a) A city government wants to know how residents of a neighborhood feel about redevelopment in that neighborhood.

(b) A department of highway safety wants to know the percentage of cars on a highway which are equipped with safety devices.

(c) A firm that manufactures food for pets wants to know whether there is commercial value in manufacturing food for hamsters, white mice, and the like.

(d) The government of a small country wants to know the size of its population. The country contains one sizeable city, and a few small towns, but most of its residents live on farms or in farming villages. There are no reliable maps for the countryside.

12.2. Are the following instances of unbiased random selection? Explain your response.

(a) It is desired to sample users of a toll highway. Every one-hundredth car coming to the toll barrier is sampled.

(b) It is desired to sample individuals who will vote in a forthcoming election. The telephone book is used as a list, and the first name on every tenth page is selected into the sample.

(c) It is desired to learn the attitudes toward a proposed program among individuals active in community organizations. Rather than make up a list of all individuals in all community organizations, we first sample organizations, then obtain their membership lists and then sample from their lists. (Question: what about individuals who are members of more than one community organization?)

12.3. Suppose the actual mean age of women in a population is 41 years and the standard deviation of their ages is 5 years. We take samples of size 100, with replacement (so the correction for finite sampling is irrelevant). Within what range would we expect 95% of our sample means?

12.4. The 64 boys in a particular eighth grade have an average height of 60 inches, with a standard deviation of three inches. Treating this eighth grade as a simple random sample, develop a confidence interval within which you would be willing to assert, at the 95% level of confidence, that the average height of all eighth grade students falls.

(a) Criticize the assumption that this eighth grade is a simple random sample of heights.

(b) Would you be willing to generalize from this sample to all eighth grade students in a study of metabolism rates (rates at which the body uses energy)? Explain.

12.5. In the samples of ages of women reported in Table 12.3, treat the first two samples as a single sample of 20, and the second two samples as another sample of 20. For each sample calculate 95% and 99% confidence intervals for the mean.

12.6. Suppose that you are predicting an election, and have taken a simple random sample of 100 voters. How large a proportion in favor of your candidate would you want, in order to be 95% sure that your candidate will actually win?

(a) Suppose that you had taken a simple random sample of 900 voters. How large a proportion in favor of your candidate would you want, in order to be 95% sure that your candidate will win?

Chapter 13

Testing Hypotheses

The problem of estimating a population value from a sample, discussed in Chapter 12, is one form of the more general problem of developing inferences from observations. We shall now examine a second form of this problem, in which we shall consider a method for affirming or rejecting hypotheses on the basis of observations.

We are given a set of observations, which may have resulted from a survey or an experiment, and we are required to judge, in the light of these observations, the validity of an hypothesis. For example, we might be told the number of couples in which wives are more friendly than husbands to a new family in the neighborhood, and the number in which the reverse is the case, and on the basis of this information be asked to decide whether we can affirm that wives in general, and not just in the sample available to us, are more friendly to newcomers than husbands. Several systems have been developed for describing the confidence that may be placed in an inference from observations, and there is at this time active and fruitful dispute among statisticians over which system is preferable. The system developed by Neyman and Pearson is presently being used by most research people, and is the system described in this chapter, but strong arguments may be made for other approaches as well.[1]

The Framework of the Approach

Our approach requires us first to make explicit not a single hypothesis we want our data to confirm or disconfirm, but rather two alternative

[1] The discussions of alternative systems of statistical inference are highly technical, and inaccessible to a reader without advanced training in statistics. Some sense of the issues may be gained from R. L. Plackett, "Current Trends in Statistical Inference," in *Journal of the Royal Statistical Society*, **129**(**2**), (1966), pp. 249–267. The Bayesian approach to hypothesis testing is described in elementary terms in *Probability and Statistics*, by Frederick Mosteller, Robert E. K. Rourke, and George B. Thomas, Jr. (Reading, Mass.: Addison-Wesley, 1961). See especially Chapters IV, V, and VIII.

hypotheses, which between them represent whatever might happen. We decide on one of these as the *hypothesis of interest*, and, if the data are compatible with it, we ask the extent to which the data are also compatible with the other, which we call the *tested hypothesis*. If the data are also compatible with the tested hypothesis, we say it is "no contest"; we cannot decide. If the data are incompatible with the tested hypothesis, then we can reject it in favor of the hypothesis of interest.

Suppose that we are interested in discovering whether it is raining outside. Rather than go outside ourselves, we call in the dog, and feel his coat. We reason that the chance of the dog's coat being wet if it is dry outside is slight. Of course the dog's coat might be dry even if it is raining; he might have been on the porch or otherwise sheltered. We set up as the hypothesis tested, that it is dry outside; the alternative hypothesis then, which we referred to above as the hypothesis of interest, is that it is raining. The dog, when he comes in, is wet. This is compatible with the alternative hypothesis. Since it is also incompatible with the tested hypothesis, we reject the latter in favor of the alternative, and decide that it is raining. If the dog had come in dry, we would not then have said that it was not raining, but only that the data were not incompatible with the tested hypothesis, and since we could not reject the tested hypothesis, we were unable to make any positive statement.

Many texts refer to what is here called the "tested hypothesis" as the "null hypothesis"; that is, the hypothesis that there is an absence of the phenomenon of interest. In the above example, the hypothesis that it is dry outside would be a null hypothesis. As Neyman notes, however, the term "tested hypothesis" seems more descriptive; in addition, in certain circumstances, the term "null hypothesis" can be misleading.[2]

The second step in hypothesis testing, after we have made explicit the hypothesis we wish to test and its alternative, is to decide on the observations on which we will base our assessment. We decide what data are relevant, and also choose a single measure based on these data which we may use as a *test statistic*. The test statistic functions like a pointer on a dial, telling us how far the data lean away from support for the tested hypothesis and toward support for the alternative hypothesis. The third step, usually handled informally, is to set up *decision rules:* rules for

---

[2] Jerzy Neyman, *First Course in Probability and Statistics* (New York: Holt, 1950). The difference in nomenclature becomes important when (a) there is no clear "null" hypothesis, as in this example; or (b) it is the "null" hypothesis which is the assertion of interest, and we want the other hypothesis to be the tested hypothesis. This would be the case if we wanted to assert positively that there was no difference between population means, for example, using as the tested hypothesis that they were 0.5 sigma units or more distant from each other. In either of these two circumstances the "null"-"alternative" designation creates some confusion.

deciding on the basis of the test statistic whether we shall be able to reject the tested hypothesis in favor of the alternative hypothesis. Almost always, we shall reject the tested hypothesis only if the data are clearly incompatible with it. The decision rules state just how incompatible it is necessary for the data to be, in order for us to reject the tested hypothesis in favor of the alternative. In the example of the weather-indicating dog, the test statistic was whether the dog's coat was wet or not. The decision rules were to reject the hypothesis that it was not raining if the dog's coat was wet, but not to reject this hypothesis otherwise.

The final step in hypothesis testing is the crucial one of evaluating the worth of the entire procedure by determining the probability that the decision rules will lead us to reject the tested hypothesis if, in fact, it is true. Here we should evaluate the probability of being led to reject the hypothesis that it was dry outside even if this is exactly what it was, and the dog had gotten wet by walking under a garden hose or falling in a tub, or something of this order. If this probability is low, then the support for the alternative hypothesis may be trusted; it could hardly have come about, if the state of the world were as described in the tested hypothesis.

We call the probability of a test procedure causing us to reject a tested hypothesis when it is true, the *level of significance* of the procedure. Obviously, the lower the level of significance, the more confident we may be that it will not lead us to reject the tested hypothesis mistakenly. We might also want to know what the probability is of our procedure causing us to reject the tested hypothesis when it is false. This probability is called the *power* of the procedure. We should like this to be as great as possible.

Let H_1 stand for the tested hypothesis, whatever it is, and H_2 stand for the alternative hypothesis, the hypothesis of interest. Then the level of significance of the procedure is the probability of rejecting H_1 in favor of H_2 when H_1 is actually the case, and the power of the procedure is the probability of rejecting H_1 in favor of H_2 when H_2 is actually the case. We can express these concepts in symbolic terms by recognizing that each refers to a conditional probability:

$$\text{Level of significance} = P(H_2/H_1)$$

$$\text{Power} = P(H_2/H_2)$$

It is general practice for investigators, whenever they have a choice between testing procedures, to choose that one which has the most power. Once having chosen a testing procedure, the investigator designs his decision rules to give him an acceptable level of significance.

A testing procedure that has a high level of significance is a worthless procedure. A high level of significance does *not* indicate that the tested hypothesis is true. It does indicate that the data are not incompatible with the tested hypothesis, but the data could also be not incompatible with the alternative hypothesis. Someone who is always cheery, whether things are good or bad, is like a test with a high level of significance; we cannot infer the state of the world from his appearance.

Limits of Generalization

Suppose we do not know whether a coin has been altered so that it will more often come up on one side than the other. Its edges may have been beveled, or the coin may have been bent, but we are not sure. Inspection does not help. We decide on an experimental test.

Our hypothesis set is:

Hypothesis 1: The probability of a head is equal to 1/2.
Hypothesis 2: The probability of a head is different from 1/2.

We decide that we will flip the coin 100 times. If Hypothesis 1 is correct, then approximately 50 of the results should be heads. If the results depart far from 50, this would offer support for Hypothesis 2. (In this situation it would be reasonable to refer to Hypothesis 1 as a "null" hypothesis.) We want to know how far away from 50 heads we have to go in order to be able to reject Hypothesis 1 at a reasonable level of significance. Intuitively, we should think that the probability of 5 heads or fewer, or of 95 heads or more, would be very small on the assumption of Hypothesis 1. But what about 40 heads or fewer?

In Chapter 8, it is pointed out that if Hypothesis 1 is the case, and if we follow the procedure of flipping the coin one hundred times and counting the number of heads which results, then the distribution of results will be binomial with mean equal to fifty and standard deviation equal to five. Chapter 8 also points out that, given this many trials, the normal distribution of the same mean and standard deviation is an excellent approximation to the binomial distribution. We can therefore refer to tabulations of the normal distribution which show that approximately 95% of the cases will be discovered between $(\bar{x} - 2\sigma)$ and $(\bar{x} + 2\sigma)$. In this particular case, σ is 5%, and so we can say: "If Hypothesis 1 were true, then 95% of the time we should find between $50 - 2(5)$ heads and $50 + 2(5)$ heads in a trial of 100 flips. Therefore, we can reject Hypothesis 1 if there are 39 or fewer heads, or 61 or more heads, at a 5% level of significance."

We now proceed with the test, flip the coin 100 times, and find that 30 heads result. We reject the hypothesis that this is a fair coin in favor of the alternative that it is unfair. These results, we say, could not have happened by chance; there is something wrong with the coin.

We have rejected the hypothesis that the probability of a head is equal to 1/2. But what if we arrange for the coin to fall, not on a hard surface, but into a bowl of mush? Now a bevel or bend would not matter, and we would expect even a doctored coin to have a probability of 1/2 of showing a head. What if we were to allow the coin to drop on sponge rubber? This modification introduces uncertainty; it is difficult to guess.

The point is that our inference is completely trustworthy only for the procedure specified in the test, and can be extrapolated only to the population of instances generated by the procedure specified in the test. The greater the modification in our procedure—the farther we depart from the population of which we have a sample in our test—the less security we can have in the trustworthiness of the generalization. Nor can we assign a probability to the likelihood of the generalization holding good for a particular modification. Substituting mush obviously changes the conditions in an important way. Does substituting sponge rubber? We must rely on our judgment.

Similarly, an association between attributes which is found to hold good among American college sophomores may or may not hold good for humanity at large. We must ask whether we depart in an important way from the population of which a sample was tested, given the characteristics in which we are interested. And, again, judgment is involved.

Test Statistics and Sampling Distributions

We have mentioned, briefly, that a test statistic is a measure based on our observations that we examine to decide whether we can reject the tested hypothesis in favor of its alternative. We calculate the level of significance of our procedure by determining the probability of the test statistic having a value that offers as much support or more support for the alternative hypothesis as the value actually observed, on the assumption that the tested hypothesis is the case. Often, to make this calculation of level of significance, we must deal with the sampling distribution that the test statistic would have if the tested hypothesis were true. That is, we must concern ourselves with the distribution of possible values of the test statistic that might arise, assuming whatever parent populations are specified in the tested hypothesis.

Suppose that we want to decide whether data we have observed which deal with the correlation between ordinal characteristics (say, grade point average and general state of health) support the hypothesis that there is a correlation between these characteristics in general, and not just in our sample. We calculate tau, a measure of correlation between ordinal characteristics. This is our test statistic. Our tested hypothesis (the "null" hypothesis) is that there is no relation between the characteristics in the population of which we have a sample. We want to calculate the probability of a tau occurring as great or greater than the one we observe, if the tested hypothesis of no relation is the case. To make this calculation, we must know the sampling distribution of taus in samples taken from a population in which the characteristics are not associated. With knowledge of this sampling distribution of taus, we can state what values of tau are exceeded, in samples from a "null" population, no more than 5% of the time, and therefore what values of tau are necessary in order to reject the tested hypothesis at the 5% level.

In the following chapters, we consider a number of possible test statistics: chi-square, the difference between means, and others. In each case we also describe the sampling distribution of this test statistic, on the assumption that the usual tested hypothesis, a "null" hypothesis, is true.

One-Sided versus Two-Sided Tests

When we compare one group with another, we may phrase the hypothesis alternative to the tested hypothesis in either of two ways: we may phrase it either as "the one group is different from the other," or "the one group is greater in some respect than the other." The second phrasing produces a "directional" test of the hypothesis. In it, we assert as the alternative to the tested hypothesis not only that the groups are different, but that one of the groups is the greater.

A nondirectional hypothesis set would have the form:

Hypothesis 1: Group A and Group B are not different.
Hypothesis 2: Group A and Group B are different.

A directional hypothesis set would have the form:

Hypothesis 1: Group A is the same or less than Group B.
Hypothesis 2: Group A is greater than Group B.

In each of the above sets, the first would be the tested hypothesis (or "null" hypothesis), the second the alternative to it.

Suppose that we wonder whether psychotherapy makes a difference in self-knowledge. We administer a test of knowledge of self to prospective patients before and after psychotherapy. If their scores are higher after psychotherapy, we score it a plus; if lower, a minus. If they are just the same, we discard the case.

The nondirectional hypothesis set is:

Hypothesis 1: The probability of a case being a plus is 1/2.
Hypothesis 2: The probability of a case being a plus is different
from 1/2.

Suppose that we examine four cases, and all have higher self-knowledge scores after psychotherapy. This is obviously support for Hypothesis 2. What is the level of significance of the support? It is the probability of getting support this strong or stronger for Hypothesis 2, if Hypothesis 1 is the case. This is just the chance of a plus occurring four times running, *or not occurring four times running.* Notice that we reject Hypothesis 1 when we observe many plusses or when we observe few plusses. The level of significance is, therefore, $2(1/2 \times 1/2 \times 1/2 \times 1/2)$, or $1/8$, or $12\,1/2\%$. The directional hypothesis set is:

> *Hypothesis 1:* The probability of a case being a plus is $1/2$ or less.
> *Hypothesis 2:* The probability of a case being a plus is more than $1/2$.

The only data that support Hypothesis 2 are many plusses. Few plusses support Hypothesis 1, against the alternative of Hypothesis 2. If we have four cases, in all of which there is greater self-knowledge after psychotherapy, this is a basis for rejecting Hypothesis 1 with a level of significance of $(1/2 \times 1/2 \times 1/2 \times 1/2)$, or $1/16$, or $6\,1/4\%$.

Notice that the level of significance at which the data support the directional hypothesis is twice as good as the level of significance at which the data support the nondirectional hypothesis. This will generally, although not always, be the case. (It depends on the sampling distribution of the test statistic being symmetric.) It virtually always is the case that the directional hypothesis can be supported at a better level of significance than the nondirectional hypothesis. For this reason, investigators often phrase their hypothesis set in directional form when they are reasonably sure which way the results will turn out.

We are justified in using a directional hypothesis set when we have decided to test a clear-cut theory that leads to directional predictions. Since psychotherapy aims at increasing self-knowledge, we should be justified in invoking the directional hypothesis here. However, investigators sometimes are tempted to try to profit from the better significance level of a directional hypothesis while not really giving up the alternative of shifting to a nondirectional hypothesis if the data make the nondirectional hypothesis seem more attractive. That is, investigators may be tempted to phrase their hypotheses in directional form, even when their theory is quite loose. Then, if the data turn out to show a tendency in the direction opposite to their hypothesis, the investigators may reverse their theoretical fields and return with a nondirectional hypothesis for test. It is better practice to insist on nondirectional phrasings of hypotheses from the beginning, except in those cases where only one direction is really of interest.

When the test we are using causes us to refer to a distribution (for instance, the normal distribution) to decide on the level of significance at which observed data might support a hypothesis of interest, then it is the area in the tails of the distribution beyond the observation that we consider. The level of significance of a nondirectional hypothesis is given by two tails of a distribution. Thus, a test of a nondirectional hypothesis is often called a "two-tailed test." The level of significance of a directional hypothesis is given by one tail of the distribution. Thus, a test of a directional hypothesis is often called a "one-tailed test."

The Use of Hypothesis Testing in Survey Research, or Any Other Exploratory Research

In most survey work, and perhaps in experimental work that has an exploratory orientation, the investigator has a general idea of what he is looking for, but cannot develop specific hypotheses before his data are collected. (Some investigators may attempt this, but the practice seems ritualistic, since they do not limit their analysis to deciding among the initial hypotheses.) In a study of the determinants of juvenile delinquency, the investigator may believe that some causal contribution can be ascribed to home conditions, but he may be unwilling to be more specific before gathering his data. He cannot say that it will be a broken home, or an ill parent, or drunkenness in the home, or parental rejection, that will be significantly associated with delinquency. Instead, he will want to investigate all these possible associations, expecting that some, but not all, will offer strong support for generalization. This practice is described by Hanan Selvin and Alan Stuart as "fishing," and they have this to say about it:

> In survey analysis, which is commonly exploratory, it is rare for precise hypotheses to be formulable independently of the data. It follows that normally no precise probabilistic interpretations can validly be given to relationships found among the survey variables. (Yet) most investigators are so accustomed to making probability statements that a survey report looks naked without them. . . .
>
> Fishing is the process of using the data to choose which of a number of candidate variables to include in an explanatory model . . . the fish which don't fall through the net are bound to be bigger than those which do, and it is fruitless to test whether they are of average size. . . . [3]

In hypothesis testing we use our data to assess the credibility of a particular hypothesis, against a particular alternative. The assumptions on which the testing is based require that we not have searched through

[3] Hanan C. Selvin and Alan Stuart, "Data Dredging Procedures in Survey Analysis," *American Statistician*, **20(3)** (June, 1966), pp. 20–23. Reprinted by permission of the authors.

study after study until we found a set of data particularly favorable to the hypothesis of interest. They also require something very similar, that we not have searched within a particular study through set after set of data, until we found a set that seemed particularly favorable to some one of a number of hypotheses of interest. Searching through many studies to find a favorable set of data, which is clearly an invalid procedure, is identical, in its contradiction of the assumptions of hypothesis testing, to searching in a particular study for data that support any one of a very large number of potentially testable hypotheses.

This does not mean that tests of hypotheses are without value in surveys; their constant use suggests that this is not the case. Rather, they must be understood as suggesting the degree of support that the data would have furnished to a hypothesis, assuming that the hypothesis was a member of the only set undergoing test. This indication of the degree of support which the data would have offered the hypothesis, under ideal conditions, can help us decide how much credence to place in the finding, understanding that the study's conditions are less than ideal. Suppose that we find that a hypothesis is supported with level of significance of less than one in ten thousand. That could hardly be the result simply of fishing for the sort of unusual patterns in data which happen by chance; we should place credence in the hypothesis, even though the significance testing model was violated by fishing. Suppose that we find that a hypothesis is supported at a level of significance of one in one hundred, and that not many hypotheses were tested in this particular study; again we should place credence in the hypothesis, since not much fishing was done, and the model was not violated very much. In other words, we use significance levels along with as much other relevant information as we can gather, including information about the way the analysis was performed, to develop some overall judgment (which cannot be expressed in probabilistic terms) about whether a hypothesis should be accepted. There is nothing at all wrong with this. To insist that significance testing be dropped, just because the model on which it is based is an idealization of reality, is surely misguided. On the other hand, recognizing that the assumptions of significance testing are rarely met in real research, we might be cautious in accepting with no further supporting evidence a conclusion that is significant at even the 0.05 level.

There are dozens, if not hundreds, of ways in which we might go about testing hypotheses. The logical framework of hypothesis testing is always the same. We set up alternative hypotheses, we decide on relevant data, and we develop decision rules that yield an acceptable level of significance. What we may take as test statistics, however, can be a difference between the mean values of two samples or the percentage of decisions made by two judges which are in agreement, or the length of a run of similar observations, or literally any other characteristic of data which is related to a hypothesis of interest. There may be so many alternatives that where the importance of the question warrants it, consultation with a statistician who is experienced in the field of the research might be valuable in deciding how hypotheses are to be tested. Yet in hypothesis testing, perhaps to a greater extent than in sampling, a little knowledge can take us quite far. There do seem to be a small number of types of hypotheses, leading to use of the same test statistics, which occur again and again. The next two chapters in this book present something of a minimum weight kit of tests for the journeyman research person. These include the chi-square test, the Fisher exact test, a test for the significance of ordinal measures, small sample and large sample tests for the difference between means, and a bit of analysis of variance. With just this much, it should be possible to manage many testing problems oneself, and also to know what is at issue when one takes an unmanageable problem to a consultant. Other sources present still other tests, and should be consulted as appropriate.[4]

PROBLEMS

13.1. It is reported in a study that there are racial differences in school achievement, with a level of significance of 0.05.

    (a) You are asked by someone without any understanding of statistics to explain what this statement means. How would you explain it?

    (b) Does this mean that the existence of racial differences has been demonstrated conclusively? What alternatives are possible? (Consider the possibility that an unlikely event has occurred, and the arguments for and against this possibility. Consider also the possibility that the result was obtained by fishing, what the evidence for or against this would be, and what difference it would make.)

13.2. A social agency is interested in whether paper and pencil tests can be substituted for interviews in assessing the readiness of clients for casework. A number of clients are interviewed and also fill out paper and pencil tests. It turns out that in the five cases where the interview and the paper and pencil test would lead to different conclusions, the interview was always the more nearly correct. This could have happened by chance only one time in thirty-two.

[4] Two excellent sources for tests that may be appropriate to a particular research situation are Sidney Siegel, *Nonparametric Statistics for the Behavioral Sciences* (New York: McGraw-Hill, 1956), and William L. Hays, *Statistics for Psychologists* (New York: Holt, Rinehart, and Winston, 1963).

(*a*) What is meant by the phrase, "happened by chance," in the last sentence?

(*b*) Set up alternative hypotheses, state decision rules, and give the level of significance at which this procedure could, in this case, lead to rejection of the tested hypothesis. Suppose that the alternative hypothesis is that the interview is superior to the paper and pencil test.

(*c*) Suppose that the alternative hypothesis was simply that one of the two, either paper and pencil test, or interview, would be superior to the other, but there was no initial commitment to one or the other. What then would be the level of significance of the procedure? Explain. (Partial answer: the level of significance would be 0.0625.)

13.3. A journal article reports a case of psychokinesis (control of matter by thought). According to the article, an individual has been able to will a coin to come up heads time after time. The level of significance of the test is reported to be better than 0.001.

(*a*) Does this constitute conclusive evidence for psychokinesis? Why or why not?

(*b*) A critic comments that the very low level of significance is conclusive evidence that something was odd in the design of the experiment. This is perhaps a cynical remark, but what is the reasoning behind it? How could it be met by those who performed the experiment?

(*c*) It has been claimed by critics that experiments on mental telepathy, psychokinesis, and the like, wait until a subject has "warmed up" before deciding that his performance will be recorded. The subject is considered to have warmed up when he begins guessing correctly. Discuss the effect this practice might have on significance testing. Is there any way in which subjects may be permitted to "warm up" without violating good statistical practice?

Chapter 14

Tests of Significance Useful
with Nominal and Ordinal Data

For the most part, the tables we examine which bear on the validity of propositions of sociological interest contain information that is nominal or, at most, ordinal in level. Tests of the kind described in this chapter thus tend to be of particular interest to sociologists; they seem particularly responsive to the nature of most sociological data.

The tests presented in this chapter, or others like them, are sometimes used with metric data because of their absence of restrictive assumptions about the nature of the data with which they may validly be used. To call attention to this property, these tests are sometimes called nonparametric. Tests described in the Chapter 15 *do* make assumptions about the population or populations from which the data have been drawn; essentially, that they are not too far from being normally distributed. When the parent population or populations are different enough from normal, nonparametric tests are preferable even when the data are metric in nature. They can validly be used with metric data even if information is lost, for metric data can always be interpreted in terms of their ordinal or nominal properties. An example of a distribution that departs enough from the normal to make justifiable the use of tests that do not require normal parent populations is the distribution of national income. In this distribution, there are many more cases many standard deviations above the mean than the normal distribution would anticipate, and the chance of a millionaire falling in a sample and drastically raising its average value is much too good.

Many different nonparametric tests have been suggested for testing particular types of hypotheses and, of course, there is no limit on the number that may yet be proposed. The tests described in this chapter will be those which have some claim to attention as most likely to be useful in situations encountered by sociologists. These are, for the most part, tests that examine the significance of association between attributes when the data are in the form of contingency tables (tables of two dimensions). In this chapter, the only other type of hypothesis discussed has to do with *goodness of fit* and even here part of the rationale for the discussion is that it serves as an introduction to the chi-square statistic, which may then be considered in relation to contingency tables.[1]

The Chi-Square Tests

The oldest and most widely used of the nonparametric tests is the chi-square test. The test has its limitations: it becomes unreliable under certain circumstances; it is responsive only to nominal level information; it tests only the degree of support for a very general hypothesis and, thus, is not exactly right for every situation. Yet it is nevertheless extremely useful. To present it, we shall discuss (1) the chi-square statistic; (2) the theoretical chi-square distributions; (3) the use of the chi-square statistic to test goodness of fit hypotheses; and (4) the use of the chi-square statistic to test hypotheses of association in contingency tables.

The chi-square statistic. Chapter 10 discusses the computation of the chi-square statistic as a component of certain measures of association: C, T, ϕ. It was there pointed out that this statistic is a plausible way of capturing the extent to which the distribution of data in a contingency table departs from what is expected on the assumption of independence. Its formula requires us to square the discrepancies between what was observed and what would have been expected on the assumption of independence, divide each squared discrepancy by the number expected, and sum the results. It is given symbolically as:

$$\chi^2 = \sum \frac{(o - e)^2}{e}$$

where o = observed frequency, e = expected frequency, and summing is over all cells.

We now want to point out that this same statistic may be formed as a way of judging the divergence of *any* set of categorized observations from a distribution that might have been expected. It is not necessary that our categories be the cells of contingency tables. We can use the chi-square statistic whenever we have a set of categories, a set of frequencies that we expect to occur within the categories, and observations

[1] For tests of other types of hypotheses see Sidney Siegel, *Nonparametric Statistics* (New York: McGraw-Hill, 1956.)

of the frequencies that actually do occur within the categories, to decide whether the observations are consonant with our expectation.

As an example of this extended use of the chi-square statistic, suppose that we want to know whether a sample of one hundred men drawn from the population of our city is divided between blue-collar and white-collar occupations in a way that makes it conceivable that the sample is a random one. We know that in our city approximately 55% of individuals are in white-collar occupations, the remainder in blue-collar occupations. We therefore should expect 55% of our sample, or 55 men, to be in white-collar occupations, and the remaining 45 to be in blue-collar occupations. We can use the chi-square statistic formed by comparing our actual observations with these expected frequencies, as a test statistic for evaluating the hypothesis of random selection against the alternative of nonrandom selection.

The sampling distribution of the chi-square statistic: the chi-square distributions. To be able to use the chi-square statistic as a test statistic, we must know the probability of this statistic taking various values simply as a result of chance fluctuations of observations from what would be expected. This is the sampling distribution of the chi-square statistic.

It can be shown mathematically that when the values expected in any category are not too small (generally taken to be five or less)[2] then the sampling distribution of the chi-square statistic is approximated by a theoretical distribution, the chi-square distribution. It must be noted that the chi-square statistic and the chi-square distribution are independently defined. The chi-square statistic is given by the formula above. The chi-square distribution is a theoretical distribution, like the normal distribution or the binomial distribution, which offers a good description of the sampling distribution of the chi-square statistic when the observed values actually do come from a population like that expected.

The chi-square distribution is closely related to the normal distribution. Let us call a variable that is normally distributed, a "normal variate." Let us now define a variate that is a sum of a number of squared normal variates; this second variate, as we have just defined it, has the chi-squared distribution. The heights of men in a large population are apt to be nearly normal in distribution. Let us select five men at random, measure the height of each, square the measures, add the squares. Then let us repeat the process again and again until we have enough results to be able to see how they are distributed. The picture that results will be a chi-square distribution. If we had included only four squared heights in our sum, the result would have been a different chi-square distribution from the

---

[2] A detailed discussion of this point in relation to contingency tables is given later in the chapter in the section on small expected values.

one we find when we include five squared heights. In general, every time we change the number of squared normal variates in our sum, we get a new chi-square distribution. We call the *number* of independent squared normal variates that have gone into a particular chi-square the *degrees of freedom* of the measure, for reasons that will be clearer in a moment. The distribution of chi-square with one degree of freedom is different from the distribution of chi-square with two degrees of freedom, and so on.

To suggest the form of these different distributions, we might begin by constructing the distribution of chi-square with one degree of freedom, starting with a population that is normally distributed on some variable. Let us transform the normal distribution to one in standard form, with mean 0 and standard deviation 1. As we noted in Chapter 8, this will not essentially alter the distribution; it will still be a normal distribution. We want to know what the distribution of the squares of the normal variates will look like. Because we are squaring, we shall have only positive values. Because the normal curve will be bulkiest around zero, the squares of normal values will also cluster around zero. The resulting curve will look like Figure 14.1.

A chi-square distribution in which each value represents the sum of four squared normal variates would look like Figure 14.2.

A section of a chi-square table is given as Table 14.1. In this table, each line lists a different chi-square distribution; the first line lists the distribution of chi-square with one degree of freedom; the second lists the distribution of chi-square with two degrees of freedom, and so on. The entries give the points in each distribution, to the right of which 0.20 or 0.10 or 0.05, and so on, of the cases will be found. For example, in a distribution of chi-square with one degree of freedom, 0.05 of the cases are to the right of (are greater than) 3.841.

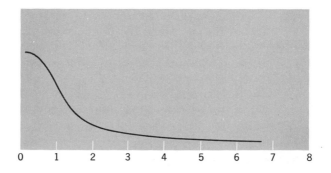

Figure 14.1 Chi-square distribution, one degree of freedom.

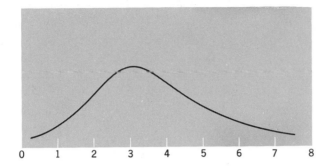

Figure 14.2   Chi-square distribution, four degrees of freedom.

To repeat, the chi-square distribution with the appropriate number of degrees of freedom may be taken as the sampling distribution of the chi-square statistic.

The chi-square goodness of fit test. A goodness of fit problem occurs when we want to compare observations with the frequencies we should have expected on the basis of a model. In this way, we may check on whether the observations are compatible with the model. The model may be the result of an empirical study, or it may be the outcome of a theo-

Table 14.1

A Section of a Chi-Square Table

Degrees of Freedom	Probability				
	0.20	0.10	0.05	0.01	0.001
1	1.642	2.706	3.841	6.635	10.827
2	3.219	4.605	5.991	9.210	13.815
3	4.642	6.251	7.815	11.341	16.268
4	5.989	7.779	9.488	13.277	18.465
5	7.289	9.236	11.070	15.086	20.517
6	8.558	10.645	12.592	16.812	22.457

Source: This table is taken from Table IV of Fisher and Yates, *Statistical Tables for Biological, Agricultural and Medical Research* (4th ed.; Edinburgh: Oliver & Boyd Ltd., 1953). Reprinted by permission of the authors and publishers.

retical analysis. As an example of comparing data with an empirically based model, we might ask whether a sample could have come from a population whose distribution of occupations was like the distribution of occupations in the United States. As an example of comparison with a theoretically based model, we might ask whether the numbers that had come up in successive spins of a roulette wheel were compatible with a horizontal distribution—the "honest wheel" distribution.

The hypothesis set when we are testing goodness of fit is:

> *Hypothesis 1:* The observations are from a population whose distribution is that given in the model.
>
> *Hypothesis 2:* The observations are not from a population whose distribution is that given in the model.

The goodness-of-fit hypothesis set is never directional; it always pits the hypothesis that observations are from the population given in the model against the alternative that observations are not from that population.

Let us suppose that we are interested in whether certain parents are more likely to have boys, while other parents are more likely to have girls. We restrict our attention to families of a certain size—say four children—and ask whether such families have three or four of one sex more often than we should expect if there were no tendency to have children of the same sex.

Our hypothesis set would be:

> *Hypothesis 1:* Our observations are drawn from a population in which the probability of a child being a boy is always 1/2.
>
> *Hypothesis 2:* Our observations are drawn from a population in which the probability of a child being a boy is not always 1/2.

Suppose we collect data from one thousand families. We need to know with what frequency we should expect no-boy families, one-boy families, etc., on the assumption that the probability of a child being a boy is always one-half. We calculate this by working out the *probability* of a no-boy family, and so on. (Ways of working out these probabilities are given in Chapter 8.) These probabilities tell us what *relative frequency* we expect, and the relative frequencies times the total tell us *how many* we expect. The table of expected values is as shown in Table 14.2.

Imagine that our observations had taken the form of Table 14.3.

Table 14.2

Expected Family Composition of One Thousand Four-Child Families

Family Composition	Probability	Expected Relative Frequency	Expected Number
(1) 0 boys, 4 girls	0.0625	0.0625	62.5
(2) 1 boy, 3 girls	0.25	0.25	250
(3) 2 boys, 2 girls	0.375	0.375	375
(4) 3 boys, 1 girl	0.25	0.25	250
(5) 4 boys, 0 girls	0.0625	0.0625	62.5
Total		1.000	1000

Table 14.3

Observed Family Composition of One Thousand Four-Child Families

Family Composition	Number
(1) 0 boys, 4 girls	85
(2) 1 boy, 3 girls	220
(3) 2 boys, 2 girls	360
(4) 3 boys, 1 girl	260
(5) 4 boys, 0 girls	75
Total	1000

We calculate the test statistic, the chi-square statistic, by squaring the discrepancy between observed and expected, dividing by the expected frequency, and summing over all cells.

$$\chi^2 = \sum \frac{(o - e)^2}{e} = \frac{(85 - 62.5)^2}{62.5} + \frac{(220 - 250)^2}{250} + \frac{(360 - 375)^2}{375}$$

$$+ \frac{(260 - 250)^2}{250} + \frac{(75 - 62.5)^2}{62.5}$$

$$\chi^2 = 15.2$$

A chi-square of 15.2 offers some support for Hypothesis 2; but how much? How likely is it that we should get a chi-square this large or larger, if Hypothesis 1 were the case? We can answer this question by consulting the proper chi-square distribution. But which one? Remembering that different chi-square distributions are identified by their degrees of freedom, how many degrees of freedom has the chi-square distribution that is appropriate for the chi-square statistic we have just calculated?

There is a rule that, in fact, follows from the definition of the chi-square variate as a sum of squared independent normal variates. The rule is:

The number of degrees of freedom to be associated with a chi-square statistic is equal to the number of independent components that entered into its calculation.

A component of a chi-square statistic would be a single term. An independent component would be one where neither observed nor expected values are determined by the frequencies in other cells.

We are told the total number of families studied and there are five categories. We can fill three of them, and still not know what number belongs in the fourth. But when we fill the fourth, we know what number belongs in the fifth. We just add up the four categories now filled and subtract the sum from the total. Four, and only four, categories are independent of each other. Therefore, the chi-square statistic that we have calculated is distributed, very nearly, by the chi-square distribution with four degrees of freedom, on the assumption that the tested hypothesis, Hypothesis 1, is true.

We consult the four degrees of freedom line in the chi-square table, and find that a value of 15.2 will not occur as often as 0.01 of the time, if Hypothesis 1 is the case, but will occur more often than 0.001 of the time. We can therefore reject Hypothesis 1, in favor of the alternative Hypothesis 2, at a level of significance of better than 0.01.

We have shown that our observations would occur less than one time in a hundred if the chances of having a boy were *always* 1/2. But now there are still two alternative possibilities: that the probability of a boy is constant, but different from 1/2; and that the probability of a boy is not always the same, but rather is greater in families that have other boys than it is in families that have girls. The data support the second alternative rather than the first. (The demonstration is left to the student. He might design two different sets of hypotheses: in the first, the hypothesis of interest would be that the probability of a boy, in the population as a whole, is different from 1/2; in the second, the hypothesis of interest would be that the probability of single-sex families is greater than would be compatible with an assumption of a constant probability of 1/2 that each child will be a boy.) The point is that the chi-square test demonstrates that the data do not fit the model, but does not specify in what respect the data diverge from it.

The chi-square statistic as a test for association in contingency tables.
Chapter 10 described methods for calculating the frequencies expected in
the cells of contingency tables on the assumption of independence—that
is, taking independence between attributes as the model of the parent
population—and for going on from there to calculate the chi-square
statistic.

The following data, describing the reading of comic books by tenth
grade boys and tenth grade girls, were presented in Table 10.3:

	Does Not Read	Reads 1–8 per Month	Reads 9 or More per Month	Total
Boys	21	39	25	85
Girls	45	51	20	116
Total	66	90	45	201

Chi-square was there shown to be 6.4.

We may treat the chi-square test for association as a special case of the
more general chi-square test for goodness of fit. The goodness of fit in
question, in this case, is with a model in which the attributes are independent of each other. In the hypothesis set, below, Hypothesis 1 is the
tested hypothesis, Hypothesis 2 the alternative to it.

> *Hypothesis 1:* The observations are from a population in which
> reading habits and sex are independent.
> *Hypothesis 2:* The observations are from a population in which
> reading habits and sex are not independent.

The test statistic, chi-square, is 6.4. We calculate the level of significance at which a value of 6.4 could be taken as a basis for rejecting
Hypothesis 1 in favor of the alternative of Hypothesis 2. We must consult
a chi-square table, and it is necessary to know which chi-square distribution is the appropriate one. How many degrees of freedom should be
associated with this chi-square statistic?

We again use the rule that the number of degrees of freedom to be
associated with a chi-square statistic is the number of independent
components on which it is based. In contingency tables where there
are r rows and c columns, the number of independent components is
$(r - 1)(c - 1)$. This is because in every row we can fill all the cells but
the last one independently; the last cell is determined by the row total
and the sum of the already filled cells. Also, in every column, we can fill
all the cells but the last one independently. After we have filled all but the
last row and column, the remaining cells are determined.

In the contingency diagram of Figure 14.3, the cells that are shaded
will be determined once the unshaded cells are filled in.

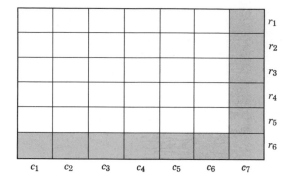

Figure 14.3 $(7 - 1)(6 - 1) = 30$ degrees of freedom may be associated with this figure.

The number of degrees of freedom (d.f.) is the number of cells that the figure would contain if one row and one column were removed; that is, if the figure had one less row and one less column.

This means that:

$$\text{d.f.} = (r - 1)(c - 1)$$

In our present example, where there are three cells in a row and two in a column, d.f. equals $(3 - 1)(2 - 1)$, or two. Referring to the chi-square table, we see that a chi-square of 6.4, with two degrees of freedom, is significant at the 0.05 level. That is, we can reject Hypothesis 1, in favor of the alternative of Hypothesis 2, on the basis of the observed chi-square, and our testing procedure will have a level of significance of 0.05.

Small expected values. The distribution of the chi-square statistic, on the assumption of independence in the parent population, is approximately, but only approximately, the chi-square distribution. Under most circumstances the approximation is a good one, and if the frequencies expected in the cells of the table are large, the approximation is excellent. However, when we expect small frequencies in some of the cells of the table, the approximation may become poor, and the calculation of the level of significance may therefore be unreliable.

This is particularly the case in 2-by-2 tables. For these tables some statisticians recommend that the chi-square test not be used if the expected value in any cell is 5 or less, and that the Fisher exact test, described in the next section, be used instead. Other statisticians would continue to use the chi-square test even though the expected number in some cells is 5 or less, if other conditions, listed below, are met, but they would introduce what has become known as "Yates' correction." This is simply a correction for continuity, required because the chi-square statistic will change in jumps, while the chi-square distribution is continuous. It consists of subtracting 0.5 from the discrepancy between the observed and the expected in every cell in which the expected value is less than 5.

The more liberal statement of when the chi-square distribution may be taken as an adequate description of the distribution of the chi-square statistic is given by Cochran.[3] He proposes that we may use the chi-square test if the table falls under any of the following three headings.

(1) In a 2-by-2 table, if the total number in the table exceeds 40. (If the expected number in any cell is 5 or less, Yates' correction should be used.)

(2) In a 2-by-2 table, if the total number in the table is between 20 and 40 and all the expected frequencies are 5 or more.

(3) In a table which has more than 2 rows or more than 2 columns, if fewer than 1/5 of the cells have expected frequencies of less than 5 and no cell has an expected frequency of less than 1.

If a contingency table fails to meet these criteria, and is 2-by-2, we may calculate a level of significance directly, using the Fisher exact test. If the table is greater than 2-by-2, we may, by collapsing categories, bring it to a table which can be tested reliably.

The Fisher Exact Test

The Fisher exact test may be used with either a directional or a nondirectional set of hypotheses.   In the first case, the hypothesis alternative to the tested hypothesis of independence is that the attributes are associated in a specific way. In the second case, the alternative hypothesis is that the two attributes are associated, without prediction of whether it is more or less of the one that goes together with more of the other.

In either the directional or nondirectional case we calculate directly the probability of evidence as inconsistent with the tested hypothesis as that observed, on the assumption that the tested hypothesis is true. (The tested hypothesis is always the hypothesis of independence.) The Fisher exact test can be used only with 2-by-2 tables.[4]

[3] W. G. Cochran, "Some Methods for Strengthening the Common Chi-Square Tests," *Biometrics*, **10** (1954), pp. 417–451. Recent empirical study shows that Yates' correction in 2-by-2 tables produces a too conservative test. See James E. Grizzle, "Continuity Correction in the χ^2 Test for 2 × 2 Tables," *The American Statistician*, **21**(**4**) (October, 1967), pp. 28–32.
[4] Exact probabilities may be calculated for other tables as well, using more advanced techniques. See William L. Hays, *Statistics for Psychologists* (New York: Holt, Rinehart, and Winston, 1963), pp. 155–156, and 598–601.

In the following discussion, we shall refer to a table whose cells and marginals are designated in this way:

	Attribute 1		
	Yes	No	
Attribute 2			
Yes	a	b	r_1
No	c	d	r_2
	c_1	c_2	n

The probability of any *single* set of frequencies arising, assuming that the two attributes are independent of each other, is given by the following formula:

$$p = \frac{r_1! r_2! c_1! c_2!}{n! a! b! c! d!}$$

The symbol $r_1!$ is read, "r-sub-one, factorial," and means the product of r_1 times $r_1 - 1$ times $r_1 - 2$ times $r_1 - 3$, and so on, until we come to 1. It is understood that $0!$ is equal to one. For example, four factorial equals 24: $4 \times 3 \times 2 \times 1$.

Let us suppose that we had wondered whether children of professionals were more likely to elect preprofessional courses than children of nonprofessionals, that we selected a sample of twenty students, and that our data looked like Table 14.4.

Let us test a nondirectional hypothesis set. Our hypotheses are:

Hypothesis 1: The occupation of the father and the course elected by the student are independent of each other.

Hypothesis 2: The occupation of the father and the course elected by the student are not independent of each other.

Table 14.4

Choice of Course and Occupation of Father, among a Sample of Students

Students	Fathers		Total
	Professional	Nonprofessional	
Preprofessional	7	2	9
Not preprofessional	5	6	11
Total	12	8	20

In the exact test, we do not calculate a test statistic. Instead, we calculate directly the probability of data displaying as much association as is observed, assuming independence in the parent population.

Table 14.4, as it stands, supports the alternative hypothesis that professional fathers have children who elect preprofessional courses. There are two other tables that would have supported this alternative hypothesis even more strongly had they been observed: one in which there was only one preprofessional student whose father is nonprofessional, and one in which there was no such preprofessional student. The three abbreviated tables, the one actually observed and the two that would have offered even stronger support for the alternative hypothesis, are as follows.

7	2	9
5	6	11
12	8	20

Actually observed

8	1	9
4	7	11
12	8	20

Even stronger support

9	0	9
3	8	11
12	8	20

Still stronger support

Since we set up our test to be nondirectional, we must also consider as support for the alternative hypothesis that occupation of father and course elected by child are related, tables that show an *inverse* relationship between the two factors. We shall have to add to our level of significance the probability of tables showing as much support for the inverse relationship as there is support for a direct relationship, on the assumption that Hypothesis 1 is true. To decide how much support is "as much support," we must calculate the probability of evidence as strongly in support of a *direct* relationship as that observed, assuming Hypothesis 1 to be true.

It is usually a good idea to begin the calculation of the probabilities with the table that offers least support for the association: that is, the actually observed table. At times we shall find, on calculating it, that it is so probable on the assumption of the tested hypothesis, that there is no point in going on.

Taking this table, and substituting in the formula,

$$p = \frac{r_1! r_2! c_1! c_2!}{n \, ! a! b! c! d!}$$

$$p = \frac{9! 11! 12! 8!}{20! 7! 6! 5! 2!}$$

Notice that the 12! in the numerator will cancel all the terms in the 20!

beginning with 12; that the 7! in the denominator will cancel all the terms in the 11! in the numerator except 11, 10, 9, and 8, and so on.

$$p = \frac{11 \times 10 \times 9 \times 8 \times 9 \times 8 \times 7 \times 8 \times 7 \times 6}{20 \times 19 \times 18 \times 17 \times 16 \times 15 \times 14 \times 13 \times 2}$$

$$p = \frac{11 \times 9 \times 7 \times 4}{19 \times 17 \times 13 \times 5}$$

$$p = 0.132$$

We might stop here and decide that the probability of even just this table, let alone the sum of this table and other tables offering equal or stronger support, is too great on the assumption of the tested hypothesis to warrant rejection of the tested hypothesis, and there is no point in proceeding further. We already can see that we cannot reject the tested hypothesis at a reasonable level of significance. But to make clear the procedure let us continue with the example.

The next stronger table in terms of support for the alternative hypothesis (that there is association between the occupation of father and course elected by child) is the second presented above. The formula now would have us calculate

$$p = \frac{9!11!12!8!}{20!8!7!4!1!}$$

Compare this with the numbers substituted in the formula for the calculation of the probability of the table of less strong support. It is identical except that we have here 8! where before we had 7!, 7! where before we had 6!, 4! where before we had 5!, and 1! where before we had 2!. The numerator remains the same, but the denominator is multiplied by:

$$\frac{(8!)\ (7!)\ (4!)\ (1!)}{(7!)\ (6!)\ (5!)\ (2!)} = \frac{8 \times 7}{5 \times 2} = \frac{28}{5}$$

The probability of this table is 5/28 of 0.132, or 0.023.

It should be apparent that the probability of the table offering strongest support for the alternative hypothesis of association is so small, on the assumption of independence, as to add little to the overall significance level. We may calculate it nevertheless, to be on the safe side. It will turn out to be 1/18 of the probability of the second table, or 0.001. The probabilities of these tables taken together are 0.132 + 0.023 + 0.001 = 0.156.

Now we must ask what the probability is, assuming the tested hypothesis, of getting support for the hypothesis of association as strong as that observed, except that occupation of parent would be *inversely* related to course election of child. Arguments may be made either for simply using the level of significance already calculated or for actually constructing the tables that would offer the same or more support as that observed, but which would display inverse association, and then calculating their probability. The first is the usual practice,[5] and is likely to be the more conservative. The second seems more in keeping with the idea of the test, but the issue is a difficult one. Let us here follow current practice and double the significance level calculated for the directional hypothesis to obtain the significance level of a nondirectional hypothesis.

Level of significance $= 2(0.156)$

Level of significance $= 0.31$

A procedure with so high a level of significance is absolutely worthless as a test of any hypothesis. We may therefore say that on the basis of this test we cannot reject the tested hypothesis, when the alternative hypothesis is one of association.

Tables giving probability levels for the exact test, for various combinations of observed table entries, may be found in a number of texts.[6] Unless there are several tables to be worked on, it may well be more convenient to calculate probabilities directly rather than hunt up the appropriate reference table.

Significance Tests for Gamma and Tau

As was pointed out in Chapter 11, gamma, tau_a and tau_b all involve the same numerator, S, the difference between the number of positive and negative pairs, and differ only in their denominator. We may take the denominator in each case as being fixed: an estimate of the maximum value S can take. We may therefore concern ourselves only with the distribution of S. If S is large enough to offer firm support for the hypothesis of association, we may say that gamma or tau, whichever we are working with, is also large enough. In other words, we may use S as our statistic for testing hypotheses involving either gamma or tau_a or tau_b.[7]

Let us return to the table in Chapter 11 relating ordinal position and pilot effectiveness. It took the form shown in Table 14.5.

It was there shown that there was an inverse association between

---

[5] See Sydney Siegel, *Nonparametric Statistics, op. cit.*, p. 103.

[6] *Ibid.*, for one.

[7] This approach follows that of Kendall's *Rank Correlation Methods* (New York: Hafner, 1955), Chapter IV. Goodman and Kruskal present expressions for the standard deviation of the sampling distribution of gamma, in their "Measure of Association for Cross-Classifications; III: Approximate Sampling Theory" *op. cit.* These may be preferable if gamma is the measure being used, and if the investigator is interested in developing confidence intervals for the population gamma.

Table 14.5

Ordinal Position and Fighter Pilot Effectiveness

Ordinal Position in Family	Fighter Pilot Effectiveness			Total
	Ace	Near-Ace	Non-Ace	
First-born	1	1	3	5
Second-born	1	4	1	6
Third-born	4	4	2	10
Fourth-born	4	2	2	8
Total	10	11	8	29

ordinal position and effectiveness, and that $\gamma = -0.33$, and $\tau_b = -0.24$. We now ask how trustworthy is this evidence as a basis for supporting the alternative hypothesis that ordinal position and pilot effectiveness are inversely associated, against the tested hypothesis that they are not associated, or are positively associated. (We use the directional hypothesis set in deference to the coherent theory that led to the examination of these data.)

The value of S for the above data was found in Chapter 11 to be -70. Kendall[8] shows that the distribution of S, in a population of samples drawn from a parent population in which attributes are uncorrelated, is approximated by a normal curve with mean zero and standard deviation given by the complicated formula below. The approximation is fair when the samples are as small as 12.[9] We may assume that it is quite good when our table includes as many as 30 or so individuals.

To state the formula for the standard deviation of the sampling distribution of S, we shall refer to a general contingency table in which column marginals are referred to as c_1, c_2, etc. to c_r and row marginals are referred to as r_1, r_2, etc. to r_c. The table might be diagrammed as shown in Figure 14.4.

The standard deviation of the sampling distribution of S (which can

---

[8] In *Rank Correlation Methods, op. cit.*

[9] E. J. Burr shows that when n is 12, and ties are distributed fairly evenly across categories, the normal approximation is, at worst, no more than 1% from the proper value for S near the 5% level; for example, when the true probability of an observed S, on the hypothesis of independence in the parent population, is 0.03, the normal approximation gives 0.023. See E. J. Burr, "The Distribution of Kendall's Score S for a Pair of Tied Rankings," *Biometrika*, **47**, (June, 1960), pp. 151–175.

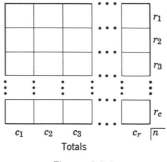

Figure 14.4

also be referred to as the sampling error of S) is:

$$
\sigma_s = \sqrt{\left\{ \frac{1}{18} \left[n(n-1)(2n+5) - \sum_{i=1}^{r} c_i(c_i-1)(2c_i+5) \right. \right.}
$$

$$
\left. - \sum_{j=1}^{c} r_j(r_j-1)(2r_j+5) \right] + \frac{1}{9n(n-1)(n-2)} \left[\sum_{i=1}^{r} c_i(c_i-1)(c_i-2) \right]
$$

$$
\left. \left[\sum_{j=1}^{c} r_j(r_j-1)(r_j-2) \right] + \frac{1}{2n(n-1)} \left[\sum_{i=1}^{r} c_i(c_i-1) \right] \left[\sum_{j=1}^{c} r_j(r_j-1) \right] \right\}
$$

Although forbidding in appearance, this standard deviation really involves just three kinds of terms: terms in which row or column totals or the grand total are multiplied by the total minus one and then again by twice the total plus five; terms in which totals are multiplied by themselves minus one and then again by themselves minus two; and terms in which totals are multiplied by themselves minus one. These terms are then grouped into sums. A working form for carrying out the calculations is suggested in Table 14.6. The marginal values are listed in the first column. Other columns list the terms to be formed and the sums. The data are those of Table 14.5.

The standard deviation of the normal distribution, which would approximate the sampling distribution of S (on the assumption that in the parent population S is zero), is 46.6. The observed S of -70 is then 1.50σ beyond the mean. It would take a value that was 1.65σ to establish a level of significance of 5%. We see that we cannot quite affirm the hypothesis that S in the parent population is different from zero with a level of significance of 0.05 or less.

Actually, however, we cannot fit the normal distribution to the dis-

Table 14.6

Worksheet for Calculation of Standard Deviation of Distribution of S in Sample from Uncorrelated Parent Population

			Types of Terms			
Table Marginals	$x(x-1)$	Sum	$x(x-1)(x-2)$	Sum	$x(x-1)(2x+5)$	Sum
Total 29	812	812	21,924	21,924	51,156	51,156
Column 10	90 ⎫		720 ⎫		2,250 ⎫	
11	110 ⎬	256	990 ⎬	2,046	2,970 ⎬	6,396
8	56 ⎭		336 ⎭		1,176 ⎭	
Row 5	20 ⎫		60 ⎫		900 ⎫	
6	30 ⎪		120 ⎪		2,040 ⎪	
10	90 ⎬	196	720 ⎬	1,236	2,250 ⎬	6,366
8	56 ⎭		336 ⎭		1,176 ⎭	

$$\sigma_S = \sqrt{\frac{1}{18}[51{,}156 - 6396 - 6366] + \frac{1}{9(21{,}924)}[(2046)(1236)]}$$

$$+ \frac{1}{2(812)}[(256)(196)]$$

$$\sigma_S = \sqrt{2132.4 + 12.8 + 30.9}$$

$$\sigma_S = \sqrt{2176.1}$$

$$\sigma_S = 46.6$$

tribution of S so simply. The problem is that S increases in jumps, while the normal distribution is continuous. If we interchange one case between adjoining cells in the table for which we have calculated S, and then recalculate this value, we find that S moves quite far from −70. For example, moving one case out of the upper left corner into an adjoining cell changes S to −77; this single interchange increases the absolute value of S by 7. A different interchange might decrease the absolute value of S by a like amount. A correction for continuity is thus quite important. We want to ask the significance not of the S actually observed, but of a value midway between the observed S and the S that is next smaller in absolute value.

To work out the next smaller value, we make use of a fact which can be demonstrated by simple algebra: if we take any four adjoining cells and change the cell frequencies in each by a single case without changing the total number of cases in the four cells—this is the smallest change we can make in the original table—then we shall change S by the sum of the frequencies in all four cells.

This leads to the following rule for finding the correction for continuity. To find the correction for continuity of the observed S, select the four adjoining cells whose sum is a minimum:

(a) If no one of them is zero, then half their sum is the correction for continuity.

(b) If one of them is zero, then check that it is possible to shift cases in a direction which will reduce the absolute value of S. If it is, then again half their sum is the correction for continuity. If it is not, then another set must be chosen.

In Table 14.5, shown above, the minimum sum of four adjoining cells is given by the four cells in the upper left corner, 1, 1, 1, 4, which sum to 7. The four cells in the second and third column and upper two lines, 1, 3, 4, 1, sum to 9, and similarly it will be found that there is no set of four adjoining cells which sum to less than 7. Therefore, the correction for continuity is 3 1/2, and the value that should be assigned to S, used as a test statistic, is 66 1/2.

To show the use of part (b) of the rule, suppose that no first-born son had become an ace: that there was a zero in the upper left hand cell. Then the minimum value would be the sum of these four cells, 0, 1, 1, 4, and would be 6. But we should have to check that it was possible to shift cases in a direction that reduced the absolute value of S. Since S is -70, we have to check that we can shift cases in a direction that would add positive cases. We should be adding positive cases if we shifted a case into the upper left hand cell, and since this is possible, this group of four cells may be used for deciding the correction for continuity. If the overall S had been $+70$, and there had been a zero in the upper left cell, we should not be able to use the group of four cells which include it.

It should be immediately apparent that in a 2×2 table, the correction for continuity is $n/2$.

Further Notes on the Significance Test Involving S

The standard deviation given above is an adequate statement of the standard deviation of the sampling distribution of S, on the assumption that the qualities are uncorrelated in the parent population. It can be used to test the hypothesis that the qualities are uncorrelated in the parent population against the alternative that there is such correlation. Other hypotheses about S, however—that it is above a certain level in the parent population, for example—cannot be tested using this standard deviation.[10]

No formal proof exists that the sampling distribution of S becomes normal as n increases indefinitely when there are tied rankings, but repeated comparisons of results obtained by direct calculation of probabilities with results obtained by use of the normal approximation make it clear that even with quite small numbers of cases—as few as eight—and with a fairly wide variety of marginal distributions, the approximation is not bad. There may be some danger in using the normal approximation when the very great bulk of cases in a table is concentrated in a single cell. But even then there is no clear counterindication; rather, we are not sure.[11]

PROBLEMS

14.1. The statistic Q, $\dfrac{P - Q}{P + Q}$, is obviously a special case of γ. The discussion of this chapter suggests a test of significance for Q.

(a) What should the test statistic be? What is its standard error?

(b) What should be the correction for continuity? (*Ans.: n/2.*)

14.2. State alternative hypotheses that might have led to the examination of each of the following sets of data. Decide for each set at what level of significance it would permit rejection of the tested hypothesis. State your conclusions.

(a) Relation between hours of study and grade (Table 14.7).

Table 14.7

Numbers of Students, Classified by Hours of Study and Grade in Class[a]

Hours of Study	Grade				
	A	B	C	D	Total
Above average	5	3	4	0	12
Average	3	6	3	0	12
Below average	2	5	3	2	12
Total	10	14	10	2	36

[a] Fictitious.

[10] Kendall, however, gives an expression for the maximum value the standard deviation can take, in his *Rank Correlation Methods, op. cit.*, p. 51.

[11] This discussion is based on the article by Burr, *op. cit.*

(b) Marital status and happiness (Table 14.8).

Table 14.8

Self-Ratings of Men Regarding Their Happiness, by Marital Status

| Marital Status | Level of Happiness | | |
	Very Happy or Pretty Happy	Not Too Happy	Total
Married	683	111	794
Single	29	13	42
Divorced or separated	16	10	26
Widowed	13	10	23
Total	741	144	885

Source: The table is adapted from tables presented in Norman M. Bradburn and David Caplovitz, *Reports on Happiness* (Chicago, Aldine, 1965), p. 13.

(c) Anxiety and happiness (Table 14.9).

Table 14.9

Self-Ratings of Happiness and Anxiety Score, Entire Population

| Self-Rating of Happiness | Anxiety Score | | | |
	Low	Medium	High	Total
Very happy	145	193	139	477
Pretty happy	228	434	523	1185
Not too happy	41	80	209	330
Total	414	707	871	1992

Source: Bradburn and Caplovitz, *ibid.*, p. 29.

Chapter 15

Tests Useful with Metric Data

The tests described in this chapter require that we assume that the population from which the data come is normally distributed. An example of a population that is far from normal is the distribution of annual incomes; this distribution generally shows a peak at the very low end, then sags for a bit, to rise to a second, higher, peak a few thousand dollars on, and finally trail off for many thousands of dollars. With a distribution so severely nonnormal, we may either attempt to find some mathematical device for reinterpreting the data so that the transformed measures approach a normal distribution, or we may neglect the metric qualities of the data and use nonparametric tests such as those described in the preceding chapter. However, if a distribution of data seems to approach the normal—that is, has a single mode near its median, and is reasonably symmetric—little error will result from accepting it as near enough to satisfy the assumptions of the tests discussed in this chapter.

Testing the Difference between Means

One of the more common hypothesis sets in sociological work tests the hypothesis that two groups are the same in some characteristic against the alternative that they are different; or, in directional version, against the alternative that one group is greater than the other. When the characteristic at issue is measured on a metric scale, it seems reasonable to phrase our concern in terms of means and ask whether, on the basis of the information in our samples, we can reject the hypothesis that the means of the populations are the same, in favor of a nondirectional or directional alternative. We should need to test the difference between means, of course, only if we view our two groups as samples from some larger population of possible observations. If we take the two groups as populations in themselves, we can know for certain whether

276

there is a difference. Only if we are concerned with inference from the two groups taken as samples must we investigate whether the difference between their means is sufficiently large to give support to the belief that the populations they represent differ in their mean value.

The statistic we use as a test statistic, in the difference between means test, is just the difference between the means of the two samples, $\bar{x}_1 - \bar{x}_2$. The question we shall ask, when we work out the level of significance of an observed $\bar{x}_1 - \bar{x}_2$, will be the probability of a difference of that magnitude arising when the mean of the population from which the first sample was drawn is the same as the mean of the population from which the second sample was drawn, and the true difference between population means is therefore zero. Imagine that we repeatedly took pairs of samples from populations that had the same mean, calculated $\bar{x}_1$ and $\bar{x}_2$, and subtracted one from the other. Generally, $\bar{x}_1 - \bar{x}_2$ would be close to zero, but occasionally one sample would have a mean somewhat larger than the other. The statistic, $\bar{x}_1 - \bar{x}_2$, would have a sampling distribution. It can be shown that if the parent populations are normal, have the same mean, and have a standard deviation of, respectively, σ_1 and σ_2, then the sampling distribution of $\bar{x}_1 - \bar{x}_2$ will be normal, with mean at zero (the difference between the means of the parent population), and standard deviation given by the following expression:

$$\sigma_{\bar{x}_1 - \bar{x}_2} = \sqrt{\frac{\sigma_{x_1}^2}{n_1} + \frac{\sigma_{x_2}^2}{n_2}}$$

The standard deviation of the difference between sample means will be the square root of the sum of the squares of the standard deviations of the parent population, each divided by its sample size.

Almost always we have to estimate the standard deviations of the parent populations from the samples themselves. It would be preferable to use the standard deviations of the populations from which the samples come, if we could, but we hardly ever have this information. Where samples are size thirty or larger, we may take the estimates formed on the basis of the sample data as fairly reliable, but where samples are smaller than thirty, we must treat the estimates themselves as having a range of variability. We thus have two cases in testing the difference between means: a large sample case and a small sample case. Should it somehow happen that we possess information about the standard deviation in the parent population or populations, we can proceed as in the large sample case, irrespective of the size of the samples.

In the large sample case, if the sample sizes are much larger than thirty, some departure from normality in the parent populations will not introduce serious error into our estimates of level of significance. However, even as much departure as is shown by the usual income curve will introduce serious errors in estimates of level of significance in samples of size thirty.[1]

The Large Sample Case

Suppose that, in a study of educational levels, we find that the mean number of years of schooling in a rural region is 9.0, and the mean number of years of schooling in an urban region is 10.0. We have samples of 400 in the rural region and 450 in the urban region; the standard deviation of the rural sample is 2.0 and the standard deviation of the urban sample is 3.0. In a table, our data would be:

Region	Mean	Standard Deviation	Sample Size
Urban	10.0	3.0	450
Rural	9.0	2.0	400

We find that $\bar{x}_u - \bar{x}_r = 1.0$.

The hypothesis set is:

H_1: The population means are the same.
H_2: The population means are different.

At what level of significance can we reject H_1 in favor of the alternative of H_2, given evidence against H_1 and in favor of H_2 no less strong than that observed? We want to work out the probability of evidence as strong or stronger than that observed arising from populations in which there was no real difference between their mean values—the situation described in H_1.

The sample sizes are large enough to allow us to assume that the distribution of differences between sample means is normal, even though the distribution of education level in the parent population is undoubtedly far from normal. We calculate an estimate of the standard deviation of this distribution of differences between sample means: that is, of the standard error of the difference between means.

$$\sigma_{\bar{x}_1 - \bar{x}_2} = \sqrt{\frac{\sigma_{x_1}^2}{n_1} + \frac{\sigma_{x_2}^2}{n_2}}$$

$$\sigma_{\bar{x}_1 - \bar{x}_2} = \sqrt{\frac{9}{450} + \frac{4}{400}}$$

$$\sigma_{\bar{x}_1 - \bar{x}_2} = 0.17$$

[1] This is shown in an unpublished memorandum by Benjamin Tepping.

If Hypothesis 1 were true, then the mean value of the sampling distribution of differences would be 0. We have just found that the standard deviation of this sampling distribution may be estimated as 0.17, and we have stated that the sampling distribution may be taken as normal. Now we can work out the probability, if H_1 is the case, of evidence no less strong in favor of H_2 than that observed. It is the probability of an observation which is at least 1.0/0.17 standard deviation units from the mean, in a normal distribution. The probability of observations at least 1.0/0.17 or 6 standard deviation units from the mean is less than 0.001: very slight indeed. We can reject H_1, in favor of the alternative of H_2, at a very stringent level of significance.

The Small Sample Case

In the large sample case, using an estimate of the population standard deviation based on sample values does not introduce an important amount of unreliability. When we deal with small samples, we cannot assume this. In the small sample case, we must refer our differences to a distribution that recognizes this second source of sampling variation, and is therefore different from the normal distribution. It is named the *t distribution*.

Like chi-square distributions, t distributions have different shapes, depending on their number of *degrees of freedom*. The fewer the degrees of freedom, the flatter the t distribution, and the more frequent the occurrence of values far from the mean. As the number of degrees of freedom increases, the t distribution approaches closer and closer to the normal distribution. A portion of a table of the t distribution is given as Table 15.1. Notice that when we reach 30 degrees of freedom the values of the t distribution differ only slightly from the values of the normal distribution.

The degrees of freedom to be associated with a t distribution, just as was true in connection with the chi-square distribution, refers to the number of independent components that contribute to the statistic. Our statistic in the difference between means test is

$$\frac{\bar{x}_1 - \bar{x}_2}{\sigma_{\bar{x}_1 - \bar{x}_2}}$$

This is the number of standard deviation units our observation is away from $\bar{x}_1 - \bar{x}_2 = 0$. When the standard deviation in the denominator is calculated from the sample there are $n_1 + n_2 - 2$ independent components contributing to it; the -2 recognizes that the differences on which the standard deviation is based are taken from the sample mean, rather than from the population mean, in each of the two samples, so that one difference in each sample is determined by the others. To state this as a formula: in small sample tests of the difference between means,

Table 15.1

A Portion of a Table of the t Distribution[a]

Degrees of Freedom	10%	5%	1%
1	6.314	12.706	63.657
2	2.920	4.303	9.925
3	2.353	3.182	5.841
4	2.132	2.776	4.604
5	2.015	2.571	4.032
6	1.943	2.447	3.707
7	1.895	2.365	3.499
8	1.860	2.306	3.355
30	1.697	2.042	2.750

[a] Level of significance for two-tailed test (see Appendix 1 for a full table).

degrees of freedom are given by this formula:

$$\text{d.f.} = n_1 + n_2 - 2$$

In the large sample case we accepted the standard deviation of each sample as an adequate estimate of the standard deviation of its parent population. In the small sample case we generally prefer to assume that the standard deviations of the parent populations of the two samples are either the same or nearly so, and to use the data from both samples to arrive at a pooled estimate of the common value.[2] We form this pooled estimate by adding together all the squared differences of observations from their sample means, and dividing by the combined sample sizes, and then taking the square root. That is,

$$\text{pooled estimate } \sigma_{\text{pop.}} = \sqrt{\frac{\Sigma(x_1 - \bar{x}_1)^2 + \Sigma(x_2 - \bar{x}_2)^2}{n_1 + n_2}}$$

Let us recall the remark in the discussion of sampling, in Chapter 12, that the standard deviation of a sample is an underestimate of the standard deviation of the population from which the sample comes. When the sample size is large, this underestimation is not serious, but

[2] A rationale for this procedure is discussed by Morris Zelditch, Jr. in his *Basic Course in Sociological Statistics* (New York: Holt, 1959), p. 246.

for small samples it is, and so it is necessary to introduce a correction factor. As is shown in Chapter 12, an unbiased estimate of the population standard deviation is given if, instead of dividing the squared discrepancies from the mean by n, we divide by $n - 1$. In this case, we replace the $n_1 + n_2$ in the denominator by $n_1 + n_2 - 2$. This gives us

$$\text{unbiased pooled estimate } \sigma_{\text{pop.}} = \sqrt{\frac{\Sigma(x_1 - \bar{x}_1)^2 + \Sigma(x_2 - \bar{x}_2)^2}{n_1 + n_2 - 2}}$$

Suppose that we are interested in whether the average age at which delinquent youths complete eighth grade is different from the average age at which nondelinquent youths complete eighth grade. We are given the average ages at which eighth grade was completed for ten delinquent and ten nondelinquent boys. We are reasonably assured that we may take each group as a good sample of the delinquent and nondelinquent youths who have attended a certain school over the past six years. We list their ages of completion and find Table 15.2.

Table 15.2

Ages of Completion of Eighth Grade (Fictitious)

Delinquent Youths	Nondelinquent Youths
16	13
13	15
14	14
15	15
15	16
16	13
16	14
15	12
16	13
14	15
$\bar{x}_D = 15$	$\bar{x}_{ND} = 14$

Our hypotheses are:

H_1: The two samples are from populations whose means are the same.

H_2: The two samples are from populations whose means are different.

Our test statistic will be

$$\frac{\bar{x}_1 - \bar{x}_2}{\text{est. } \sigma_{\bar{x}_1 - \bar{x}_2}}$$

We see that $\bar{x}_1 - \bar{x}_2 = 1$.

To calculate an estimate of $\sigma_{\bar{x}_1 - \bar{x}_2}$ we first calculate a pooled estimate of the population standard deviation:

$$\text{Unbiased pooled estimate } \sigma_{\text{pop.}} = \sqrt{\frac{\Sigma(x_1 - \bar{x}_1)^2 + \Sigma(x_2 - \bar{x}_2)^2}{n_1 + n_2 - 2}}$$

$$\text{est. } \sigma_{\text{pop.}} = \sqrt{\frac{10 + 14}{18}}$$

$$\text{est. } \sigma_{\text{pop.}} = \sqrt{\frac{24}{18}} = \sqrt{1.33}$$

We next calculate estimated $\sigma_{\bar{x}_1 - \bar{x}_2}$, the estimate of the sampling error of the differences, using the same formula we used in the large sample case.

$$\text{est. } \sigma_{\bar{x}_1 - \bar{x}_2} = \sqrt{\frac{(\text{est. } \sigma_{\text{pop.}_1})^2}{n_1} + \frac{(\text{est. } \sigma_{\text{pop.}_2})^2}{n_2}}$$

$$\text{est. } \sigma_{\bar{x}_1 - \bar{x}_2} = \sqrt{\frac{1.33}{10} + \frac{1.33}{10}}$$

$$\text{est. } \sigma_{\bar{x}_1 - \bar{x}_2} = \sqrt{0.266}$$

$$\text{est. } \sigma_{\bar{x}_1 - \bar{x}_2} = 0.52$$

The test statistic is, then, $1/0.52 = 1.94$. This has a t distribution with $n_1 + n_2 - 2 = 18$ degrees of freedom.

We consult the table of the t distribution and find that a statistic which has a t distribution with 18 degrees of freedom might have an absolute value of at least 1.94 more than 5% of the time, but less than 10% of the time. Therefore, on the basis of this evidence, we cannot reject the hypothesis of no difference in favor of a nondirectional alternative at the 5% level of significance, but we can, if we wish, reject it at the 10% level. (The 10% level, it may be noted, is not a very stringent one.)

Analysis of Variance

Tests of the difference between means compare the variation of observations *between* samples with variation of observations *within* samples.

The between sample variation is stated by the difference between sample means. The within sample variation is stated by the estimated standard deviation within the samples, on the basis of which we develop an estimated standard error of the difference between means. Our test statistic is the ratio of the one to the other.

We can generalize this idea of comparing variation between samples with variation within samples to more than just the case of two samples. The technique for doing so is called the analysis of variance, and is one of the most powerful and flexible approaches available for the analysis of metric data.[3] Adaptations of the technique for other forms of data have also been made. The present discussion is introductory, intended only to make clear the essential ideas of the approach.

When we have more than two samples, we cannot use the difference between means to judge the variation among the samples. Instead, we use the square of the standard deviation, the variance, of the sample means. To judge whether the variation between samples is greater than the variation within samples, we compare the variance of the sample means with the variance of observations within samples.

We must begin by answering the question, what would be the relationship between the variance of sample means and the variance of observations within samples, if the samples were each from the same population?[4]

Chapter 12 stated the relation between the variance of the distribution of sample means and the variance of the distribution of observations in the parent population. There it was pointed out that the standard deviation of the distribution of sample means was $1/\sqrt{n}$ of the standard deviation of the parent population, when the samples were of size n. The variance of the distribution of sample means would, in consequence, be $1/n$ of the variance of the parent population.

To see how this relation can be used here, let us assume that we have three samples, of n observations each. Let us say that the first observation in the first sample will be x_{11} and the second observation in the first sample will be x_{12} and so on. Our complete set of observations and means will be as shown in Table 15.3.

[3] The analysis of variance was first proposed by Ronald A. Fisher, one of the most important contributors to modern statistics. An excellent treatment accessible to nonmathematicians is given by M. J. Moroney, *Facts from Figures* (Baltimore: Penguin, 1951). A more complete discussion of underlying mathematical models is given by William Hays, *Statistics for Psychologists, op. cit.*
[4] Note the minor change in the phrasing of the tested hypothesis from the phrasing in testing the difference between means. We assume here that samples are from the same population rather than from populations with the same mean.

Table 15.3

A Schematic Tabling of Three Samples of n Observations Each

	Samples			
	No. 1	No. 2	No. 3	
	x_{11}	x_{21}	x_{31}	
	x_{12}	x_{22}	x_{32}	
	x_{13}	x_{23}	x_{33}	
	x_{14}	x_{24}	x_{34}	
	x_{1n}	x_{2n}	x_{3n}	
Total:	n_1	n_2	n_3	n
Mean:	$\bar{x}_1$	$\bar{x}_2$	$\bar{x}_3$	$\bar{x}$

It was noted earlier in this chapter that we may form a pooled estimate of the population standard deviation, if we have two samples, by use of this formula:

$$\text{Unbiased pooled est. } \sigma_{\text{pop.}} = \sqrt{\frac{\Sigma(x_{1i} - \bar{x}_1)^2 + \Sigma(x_{2i} - \bar{x}_2)^2}{n_1 + n_2 - 2}}$$

We may form a pooled estimate of the variance of the population by squaring the above. We may form a pooled estimate of the variance of the population based on three samples, by a simple extension of the basic idea:

$$\text{Unbiased pooled est. } \sigma_{\text{pop.}}^2 = \frac{\Sigma(x_{1i} - \bar{x}_1)^2 + \Sigma(x_{2i} - \bar{x}_2)^2 + \Sigma(x_{3i} - \bar{x}_3)^2}{n_1 + n_2 + n_3 - 3}$$

or, since sample sizes are here the same,

$$\text{est. } \sigma_{\text{pop.}}^2 = \frac{\Sigma(x_{1i} - \bar{x}_1)^2 + \Sigma(x_{2i} - \bar{x}_2)^2 + \Sigma(x_{3i} - x_3)^2}{3n - 3}$$

The above formula gives us an estimate of $\sigma_{pop.}^2$ based on within sample variation.

If the samples are all from the same population, we may form an independent estimate of the population variance by first estimating the variance of the distribution of sample means. The estimate of the variance of the distribution of sample means is:

$$\text{Unbiased est. } \sigma_{\bar{x}}^2 = \frac{(\bar{x}_1 - \bar{x})^2 + (\bar{x}_2 - \bar{x})^2 + (\bar{x}_3 - \bar{x})^2}{k - 1}$$

where k = number of groups. Here $k = 3$.

Since this estimate is based on samples of size n, we can multiply it by n to get an estimate of the population variance, based on the variance of the sample means. Assuming that the samples are from the same population:

$$\text{est. } \sigma_{\text{pop.}}^2 = \frac{n[(\bar{x}_1 - \bar{x})^2 + (\bar{x}_2 - \bar{x})^2 + (\bar{x}_3 - \bar{x})^2]}{2}$$

The above formula gives us an estimate of $\sigma_{pop.}^2$ based on between sample variation.

The expression above is an estimate of the variance of the parent population *only* if samples are from the same population. Otherwise, it will tend to be larger than the variance of the parent population. We can form a test statistic that will help us decide whether our observations are compatible with the hypothesis that the samples are from the same population by taking the ratio between the variance estimate based on the variation among means between samples, and the variance estimate based on the variation among observations within samples. The ratio of these two variance estimates is called F, after Fisher.

$$F = \frac{\text{est. } \sigma_{\text{pop.}}^2\text{, based on sample means}}{\text{est. } \sigma_{\text{pop.}}^2\text{, based on observations within samples}}$$

If the samples were from populations with different means, then their mean values would be more divergent than we should expect simply as a result of sampling variation. The F ratio, as a result, would be greater than one. If there is no reason for sample means to differ among themselves other than sampling variation, then the F should not be too far from one. The level of significance question is: how large must F be, in order to be incompatible, at a reasonable level of significance, with the hypothesis that the differences among sample means reflect only sampling variations, that is, that the samples are all from the same parent population?

We may recognize that both the numerator and the denominator of F are quantities that will have a sampling distribution. The nature of the sampling distribution for each will vary, depending on its degrees of freedom. Again, as in the discussion of the chi-square and t distributions, "degrees of freedom" refers to the number of independent components that contribute to the estimate. There will be a different F distribution for different values of degrees of freedom in both numerator and denominator. In order to specify the F distribution that would be appropriate, we must state the number of degrees of freedom in the variance estimates in both the numerator and in the denominator.

To calculate the level of significance of an analysis of variance we need to know the probability of a particular F value, on the assumption that there is no real difference between samples. We need to be able to refer to a tabulation of the probabilities of F values that result from taking the ratio of two different independent estimates of the same variance. Appendix Table 1.5 presents just the 5% points of 510 of these F distributions. That is, the table lists, for each of 510 distributions of F ratios, each resulting from independent samples from the same population, the values that will be exceeded by only 5% of the ratios.

Degrees of freedom may be determined for the within sample vari-

Table 15.4

A Schematic Analysis of Variance Table. One-Way Analysis of Variance, Equal-Sized Samples[a]

Source	Variance Estimate	Degrees of Freedom	F
Within groups	$\dfrac{\sum\limits_{i=1}^{k} \sum\limits_{j=1}^{n} (x_{ij} - \bar{x}_i)^2}{N - k}$	$N - k$	
Between groups	$\dfrac{n \sum\limits_{i=1}^{k} (\bar{x}_i - \bar{x})^2}{k - 1}$	$k - 1$	$F = \dfrac{\dfrac{n \sum\limits_{i=1}^{k} (\bar{x}_i - \bar{x})^2}{k - 1}}{\dfrac{\sum\limits_{i=1}^{k} \sum\limits_{j=1}^{n} (x_{ij} - \bar{x}_i)^2}{N - k}}$

[a] Where n = number in each group; k = number of groups; N = total number of observations; x_{ij} = an observation in the ith group; $\bar{x}_i$ = the mean of the ith group; and $\bar{x}$ = the grand mean.

ance, by noting that one degree of freedom is lost in each sample, just as was the case in the t test. As a result, if there are N observations altogether and k samples, there are $N - k$ degrees of freedom in the variance estimate based on within-group variation. For the between group variance, there are $k - 1$ independent differences between sample means and the grand mean, and so there will be $k - 1$ degrees of freedom.

The important elements in an analysis of variance are often presented in an analysis of variance table. If we wanted to present the variance estimates, the degrees of freedom, and the F ratio for an analysis of variance like the one here discussed, we should make up a table like Table 15.4, putting numbers in place of the formulas.

The particular form of analysis of variance discussed to this point may be called "one-way analysis of variance" because we have examined the effects of only one way of clustering observations. In addition, we are dealing with the simplest case, where there are equal numbers in the groups.

Notice that the numerator of the variance estimates is a sum of squared differences from the mean. Many analysis of variance tables present these numerators in a separate column, headed SS, or "sum of squares." These tables may also refer to what is here called the variance estimate as the "mean square," sometimes abbreviating this to MS. Such a table might be schematized in this way:

Source	*SS*	*DF*	*MS*
Within Groups	$\sum_{i=1}^{k} \sum_{j=1}^{n} (x_{ij} - \bar{x}_i)^2$	$N - k$	$\dfrac{\sum_{i=1}^{k} \sum_{j=1}^{n} (x_{ij} - \bar{x}_i)^2}{N - k}$
Between Groups	$n \sum_{i=1}^{k} (\bar{x}_i - \bar{x})^2$	$k - 1$	$\dfrac{n \sum_{i=1}^{k} (\bar{x}_i - \bar{x})^2}{k - 1}$

Working out squared differences from a mean almost always turns out to be computationally awkward. We encountered just this problem in the calculation of the standard deviation (see Chapter 7) and there found the following equivalence useful for calculation:

$$\Sigma(x - \bar{x})^2 = \frac{1}{n} [n\Sigma x^2 - (\Sigma x)^2]$$

The following computational formulas are based on extension of the above equivalence to the analysis of variance situation. By introduction of a weighting procedure, we shall also develop formulas that may be used even though samples are not all equal in size.

Table 15.5

A Schematic Tabling of k Samples of n_k Observations Each

Samples[a]			
1	2	3	k
x_{11}	x_{21}	x_{31}	x_{k1}
x_{12}	x_{22}	x_{32}	x_{k2}
—	—	—	—
—	—	—	—
x_{1n_1}	x_{2n_2}	x_{3n_3}	x_{kn_k}

[a] There are k samples. In the first sample, there are n_1 observations, in the second n_2, etc. In the kth sample, there are n_k observations.

We work out these quantities, using a calculator when necessary:

(a) $\quad N = n_1 + n_2 + n_3 + \cdots + n_k$

(b) $\quad \Sigma x_{1i} = x_{11} + x_{12} + \cdots + x_{1n_1}$

$\quad \Sigma x_{2i} = x_{21} + x_{22} + \cdots + x_{2n_2}$
$$\text{etc.}$$

(c) $\quad \Sigma x = \Sigma x_{1i} + \Sigma x_{2i} + \cdots + \Sigma x_{ki}$

(d) $\quad \Sigma x_{1i}^2 = x_{11}^2 + x_{12}^2 - \cdots x_{1n_1}^2$

$\quad \Sigma x_{2i}^2 = x_{21}^2 + x_{22}^2 + \cdots x_{2n_2}^2$
$$\text{etc.}$$

(e) $\quad \Sigma x^2 = \Sigma x_{1i}^2 + \Sigma x_{2i}^2 + \cdots + \Sigma x_{ki}^2$

Now we calculate

$$SS\ Between = \left[\frac{(\Sigma x_{1i})^2}{n_1} + \frac{(\Sigma x_{2i})^2}{n_2} + \cdots + \frac{(\Sigma x_{ki})^2}{n_k}\right] - \frac{(\Sigma x)^2}{N}$$

$$SS\ Within = \Sigma x^2 - \left[\frac{(\Sigma x_{1i})^2}{n_1} + \frac{(\Sigma x_{2i})^2}{n_2} + \cdots + \frac{(\Sigma x_{ki})^2}{n_k}\right]$$

It might be noted that the sum within brackets in the formula for the *SS Between* also occurs in the formula for the *SS Within,* and need be calculated only once.

Suppose that we wanted to decide whether where a child lives in a community makes any difference in the age at which he completes eighth grade. We take samples of ten from a suburb, from a good residential area in the city, and from a poor area. Two of the suburban cases are recent transfers and we decide not to count them; we therefore have eight suburban cases. (In any real study, we would have many more observations in our samples than 8, 10, and 10.)

Table 15.6

Ages of Completion of Eighth Grade in Three Areas

Suburb	Good Area	Poor Area
14	14	16
14	14	16
14	14	15
14	13	15
13	13	15
13	13	14
13	13	14
12	13	14
	12	13
	12	12

Our hypothesis set is:

H_1: The samples are from the same parent population.
H_2: The samples are from different parent populations.

Remember that in the discussion of standard deviations it was noted that the standard deviation was unaffected by any addition or subtraction of a constant to all the observations. We can make our calculations simpler by subtracting 14 from all observations, as is shown in Table 15.7. (We could also multiply or divide all observations by a constant without changing the F ratio.)

Table 15.7

Ages of Completion Less 14 (See Table 15.6)

Suburb		Good Area		Poor Area	
x_{1i}	x_{1i}^2	x_{2i}	x_{2i}^2	x_{3i}	x_{3i}^2
0	0	0	0	2	4
0	0	0	0	2	4
0	0	0	0	1	1
0	0	−1	1	1	1
−1	1	−1	1	1	1
−1	1	−1	1	0	0
−1	1	−1	1	0	0
−2	4	−1	1	0	0
		−2	4	−1	1
		−2	4	−2	4
−5	7	−9	13	4	16

We proceed to calculate the quantities required in the formulas.

(a) $N = 8 + 10 + 10 = 28$

(b) $\Sigma x_{1i} = -5$

$\Sigma x_{2i} = -9$

$\Sigma x_{3i} = 4$

(c) $\Sigma x = -5 - 9 + 4 = -10$

(d) $\Sigma x_{1i}^2 = 7$

$\Sigma x_{2i}^2 = 13$

$\Sigma x_{3i}^2 = 16$

(e) $\Sigma x^2 = 7 + 13 + 16 = 36$

$$SS\ Between = \frac{(-5)^2}{8} + \frac{(-9)^2}{10} + \frac{(4)^2}{10} - \frac{(-10)^2}{28}$$

$$= 3.12 + 8.1 + 1.6 - 3.57 = 9.25$$

$$SS\ Within = 36 - [3.12 + 8.1 + 1.6] = 36 - [12.82] = 23.18$$

Table 15.8

Analysis of Variance, Data of Table 15.6

Source	SS	DF	MS	F
Between	9.25	2	4.62	$\dfrac{4.62}{0.93} = 5.0$
Within	23.18	25	0.93	

The analysis of variance table would be as shown in Table 15.8.

Referring to Appendix Table 1.5, we see that an F of 5.0 with 2 and 25 degrees of freedom is significant at the 5% level. We can, therefore, at the 5% level, reject the hypothesis that the samples are from the same parent population in favor of the hypothesis that the samples are from populations in which the ages at which students complete eighth grade differ.

Two-Way Analysis of Variance

There is a second way in which the analysis of variance is a more flexible and powerful technique than the difference between means test; not only can it deal with more than two samples at a time, but it can also deal with more than a single characteristic. In the difference between means test, we could compare groups distinguished by age, contrasting perhaps the educational level attained by young adults and older adults, or we could work with groups distinguished by social class, or groups distinguished by sex, but we could not in a single analysis of the data assess the effect of age *and* class *and* sex on educational attainment. Using analysis of variance, that is just what we can do. Analysis of variance is a technique that can consider many variables at once; it is a way of doing *multivariate analysis.*

To suggest how the effects of two or more possible independent variables can be judged simultaneously, we shall discuss two-way analysis of variance. Analyses of the effects of four or five independent variables are fairly common, and computer programs have been written that investigate the effects of more. The approach is, in principle, no different, irrespective of the number of independent variables involved.

Suppose that in the previous example we had not been interested only in the effect of region of residence on age at graduation from eighth grade, but that we had also been interested in the effect of the sex of the youngster. We might wonder whether boys were more likely than girls to

Table 15.9

General Format, Two-Way Analysis of Variance

Characteristic B	Characteristic A			
	Level 1	Level 2	Level 3	Level c
Level 1	x_{111}	x_{121}	x_{131}	x_{1c1}
	x_{112}	x_{122}	x_{132}	x_{1c2}
	—	—	—	—
	x_{11n}	x_{12n}	x_{13n}	x_{1cn}
	x_{211}	x_{221}	x_{231}	x_{2c1}
Level 2	x_{212}	x_{222}	x_{232}	x_{2c2}
	—	—	—	—
	x_{21n}	x_{22n}	x_{23n}	x_{2cn}
	x_{311}	x_{321}	x_{331}	x_{3c1}
Level 3	x_{312}	x_{322}	x_{332}	x_{3c2}
	—	—	—	—
	x_{31n}	x_{32n}	x_{33n}	x_{3cn}
	x_{r11}	x_{r21}	x_{r31}	x_{rc1}
Level r	x_{r12}	x_{r22}	x_{r32}	x_{rc2}
	—	—	—	—
	x_{r1n}	x_{r2n}	x_{r3n}	x_{rcn}

be skipped, or alternatively, to be held back. We should be interested in the effects of two characteristics, region of residence and sex.

Table 15.9 is a two-way table in which there are the same number of observations in every cell. When working with more than one independent variable, the analysis becomes complicated if cell frequencies are unequal.[5]

Our data on age of graduation of eighth grade might be displayed as in Table 15.9. Assume two or more observations have been added to the suburban school, to allow equal ns in the cells (Table 15.10).

The data are the same as in the example of one-way analysis of variance (except for the additional cases in the suburban group), but now there are two bases for classification.

We again can estimate the variance of observations within groups,

[5] For a treatment of this case, see George W. Snedecor, *Statistical Methods* (Iowa State University Press, 1957).

Table 15.10

Ages of Completion of Eighth Grade, by Region and Sex

		Region	
Sex	Suburb	Good Area	Poor Area
Male	15	14	16
	14	14	15
	14	13	15
	13	13	14
	13	12	13
Female	14	14	16
	14	13	15
	13	13	14
	13	13	14
	12	12	12

but now we can compare with this not only the variance among regional means, but also the variance between averages for sex classifications.

The estimate of the variance within cells is given by pooling the estimates based on differences of observations within each cell from the cell mean. The calculating formula is the same as in the one-way analysis of variance:

$$Within \ SS = \Sigma x^2 - \left[\frac{(\Sigma x_{11})^2}{n} + \frac{(\Sigma x_{12})^2}{n} + \cdots + \frac{(\Sigma x_{rc})^2}{n} \right]$$

$$= \Sigma x^2 - \frac{1}{n} [(\Sigma x_{11})^2 + (\Sigma x_{12})^2 + \cdots + (\Sigma x_{rc})^2]$$

where Σx^2 is the sum of squares of all observations; Σx_{11} is the sum of observations in cell 11; Σx_{12} is the sum of observations in cell 12, and so on; and n is the number in a cell.

There are as many degrees of freedom in this as there are observations in the table as a whole, minus one for every mean involved, which means minus one for every cell. Therefore, within degrees of freedom $= N - k$, where $N =$ total number of observations, and $k =$ number of cells.

There are two *Between SS*. We may refer to one as the *Column SS*, the other as the *Row SS*. In the illustrative table, region is the column dimension; sex is the row dimension.

The calculating formulas again are like the formula for *SS Between* in the one-way analysis of variance:

$$SS\ Columns = \frac{1}{nr}\left[(\Sigma x_{1i})^2 + (\Sigma x_{2i})^2 + \cdots + (\Sigma x_{ci})^2\right] - \frac{(\Sigma x)^2}{N}$$

where r = number of observations in a column (also the number of rows in the table).

$(\Sigma x_{1i})^2$ = square of sum of observations in the first column

$(\Sigma x_{2i})^2$ = square of sum of observations in the second column

etc.

$$SS\ Rows = \frac{1}{nc}\left[(\Sigma x_{i1})^2 + (\Sigma x_{i2})^2 + \cdots + (\Sigma x_{ir})^2\right] - \frac{(\Sigma x)^2}{N}$$

where c = number of observations in a row (also the number of columns in the table).

$(\Sigma x_{i1})^2$ = square of sum of observations in the first row

$(\Sigma x_{i2})^2$ = square of sum of observations in the second row

etc.

The degrees of freedom in variance estimates based on both column and row means will be the number of means—the number of columns or number of rows—minus one, for the grand mean.

We can collect these assertions in an analysis of variance table:

Two-Way Analysis of Variance, Equal Numbers in Cells

Source	SS	DF	MS
Columns	$\dfrac{1}{nr}\left[(\Sigma x_{i1})^2 + (\Sigma x_{i2})^2 + \cdots\right] - \dfrac{(\Sigma x)^2}{N}$	$c-1$	$\dfrac{SS\ Columns}{c-1}$
Rows	$\dfrac{1}{nc}\left[(\Sigma x_{1i})^2 + (\Sigma x_{2i})^2 + \cdots\right] - \dfrac{(\Sigma x)^2}{N}$	$r-1$	$\dfrac{SS\ Rows}{r-1}$
Within	$\Sigma x^2 - \dfrac{1}{n}\left[(\Sigma x_{11})^2 + (\Sigma x_{12})^2 + \cdots + (\Sigma x_{rc})^2\right]$	$N-cr$	$\dfrac{SS\ Within}{N-cr}$

We can stop here, if we wish, in our analysis of variance, with the assessment of row and column effects. However, when we have a two-way or still more complex analysis of variance, we can ask yet another ques-

Table 15.11

Ages of Completion of Eighth Grade

		Suburbs	Good Area	Poor Area
Boys	13		14	15
	13		14	15
	13		14	15
	13		14	15
	13		14	15
Girls	15		14	13
	15		14	13
	15		14	13
	15		14	13
	15		14	13

tion: do certain conjunctions of values of the two characteristics have some special effect? For example, do boys in poor regions graduate late, whereas girls in these regions do not? A question like this has to do with *interaction* effects.

As an example of what is meant by interaction, in Table 15.11 there are absolutely no region effects, no sex effects, and no variation within cells, but there are interaction effects. All the variation among observations within the table is due to interaction. Of course, no data like these will ever actually occur, but the illustration may nevertheless serve to make clear the nature of interaction.

In Table 15.11 all the entries in a given cell are the same, so there is no *Within SS*. All the row means are the same, so there is no *Row SS*. All the column means are the same, so there is no *Column SS*. There is variation among the observations, but it is all associated with certain *combinations* of levels of the independent variables. This is what inter-action is about.

The computing formula for *Interaction SS* is:

$$Interaction\ SS = \frac{1}{n}[(\Sigma x_{11})^2 + (\Sigma x_{12})^2 + (\Sigma x_{13})^2 + \cdots + (\Sigma x_{rc})^2]$$

$$- \frac{1}{cn}[(\Sigma x_{1i})^2 + (\Sigma x_{2i})^2 + \cdots]$$

$$- \frac{1}{rn}[(\Sigma x_{i1})^2 + (\Sigma x_{i2})^2 + \cdots] + \frac{1}{N}(\Sigma x)^2$$

The number of degrees of freedom to be associated with interaction is not obvious. However, notice that the interaction term stems from systematic differences in the cells from what would be expected on the basis of row means and column means. If we think of a "cell effect" as the difference between the cell means and the grand mean, and a "row effect" and "column effect" as the difference between row and column means and the grand mean, then interaction is the difference between the cell effects and the sum of the row and column effects. Each difference of this sort is a contribution to interaction; but not all these differences are independent of each other. In fact there are only $(r - 1)(c - 1)$ independent differences, because the differences involving the "border" cells are determined, once the differences involving the "inside" cells are known. (See the discussion of degrees of freedom in a contingency

Table 15.12

Schematic Analysis of Variance Table, Two Dimensions of Classification

Source	SS	DF	MS
Rows	$\dfrac{1}{nc}[(\Sigma x_{1i})^2 + (\Sigma x_{2i})^2 + \cdots$ $+ (\Sigma x_{ri})^2] - \dfrac{(\Sigma x)^2}{N}$	$r - 1$	$\dfrac{\text{Rows SS}}{r - 1}$
Columns	$\dfrac{1}{nr}[(\Sigma x_{i1})^2 + (\Sigma x_{i2})^2 + \cdots$ $+ (\Sigma x_{ic})^2] - \dfrac{(\Sigma x)^2}{N}$	$c - 1$	$\dfrac{\text{Columns SS}}{c - 1}$
Interaction	$\dfrac{1}{n}[(\Sigma x_{11})^2 + (\Sigma x_{12})^2 + (\Sigma x_{13})^2 + \cdots$ $+ (\Sigma x_{rc})^2] - \dfrac{1}{cn}[(\Sigma x_{1i})^2 + (\Sigma x_{2i})^2 +$ $\cdots + (\Sigma x_{ri})^2] - \dfrac{1}{rn}[(\Sigma x_{i1})^2$ $+ (\Sigma x_{i2})^2 + \cdots + (\Sigma x_{ic})^2] + \dfrac{(\Sigma x)^2}{N}$	$(r - 1)(c - 1)$	$\dfrac{\text{Interaction SS}}{(r - 1)(c - 1)}$
Within	$\Sigma x^2 - \dfrac{1}{n}[(\Sigma x_{11})^2 + (\Sigma x_{12})^2 +$ $\cdots + (\Sigma x_{rc})^2]$	$N - rc$	$\dfrac{\text{Within SS}}{N - rc}$

table, in Chapter 14.) So *Interaction SS* has $(r - 1)(c - 1)$ degrees of freedom.

A schematic analysis of variance table for a two-way analysis of variance is given as Table 15.12.

As an example, we may analyse the data presented in Table 15.10. To repeat the table:

Sex	Suburb	Region Good Area	Poor Area
Male	15	14	16
	14	14	15
	14	13	15
	13	13	14
	13	12	13
Female	14	14	16
	14	13	15
	13	13	14
	13	13	14
	12	12	12

We can subtract a constant from all observations without affecting our mean squares, and so we subtract 14, to simplify the calculations, and produce Table 15.13.

Table 15.13

Ages of Completion Less 14 Years

Sex	Suburb	Region Good Area	Poor Area
Male	1	0	2
	0	0	1
	0	−1	1
	−1	−1	0
	−1	−2	−1
Female	0	0	2
	0	−1	1
	−1	−1	0
	−1	−1	0
	−2	−2	−2

We shall need the sums of squares of (a) observations; (b) cell totals; (c) row totals; (d) column totals; and (e) the grand total.

A. Totals of squares:

     (a)   Observations = 38

      (b)   Cell totals = $1 + 16 + 9 + 16 + 25 + 1 = 68$

      (c)   Row totals = $4 + 64 = 68$

    (d)   Column totals = $25 + 81 + 16 = 122$

  (e)   Grand total squared = 100

B. Formulas for calculation of sums of squares of deviations from appropriate means:

$$Row\ SS = \frac{1}{15}[68] - \frac{100}{30} = 1.20$$

$$Column\ SS = \frac{1}{10}[122] - \frac{100}{30} = 8.87$$

$$Interaction\ SS = \frac{1}{5}[68] - \frac{1}{15}[68] - \frac{1}{10}[122] + \frac{100}{30}$$

$$= 13.60 - 4.53 - 12.2 + 3.33$$

$$= 0.20$$

$$Within\ SS = 38 - \frac{1}{5}[68]$$

$$= 24.4$$

C. Analysis of Variance Table:

Source	SS	DF	MS
Rows	1.20	1	1.20
Columns	8.87	2	4.43
Interaction	0.20	2	0.10
Within	24.4	24	1.02

$$F_{Rows} = \frac{1.20}{1.02} = 1.18 \text{ with 1 and 24 } df,\ p > 0.05$$
$$\text{and not significant at } 5\% \text{ level}$$

$$F_{Columns} = \frac{4.43}{1.02} = 4.22 \text{ with 2 and 24 } df,\ p < 0.05$$
$$\text{therefore significant at } 5\% \text{ level}$$

$$F_{Interaction} = \frac{0.20}{1.02} < 1.00 \text{ and therefore not significant}$$

We conclude that region has a definite effect, significant at the 5% level, but that we cannot reject the hypothesis of no effect for either sex or the interaction of sex and region at this level of significance.

Other Ideas in Analysis of Variance

The preceding discussion has presented some of the basic ideas of the analysis of variance, but it has nevertheless been only an introduction to this statistical approach. As presented here, it was assumed that particular levels of the independent variable represented distinct samples. This is only one possible model—the fixed effects model. In some problems, it may be preferable to assume that the levels of the independent variable themselves are a sample of a range of possible values. This leads to the random effects model and, in complex problems, to different ways of testing hypotheses.[6] Still another variation of analysis of variance (analysis of covariance) results from the attempt to correct observations of effects for the contribution of some independent variable that is correlated with the effects. An offshoot of analysis of variance, to which much attention has been given, is the arrangement of the conjunction of possible independent variables to produce the maximum of useful information for a given number of observations. This work is referred to as experimental design.

PROBLEMS

15.1. A study[7] is aimed at discovering whether conformity to the opinion of others is associated with responding to a great variety of stimuli, while relative invulnerability to the opinions of others is associated with a restriction of attention. An experiment was performed in which individuals were asked to make judgments which could be influenced by others. If they accepted the influence, they were called conforming, if they rejected the influence, they were called resisting. A control group was not exposed to the influence of others at all. All three groups, conformers, resisters, and controls, were asked to recall pictures about which they had not made judgments, which were shown along with the material about which they had made judgments. The means and standard deviations of the number of pictures recalled, along with the number of individuals in each group, are listed below:

[6] See Hays, *Statistics for Psychologists, op. cit.*
[7] Morton Goldman, Bernard J. Haberlein, and Gloria J. Feder, "Conformity and Resistance to Group Pressure," *Sociometry*, **28(2)** (June, 1965), pp. 220–227. Reprinted by permission of The American Sociological Association.

	Controls	Conformers	Resisters
Mean number of pictures recalled	5.75	4.40	2.75
Standard deviation of number recalled	1.7	1.6	1.4
Number in group	12	15	15

(a) Is the difference between the resisters and the conformers in number of pictures recalled a significant one?

(b) Is the difference between resisters and controls in number of pictures recalled a significant one?

15.2. The analysis of variance table for the study above is:

Source	DF	SS	MS
Between	2	61.56	30.78
Within	39	96.82	2.49

(a) Calculate the F ratio, and interpret its meaning.

(b) Justify the values given for the between degrees of freedom and the within degrees of freedom.

15.3. In another study of attitude change,[8] it was hypothesized that the more individuals liked each other, and also the more the apparent discrepancy between their judgments, the more they would change their attitudes. Attitude change was measured by movement along a scale. The analysis of variance table was the following:

Source	DF	Attitude Change MS
1. Liking	1	7.79
2. Discrepancy	2	0.49
3. Liking × discrepancy	2	0.11
4. Within groups	66	1.25

(a) Are the effects of either of the independent variables significant? Interpret.

(b) Is interaction significant? Interpret.

15.4. Using the data in Appendix 2, can you support the proposition that the educational level of younger women is different from that of older women?

(a) What if you divide the women into those who have some college, those who have graduated high school but do not have college, and those who have not graduated high school? Is there any difference in age among these three groups? Interpret.

[8] Leonard Berkowitz and Richard E. Goranson, "Motivational and Judgmental Determinants of Social Perception," *Journal of Abnormal and Social Psychology*, **69(3)** (1964), pp. 296–302.

Chapter 16

The Report

The research task is not completed until the report has been written. The most brilliant hypothesis, the most carefully designed and conducted study, the most striking findings, are of little import unless they are communicated to others. Many social scientists seem to regard the writing of a report as an unpleasant chore tacked on the end of the research process but not really an inherent part of it. To be sure, this stage requires a set of skills somewhat different from those called for by earlier stages of research; and much of the excitement of discovery may have worn off by the time the investigator shifts the focus of his attention from analysis of the data to preparation of the report. Nevertheless, communication of the results so that they enter the general store of knowledge is an essential part of the investigator's responsibilities, which should receive the same careful attention that earlier stages do.[1]

The final, and critical, part of a study is the report which makes available to a reader what the study has produced—its findings, and their implications.

A well-organized quantitative report should move smoothly from introduction to final summary and conclusion, with statement and supporting data clearly related to each other throughout, with speculation and inference developed naturally from the findings and of interest and relevance to important larger issues, and with the topics of the report integrated logically so that the total represents a coherent whole. There are several styles in which this may be done, but no matter which is adopted, the task of developing a coherent report can only in the most general terms be reduced to a series of steps. One of the very best discussions in the literature of the way in which an integrated report was developed from the discrete, unconnected findings produced by data analysis, mentions a period during which the study director was immersed

[1] Claire Selltiz, Marie Jahoda, Morton Deutsch, and Stuart Cook, *Research Methods in Social Relations* (New York: Henry Holt and Co., 1959), p. 442.

in the data, but unable, for the time, to say what they amounted to. The author speculates that:

. . . such a period is necessary . . . in order to carry out synthesis. The synthesis necessary in any coherent research is often neglected in our examination of research activity. We can teach methods of analysis, yet any extensive research . . . requires something equally important: an organization or synthesis which provides the essential structure into which the pieces of analysis fit.[2]

During such a period of intensive study of his materials, a possible approach the investigator might try is to organize the tables containing his findings so that those that deal with the same or related material are placed together. He might then try to develop a conceptual scheme for relating his tables, or rather the findings they embody, to each other. He might ask whether the findings support one another, and in what way, or whether any of the data require that he modify an argument that might be based on other data. Once he is fairly certain of what the data add up to, the investigator may concern himself with a strategy of presentation. He might imagine himself addressing an audience that he must familiarize with his results. Which result must be presented first? Should the investigator tell the audience the general nature of his sample, and then show the distributions of the dependent variable, and then tell what independent variables seem to determine the level of the dependent variable; or should some other scheme be adopted? And, if this approach is used, in what order should the independent variables be presented, and how are they to be related to each other? These are the types of questions that must be dealt with as the investigator organizes the report in his mind.

Often, the process of synthesis begins long before the investigator sits down to write his report. Some investigators try to plan their chapter headings even as they design their questionnaires. In any event, preliminary analyses will point the way to one or another emphasis in the final report. When the final report stage is reached, it is almost always helpful to develop a rough draft just as quickly as possible. The process of turning out the rough draft will make clear whether the logical scheme that has been developed for the report is adequate, and will enormously facilitate its revision should it prove not to be. A first draft is, in fact, a first organization, rather than a first writing; the material may be totally rewritten in the second draft, and yet the first draft will have been worthwhile if it made clear how the second should be organized. Clear

[2] James S. Coleman, "Research Chronicle: The Adolescent Society," in *Sociologists at Work*, ed. Phillip E. Hammond (New York: Basic Books, 1964), p. 204. Reprinted by permission of Basic Books, Inc., publishers.

and detailed outlines are helpful, but an outline is something of a prospectus; a draft makes it clear whether the goods are on hand.

There is no widely accepted category system of reporting styles, but some rather general types of report may be identified. Studies sometimes are divided into those that have descriptive aims, and those that aim at explanation, and reports may be divided in the same way. The essential difference between the two is not that one contains only findings and the other only interpretations, since each will contain both, but rather that in the descriptive report the focus of attention will be on the findings, with interpretation auxiliary, while in the explanatory report the focus of attention will be on the general statements, with findings serving a secondary role as evidence.

The Descriptive Report

The problem in writing a descriptive report is to communicate to an audience a good many often discrete facts about the population studied. Some findings of the study may possibly be disregarded as trivial or of peripheral interest, but descriptive reports generally are not particularly selective. Just because of this there is a need for organization of the materials, and the development of a narrative to accompany the tabulations that present the findings which will direct a reader's attention to the findings' main features.

In a descriptive report the author is like a guide, accompanying his readers through the collection of his findings. The findings should be organized in the way that makes it easiest for the readers to grasp them. For example, one way of developing some coherence among the findings is to show how questions suggested by one finding may be dealt with by another finding. The author helps by pointing out particularly important findings, and by suggesting possible interpretations and implications. Like the guide, if the author has some idea of the interests and level of sophistication of the audience he will reach, he is that much better able to develop a useful presentation.

In putting together descriptive reports, it is a great temptation to stint on tables and instead to have many charts and pictorial representations. The justification may be that an audience will not take the trouble to puzzle out the tables, and the charts and pictures will make the report easier to read. While there is much to be said for picturing important findings, too many pictures make it difficult to emphasize any one of them, and then the dramatic value of pictorial representation is lost. In addition, it probably is true that it is not much more dismaying to have to work through a set of tables than it is to have to work through a set of charts, especially if the tables are accompanied by truly informative text.

A descriptive report might begin with orienting information: descriptions of the aims of the study, the sample, and the instruments used to collect data. It might then move to the presentation of findings having to do with some single aspect of the population studied; for example, in a study of attitudes toward an organization among the organization's members, the first data section might deal with levels of participation, and present findings having to do with hours spent on organization business. A next section could then turn to the attitudes of members to the organization and compare the views of active and inactive members, and so on. Within each of these sections the emphasis would be on the presentation of findings, but there would be sufficient narrative to inform the reader of the main points of tables and of their implications. (Or, from another point of view, the evidence supporting the interpretations would be presented in the tables and brought to the reader's attention as required.) Finally there might be a summarizing chapter which would also try to phrase the most general conclusions the study may support, and perhaps suggest implications of these conclusions for theory or action or, in a phrase that has become trite and perhaps long was empty, for further research.

Explanatory Reports

There are a number of different frameworks within which the results of a study may be marshalled to provide support for generalization. Three of these, each stemming from a different original design, may be referred to as hypothesis testing, focused argument, and the development of a system or structural model.

Hypothesis Testing

An investigator is fortunate if he has been able to conduct a study whose results bear on the validity of a small number of concrete hypotheses, themselves derived from a well-developed theory. The report of such a study can be compact and direct. It may begin by justifying the hypotheses, perhaps showing how they are implied in the theory. It may then describe the methods used, present the data, and, finally, judge the validity of the hypotheses in light of the research results. A concluding section might offer some reassessment of both hypotheses and theory.

This method of presenting material is sometimes thought to be the model for any proper explanatory report. As Kaplan puts it, it is the approved reconstructed logic for communicating scientific results.[3] At times, investigators find this method so appealing that they use it to present their data even though they had no particular hypothesis in mind

[3] Abraham Kaplan, *The Conduct of Inquiry* (San Francisco: Chandler, 1964), Chapter 1.

when they collected them. The result, often, is a report that seems awkward and pseudo-scientific.

Focused Argument

Another model for an explanatory report is the legal brief. To the investigator, the data may all seem to contribute to a single conclusion, and to support a single central proposition. The investigator may feel then that his task in his report is to win the assent of his readers to the general conclusion. The legal brief simile is inaccurate in one important respect: the lawyer is an advocate for a position, while the investigator must present doubts as effectively as he presents supporting evidence. A focused argument is like a legal brief in its concern with a central issue and its examination of evidence in terms of its bearing on that issue; it differs in the demand that the investigator present all relevant data, and not only all favorable data.

Durkeim's *Suicide* can be viewed as an instance of a focused argument. He concluded, on examination of his data, before he presented them, that suicide is a response to the nature of the social fabric. He began his argument by proposing alternative theories, and by then showing that the evidence failed to support them. He then presented new data and argued that it led to the presumption that the suicide-social fabric theory was correct. He then presented additional data showing that implications of this theory were supported, and then still more data that suggested modifications and specifications of this theory. The reader, when he has finished the report, feels sure that all data that were relevant and available to the author have been examined and represented honestly, and that the theory is sound.

In a presentation of this sort, the *line of argument* is extremely important. The investigator may imagine himself addressing a somewhat skeptical audience, to whom he must make his case step by step, including all relevant data, treating them fairly, and moving toward his general conclusion in a logical and steady progression. For example, in a study of the sources of adolescent views of the world, the investigator might decide that the overall conclusion of his data is that adolescents are selective, absorbing some of their views from their parents, some from peers, and adding their own individual appraisals of the meaning of observations. The reader might be led to this conclusion in a report that first presented the problem to him, then showed that in some areas views were most like those of peers, then showed that in other areas views were most like those of parents, then discussed the ways in which individual differences asserted themselves, and finally summed up what had been demonstrated.

A report in this style is like a descriptive report, in its presentation of a great deal of data, and its attempt to develop a narrative that moves the reader from point to point until a terrain has been covered. It differs in its concern for the implications findings have for a central issue. Where the descriptive report presents findings for their own sake, because each makes clear some aspect of the object of study, the focused argument presents findings because each has bearing on the nature or validity of the central proposition.

Structural or System Models

Perhaps the most difficult of conceptual frameworks to manage for the presentation of quantitative data is one that proposes a structural or systemlike model of an institution that has been studied—school or hospital or neighborhood—and uses the data to support or illuminate this model. This is the sort of task that traditionally has been the domain of qualitative research; it is most difficult with the standardized materials of a quantitative study. A report of this sort might first concern itself with structural aspects: the numbers of personnel, their positions, their responsibilities; the goals and atmosphere of the system. It might then consider what might be more nearly aspects of functioning within the system: the attitudes and beliefs of individuals in particular roles; the effects on them that membership in the system seems to have.

It is difficult to describe this approach in general terms. Much depends on the quality of the underlying model, and much, too, on the existence of quantitative data that can be coordinated to a great many of its points.[4]

Audiences

One of the problems in report writing is deciding on the audience to address. It is distressing to read a report that appears now to be directed to a lay audience, now to colleagues of the author, and now to representatives of an agency that originally sponsored the research. The multipurpose report rarely has much success. The most useful approach is to choose a single audience, and then to include material of interest to other audiences, or to write on a level appropriate to other audiences, only if it does not interfere with the primary communication. Material that would not be appropriate for the primary audience might be set off from the body of the report in footnotes or an appendix.

[4] As an instance of this approach, a reader may want to consider James S. Coleman's *Adolescent Society* (New York: Free Press, 1960).

Learning to Write Reports

The communication of findings is perhaps more of an art than is any other aspect of quantitative research. Learning to write reports has much in common with learning an art. A certain amount of native talent seems most useful, and some individuals seem so talented to begin with that almost without instruction they are able to produce respectable work. Most investigators learn to write reports in much the way they learn to conduct other aspects of studies: by an apprenticeship in which their work is criticized by those in the field, by continued efforts, and by study of the work of their colleagues. Some learning can take place only through practice, through producing reports, and experiencing the reactions to them. Some learning is possible through close attention to the way in which other investigators communicate their findings. An investigator who encounters the report of a colleague that seems unusually good may take time to work out just where its merits lie, and in this way add to his understanding of how good reports are written. There probably is no point in trying to develop general rules regarding what would be a good report, but the study of the work of one's colleagues should be the post-graduate education of the artist and research worker alike.

Appendix **1**

TABLES

Table 1

Squares and Square Roots*

N	N^2	$\sqrt{N}$	$\sqrt{10N}$	N	N^2	$\sqrt{N}$	$\sqrt{10N}$
1.00	1.0000	1.00000	3.16228	**1.50**	2.2500	1.22474	3.87298
1.01	1.0201	1.00499	3.17805	1.51	2.2801	1.22882	3.88587
1.02	1.0404	1.00995	3.19374	1.52	2.3104	1.23288	3.89872
1.03	1.0609	1.01489	3.20936	1.53	2.3409	1.23693	3.91152
1.04	1.0816	1.01980	3.22490	1.54	2.3716	1.24097	3.92428
1.05	1.1025	1.02470	3.24037	1.55	2.4025	1.24499	3.93700
1.06	1.1236	1.02956	3.25576	1.56	2.4336	1.24900	3.94968
1.07	1.1449	1.03441	3.27109	1.57	2.4649	1.25300	3.96232
1.08	1.1664	1.03923	3.28634	1.58	2.4964	1.25698	3.97492
1.09	1.1881	1.04403	3.30151	1.59	2.5281	1.26095	3.98748
1.10	1.2100	1.04881	3.31662	**1.60**	2.5600	1.26491	4.00000
1.11	1.2321	1.05357	3.33167	1.61	2.5921	1.26886	4.01248
1.12	1.2544	1.05830	3.34664	1.62	2.6244	1.27279	4.02492
1.13	1.2769	1.06301	3.36155	1.63	2.6569	1.27671	4.03733
1.14	1.2996	1.06771	3.37639	1.64	2.6896	1.28062	4.04969
1.15	1.3225	1.07238	3.39116	1.65	2.7225	1.28452	4.06202
1.16	1.3456	1.07703	3.40588	1.66	2.7556	1.28841	4.07431
1.17	1.3689	1.08167	3.42053	1.67	2.7889	1.29228	4.08656
1.18	1.3924	1.08628	3.43511	1.68	2.8224	1.29615	4.09878
1.19	1.4161	1.09087	3.44964	1.69	2.8561	1.30000	4.11096
1.20	1.4400	1.09545	3.46410	**1.70**	2.8900	1.30384	4.12311
1.21	1.4641	1.10000	3.47851	1.71	2.9241	1.30767	4.13521
1.22	1.4884	1.10454	3.49285	1.72	2.9584	1.31149	4.14729
1.23	1.5129	1.10905	3.50714	1.73	2.9929	1.31529	4.15933
1.24	1.5376	1.11355	3.52136	1.74	3.0276	1.31909	4.17133
1.25	1.5625	1.11803	3.53553	1.75	3.0625	1.32288	4.18330
1.26	1.5876	1.12250	3.54965	1.76	3.0976	1.32665	4.19524
1.27	1.6129	1.12694	3.56371	1.77	3.1329	1.33041	4.20714
1.28	1.6384	1.13137	3.57771	1.78	3.1684	1.33417	4.21900
1.29	1.6641	1.13578	3.59166	1.79	3.2041	1.33791	4.23084
1.30	1.6900	1.14018	3.60555	**1.80**	3.2400	1.34164	4.24264
1.31	1.7161	1.14455	3.61939	1.81	3.2761	1.34536	4.25441
1.32	1.7424	1.14891	3.63318	1.82	3.3124	1.34907	4.26615
1.33	1.7689	1.15326	3.64692	1.83	3.3489	1.35277	4.27785
1.34	1.7956	1.15758	3.66060	1.84	3.3856	1.35647	4.28952
1.35	1.8225	1.16190	3.67423	1.85	3.4225	1.36015	4.30116
1.36	1.8496	1.16619	3.68782	1.86	3.4596	1.36382	4.31277
1.37	1.8769	1.17047	3.70135	1.87	3.4969	1.36748	4.32435
1.38	1.9044	1.17473	3.71484	1.88	3.5344	1.37113	4.33590
1.39	1.9321	1.17898	3.72827	1.89	3.5721	1.37477	4.34741
1.40	1.9600	1.18322	3.74166	**1.90**	3.6100	1.37840	4.35890
1.41	1.9881	1.18743	3.75500	1.91	3.6481	1.38203	4.37035
1.42	2.0164	1.19164	3.76829	1.92	3.6864	1.38564	4.38178
1.43	2.0449	1.19583	3.78153	1.93	3.7249	1.38924	4.39318
1.44	2.0736	1.20000	3.79473	1.94	3.7636	1.39284	4.40454
1.45	2.1025	1.20416	3.80789	1.95	3.8025	1.39642	4.41588
1.46	2.1316	1.20830	3.82099	1.96	3.8416	1.40000	4.42719
1.47	2.1609	1.21244	3.83406	1.97	3.8809	1.40357	4.43847
1.48	2.1904	1.21655	3.84708	1.98	3.9204	1.40712	4.44972
1.49	2.2201	1.22066	3.86055	1.99	3.9601	1.41067	4.46094
1.50	2.2500	1.22474	3.87298	**2.00**	4.0000	1.41421	4.47214
N	N^2	$\sqrt{N}$	$\sqrt{10N}$	N	N^2	$\sqrt{N}$	$\sqrt{10N}$

Table 1 (*Continued*)

N	N^2	$\sqrt{N}$	$\sqrt{10N}$	N	N^2	$\sqrt{N}$	$\sqrt{10N}$
2.00	4.0000	1.41421	4.47214	**2.50**	6.2500	1.58114	5.00000
2.01	4.0401	1.41774	4.48330	2.51	6.3001	1.58430	5.00999
2.02	4.0804	1.42127	4.49444	2.52	6.3504	1.58745	5.01996
2.03	4.1209	1.42478	4.50555	2.53	6.4009	1.59060	5.02991
2.04	4.1616	1.42829	4.51664	2.54	6.4516	1.59374	5.03984
2.05	4.2025	1.43178	4.52769	2.55	6.5025	1.59687	5.04975
2.06	4.2436	1.43527	4.53872	2.56	6.5536	1.60000	5.05964
2.07	4.2849	1.43875	4.54973	2.57	6.6049	1.60312	5.06952
2.08	4.3264	1.44222	4.56070	2.58	6.6564	1.60624	5.07937
2.09	4.3681	1.44568	4.57165	2.59	6.7081	1.60935	5.08920
2.10	4.4100	1.44914	4.58258	**2.60**	6.7600	1.61245	5.09902
2.11	4.4521	1.45258	4.59347	2.61	6.8121	1.61555	5.10882
2.12	4.4944	1.45602	4.60435	2.62	6.8644	1.61864	5.11859
2.13	4.5369	1.45945	4.61519	2.63	6.9169	1.62173	5.12835
2.14	4.5796	1.46287	4.62601	2.64	6.9696	1.62481	5.13809
2.15	4.6225	1.46629	4.63681	2.65	7.0225	1.62788	5.14782
2.16	4.6656	1.46969	4.64758	2.66	7.0756	1.63095	5.15752
2.17	4.7089	1.47309	4.65833	2.67	7.1289	1.63401	5.16720
2.18	4.7524	1.47648	4.66905	2.68	7.1824	1.63707	5.17687
2.19	4.7961	1.47986	4.67974	2.69	7.2361	1.64012	5.18652
2.20	4.8400	1.48324	4.69042	**2.70**	7.2900	1.64317	5.19615
2.21	4.8841	1.48661	4.70106	2.71	7.3441	1.64621	5.20577
2.22	4.9284	1.48997	4.71169	2.72	7.3984	1.64924	5.21536
2.23	4.9729	1.49332	4.72229	2.73	7.4529	1.65227	5.22494
2.24	5.0176	1.49666	4.73286	2.74	7.5076	1.65529	5.23450
2.25	5.0625	1.50000	4.74342	2.75	7.5625	1.65831	5.24404
2.26	5.1076	1.50333	4.75395	2.76	7.6176	1.66132	5.25357
2.27	5.1529	1.50665	4.76445	2.77	7.6729	1.66433	5.26308
2.28	5.1984	1.50997	4.77493	2.78	7.7284	1.66733	5.27257
2.29	5.2441	1.51327	4.78539	2.79	7.7841	1.67033	5.28205
2.30	5.2900	1.51658	4.79583	**2.80**	7.8400	1.67332	5.29150
2.31	5.3361	1.51987	4.80625	2.81	7.8961	1.67631	5.30094
2.32	5.3824	1.52315	4.81664	2.82	7.9524	1.67929	5.31037
2.33	5.4289	1.52643	4.82701	2.83	8.0089	1.68226	5.31977
2.34	5.4756	1.52971	4.83735	2.84	8.0656	1.68523	5.32917
2.35	5.5225	1.53297	4.84768	2.85	8.1225	1.68819	5.33854
2.36	5.5696	1.53623	4.85798	2.86	8.1796	1.69115	5.34790
2.37	5.6169	1.53948	4.86826	2.87	8.2369	1.69411	5.35724
2.38	5.6644	1.54272	4.87852	2.88	8.2944	1.69706	5.36656
2.39	5.7121	1.54596	4.88876	2.89	8.3521	1.70000	5.37587
2.40	5.7600	1.54919	4.89898	**2.90**	8.4100	1.70294	5.38516
2.41	5.8081	1.55242	4.90918	2.91	8.4681	1.70587	5.39444
2.42	5.8564	1.55563	4.91935	2.92	8.5264	1.70880	5.40370
2.43	5.9049	1.55885	4.92950	2.93	8.5849	1.71172	5.41295
2.44	5.9536	1.56205	4.93964	2.94	8.6436	1.71464	5.42218
2.45	6.0025	1.56525	4.94975	2.95	8.7025	1.71756	5.43139
2.46	6.0516	1.56844	4.95984	2.96	8.7616	1.72047	5.44059
2.47	6.1009	1.57162	4.96991	2.97	8.8209	1.72337	5.44977
2.48	6.1504	1.57480	4.97996	2.98	8.8804	1.72627	5.45894
2.49	6.2001	1.57797	4.98999	2.99	8.9401	1.72916	5.46809
2.50	6.2500	1.58114	5.00000	**3.00**	9.0000	1.73205	5.47723
N	N^2	$\sqrt{N}$	$\sqrt{10N}$	N	N^2	$\sqrt{N}$	$\sqrt{10N}$

(*Continued*)

Table 1 (*Continued*)

N	N^2	$\sqrt{N}$	$\sqrt{10N}$	N	N^2	$\sqrt{N}$	$\sqrt{10N}$
3.00	9.0000	1.73205	5.47723	**3.50**	12.2500	1.87083	5.91608
3.01	9.0601	1.73494	5.48635	3.51	12.3201	1.87350	5.92453
3.02	9.1204	1.73781	5.49545	3.52	12.3904	1.87617	5.93296
3.03	9.1809	1.74069	5.50454	3.53	12.4609	1.87883	5.94138
3.04	9.2416	1.74356	5.51362	3.54	12.5316	1.88149	5.94979
3.05	9.3025	1.74642	5.52268	3.55	12.6025	1.88414	5.95819
3.06	9.3636	1.74929	5.53173	3.56	12.6736	1.88680	5.96657
3.07	9.4249	1.75214	5.54076	3.57	12.7449	1.88944	5.97495
3.08	9.4864	1.75499	5.54977	3.58	12.8164	1.89209	5.98331
3.09	9.5481	1.75784	5.55878	3.59	12.8881	1.89473	5.99166
3.10	9.6100	1.76068	5.56776	**3.60**	12.9600	1.89737	6.00000
3.11	9.6721	1.76352	5.57674	3.61	13.0321	1.90000	6.00833
3.12	9.7344	1.76635	5.58570	3.62	13.1044	1.90263	6.01664
3.13	9.7969	1.76918	5.59464	3.63	13.1769	1.90526	6.02495
3.14	9.8596	1.77200	5.60357	3.64	13.2496	1.90788	6.03324
3.15	9.9225	1.77482	5.61249	3.65	13.3225	1.91050	6.04152
3.16	9.9856	1.77764	5.62139	3.66	13.3956	1.91311	6.04979
3.17	10.0489	1.78045	5.63028	3.67	13.4689	1.91572	6.05805
3.18	10.1124	1.78326	5.63915	3.68	13.5424	1.91833	6.06630
3.19	10.1761	1.78606	5.64801	3.69	13.6161	1.92094	6.07454
3.20	10.2400	1.78885	5.65685	**3.70**	13.6900	1.92354	6.08276
3.21	10.3041	1.79165	5.66569	3.71	13.7641	1.92614	6.09098
3.22	10.3684	1.79444	5.67450	3.72	13.8384	1.92873	6.09918
3.23	10.4329	1.79722	5.68331	3.73	13.9129	1.93132	6.10737
3.24	10.4976	1.80000	5.69210	3.74	13.9876	1.93391	6.11555
3.25	10.5625	1.80278	5.70088	3.75	14.0625	1.93649	6.12372
3.26	10.6276	1.80555	5.70964	3.76	14.1376	1.93907	6.13188
3.27	10.6929	1.80831	5.71839	3.77	14.2129	1.94165	6.14003
3.28	10.7584	1.81108	5.72713	3.78	14.2884	1.94422	6.14817
3.29	10.8241	1.81384	5.73585	3.79	14.3641	1.94679	6.15630
3.30	10.8900	1.81659	5.74456	**3.80**	14.4400	1.94936	6.16441
3.31	10.9561	1.81934	5.75326	3.81	14.5161	1.95192	6.17252
3.32	11.0224	1.82209	5.76194	3.82	14.5924	1.95448	6.18061
3.33	11.0889	1.82483	5.77062	3.83	14.6689	1.95704	6.18870
3.34	11.1556	1.82757	5.77927	3.84	14.7456	1.95959	6.19677
3.35	11.2225	1.83030	5.78792	3.85	14.8225	1.96214	6.20484
3.36	11.2896	1.83303	5.79655	3.86	14.8996	1.96469	6.21289
3.37	11.3569	1.83576	5.80517	3.87	14.9769	1.96723	6.22093
3.38	11.4244	1.83848	5.81378	3.88	15.0544	1.96977	6.22896
3.39	11.4921	1.84120	5.82237	3.89	15.1321	1.97231	6.23699
3.40	11.5600	1.84391	5.83095	**3.90**	15.2100	1.97484	6.24500
3.41	11.6281	1.84662	5.83952	3.91	15.2881	1.97737	6.25300
3.42	11.6964	1.84932	5.84808	3.92	15.3664	1.97990	6.26099
3.43	11.7649	1.85203	5.85662	3.93	15.4449	1.98242	6.26897
3.44	11.8336	1.85472	5.86515	3.94	15.5236	1.98494	6.27694
3.45	11.9025	1.85742	5.87367	3.95	15.6025	1.98746	6.28490
3.46	11.9716	1.86011	5.88218	3.96	15.6816	1.98997	6.29285
3.47	12.0409	1.86279	5.89067	3.97	15.7609	1.99249	6.30079
3.48	12.1104	1.86548	5.89915	3.98	15.8404	1.99499	6.30872
3.49	12.1801	1.86815	5.90762	3.99	15.9201	1.99750	6.31664
3.50	12.2500	1.87083	5.91608	**4.00**	16.0000	2.00000	6.32456
N	N^2	$\sqrt{N}$	$\sqrt{10N}$	N	N^2	$\sqrt{N}$	$\sqrt{10N}$

Table 1 (*Continued*)

N	N^2	$\sqrt{N}$	$\sqrt{10N}$	N	N^2	$\sqrt{N}$	$\sqrt{10N}$
4.00	16.0000	2.00000	6.32456	**4.50**	20.2500	2.12132	6.70820
4.01	16.0801	2.00250	6.33246	4.51	20.3401	2.12368	6.71565
4.02	16.1604	2.00499	6.34035	4.52	20.4304	2.12603	6.72309
4.03	16.2409	2.00749	6.34823	4.53	20.5209	2.12838	6.73053
4.04	16.3216	2.00998	6.35610	4.54	20.6116	2.13073	6.73795
4.05	16.4025	2.01246	6.36396	4.55	20.7025	2.13307	6.74537
4.06	16.4836	2.01494	6.37181	4.56	20.7936	2.13542	6.75278
4.07	16.5649	2.01742	6.37966	4.57	20.8849	2.13776	6.76018
4.08	16.6464	2.01990	6.38749	4.58	20.9764	2.14009	6.76757
4.09	16.7281	2.02237	6.39531	4.59	21.0681	2.14243	6.77495
4.10	16.8100	2.02485	6.40312	**4.60**	21.1600	2.14476	6.78233
4.11	16.8921	2.02731	6.41093	4.61	21.2521	2.14709	6.78970
4.12	16.9744	2.02978	6.41872	4.62	21.3444	2.14942	6.79706
4.13	17.0569	2.03224	6.42651	4.63	21.4369	2.15174	6.80441
4.14	17.1396	2.03470	6.43428	4.64	21.5296	2.15407	6.81175
4.15	17.2225	2.03715	6.44205	4.65	21.6225	2.15639	6.81909
4.16	17.3056	2.03961	6.44981	4.66	21.7156	2.15870	6.82642
4.17	17.3889	2.04206	6.45755	4.67	21.8089	2.16102	6.83374
4.18	17.4724	2.04450	6.46529	4.68	21.9024	2.16333	6.84105
4.19	17.5561	2.04695	6.47302	4.69	21.9961	2.16564	6.84836
4.20	17.6400	2.04939	6.48074	**4.70**	22.0900	2.16795	6.85565
4.21	17.7241	2.05183	6.48845	4.71	22.1841	2.17025	6.86294
4.22	17.8084	2.05426	6.49615	4.72	22.2784	2.17256	6.87023
4.23	17.8929	2.05670	6.50384	4.73	22.3729	2.17486	6.87750
4.24	17.9776	2.05913	6.51153	4.74	22.4676	2.11715	6.88477
4.25	18.0625	2.06155	6.51920	4.75	22.5625	2.17945	6.89202
4.26	18.1476	2.06398	6.52687	4.76	22.6576	2.18174	6.89928
4.27	18.2329	2.06640	6.53452	4.77	22.7529	2.18403	6.90652
4.28	18.3184	2.06882	6.54217	4.78	22.8484	2.18632	6.91375
4.29	18.4041	2.07123	6.54981	4.79	22.9441	2.18861	6.92098
4.30	18.4900	2.07364	6.55744	**4.80**	23.0400	2.19089	6.92820
4.31	18.5761	2.07605	6.56506	4.81	23.1361	2.19317	6.93542
4.32	18.6624	2.07846	6.57267	4.82	23.2324	2.19545	6.94262
4.33	18.7489	2.08087	6.58027	4.83	23.3289	2.19773	6.94982
4.34	18.8356	2.08327	6.58787	4.84	23.4256	2.20000	6.95701
4.35	18.9225	2.08567	6.59545	4.85	23.5225	2.20227	6.96419
4.36	19.0096	2.08806	6.60303	4.86	23.6196	2.20454	6.97137
4.37	19.0969	2.99045	6.61060	4.87	23.7169	2.20681	6.97854
4.38	19.1844	2.09284	6.61816	4.88	23.8144	2.20907	6.98570
4.39	19.2721	2.09523	6.62571	4.89	23.9121	2.21133	6.99285
4.40	19.3600	2.09762	6.63325	**4.90**	24.0100	2.21359	7.00000
4.41	19.4481	2.10000	6.64078	4.91	24.1081	2.21585	7.00714
4.42	19.5364	2.10238	6.64831	4.92	24.2064	2.21811	7.01427
4.43	19.6249	2.10476	6.65582	4.93	24.3049	2.22036	7.02140
4.44	19.7136	2.10713	6.66333	4.94	24.4036	2.22261	7.02851
4.45	19.8025	2.10950	6.67083	4.95	24.5025	2.22486	7.03562
4.46	19.8916	2.11187	6.67832	4.96	24.6016	2.22711	7.04273
4.47	19.9809	2.11424	6.68581	4.97	24.7009	2.22935	7.04982
4.48	20.0704	2.11660	6.69328	4.98	24.8004	2.23159	7.05691
4.49	20.1601	2.11896	6.70075	4.99	24.9001	2.23383	7.06399
4.50	20.2500	2.12132	6.70820	**5.00**	25.0000	2.23607	7.07107
N	N^2	$\sqrt{N}$	$\sqrt{10N}$	N	N^2	$\sqrt{N}$	$\sqrt{10N}$

(*Continued*)

Table 1 (*Continued*)

N	N^2	$\sqrt{N}$	$\sqrt{10N}$	N	N^2	$\sqrt{N}$	$\sqrt{10N}$
5.00	25.0000	2.23607	7.07107	**5.50**	30.2500	2.34521	7.41620
5.01	25.1001	2.23830	7.07814	5.51	30.3601	2.34734	7.42294
5.02	25.2004	2.24054	7.08520	5.52	30.4704	2.34947	7.42967
5.03	25.3009	2.24277	7.09225	5.53	30.5809	2.35160	7.43640
5.04	25.4016	2.24499	7.09930	5.54	30.6916	2.35372	7.44312
5.05	25.5025	2.24722	7.10634	5.55	30.8025	2.35584	7.44983
5.06	25.6036	2.24944	7.11337	5.56	30.9136	2.35797	7.45654
5.07	25.7049	2.25167	7.12039	5.57	31.0249	2.36008	7.46324
5.08	25.8064	2.25389	7.12741	5.58	31.1364	2.36220	7.46994
5.09	25.9081	2.25610	7.13442	5.59	31.2481	2.36432	7.47663
5.10	26.0100	2.25832	7.14143	**5.60**	31.3600	2.36643	7.48331
5.11	26.1121	2.26053	7.14843	5.61	31.4721	2.36854	7.48999
5.12	26.2144	2.26274	7.15542	5.62	31.5844	2.37065	7.49667
5.13	26.3169	2.26495	7.16240	5.63	31.6969	2.37276	7.50333
5.14	26.4196	2.26716	7.16938	5.64	31.8096	2.37487	7.50999
5.15	26.5225	2.26936	7.17635	5.65	31.9225	2.37697	7.51665
5.16	26.6256	2.27156	7.18331	5.66	32.0356	2.37908	7.52330
5.17	26.7289	2.27376	7.19027	5.67	32.1489	2.38118	7.52994
5.18	26.8324	2.27596	7.19722	5.68	32.2624	2.38328	7.53658
5.19	26.9361	2.27816	7.20417	5.69	32.3761	2.38537	7.54321
5.20	27.0400	2.28035	7.21110	**5.70**	32.4900	2.38747	7.54983
5.21	27.1441	2.28254	7.21803	5.71	32.6041	2.38956	7.55645
5.22	27.2484	2.28473	7.22496	5.72	32.7184	2.39165	7.56307
5.23	27.3529	2.28692	7.23187	5.73	32.8329	2.39374	7.56968
5.24	27.4576	2.28910	7.23878	5.74	32.9476	2.39583	7.57628
5.25	27.5625	2.29129	7.24569	5.75	33.0625	2.39792	7.58288
5.26	27.6676	2.29347	7.25259	5.76	33.1776	2.40000	7.58947
5.27	27.7729	2.29565	7.25948	5.77	33.2929	2.40208	7.59605
5.28	27.8784	2.29783	7.26636	5.78	33.4084	2.40416	7.60263
5.29	27.9841	2.30000	7.27324	5.79	33.5241	2.40624	7.60920
5.30	28.0900	2.30217	7.28011	**5.80**	33.6400	2.40832	7.61577
5.31	28.1961	2.30434	7.28697	5.81	33.7561	2.41039	7.62234
5.32	28.3024	2.30651	7.29383	5.82	33.8724	2.41247	7.62889
5.33	28.4089	2.30868	7.30068	5.83	33.9889	2.41454	7.63544
5.34	28.5156	2.31084	7.30753	5.84	34.1056	2.41661	7.64199
5.35	28.6225	2.31301	7.31437	5.85	34.2225	2.41868	7.64853
5.36	28.7296	2.31517	7.32120	5.86	34.3396	2.42074	7.65506
5.37	28.8369	2.31733	7.32803	5.87	34.4569	2.42281	7.66159
5.38	28.9444	2.31948	7.33485	5.88	34.5744	2.42487	7.66812
5.39	29.0521	2.32164	7.34166	5.89	34.6921	2.42693	7.67463
5.40	29.1600	2.32379	7.34847	**5.90**	34.8100	2.42899	7.68115
5.41	29.2681	2.32594	7.35527	5.91	34.9281	2.43105	7.68765
5.42	29.3764	2.32809	7.36206	5.92	35.0464	2.43311	7.69415
5.43	29.4849	2.33024	7.36885	5.93	35.1649	2.43516	7.70065
5.44	29.5936	2.33238	7.37564	5.94	35.2836	2.43721	7.70714
5.45	29.7025	2.33452	7.38241	5.95	35.4024	2.43926	7.71362
5.46	29.8116	2.33666	7.38918	5.96	35.5216	2.44131	7.72010
5.47	29.9209	2.33880	7.39594	5.97	35.6409	2.44336	7.72658
5.48	30.0304	2.34094	7.40270	5.98	35.7604	2.44540	7.73305
5.49	30.1401	2.34307	7.40945	5.99	35.8801	2.44745	7.73951
5.50	30.2500	2.34521	7.41620	**6.00**	36.0000	2.44949	7.74597
N	N^2	$\sqrt{N}$	$\sqrt{10N}$	N	N^2	$\sqrt{N}$	$\sqrt{10N}$

Table 1 (*Continued*)

N	N²	√N	√10N	N	N²	√N	√10N
6.00	36.0000	2.44949	7.74597	**6.50**	42.2500	2.54951	8.06226
6.01	36.1201	2.45153	7.75242	6.51	42.3801	2.55147	8.06846
6.02	36.2404	2.45357	7.75887	6.52	42.5104	2.55343	8.07465
6.03	36.3609	2.45561	7.76531	6.53	42.6409	2.55539	8.08084
6.04	36.4816	2.45764	7.77174	6.54	42.7716	2.55734	8.08703
6.05	36.6025	2.45967	7.77817	6.55	42.9025	2.55930	8.09321
6.06	36.7236	2.46171	7.78460	6.56	43.0336	2.56125	8.09938
6.07	36.8449	2.46374	7.79102	6.57	43.1649	2.56320	8.10555
6.08	36.9664	2.46577	7.79744	6.58	43.2964	2.56515	8.11172
6.09	37.0881	2.46779	7.80385	6.59	43.4281	2.56710	8.11788
6.10	37.2100	2.46982	7.81025	**6.60**	43.5600	2.56905	8.12404
6.11	37.3321	2.47184	7.81665	6.61	43.6921	2.57099	8.13019
6.12	37.4544	2.47386	7.82304	6.62	43.8244	2.57294	8.13634
6.13	37.5769	2.47588	7.82943	6.63	43.9569	2.57488	8.14248
6.14	37.6996	2.47790	7.83582	6.64	44.0896	2.57682	8.14862
6.15	37.8225	2.47992	7.84219	6.65	44.2225	2.57876	8.15475
6.16	37.9456	2.48193	7.84857	6.66	44.3556	2.58070	8.16088
6.17	38.0689	2.48395	7.85493	6.67	44.4889	2.58263	8.16701
6.18	38.1924	2.48596	7.86130	6.68	44.6224	2.58457	8.17313
6.19	38.3161	2.48797	7.86766	6.69	44.7561	2.58650	8.17924
6.20	38.4400	2.48998	7.87401	**6.70**	44.8900	2.58844	8.18535
6.21	38.5641	2.49199	7.88036	6.71	45.0241	2.59037	8.19146
6.22	38.6884	2.49399	7.88670	6.72	45.1584	2.59230	8.19756
6.23	38.8129	2.49600	7.89303	6.73	45.2929	2.59422	8.20366
6.24	38.9376	2.49800	7.89937	6.74	45.4276	2.59615	8.20975
6.25	39.0625	2.50000	7.90569	6.75	45.5625	2.59808	8.21584
6.26	39.1876	2.50200	7.91202	6.76	45.6976	2.60000	8.22192
6.27	39.3129	2.50400	7.91833	6.77	45.8329	2.60192	8.22800
6.28	39.4384	2.50599	7.92465	6.78	45.9684	2.60384	8.23408
6.29	39.5641	2.50799	7.93095	6.79	46.1041	2.60576	8.24015
6.30	39.6900	2.50998	7.93725	**6.80**	46.2400	2.60768	8.24621
6.31	39.8161	2.51197	7.94355	6.81	46.3761	2.60960	8.25227
6.32	39.9424	2.51396	7.94984	6.82	46.5124	2.61151	8.25833
6.33	40.0689	2.51595	7.95613	6.83	46.6489	2.61343	8.26438
6.34	40.1956	2.51794	7.96241	6.84	46.7856	2.61534	8.27043
6.35	40.3225	2.51992	7.96869	6.85	46.9225	2.61725	8.27647
6.36	40.4496	2.52190	7.97496	6.86	47.0596	2.61916	8.28251
6.37	40.5769	2.52389	7.98123	6.87	47.1969	2.62107	8.28855
6.38	40.7044	2.52587	7.98749	6.88	47.3344	2.62298	8.29458
6.39	40.8321	2.52784	7.99375	6.89	47.4721	2.62488	8.30000
6.40	40.9600	2.52982	8.00000	**6.90**	47.6100	2.62679	8.30662
6.41	41.0881	2.53180	8.00625	6.91	47.7481	2.62869	8.31264
6.42	41.2164	2.53377	8.01249	6.92	47.8864	2.63059	8.31865
6.43	41.3449	2.53574	8.01873	6.93	48.0249	2.63249	8.32466
6.44	41.4736	2.53772	8.02496	6.94	48.1636	2.63439	8.33067
6.45	41.6025	2.53969	8.03119	6.95	48.3025	2.63629	8.33667
6.46	41.7316	2.54165	8.03741	6.96	48.4416	2.63818	8.34266
6.47	41.8609	2.54362	8.04363	6.97	48.5809	2.64008	8.34865
6.48	41.9904	2.54558	8.04984	6.98	48.7204	2.64197	8.35464
6.49	42.1201	2.54755	8.05605	6.99	48.8601	2.64386	8.36062
6.50	42.2500	2.54951	8.06226	**7.00**	49.0000	2.64575	8.36660
N	N²	√N	√10N	N	N²	√N	√10N

(*Continued*)

Table 1 (*Continued*)

N	N^2	$\sqrt{N}$	$\sqrt{10N}$	N	N^2	$\sqrt{N}$	$\sqrt{10N}$
7.00	49.0000	2.64575	8.36660	**7.50**	56.2500	2.73861	8.66025
7.01	49.1401	2.64764	8.37257	7.51	56.4001	2.74044	8.66603
7.02	49.2804	2.64953	8.37854	7.52	56.5504	2.74226	8.67179
7.03	49.4209	2.65141	8.38451	7.53	56.7009	2.74408	8.67756
7.04	49.5616	2.65330	8.39047	7.54	56.8516	2.74591	8.68332
7.05	49.7025	2.65518	8.39643	7.55	57.0025	2.74773	8.68907
7.06	49.8436	2.65707	8.40238	7.56	57.1536	2.74955	8.69483
7.07	49.9849	2.65895	8.40833	7.57	57.3049	2.75136	8.70057
7.08	50.1264	2.66083	8.41427	7.58	57.4564	2.75318	8.70632
7.09	50.2681	2.66271	8.42021	7.59	57.6081	2.75500	8.71206
7.10	50.4100	2.66458	8.42615	**7.60**	57.7600	2.75681	8.71780
7.11	50.5521	2.66646	8.43208	7.61	57.9121	2.75862	8.72353
7.12	50.6944	2.66833	8.43801	7.62	58.0644	2.76043	8.72926
7.13	50.8369	2.67021	8.44393	7.63	58.2169	2.76225	8.73499
7.14	50.9796	2.67208	8.44985	7.64	58.3696	2.76405	8.74071
7.15	51.1225	2.67395	8.45577	7.65	58.5225	2.76586	8.74643
7.16	51.2656	2.67582	8.46168	7.66	58.6756	2.76767	8.75214
7.17	51.4089	2.67769	8.46759	7.67	58.8289	2.76948	8.75785
7.18	51.5524	2.67955	8.47349	7.68	58.9824	2.77128	8.76356
7.19	51.6961	2.68142	8.47939	7.69	59.1361	2.77308	8.76926
7.20	51.8400	2.68328	8.48528	**7.70**	59.2900	2.77489	8.77496
7.21	51.9841	2.68514	8.49117	7.71	59.4441	2.77669	8.78066
7.22	52.1284	2.68701	8.49706	7.72	59.5984	2.77849	8.78635
7.23	52.2729	2.68887	8.50294	7.73	59.7529	2.78029	8.79204
7.24	52.4176	2.69072	8.50882	7.74	59.9076	2.78209	8.79773
7.25	52.5625	2.69258	8.51469	7.75	60.0625	2.78388	8.80341
7.26	52.7076	2.69444	8.52056	7.76	60.2176	2.78568	8.80909
7.27	52.8529	2.69629	8.52643	7.77	60.3729	2.78747	8.81476
7.28	52.9984	2.69815	8.53229	7.78	60.5284	2.78927	8.82043
7.29	53.1441	2.70000	8.53815	7.79	60.6841	2.79106	8.82610
7.30	53.2900	2.70185	8.54400	**7.80**	60.8400	2.79285	8.83176
7.31	53.4361	2.70370	8.54985	7.81	60.9961	2.79464	8.83742
7.32	53.5824	2.70555	8.55570	7.82	61.1524	2.79643	8.84308
7.33	53.7289	2.70740	8.56154	7.83	61.3089	2.79821	8.84873
7.34	53.8756	2.70924	8.56738	7.84	61.4656	2.80000	8.85438
7.35	54.0225	2.71109	8.57321	7.85	61.6225	2.80179	8.86002
7.36	54.1696	2.71293	8.57904	7.86	61.7796	2.80357	8.86566
7.37	54.3169	2.71477	8.58487	7.87	61.9369	2.80535	8.87130
7.38	54.4644	2.71662	8.59069	7.88	62.0944	2.80713	8.87694
7.39	54.6121	2.71846	8.59651	7.89	62.2521	2.80891	8.88257
7.40	54.7600	2.72029	8.60233	**7.90**	62.4100	2.81069	8.88819
7.41	54.9081	2.72213	8.60814	7.91	62.5681	2.81247	8.89382
7.42	55.0564	2.72397	8.61394	7.92	62.7264	2.81425	8.89944
7.43	55.2049	2.72580	8.61974	7.93	62.8849	2.81603	8.90505
7.44	55.3536	2.72764	8.62554	7.94	63.0436	2.81780	8.91067
7.45	55.5025	2.72947	8.63134	7.95	63.2025	2.81957	8.91628
7.46	55.6516	2.73130	8.63713	7.96	63.3616	2.82135	8.92188
7.47	55.8009	2.73313	8.64292	7.97	63.5209	2.82312	8.92749
7.48	55.9504	2.73496	8.64870	7.98	63.6804	2.82489	8.93308
7.49	56.1001	2.73679	8.65448	7.99	63.8401	2.82666	8.93868
7.50	56.2500	2.73861	8.66025	**8.00**	64.0000	2.82843	8.94427
N	N^2	$\sqrt{N}$	$\sqrt{10N}$	N	N^2	$\sqrt{N}$	$\sqrt{10N}$

Table 1 (*Continued*)

N	N^2	$\sqrt{N}$	$\sqrt{10N}$	N	N^2	$\sqrt{N}$	$\sqrt{10N}$
8.00	64.0000	2.82843	8.94427	**8.50**	72.2500	2.91548	9.21954
8.01	64.1601	2.83019	8.94986	8.51	72.4201	2.91719	9.22497
8.02	64.3204	2.83196	8.95545	8.52	72.5904	2.91890	9.23038
8.03	64.4809	2.83373	8.96103	8.53	72.7609	2.92062	9.23580
8.04	64.6416	2.83549	8.96660	8.54	72.9316	2.92233	9.24121
8.05	64.8025	2.83725	8.97218	8.55	73.1025	2.92404	9.24662
8.06	64.9636	2.83901	8.97775	8.56	73.2736	2.92575	9.25203
8.07	65.1249	2.84077	8.98332	8.57	73.4449	2.92746	9.25743
8.08	65.2864	2.84253	8.98888	8.58	73.6164	2.92916	9.26283
8.09	65.4481	2.84429	8.99444	8.59	73.7881	2.93087	9.26823
8.10	65.6100	2.84605	9.00000	**8.60**	73.9600	2.93258	9.27362
8.11	65.7721	2.84781	9.00555	8.61	74.1321	2.93428	9.27901
8.12	65.9344	2.84956	9.01110	8.62	74.3044	2.93598	9.28440
8.13	66.0969	2.85132	9.01665	8.63	74.4769	2.93769	9.28978
8.14	66.2596	2.85307	9.02219	8.64	74.6496	2.93939	9.29516
8.15	66.4225	2.85482	9.02774	8.65	74.8225	2.94109	9.30054
8.16	66.5856	2.85657	9.03327	8.66	74.9956	2.94279	9.30591
8.17	66.7489	2.85832	9.03881	8.67	75.1689	2.94449	9.31128
8.18	66.9124	2.86007	9.04434	8.68	75.3424	2.94618	9.31665
8.19	67.0761	2.86182	9.04986	8.69	75.5161	2.94788	9.32202
8.20	67.2400	2.86356	9.05539	**8.70**	75.6900	2.94958	9.32738
8.21	67.4041	2.86531	9.06091	8.71	75.8641	2.95127	9.33274
8.22	67.5684	2.86705	9.06642	8.72	76.0384	2.95296	9.33809
8.23	67.7329	2.86880	9.07193	8.73	76.2129	2.95466	9.34345
8.24	67.8976	2.87054	9.07744	8.74	76.3876	2.95635	9.34880
8.25	68.0625	2.87228	9.08295	8.75	76.5625	2.95804	9.35414
8.26	68.2276	2.87402	9.08845	8.76	76.7376	2.95973	9.35949
8.27	68.3929	2.87576	9.09395	8.77	76.9129	2.96142	9.36483
8.28	68.5584	2.87750	9.09945	8.78	77.0884	2.96311	9.37017
8.29	68.7241	2.87924	9.10494	8.79	77.2641	2.96479	9.37550
8.30	68.8900	2.88097	9.11043	**8.80**	77.4400	2.96648	9.38083
8.31	69.0561	2.88271	9.11592	8.81	77.6161	2.96816	9.38616
8.32	69.2224	2.88444	9.12140	8.82	77.7924	2.96985	9.39149
8.33	69.3889	2.88617	9.12688	8.83	77.9689	2.97153	9.39681
8.34	69.5556	2.88791	9.13236	8.84	78.1456	2.97321	9.40213
8.35	69.7225	2.88964	9.13783	8.85	78.3225	2.97489	9.40744
8.36	69.8896	2.89137	9.14330	8.86	78.4996	2.97658	9.41276
8.37	70.0569	2.89310	9.14877	8.87	78.6769	2.97825	9.41807
8.38	70.2244	2.89482	9.15423	8.88	78.8544	2.97993	9.42338
8.39	70.3921	2.89655	9.15969	8.89	79.0321	2.98161	9.42868
8.40	70.5600	2.89828	9.16515	**8.90**	79.2100	2.98329	9.43398
8.41	70.7281	2.90000	9.17061	8.91	79.3881	2.98496	9.43928
8.42	70.8964	2.90172	9.17606	8.92	79.5664	2.98664	9.44458
8.43	71.0649	2.90345	9.18150	8.93	79.7449	2.98831	9.44987
8.44	71.2336	2.90517	9.18695	8.94	79.9236	2.98998	9.45516
8.45	71.4025	2.90689	9.19239	8.95	80.1025	2.99166	9.46044
8.46	71.5716	2.90861	9.19783	8.96	80.2816	2.99333	9.46573
8.47	71.7409	2.91033	9.20326	8.97	80.4609	2.99500	9.47101
8.48	71.9104	2.91204	9.20869	8.98	80.6404	2.99666	9.47629
8.49	72.0801	2.91376	9.21412	8.99	80.8201	2.99833	9.48156
8.50	72.2500	2.91548	9.21954	**9.00**	81.0000	3.00000	9.48683
N	N^2	$\sqrt{N}$	$\sqrt{10N}$	N	N^2	$\sqrt{N}$	$\sqrt{10N}$

(*Continued*)

Table 1 (*Continued*)

N	N²	√N	√10N	N	N²	√N	√10N
9.00	81.0000	3.00000	9.48683	**9.50**	90.2500	3.08221	9.74679
9.01	81.1801	3.00167	9.49210	9.51	90.4401	3.08383	9.75192
9.02	81.3604	3.00333	9.49737	9.52	90.6304	3.08545	9.75705
9.03	81.5409	3.00500	9.50263	9.53	90.8209	3.08707	9.76217
9.04	81.7216	3.00666	9.50789	9.54	91.0116	3.08869	9.76729
9.05	81.9025	3.00832	9.51315	9.55	91.2025	3.09031	9.77241
9.06	82.0836	3.00998	9.51840	9.56	91.3936	3.09192	9.77753
9.07	82.2649	3.01164	9.52365	9.57	91.5849	3.09354	9.78264
9.08	82.4464	3.01330	9.52890	9.58	91.7764	3.09516	9.78775
9.09	82.6281	3.01496	9.53415	9.59	91.9681	3.09677	9.79285
9.10	82.8100	3.01662	9.53939	**9.60**	92.1600	3.09839	9.79796
9.11	82.9921	3.01828	9.54463	9.61	92.3521	3.10000	9.80306
9.12	83.1744	3.01993	9.54987	9.62	92.5444	3.10161	9.80816
9.13	83.3569	3.02159	9.55510	9.63	92.7369	3.10322	9.81326
9.14	83.5396	3.02324	9.56033	9.64	92.9296	3.10483	9.81835
9.15	83.7225	3.02490	9.56556	9.65	93.1225	3.10644	9.82344
9.16	83.9056	3.02655	9.57079	9.66	93.3156	3.10805	9.82853
9.17	84.0889	3.02820	9.57601	9.67	93.5089	3.10966	9.83362
9.18	84.2724	3.02985	9.58123	9.68	93.7024	3.11127	9.83870
9.19	84.4561	3.03150	9.58645	9.69	93.8961	3.11288	9.84378
9.20	84.6400	3.03315	9.59166	**9.70**	94.0900	3.11448	9.84886
9.21	84.8241	3.03480	9.59687	9.71	94.2841	3.11609	9.85393
9.22	85.0084	3.03645	9.60208	9.72	94.4784	3.11769	9.85901
9.23	85.1929	3.03809	9.60729	9.73	94.6729	3.11929	9.86408
9.24	85.3776	3.03974	9.61249	9.74	94.8676	3.12090	9.86914
9.25	85.5625	3.04138	9.61769	9.75	95.0625	3.12250	9.87421
9.26	85.7476	3.04302	9.62289	9.76	95.2576	3.12410	9.87927
9.27	85.9329	3.04467	9.62808	9.77	95.4529	3.12570	9.88433
9.28	86.1184	3.04631	9.63328	9.78	95.6484	3.12730	9.88939
9.29	86.3041	3.04795	9.63846	9.79	95.8441	3.12890	9.89444
9.30	86.4900	3.04959	9.64365	**9.80**	96.0400	3.13050	9.89949
9.31	86.6761	3.05123	9.64883	9.81	96.2361	3.13209	9.90454
9.32	86.8624	3.05287	9.65401	9.82	96.4324	3.13369	9.90959
9.33	87.0489	3.05450	9.65919	9.83	96.6289	3.13528	9.91464
9.34	87.2356	3.05614	9.66437	9.84	96.8256	3.13688	9.91968
9.35	87.4225	3.05778	9.66954	9.85	97.0225	3.13847	9.92472
9.36	87.6096	3.05941	9.67471	9.86	97.2196	3.14006	9.92975
9.37	87.7969	3.06105	9.67988	9.87	97.4169	3.14166	9.93479
9.38	87.9844	3.06268	9.68504	9.88	97.6144	3.14325	9.93982
9.39	88.1721	3.06431	9.69020	9.89	97.8121	3.14484	9.94485
9.40	88.3600	3.06594	9.69536	**9.90**	98.0100	3.14643	9.94987
9.41	88.5481	3.06757	9.70052	9.91	98.2081	3.14802	9.95490
9.42	88.7364	3.06920	9.70567	9.92	98.4064	3.14960	9.95992
9.43	88.9249	3.07083	9.71082	9.93	98.6049	3.15119	9.96494
9.44	89.1136	3.07246	9.71597	9.94	98.8036	3.15278	9.96995
9.45	89.3025	3.07409	9.72111	9.95	99.0025	3.15436	9.97497
9.46	89.4916	3.07571	9.72625	9.96	99.2016	3.15595	9.97998
9.47	89.6809	3.07734	9.73139	9.97	99.4009	3.15753	9.98499
9.48	89.8704	3.07896	9.73653	9.98	99.6004	3.15911	9.98999
9.49	90.0601	3.08058	9.74166	9.99	99.8001	3.16070	9.99500
9.50	90.2500	3.08221	9.74679	**10.00**	100.000	3.16228	10.0000
N	N²	√N	√10N	N	N²	√N	√10N

* From Paul G. Hoel, *Introduction to Mathematical Statistics* (3rd ed.; New York: John Wiley. 1962).

Table 2

Areas Under the Normal Curve to the Right of Given Sigma-Distance From the Mean

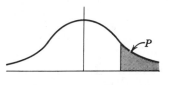

z	0.00	0.01	0.02	0.03	0.04	0.05	0.06	0.07	0.08	0.09
0.0	0.5000	0.4960	0.4920	0.4880	0.4840	0.4801	0.4761	0.4721	0.4681	0.4641
0.1	0.4602	0.4562	0.4522	0.4483	0.4443	0.4404	0.4364	0.4325	0.4286	0.4247
0.2	0.4207	0.4168	0.4129	0.4090	0.4052	0.4013	0.3974	0.3936	0.3897	0.3859
0.3	0.3821	0.3783	0.3745	0.3707	0.3669	0.3632	0.3594	0.3557	0.3520	0.3483
0.4	0.3446	0.3409	0.3372	0.3336	0.3300	0.3264	0.3228	0.3192	0.3156	0.3121
0.5	0.3085	0.3050	0.3015	0.2981	0.2946	0.2912	0.2877	0.2843	0.2810	0.2776
0.6	0.2743	0.2709	0.2676	0.2643	0.2611	0.2578	0.2546	0.2514	0.2483	0.2451
0.7	0.2420	0.2389	0.2358	0.2327	0.2296	0.2266	0.2236	0.2206	0.2177	0.2148
0.8	0.2119	0.2090	0.2061	0.2033	0.2005	0.1977	0.1949	0.1922	0.1894	0.1867
0.9	0.1841	0.1814	0.1788	0.1762	0.1736	0.1711	0.1685	0.1660	0.1635	0.1611
1.0	0.1587	0.1562	0.1539	0.1515	0.1492	0.1469	0.1446	0.1423	0.1401	0.1379
1.1	0.1357	0.1335	0.1314	0.1292	0.1271	0.1251	0.1230	0.1210	0.1190	0.1170
1.2	0.1151	0.1131	0.1112	0.1093	0.1075	0.1056	0.1038	0.1020	0.1003	0.0985
1.3	0.0968	0.0951	0.0934	0.0918	0.0901	0.0885	0.0869	0.0853	0.0838	0.0823
1.4	0.0808	0.0793	0.0778	0.0764	0.0749	0.0735	0.0721	0.0708	0.0694	0.0681
1.5	0.0668	0.0655	0.0643	0.0630	0.0618	0.0606	0.0594	0.0582	0.0571	0.0559
1.6	0.0548	0.0537	0.0516	0.0516	0.0505	0.0495	0.0485	0.0475	0.0465	0.0455
1.7	0.0446	0.0436	0.0427	0.0418	0.0409	0.0401	0.0392	0.0384	0.0375	0.0367
1.8	0.0359	0.0351	0.0344	0.0336	0.0329	0.0322	0.0314	0.0307	0.0301	0.0294
1.9	0.0287	0.0281	0.0274	0.0268	0.0262	0.0256	0.0250	0.0244	0.0239	0.0233
2.0	0.0228	0.0222	0.0217	0.0212	0.0207	0.0202	0.0197	0.0192	0.0188	0.0183
2.1	0.0179	0.0174	0.0170	0.0166	0.0162	0.0158	0.0154	0.0150	0.0146	0.0143
2.2	0.0139	0.0136	0.0132	0.0129	0.0125	0.0122	0.0199	0.0166	0.0133	0.0110
2.3	0.0107	0.0104	0.0102	0.00990	0.00964	0.00939	0.00914	0.00889	0.00866	0.00842
2.4	0.00820	0.00798	0.00776	0.00755	0.00734	0.00714	0.00695	0.00676	0.00657	0.00639
2.5	0.00621	0.00604	0.00587	0.00570	0.00554	0.00539	0.00523	0.00508	0.00494	0.00480
2.6	0.00466	0.00453	0.00440	0.00427	0.00415	0.00402	0.00391	0.00379	0.00368	0.00357
2.7	0.00437	0.00336	0.00326	0.00317	0.00307	0.00298	0.00289	0.00280	0.00272	0.00264
2.8	0.00256	0.00248	0.00240	0.00233	0.00226	0.00219	0.00212	0.00205	0.00199	0.00193
2.9	0.00187	0.00181	0.00175	0.00169	0.00164	0.00159	0.00154	0.00149	0.00144	0.00139

Source: Reproduced by permission from *Tables of Areas in Two Tails and in One Tail of the Normal Curve*, by Frederick E. Croxton. Copyright, 1949, by Prentice-Hall, Inc., Englewood Cliffs, N.J.

Table 3

Chi Square Distribution

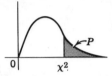

VALUES OF χ^2 FOR VARIOUS VALUES OF P
AND DEGREES OF FREEDOM n

Degrees of Freedom n	P			
	0.10	0.05	0.02	0.01
1	2.706	3.841	5.412	6.635
2	4.605	5.991	7.824	9.210
3	6.251	7.815	9.837	11.341
4	7.779	9.488	11.668	13.277
5	9.236	11.070	13.388	15.086
6	10.645	12.592	15.033	16.812
7	12.017	14.067	16.622	18.475
8	13.362	15.507	18.168	20.090
9	14.684	16.919	19.679	21.666
10	15.987	18.307	21.161	23.209
11	17.275	19.675	22.618	24.725
12	18.549	21.026	24.054	26.217
13	19.812	22.362	25.472	27.688
14	21.064	23.685	26.873	29.141
15	22.307	24.996	28.259	30.578
16	23.542	26.296	29.633	32.000
17	24.769	27.587	30.995	33.409
18	25.989	28.869	32.346	34.805
19	27.204	30.144	33.687	36.191
20	28.412	31.410	35.020	37.566
21	29.615	32.671	36.343	38.932
22	30.813	33.924	37.659	40.289
23	32.007	35.172	38.968	41.638
24	33.196	36.415	40.270	42.980
25	34.382	37.652	41.566	44.314
26	35.563	36.885	42.856	45.642
27	36.741	40.113	44.140	46.963
28	37.916	41.337	45.419	48.278
29	39.087	42.557	46.693	49.588
30	40.256	43.773	47.962	50.892

Source: Abridged from Table IV of Fisher and Yates, *Statistical Tables for Biological, Agricultural, and Medical Research,* published by Oliver and Boyd, Ltd., Edinburgh, and from Catherine M. Thompson, *Biometrika,* Vol. XXXII, Part II, October 1941, pp. 187–191, "Tables of Percentage Points of the χ^2 Distribution," by permission of the authors and publishers.

Table 4

Student's t Distribution

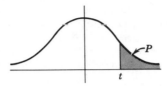

VALUES OF t CORRESPONDING TO GIVEN VALUES OF P
AND n DEGREES OF FREEDOM
P (One-tailed)

Degrees of Freedom n	0.01	0.025	0.05	0.10
1	31.821	12.706	6.314	3.078
2	6.965	4.303	2.920	1.886
3	4.541	3.182	2.353	1.638
4	3.747	2.776	2.132	1.553
5	3.365	2.571	2.015	1.476
6	3.143	2.447	1.943	1.440
7	2.998	2.365	1.895	1.415
8	2.896	2.306	1.860	1.397
9	2.821	2.262	1.833	1.383
10	2.764	2.228	1.812	1.372
11	2.718	2.201	1.796	1.363
12	2.681	2.179	1.782	1.356
13	2.650	2.160	1.771	1.350
14	2.624	2.145	1.761	1.345
15	2.602	2.131	1.753	1.341
16	2.583	2.120	1.746	1.337
17	2.567	2.110	1.740	1.333
18	2.552	2.101	1.734	1.330
19	2.539	2.093	1.729	1.328
20	2.528	2.086	1.725	1.325
21	2.518	2.080	1.721	1.323
22	2.508	2.074	1.717	1.321
23	2.500	2.069	1.714	1.319
24	2.492	2.064	1.711	1.318
25	2.485	2.060	1.708	1.316
26	2.479	2.056	1.706	1.315
27	2.473	2.052	1.703	1.314
28	2.467	2.048	1.701	1.313
29	2.462	2.045	1.699	1.311
30	2.457	2.042	1.697	1.310
∞	2.326	1.960	1.645	1.282

Source: Abridged from Table III of Fisher and Yates, *Statistical Tables for Biological, Agricultural, and Medical Research,* published by Oliver and Boyd, Ltd., Edinburgh, by permission of the authors and publishers.

Table 5

The F Distribution

VALUES OF F CORRESPONDING TO A P OF .05,
FOR VARIOUS DEGREES OF FREEDOM IN
NUMERATOR AND DENOMINATOR

Degrees of Freedom, Denominator	Degrees of Freedom, Numerator									
	1	2	3	4	5	6	8	12	24	∞
1	161.4	199.5	215.7	224.6	230.2	234.0	238.9	243.9	249.0	254.3
2	18.51	19.00	19.16	19.25	19.30	19.33	19.37	19.41	19.45	19.50
3	10.13	9.55	9.28	9.12	9.01	8.94	8.84	8.74	8.64	8.53
4	7.71	6.94	6.59	6.39	6.26	6.16	6.04	5.91	5.77	5.63
5	6.61	5.79	5.41	5.19	5.05	4.95	4.82	4.68	4.53	4.36
6	5.99	5.14	4.76	4.53	4.39	4.28	4.15	4.00	3.84	3.67
7	5.59	4.74	4.35	4.12	3.97	3.87	3.73	3.57	3.41	3.23
8	5.32	4.46	4.07	3.84	3.69	3.58	3.44	3.28	3.12	2.93
9	5.12	4.26	3.86	3.63	3.48	3.37	3.23	3.07	2.90	2.71
10	4.96	4.10	3.71	3.48	3.33	3.22	3.07	2.91	2.74	2.54
11	4.84	3.98	3.59	3.36	3.20	3.09	2.95	2.79	2.61	2.40
12	4.75	3.88	3.49	3.26	3.11	3.00	2.85	2.69	2.50	2.30
13	4.67	3.80	3.41	3.18	3.02	2.92	2.77	2.60	2.42	2.21
14	4.60	3.74	3.34	3.11	2.96	2.85	2.70	2.53	2.35	2.13
15	4.54	3.68	3.29	3.06	2.90	2.79	2.64	2.48	2.29	2.07
16	4.49	3.63	3.24	3.01	2.85	2.74	2.59	2.42	2.24	2.01
17	4.45	3.59	3.20	2.96	2.81	2.70	2.55	2.38	2.19	1.96
18	4.41	3.55	3.16	2.93	2.77	2.66	2.51	2.34	2.15	1.92
19	4.38	3.52	3.13	2.90	2.74	2.63	2.48	2.31	2.11	1.88
20	4.35	3.49	3.10	2.87	2.71	2.60	2.45	2.28	2.08	1.84
21	4.32	3.47	3.07	2.84	2.68	2.57	2.42	2.25	2.05	1.81
22	4.30	3.44	3.05	2.82	2.66	2.55	2.40	2.23	2.03	1.78
23	4.28	3.42	3.03	2.80	2.64	2.53	2.38	2.20	2.00	1.76
24	4.26	3.40	3.01	2.78	2.62	2.51	2.36	2.18	1.98	1.73
25	4.24	3.38	2.99	2.76	2.60	2.49	2.34	2.16	1.96	1.71
26	4.22	3.37	2.98	2.74	2.59	2.47	2.32	2.15	1.95	1.69
27	4.21	3.35	2.96	2.73	2.57	2.46	2.30	2.13	1.93	1.67
28	4.20	3.34	2.95	2.71	2.56	2.44	2.29	2.12	1.91	1.65
29	4.18	3.33	2.93	2.70	2.54	2.43	2.28	2.10	1.90	1.64
30	4.17	3.32	2.92	2.69	2.53	2.42	2.27	2.09	1.89	1.62
40	4.08	3.23	2.84	2.61	2.45	2.34	2.18	2.00	1.79	1.51
60	4.00	3.15	2.76	2.52	2.37	2.25	2.10	1.92	1.70	1.39
120	3.92	3.07	2.68	2.45	2.29	2.17	2.02	1.83	1.61	1.25
∞	3.84	2.99	2.60	2.37	2.21	2.09	1.94	1.75	1.52	1.00

Source: Abridged from Table V of Fisher and Yates, *Statistical Tables for Biological, Agricultural, and Medical Research*, Oliver and Boyd, Ltd., Edinburgh, by permission of the authors and publishers.

Appendix **2**

Data[1]

[1] From a national sample study of women living in urbanized areas of the United States, 1955.

CODE

1. Interview number.
2. Age—of respondent, in years.
3. Are you employed?
   Y—Yes
   N—No
4. (If *yes* to question 3). What kind of work are you now doing?
5. (Married women only). Did you work before your marriage?
   Y—Yes
   N—No
6. (If *yes* to question 5) What kind of work were you doing before marriage?
7. Have you ever wanted a career?
   Y—Yes
   N—No
8. Would you like to work in the future?
   Y—Yes
   N—No
9. Now, thinking about a woman's life, how is a woman's life changed by having children?
10. In bringing up your children, what do (would) you try to do?
11. Marital status—of respondent.
    M—married
    Si—single
    D—divorced
    Sp—separated
    W—widowed
12. Education—of respondent, in years.
    C—college
13. Father's usual occupation while woman was growing up.
14. Religious preference.
    P—Protestant
    C—Catholic
    J—Jewish
15. Family income.
16. How many children do you have?
17. Age of youngest child.
18. Husband's occupation.

1 Interview #	2 Age	3 Employed?	4 If yes, kind of work	5 Work before marriage?	6 If yes, kind of work	7 Wanted career?	8 Desire future work?	9 How life changed by children?	10 What try to do in bringing up children?	11 Marital status	12 Education	13 Father's Occupation	14 Religion	15 Family Income	16 # of children	17 Age youngest child	18 Husband's Occupation
1	49	N	—	Y	office work	N	Y	So completely I couldn't even start to say. (try) Fuller, more interesting, no chance of getting the doldrums! I wouldn't know what else to say.	That they are well-balanced. I aim at that, don't know if accomplish. (mean) Charity be their watchword in dealings with people. (Mean by well-balanced?) Well, have a place for religion, morals & emotional life in right places. Don't know how to explain better. Religion has to have part in their lives	M	10	owned fruit store	C	4000–4999	4	4	boiler engineer
2	54	N	—	Y	bookkeeper & secretary	Y	Y	You spend more time at home naturally—your interests are for	We promoted education & religion, social life & friendship.	M	C	real estate man	C	15,000–19,999	3	—	doctor

3	28	N	—	Y	inspector in factory	N	N	the future more so you become interested in their activities instead of your own. / Mine hasn't much —only I don't go places like I used to. I go no place without them— guess that is why I don't know nothing.	I try to teach them right from wrong & to believe in the Lord.	M	7	farmer	P	DK	4	2	fireman for box co.
4	31	N	—	N	—	N	Y	Don't see much change—only more work to do.	The main thing I'd say is in the church and by teaching of the Bible.	M	11	farmer	P	5000– 5999	1	10	farmer
5	44	Y	canteen truck driver	Y	dieti- cian	Y	N	That's the $64,-000 question. It brings her closer to home, closer to her husband, closer to her children.	I try to discipline them as much as I can. I make them honest & to do what's right.	M	C	truck driver	C	2000– 2999	5	9	crane opera- tor

Interview # 1	Age 2	Employed? 3	If yes, kind of work 4	Work before marriage? 5	If yes, kind of work 6	Wanted career? 7	Desire future work? 8	How life changed by children? 9	What try to do in bringing up children? 10	Marital status 11	Education 12	Father's Occupation 13	Religion 14	Family Income 15	# of children 16	Age youngest child 17	Husband's Occupation 18
6	52	N	—	Y	factory work	N	N	There is more nearness—there is more of a closeness in your home—a companionship. More working together. It seems as if you've got something to work for. I think you have greater love too.	First I tried to teach them right way of living & doing things—to be kind to each other & to always respect your elders.	M	8	farmer	P	4000–4999	2	—	retired
7	31	N	—	Y	insurance agent	N	N	Well, you have so much more responsibilities. Everything you do you have to think in relation to your children. Even in going downtown shop-	Try to help each one of them grow up to be a responsible decent person. We try to bring them up with a sense of responsibility, with a sense of re-	M	C	cowboy	C	10,000–14,999	2	6	insurance salesman

8 56	N	—	Y	shoe store clerk	N	ping or to the grocery store, you have to consider your children & of course there's more work involved. One big change is you no longer think of yourself in all things—children come first.	sponsibility to God: to be fair—we want them to behave in school & all that sort of thing but I don't know how to put it. We also want to help them make their own decisions as far as careers go.	M	C	stage coach driver, surveyor, printer, woodsman		4000–4999	2	—	truck loader
9 42	Y	typist	Y	same	Y	I couldn't answer that. (It makes a difference?) I presume so. I had mine so young I can't remember how it was before. / She is kept out of mischief.	(shrugged shoulders) Just brought them up. (Any specific aim?) No. / I am trying to instill a rigid code of ethics in her—first honesty—not to touch what isn't hers.	W	C	Navy ward officer & car inspector	C	under 1000	1	4	male nurse

1 Interview #	2 Age	3 Employed?	4 If yes, kind of work	5 Work before marriage?	6 If yes, kind of work	7 Wanted career?	8 Desire future work	9 How life changed by children?	10 What try to do in bringing up children?	11 Marital status	12 Education	13 Father's Occupation	14 Religion	15 Family Income	16 # of children	17 Age youngest child	18 Husband's Occupation
10	36	Y	practical nurse	—	—	N	Y	Oh goodness. Becomes a fuller life. A woman has to learn to share her time, more than just a wife—be a nurse, philosopher, doctor, psychologist.	Raise them to be good & honest, do things well. Be gentlemen. Understanding—work out problems with them.	W	12	rancher	P	3000–3999	2	11	—
11	49	N	—	N	—	N	N	Becomes happier, busier.	Give them good education—to learn how to work—be good children so be good grownups.	M	8	farmer	P	4000–4999	2	—	carpenter
12	50	N	—	Y	house-work	N	N	She's kept more busy & she has to watch what she says & does because children copy you & a	Taught them to go to church & Sunday school & taught them to be good & kind & to be clean morally	M	8	farmer	C	3000–3999	3	—	farmer

(continued from previous row) & physically. … woman is more happy when she has children & she stays young. I don't know what I'd do without children.

No.	Age						Attitude about married women working	What parents try to teach children	Spouse		Spouse occ.	Income		No. ch.	Ages	Occupation
13	53	N	—	N	—	N	You're tied down a lot, but then it's worth it. Also a woman's interests are changed. She's more interested in getting educated to keep up with her children.	To be polite & honest & to go to church & believe in God & I also teach them to respect their parents & their elders.	M	8	farmer	C	4000–4999	7	—	farmer
14	58	Y	factory work	Y	domestic	Y	Not much more changes—just more responsibility—& we lived & played together.	I've tried to bring them up the right way—on Sundays we always had programs together & people used to say we would teach them so much at home.	M	12	laborer	P	5000–5999	8	17	packer in tobacco co.
15	34	N	—	N	—	N	She is tied down more. She has more work to do.	Keep them clean & well fed & healthy.	M	10	farmer	P	4000–4999	3	3	riveter

1 Interview #	2 Age	3 Employed?	4 If yes, kind of work	5 Work before marriage?	6 If yes, kind of work	7 Wanted career?	8 Desire future work?	9 How life changed by children?	10 What try to do in bringing up children?	11 Marital status	12 Education	13 Father's Occupation	14 Religion	15 Family Income	16 # of children	17 Age youngest child	18 Husband's Occupation
16	30	N	—	Y	librarian	Y	N	Well, of course your responsibility is multiplied I don't know how many times.	Well, I think the main thing is to try to get them to understand right & wrong but also to be able to be independent & stand on their own 2 feet & make decisions & assume their own responsibilities.	M	C	truck driver	C	3000–3999	1	4	librarian
17	37	Y	book-keeper	N	—	N	Y	The responsibilities. (else?) You have to schedule & there's less money for fun; medical expenses & food are more.	I try to see that they go to church & teach them good manners & try to teach them the things that will make them good citizens. (such as?) Obeying the laws & re-	M	12	tele-phone lineman	P	5000–5999	2	9	Army

...specting other people.

18	38	N	—	Y	sales-clerk	Y	Y	It is a rich experience. It brings a fulfillment every girl dreams of. But it does tie her down an awful lot. It puts her in a different circle of friends.	I try to see & help them live their own lives—not tie them down. I want to teach them how to overcome danger & be ready to make a life of their own.	M	C	carpenter	P 7500–9999	4	4	salesman
19	37	N	—	Y	payroll clerk	Y	N	It gives her responsibility for another life & gives her responsibilities for physical, mental and spiritual development. (other?) Helps to mature—to have them dependent—you stop thinking about yourself.	I try to take care of them physically & try to teach the rules of hygiene & nutrition—to teach them the needs of spiritual—the Bible & teachings & also their relationship to other people.	M	C	mechanical engineer	P 6000–7499	4	5	bus co. foreman
20	59	N	—	Y	factory work	Y	Y	It don't change it in no special way.	I tried to bring them up right. (what do you mean right?) To mind people & not destroy things.	M	4	RR conductor	P 1000–1999	1	—	retired

| Interview # | Age | Employed? | If yes, kind of work | Work before marriage? | If yes, kind of work | Wanted career? | Desire future work | How life changed by children? | What try to do in bringing up children? | Marital status | Education | Father's Occupation | Religion | Family Income | # of children | Age youngest child | Husband's Occupation |
1	2	3	4	5	6	7	8	9	10	11	12	13	14	15	16	17	18
21	62	N	—	Y	comptometer operator	—	N	Mine wasn't. I've always had youngsters around—younger brothers & sisters—I've enjoyed having children & learned a lot from them.	Interest them in school activities—never let them run too wild but give them some freedom.	M	11	coal yard foreman	P	under 1000	5	—	retired
22	58	N	—	N	—	N	N	I think it's really more confining by having children.	I think they should try to make them mind.	M	5	dairy farmer	C	2000–2999	5	—	carpenter
23	36	Y	waitress	Y	same	N	Y	It's a lot more work & you have to stay home. You can't go every place you want to.	Making them mind.	M	12	farmer		5000–5999	2	8	prison guard
24	70	N	—	—	—	Y	N	The immediate thing that faces us in our old age is the fact that without children there	I think it is very important if you can strike a happy medium. There must be disci-	M	C	farmer	P	10,000–14,999	0	—	professor

| 25 | 28 | N | — | Y | lab tech-nician | Y | N | is an emptiness in our life. You have more interests in life. The change would be a great deal greater if you had a career. It would have to take a back seat. I regret that we had no children but I was married rather late in life. We have so few left of our families. I'm quite sure that if we had had children our life would have been changed. We have one another's companionship but children would have filled a great void.

Oh, she's tied down. | pline—not slavish obedience—but the children must learn that the world does not revolve around them. Try to let him know of love & affection. He should learn these things as fast as possible.

Put the right thoughts in their heads, teach them right from wrong. | M | 12 | owned meat business | J | — | 3 | 7 mos | sales-man |

1 Interview #	2 Age	3 Employed?	4 If yes, kind of work	5 Work before marriage?	6 If yes, kind of work	7 Wanted career?	8 Desire future work?	9 How life changed by children?	10 What try to do in bringing up children?	11 Marital status	12 Education	13 Father's Occupation	14 Religion	15 Family Income	16 # of children	17 Age youngest child	18 Husband's Occupation
26	42	Y	cook	Y	sales-lady	N	N	I don't know. It didn't change my life. (in general) No. Some people feel they are tied down but this doesn't affect me because I've never been one to go out.	Always teach them right. (probe) Being good in all ways. (probe) Friendly & kind.	M	10	furniture refinish. business	P	5000–5999	1	—	painter (automobiles)
27	50	N	—	Y	office work	Y	Y	I think that it ties you down more. You become interested in school affairs & have a different feeling about community problems that you wouldn't have if you didn't have a family. You plan and think about the future more when there are children.	I try to make them behave and make them understand that they have their own responsibilities. Not to be destructive. (anything else?) Try to teach them to be interested in their country and things that are going on in church.	M	12	farmer	C	5000–5999	2	9	golf green keeper

28	26	Y	nurse	Y	same	Y	Y	Well, she doesn't have as much freedom as she had before & she has more responsibilities. As a rule she can't spend as much money for clothes or have as much recreation.	I try to help them to be good Christians and help one another not to fight & to share each other's things. It's hard sometimes.	M	C	silver table ware inspector	C 4000–4999	3	1	policeman
29	34	Y	teacher	Y	same	—	Y	A lot more work & responsibility of keeping the children fed & clean. You have more to think about & plan for.	I try to teach them to obey, to keep them clean & healthy.	M	C	teacher	P 4000–4999	2	6 wks	school principal
30	61	N	—	Y	Red Cross	N	Y	You have a different kind of responsibility. You have less time to spend outside the home. You are responsible for the health, religious life, food, shelter & clothing, moral teachings of the children.	I tried to make an honest, upright, Christian citizen out of her.	M	C	farmer	P 6000–7499	1	—	plant specialist

1 Interview #	2 Age	3 Employed?	4 If yes, kind of work	5 Work before marriage?	6 If yes, kind of work	7 Wanted career?	8 Desire future work	9 How life changed by children?	10 What try to do in bringing up children?	11 Marital status	12 Education	13 Father's Occupation	14 Religion	15 Family Income	16 # of children	17 Age youngest child	18 Husband's Occupation
31	25	N	—	Y	cafeteria	Y	Y	They have to spend more time home. And then they feel more obligated—at least I do. I feel more grown up.	I try to be more careful in things I say, things I do. You have to watch the children's health especially before they start talking.	Sp	12	farmer	P	1000–1999	1	3	laborer
32	26	N	—	Y	scientific research in hospital	N	Y	I've never had any so I wouldn't know.	—	M	C	Bell Telephone	P	4000–4999	0	—	industrial relations
33	51	Y	nurse's aid	N	—	—	Y	They have to give up things after having children that they didn't before—doing things & going out	I always tried to live the right life before them—& learn them to go to church & get along with other people.	W	7	farmer	P	3000–3999	3	—	—

34	61	N	—	Y	hosiery mill	N	N	You really have a busy life when you have children & when your grandchildren come along you more busy looking after them.	Tried to teach right from wrong and never had any trouble.	M	7	farmer	P	1000–1999	3	18	retired
35	44	Y	cook	Y	waitress, factory work, housework	—	Y	More responsibility. You go to work whether you feel like it or not. You don't think of yourself. Life is less selfish c* children. If you both work together you can always get out of the house. I never stayed home too much.	First place you try to teach respect (?) respect other people's property. (?) To teach them how to keep themselves clean.	M	9	machinist	C	5000–5999	3	12	switch tender on RR
36	34	N	—	Y	waitress	N	Y	Well, I don't know. They would have to stay home & care for their children.	I'd try to give them a good education, keep them where I could watch after them, stay home c them.	M	8	farmer	P	3000–3999	0	—	laborer

* c stands for "with."

1 Interview #	2 Age	3 Employed?	4 If yes, kind of work	5 Work before marriage?	6 If yes, kind of work	7 Wanted career?	8 Desire future work?	9 How life changed by children?	10 What try to do in bringing up children?	11 Marital status	12 Education	13 Father's Occupation	14 Religion	15 Family Income	16 # of children	17 Age youngest child	18 Husband's Occupation
37	27	Y	switchboard & clerk	Y	elevator operator, managed restaurant, managed laundry	Y	Y	It don't seem to have changed many of women's lives. They still seem to participate in things they were interested in before children born. (what things?) Whatever things they participated in before.	Try to teach them right from wrong. And always respect their elders. Always carry themselves like ladies. Stay away from the rough bunch—those that are fast company. Always try to better themselves—in their company—that they keep.	M	11	barber	P	7500–9999	3	6	butcher
38	29	Y	assembly line	Y	defense work—made bombs	Y	Y	Well, before you're kinda I think I am immature. Having children you don't care about yourself—just about the kids—their welfare.	I try to be kind—try to understand them. Never spoil them. I try to make up time I don't spend c them. We always spend evenings c	M	9	auto mechanic	C	5000–5999	2	7	welder

No.	Age		Occupation		Occupation			Response	Response			Occupation	Income			Occupation
39	32	Y	sample clerk in paper mill	—	—	N	Y	I've never had children. I would think children would make your life more worthwhile but sometimes families can be too large.	them. I don't think they (are) missing too much. I try to be just c them—make friends c them. I never break promises c them. Anything parents do for kids—they are trying to do the best.	D	12	iron worker (orna-mental)	P 3000–3999	0	—	—
40	35	N	—	Y	factory work	N	Y	It makes it a lot happier.	Well, oh, teach them to be helpful & kind to their parents.	M	12	farmer	P ca. 5000	0	—	carpenter
41	42	N	—	Y	maid	N	Y	Well, she has more to do & can't go when she pleases. She has to work to help make a living for them.	Make them know the right way to live & be honest.	W	5	farmer	P under 1000	0	—	—

1 Interview #	2 Age	3 Employed?	4 If yes, kind of work	5 Work before marriage?	6 If yes, kind of work	7 Wanted career?	8 Desire future work?	9 How life changed by children?	10 What try to do in bringing up children?	11 Marital status	12 Education	13 Father's Occupation	14 Religion	15 Family Income	16 # of children	17 Age youngest child	18 Husband's Occupation
42	63	—	—	—	—	—	Y	A woman has a lot more responsibilities & she shows her love by loving her children. Of course you're kept very busy & you get more broad-mind by sharing children's education & also you stay young because you grow up with your children.	Taught him to be well mannered & to go to church & also talked to him all the time to go on the straight path & not to steal or be wild. I tried to spend as much time as I could with him & gave him a lot of love & care.	W	8	street-car lines-man	P	2000–2999	1	—	railroad laborer
43	43	N	—	Y	secre-tary	N	Y	Well, she certainly has more responsibility. (anything else?) I think life means more when you have children to care for & teach &	Teach them to lead a quiet life—to be honest.	M	8	black-smith	P	5000–5999	3	13	crane opera-tor

| 44 | 58 | Y | teacher | Y | same | — | Y | watch them grow & develop into men & women. | Your interests are different. Being a mother you can't become self-centered. It certainly made me a better teacher. You realize each child has an individuality all its own. | Teach them the difference between right & wrong. They couldn't always to be right. Be religious. Be considerate of others. | M | C | livery stable foreman | P | — | 5 | — | mule fixer in worsted mill |
| 45 | 64 | N | — | Y | teacher | N | N | A woman is not so self-centered nor so selfish after she has children. She gets used to doing for the children, she doesn't consider it a sacrifice but it is. Having children makes a woman's life much fuller. (how fuller?) Oh, she looks at things from the children's angle or how they will affect children. | Oh, I tried to give him a good religious training & we gave him advantages. (You mean?) Oh, music & well, we tried to train him to do the things that were honorable & right. | | M | C | farmer | P | 1000–1999 | 1 | — | retired postman |

Interview # 1	Age 2	Employed? 3	If yes, kind of work 4	Work before marriage? 5	If yes, kind of work 6	Wanted career? 7	Desire future work? 8	How life changed by children? 9	What try to do in bringing up children? 10	Marital status 11	Education 12	Father's Occupation 13	Religion 14	Family Income 15	# of children 16	Age youngest child 17	Husband's Occupation 18
46	32	N	—	Y	secretarial	—	Y	She's confined to the house & can't do anything outside take care of them—when they are little.	Feed them good, well-balanced meals & keep them clean & give them the proper training.	M	12	manager of construction company	P	7500–9999	2	1½	heat-treating inspector in machine shop
47	45	Y	cook	N	—	—	Y	I don't know—I never had any.	Lord, honey, I ain't never thought about it.	M	8	coal miner	P	DK	0	—	helper locomotive co.
48	26	Y	saleslady & some office work	N	—	N	Y	More responsibility but also more to look forward to in life.	First, I would try to get thru school & a good education. Also train them to have respect for others—especially older people.	M	C	carpenter	P	5000–5999	0	—	clerical
49	25	N	—	N	—	Y	Y	Will stay at home more & be more interested in the	Give them a good start in religious education & try &	M	12	pipe-fitter-plumber	P	6000–7499	0	—	carpenter

							children than any-thing else.	set a good example for them to follow.							
50	34	Y	secre-tarial	Y	same	Y	Y	Your interests are different. (in what way?) You don't go the same places & you do things to please your chil-dren—you sort of live your life over through your children. You have to.	Try to teach her right—to respect the higher ideals—to be thankful she's healthy and be happy—and that money isn't everything.	M	C	engineer fireman	P 2000-2999	1	11	account-ant
51	47	Y	cares for children	Y	same	Y	Y	You do what you can for them & it takes most of your time.	I have my children within my sight so I know what they're doing—if I go out I take them with me.	M		6 builder	P 1000-1999	6	—	retired
52	46	Y	soda foun-tain clerk	N	—	Y	Y	You realize how much trouble you were when you were small. It takes away lots of a woman's spare time—she can't do things like she used to do—she has to think of the child first.	I try to keep him in church & Sun-day school & teach him what is right thing to do.	D	8	carpen-ter	P 3000-3999	8	9	—

Interview # 1	Age 2	Employed? 3	If yes, kind of work 4	Work before marriage? 5	If yes, kind of work 6	Wanted career? 7	Desire future work? 8	How life changed by children? 9	What try to do in bringing up children? 10	Marital status 11	Education 12	Father's Occupation 13	Religion 14	Family Income 15	# of children 16	Age youngest child 17	Husband's Occupation 18
53	27	N	—	Y	plaine-meter operator	Y	Y	More confined & more responsibilities & work to be done—but is real happiness.	Try to have them happy, well trained and not spoiled.	M	C	worker in tire company	P	5000–5999	1	8 mos	Navy officer
54	25	N	—	Y	clerk typist	—	Y	It gives her more work to do.	Well, teach them to be obedient, have good manners, be polite to others.	M	12	me-chanic	C	6000–7499	2	3 mos	Army soldier
55	59	N	—	Y	domestic	N	N	Well, she takes on more things to do—it keeps her busy.	I tried to educate them and bring them up in the right way.	M	8	farmer	P	2000–2999	2	—	retired
56	34	N	—	Y	inspector for cork co.	Y	N	Well, I don't know. (what be your guess?) You have more responsibility to take care of your boy (family).	I try to do nothing but the best for him. (How mean that?) Well, I teach him religion (yes?) & to be obedient. (Tell me more about that.) Teach him to be	M	—	—		—	1	11	—

57	36	N	—	Y	N	checker in cleaning plant	N	Oh me! in every way I believe. (Tell me some of the ways.) You have a mother's responsibility for one. Seeing that they get every care—grow up right—see that they have right schooling—meet right people. (Other way?) Well, you feel older.	home on time——that's about it I guess. I guess I covered that in the other question. Seeing they get the proper schooling, meet the right people.	M	7	sales-man	C	3000–3999	—	1	7	claim adjuster for VA	—
58	40	N	—	Y	N	secre-tarial	Y	Oh, I think it's more complete. (More about that?) Well, it gives life a purpose. (Other ways?) It gives you a greater sense of responsibility & you worry more, but it's worth it.	I try to see they have a feeling of security & the advantages it's possible for me to give them. (Else?) See that they are polite, have respect for their elders.	W	12	steel mill laborer	P	—		2	13		

# Interview 1	Age 2	Employed? 3	If yes, kind of work 4	Work before marriage? 5	If yes, kind of work 6	Wanted career? 7	Desire future work? 8	How life changed by children? 9	What try to do in bringing up children? 10	Marital status 11	Education 12	Father's Occupation 13	Religion 14	Family Income 15	# of children 16	Age youngest child 17	Husband's Occupation 18
59	25	Y	sales-work in show-room	—	—	—	Y	I couldn't say. I never had any children. (Friends?) No—none of my closest friends are married yet.	Just make them behave & have nice manners. Help them with their school work.	Si	C	chemical co. worker	C	6000–7499	—	—	—
60	53	Y	clean-ing	—	—	N	Y	She is more confined and more busy at home. She is not free to go as she pleases. There are things she has to give up to be with them.	I always taught them to do the right things & to go to church and Sunday school.	W	8	farmer	P	3000–3999	1	—	—
61	24	N	—	—	—	N	Y	I don't know. Oh, you have to do more work. You have to feed the kids & take care of them—of course you have more work when you	Teach them to obey me. And have them clean? Oh boy, that's a hard one to answer. I think you just take care of them. To tell you the truth,	Si	8	laborer	C	DK	—	—	—

62	56	N	—	Y	teacher	N	N	She has more responsibility—up until then she was just one of the world—now she has produced—and that's what she's here for—has more interest then in others.	have kids. I don't like kids, I don't know what I would do with them. Useful citizens. (Anything else?) I think I did pretty good with discipline.	M	C	store-keeper	P 6000–7499	4 11	school teacher
63	26	Y	traffic clerk for Army	Y	same	N	N	She's more confined to the home. She is more interested in community & civic org.—more interested in seeing there are better schools & community parks & play grounds & more concerned about the neighborhood she lives in.	Be fair with them & stick to good discipline rules at the same time.	M	C	engi-neer	P 6000–7499	0 —	ac-count-ant

1 Interview #	2 Age	3 Employed?	4 If yes, kind of work	5 Work before marriage?	6 If yes, kind of work	7 Wanted career?	8 Desire future work?	9 How life changed by children?	10 What try to do in bringing up children?	11 Marital status	12 Education	13 Father's Occupation	14 Religion	15 Family Income	16 # of children	17 Age youngest child	18 Husband's Occupation
64	28	N	—	Y	printing press operator	N	Y	They have more responsibility; satisfied to stay home & not be on the go all the time. It brings a husband & wife closer together.	Teach them never to lie or cheat—& they get punished when they deserve it. Be polite. Not to be selfish & always thinking of themselves. Try to set a good example for them myself.	M	8	machinist	C	5000–5999	2	5	custodian
65	46	Y	store clerk	Y	housework	N	N	Well, it gives you something to love & take care of. (other ways?) It gives a lot of responsibility—that's all I know.	Bring them up right. (How mean?) Well, they should help others & never do anything wrong. (like?) Stealing or swearing.	W	8	miner	C	6000	5	7	—
66	42	N	—	Y	store clerk	Y	Y	It's the main thing in a woman's life. She has a responsibility—you are	Distinct the good things from the bad. I think discipline is import. &	M	9	miner	C	3000–3999	3	14	teacher

								more sympathetic to people.	teach them about being honest.							
67	32	Y	informa-tion clerk at hospital	Y	house-work	—	N	Yes—she always has to be caring for them.	I try to be a mother & father—it's terrible hard.	D	12	post office clerk	P 2000–2999	2	11	—
68	28	N	—	Y	office work	N	N	I don't know—I haven't had him that long, to really know.	Bring them up right.	M	—	—	—	1	3 wks	—
69	47	Y	teacher	Y	same	—	Y	Well, responsibility is greater. You should always think of them constantly. And you have more to work for and live for. (Anything else?) I think that it certainly widens the circle of woman's acquaintances because they are always bringing home people—either their friends or their parents' friends.	Teach them to be good citizens. (How mean?) Respect for other people's property. To know the difference between right & wrong.	M	C	physi-cian & drug store owner	P 7500–9999	2	16	real estate

Interview # 1	Age 2	Employed? 3	If yes, kind of work 4	Work before marriage? 5	If yes, kind of work 6	Wanted career? 7	Desire future work? 8	How life changed by children? 9	What try to do in bringing up children? 10	Marital status 11	Education 12	Father's Occupation 13	Religion 14	Family Income 15	# of children 16	Age youngest child 17	Husband's Occupation 18
70	29	Y	auditor	Y	same	Y	Y	To me having children is one of the best things that could happen to someone. I don't think anyone can feel complete until they have a family. I'd be a lot happier. (Anything else?) You spend more time at home but I think it's worth it.	I'd try to bring them up morally & in their faith. I'd want them to be worthy citizens. (How mean?) Have a realization what their country means, their freedom means. I'd never try to push them either.	Sp	12	mail carrier	C	7500–9999	0	—	insurance agent
71	44	N	—	Y	cook	N	N	You is busy all the time & you is responsible for the children in how they behave & to keep them fed & clothed.	Keep them clean & well & happy.	M	11	laborer	P	2000–2999	3	16	janitor

72	36	Y	sewing machine operator	Y	field worker on sugar farm	N	Y	No—she still works—the children when they get bigger—they work too.	(R couldn't say)	Sp	2	sugar cane farm worker	C	2000–2999	4	3	factory worker
73	43	N	—	Y	house-work	Y	Y	Lots (in what way?) Well you have a lot of responsibility—you have to try & please them all (children)—can't go out like when you were single.	Oh, I always preach to them (tell me more?) I try to explain to them how to be good & not grow wild & run around —(else?) I always tell them the least you have to say the better off you are (try to get along with everyone).	M	8	mine worker	C	—	3	12	laborer coke ovens
74	51	N	—	Y	gauged lenses on eye glasses	Y	N	It's a lot busier but a lot happier.	I try to see that they go to church & school & get active in things like the scouts & clubs.	M	8	carpenter	C	5000–5999	11	11	maintenance helper
75	36	N	—	Y	factory work, domestic & others	N	Y	It gets more busy—certainly there's always more to do.	I try to teach them to do for themselves & to respect their parents as well as each other.	M	8	farmer	C	5000–5999	4	?	external grinder machine

1 Interview #	2 Age	3 Employed?	4 If yes, kind of work	5 Work before marriage?	6 If yes, kind of work	7 Wanted career?	8 Desire future work?	9 How life changed by children?	10 What try to do in bringing up children?	11 Marital status	12 Education	13 Father's Occupation	14 Religion	15 Family Income	16 # of children	17 Age youngest child	18 Husband's Occupation
76	29	Y	clerical	Y	same	—	Y	Can only tell what I've observed in my married friends, my girl friends. Their interests are different—finances get smaller as they have children—they complain a lot. (what about?) They don't go any place, don't have any clothes—other items too numerous to mention—at times quite depressing.	Think I'd teach them outdoor manners—when they go visiting. (What mean?) Not touch things—I'd never talk baby talk—I'd try to understand them.	M	12	deceased	C	10,000–14,999	0	—	welfare worker
77	53	N	—	Y	secretary	N	Y	Her interests change to things that are of interest to children.	I tried to teach them always to be fair—to be kind and live by the golden rule—to	M	12	deceased	P	10,000–14,999	1	—	buyer

(continued from previous case) give them a well-rounded education.

Case	Age				Occupation						Occupation				Occupation
78	29	N	—	N	—	N	N	I think she is more tied down. You have to consider your children before yourself but you wouldn't want to be without them.	Made them mind. Teach them to do household duties—be considerate of others—not to be selfish!	M 12	owned shoe store prior to death	C 7500–9999	2	8	warehouse worker
79	29	N	—	Y	soda fountain clerk	—	—	Oh, I don't know—you've got more to do—keeps you working all the time but you expect to & they're worth it.	Oh, try to be a good mother—take care of them right. (What mean?) Oh, stay home & take care of them & not let them run loose all over like some kids do.	M 7	paperhanger	P 4000–4999	3	1½	truck driver
80	25	N	—	Y	coordinator in chain store	—	Y	I think a woman fulfills her destiny by having children. We are Catholics. (question repeat) It gives you something to do & it makes you feel the marriage is really consummated.	I want to bring my children up so that they will be able to have the things their grandfather wanted for his son but couldn't give him—he got caught in the depression (paternal grandfather).	M 12	owned trucking company	C 7500–9999	1	11	procedure writer in chain store group

Interview #	Age	Employed?	If yes, kind of work	Work before marriage?	If yes, kind of work	Wanted career?	Desire future work?	How life changed by children?	What try to do in bringing up children?	Marital status	Education	Father's Occupation	Religion	Family Income	# of children	Age youngest child	Husband's Occupation
1	2	3	4	5	6	7	8	9	10	11	12	13	14	15	16	17	18
81	49	N	—	N	—	N	Y	You are more happier by having children & you have a lots more to do. You think of the children and not yourself.	I tried to please them & gave them everything I could afford. I did without so they could have.	M	9	carpenter	P	300–3999	3	—	foreman telephone company
82	62	Y	housework	Y	school teacher	N	N	Well you have a great deal more work & a great deal more joy.	Teach them to love God & their neighbor.	M	10	farmer	P	under 1000	6	—	retired
83	36	Y	store clerk	Y	factory worker	N	Y	She has a great joy added to it— she is tied down more.	The same principles I was taught.	M	12	mill worker	P	7500–9999	1	16	steel mill craneman
84	31	N	—	Y	restaurant cook & waitress & checker in	N	Y	She has to do more sacrificing. (How mean?) Many things she might want like shoes or new dress, she would have to get	I would try to raise them in the right way. (How mean?) Give them all the love and affection they needed. Give them the things	M	11	furnace man in factory	P	under 1000	0	—	packer (light fixture co.)

| 85 43 | N | — | Y | leather factory worker | Y | Y | More responsibilities. More housework, you know cooking, washing, ironing etc. (anything else?) No, I think not. | them for the children & let herself go. The times she usually spent for herself she would have to spend doing (caring) for her children. | they needed—not all they wanted. | I would try to raise my children. (How mean?) I would try to teach them obedience, talk to them & try to make them understand what they should & shouldn't do. Read good books to them—teach them the Bible. (Anything else?) Teach them to have respect for others. Play with them & love them (give them affection). Try to give them a good education. | M | 8 minister prior to death | P 3000–3999 | 0 | — | printer in packing co. box dept. |

Interview # 1	Age 2	Employed? 3	If yes, kind of work 4	Work before marriage? 5	If yes, kind of work 6	Wanted career? 7	Desire future work? 8	How life changed by children? 9	What try to do in bringing up children? 10	Marital status 11	Education 12	Father's Occupation 13	Religion 14	Family Income 15	# of children 16	Age youngest child 17	Husband's Occupation 18
86	25						Y	All I can say is everything changes. You become more accustomed to the ways of life—and once you have had a child you have more reason for working, living, and doing the best you can.	Everything that I can do for their benefit & welfare. I try to teach them what's right & wrong.	D	10	mill operator	P	DK	3	7	—
87	42	Y	keeps books, cleans office, orders supplies in husband's garage	Y	sewed in silk mill	N	N	They have more obligations. They're looked up to. They must set good examples. I think motherhood is the greatest responsibility in the world.	I always believed in religious teaching when I brought my children up. I think that's very important.	M	8	miner	C	2000–2999	2	—	mechanic
88	26	N	—	Y	store clerk	Y	N	I think you have more responsi-	Keep them from fighting mostly—	M	12	foreman on RR	P	5000–5999	3	9 mos	order clerk

No.	Age				Occupation			Responsibility	Child rearing		Income			
								bility. I think your whole schedule should be changed because you have the baby to think of and work into your day and life.	but don't put that down. I see that they're fed 3 times a day & go to bed on time at night. Keep up with their regular check-up at the doctor. See that they play & keep happy during the day.					
89	53	N	—	Y	clerical	N	N	She has more to do in the home & a bigger responsibility.	Teach them good habits and honesty.	M 12 clerk	C 6000–7499	2	—	—
90	26	Y	in the field	Y	housework & worked in the field	N	N	She has to work all the time & never can go nowhere. She has to get up food & clothes for the children.	I try to keep 'em clean & make them mind & talk nice to people.	M 6 farmer	P 1000–1999	3	1	farmer
91	47	N	—	Y	shoe shop inspector	N	Y	It makes you more settled but gives you lots more responsibility—they are company for you.	I keep them in church—try to keep them in good company & see that they are in early nites—to keep clean & take care of their clothes.	M 8 baker	C 2000–2999	3	12	leather worker

1 Interview #	2 Age	3 Employed?	4 If yes, kind of work	5 Work before marriage?	6 If yes, kind of work	7 Wanted career?	8 Desire future work?	9 How life changed by children?	10 What try to do in bringing up children?	11 Marital status	12 Education	13 Father's Occupation	14 Religion	15 Family Income	16 # of children	17 Age youngest child	18 Husband's Occupation
92	59	Y	dish-washer	N	—	N	Y	I've had five. It helps you to understand things with everyone—I know some who haven't had children & they don't seem to have the patience with the younger ones.	Well, I really don't know what to say, but always tried to see they went to church—when I could.	Sp	7	farmer	P	1000–1999	5	—	—
93	36	Y	factory worker	Y	same	Y	Y	You're more tied down—she has less time for herself, less money to spend—she can't get away from home—no vacations.	I try to get her to church—I try to get her home at a reasonable hour & teach her to be clean & to know who her friends are.	Sp	9	factory worker	C	4000–4999	1	16	—
94	45	N	—	Y	secretarial	N	Y	She's more mature & has to accept responsibilities children bring. She	I try to teach them consideration for others & to do right—make out as	M	12	carpenter	C	6000–7499	2	16	group leader, Fan Dept.

95	42	N	—	Y	secre-tarial	N	N	has to do less fuss-ing with herself & concentrate more on the children & she has to manage finances better be-cause there's more expenses & plan-ning.	best they can with their allowances & not throw their money away. I've taught them to at-tend church regu-larly & they do & to be good.	M	12	sales-man	P	4000–4999	3	10	service manager
96	36	N	—	N	—	Y	N	To me it makes all the difference in the world. I don't be-lieve you could be truly happy until you have them. I pity deeply those who have no chil-dren or only one.	I guess of all the things it would be to try to make them able to judge right and wrong for themselves.	M	12	brick-layer	P	7500–9999	2	8	plumber
97	35	N	—	Y	dye sampler	Y	Y	Makes her life complete and hap-pier.	Give them train-ing to do right and how to turn away from wrong.	M	8	not home	C	5000–5999	2	5	owns lunch-eonette
98	29	N	—	—	—	Y	Y	More work! (laugh)	I'm bringing them up to be fine boys.	Si	8	porter	P	—	—	—	—

1 Interview #	2 Age	3 Employed?	4 If yes, kind of work	5 Work before marriage?	6 If yes, kind of work	7 Wanted career?	8 Desire future work?	9 How life changed by children?	10 What try to do in bringing up children?	11 Marital status	12 Education	13 Father's Occupation	14 Religion	15 Family Income	16 # of children	17 Age youngest child	18 Husband's Occupation
99	36	N	—	Y	usherette in movie theatre	N	Y	It's just fulfillment for both husband and wife—it's empty without them. It changes a woman's life altogether—it gives her interest. Before children come you belong to clubs & card clubs & go downtown shopping because you're bored to death—with children you are more interested in them, in staying at home.	I stress morals more than anything because as a child I saw the other end of things; so I stress morals first with mine. Not to hurt people—I'm always after them if I've thought they've said something to hurt somebody.	M	10	tavern owner	C	5000–5999	2	9	parts man, garage

1 Interview #	2 Age	3 Employed?	4 If yes, kind of work	5 Work before marriage?	6 If yes, kind of work	7 Wanted career?	8 Desire future work?	9 How life changed by children?	10 What try to do in bringing up children?	11 Marital status	12 Education	13 Father's Occupation	14 Religion	15 Family Income	16 # of children	17 Age youngest child	18 Husband's Occupation
100	31	N	—	Y	part-time in snack bar	Y	Y	You don't have as much free time—they take up a lot of time if they're raised like they should be.	Try to teach them self-respect & to try to get them to depend on themselves & not their parents—and that is a job! Try to teach them respect for their elders.	M	9	soldier	P	3000–3999	4	6	soldier

Index

The (t) in parentheses indicates a table; (f), a figure; (n), a footnote.